HAIL MARY
FULL OF GRACE
Our Lord is with thee;
blessed art thou a-
mongst Women, and
blessed is the fruit
of thy womb, Jesus,
Holy Mary, Mother of
God, Pray for us Sinners Now
& at the hour of our Death
AMEN
I0754218

THE
URSULINE
MANUAL.
VERY
REV. JOHN POWER, D.D.
RT. REV. JOHN HUGHES, D.D.
New-York
PUBLISHED BY EDWD. DUNIGAN,
151 FULTON ST

THE

URSULINE MANUAL,

OR A

COLLECTION,

OF

PRAYERS, SPIRITUAL EXERCISES, ETC.,

INTERSPERSED WITH

THE VARIOUS INSTRUCTIONS

NECESSARY FOR

FORMING YOUTH TO THE PRACTICE

OF

SOLID PIETY

ORIGINALLY ARRANGED FOR

THE YOUNG LADIES

EDUCATED AT THE URSULINE CONVENT, CORK.

REVISED BY THE VERY REV. JOHN POWER, D. D.,

AND APPROVED BY THE

MOST REV. JOHN HUGHES, D. D.,

Archbishop of New York.

NEW YORK:

EDWARD DUNIGAN AND BROTHER,

(JAMES B. KIRKER,)

No. 151 FULTON STREET.

1857.

INTRODUCTION TO THE NEW-YORK EDITION

OF THE

URSULINE MANUAL.

The intrinsic merits of this Prayer Book, and the high place it deservedly holds in public estimation, have induced the Publisher to reprint it in this city. Though the work was originally intended for the use of the Young Ladies educated in the famous Ursuline Convent, in the city of Cork; yet many editions of it quickly succeeded each other, both in Dublin and in London: a fact which alone bespeaks its worth; and a mere perusal of the table of its contents, will show, that no book of the same kind, contains a greater amount of pious and useful reading. The Publisher has the satisfaction to state that no pains have been spared to adapt the Work to the peculiar circumstances of this country, and that it comes before the public with strong claims on their attention. It has been carefully revised by the Very Reverend Divine whose name appears in the title page, and is approved of by the Spiritual Authority of this Diocess.

APPROBATION OF THE IRISH EDITION

By the desire of the Rt. Rev. Dr. Murphy, the R. C. Bishop of Cork, I have attentively perused the Manuscript of a Book entitled *The* Ursuline Manual; *or, a Collection of Prayers, Spiritual Exercises, &c. interspersed with the various Instructions necessary for forming Youth to the Practice of solid Piety.*

The fervent Piety, interesting Instructions, and useful Doctrinal Expositions contained in this Work, are extremely valuable; and few books appear to me better fitted than it is to advance the Cause of Religion, Morality, and Virtue. It is calculated, in my opinion, not only to be serviceable in Religious Communities, but likewise in Private Families, and as a Devotional Book to the Faithful in general.

THOMAS R. ENGLAND, P. P., &c. &c.

Cork, April 14th, 1823

CONTENTS

APPENDIX.

PREFACE.

Those who have made the human mind the object of their peculiar study, unanimously allow, that nothing contributes so materially to the happiness of society as a christian and well-directed system of education for youth. This has ever been looked upon as a public concern, a subject of universal interest; because, generally speaking, the early impressions made on the minds of children, are those which they longest retain; and the habits to which they are formed in youth, are those in which they persevere. The greatest and most enlightened Doctors of the Church, sensible that faults are corrected, and virtue inculcated, with more than ordinary facility and success in youth, have considered the cultivation of young minds as closely connected with the glory of God, and calculated to promote the temporal and eternal happiness of mankind. On that account, the greatest men were remarkable for their zeal in catechizing and instructing children. Many devoted their time and talents, not only to the religious instruction of youth, but likewise to their education, that the system pursued therein may not interfere with their more important interests; others successfully exerted themselves in providing establishments, wherein young persons may acquire profane science, useful knowledge, and accomplishments suitable to their future prospects, without any risk of losing their innocence and piety; a danger always attendant on any system of public education which is not founded on religion, conducted by religion, and directed to religion. Opportunities for attaining education, similar to those provided by the pious and the learned for the youth of past generations, are, by the providence of God, within the reach of the youth of the present day. There are now, as there were formerly, multitudes instructed and educated in religious seminaries, whose piety in their progress through life, appears to be solid and enlightened; whose minds are cultivated and formed; whose hearts are filled with the meekness and charity of Jesus Christ; and who exhibit striking evidences of the fruits which may naturally be expected from a religious education.

Unfortunately, however, there exists a strong antipathy to a religious education, founded on a misconception of its object, and tending materially to limit its advantages to much the smallest portion of society. This prejudice originates in the erroneous idea entertained by many, that this species of education is confined to such subjects as regard religion alone; that it excludes the sciences, and most branches of liberal education; and that, being incompatible with ornamental accomplishments and elegant manners, it is consequently better calculated to disqualify than to prepare any young lady for society. Such opinions are unfounded; they are entertained only by those who have no knowledge of the system pursued in conferring a christian education. In that system, religion, it is true, is always, as it should be, the first object kept in view: a thorough knowledge of the duties and obligations of a christian is imparted to youth; a deep sense of the necessity of acting on that knowledge, by the constant discharge of those obligations, is impressed on their minds; and those are held up to them uniformly as the most necessary, the most valuable and useful of all acquirements; as the source of true enjoyments here, and the only foundation for hoping eternal enjoyments hereafter. But that does not prevent due attention being paid to every branch of education, and to every accomplishment which should enter into the system of a young lady's education. It is not a little to be lamented that this truth is not more generally understood or believed, by those who naturally desire to facilitate the studies of their children; for experience has proved the necessity and the utility of accompanying the education of youth with religious instruction. It has proved, beyond a doubt, that to instruct children thoroughly in the principles of the christian doctrine, and the truths and maxims of the gospel; to teach them to apply those truths to themselves, and to make them the rule of their conduct, is an excellent method of facilitating their progress in other pursuits, and in a great measure of insuring their success. For, to say nothing of the blessing which the Almighty always gives to such studies as children are taught by religion to consecrate to his service, and to sanctify by the innocence of their lives, how could it be expected that young persons would persevere in restraining the levity, and conquering the sloth and inapplication of early years, so far as is necessary for succeeding in their studies, if not stimulated by a strong sense of duty? Beside, this precaution becomes particularly requisite with regard to female youth, for every one who has any experience concerning them knows, that unless religious instruction teach them early the comparative insignificance of human acquirements, and fill their hearts with the fear and love of God, it will be very unsafe to fill their heads with mere worldly knowledge.

In fact, the little attention paid to young ladies in this respect, is the primary cause of the vanity, levity, extravagance, neglect of duty, and unchristian lives of many young persons, who certainly received a liberal, and otherwise judicious education. In the course of that education, great care, constant attention, instruction of all kinds were perhaps lavished on them, and the utmost pains were taken to render them amiable and accomplished members of society: but in vain.

Why so? Because religious instruction, and a continual application of its principles to their conduct in early life, did not enter into the system of their education. So insensible are the generality of young persons under such circumstances to their own real interests, that they seldom co-operate with the exertions of their teachers, and consequently those exertions seldom succeed. Little acquainted with a truth, which religious instruction renders familiar to its pupils, that disappointments and afflictions are the ordinary portion of mortals in their progress through life, they long for the expiration of their school days, and will not be persuaded that they are, in reality, the most peaceful, the happiest, and even the most precious of their lives. If they do not actually lose their time, their attention is chiefly directed to such branches of education as they consider most ornamental; and they neglect the less shining, but more valuable acquirements, which are indispensable in a woman. The time allotted to their studies expires, without their having well commenced them;—they return home little acquainted with their duties to God, to society, and to themselves, and still less disposed to fulfil them; accomplished, perhaps, but not educated, and particularly ill-qualified to discharge the useful and responsible duties of society, which are the birthright of women. Those evils, which are nothing when compared to subsequent misfortunes, may evidently be traced to the want of a religious education:—for, as the Scripture says, *Those things which thou hast not gathered in thy youth, how shalt thou find them in thy old age?*

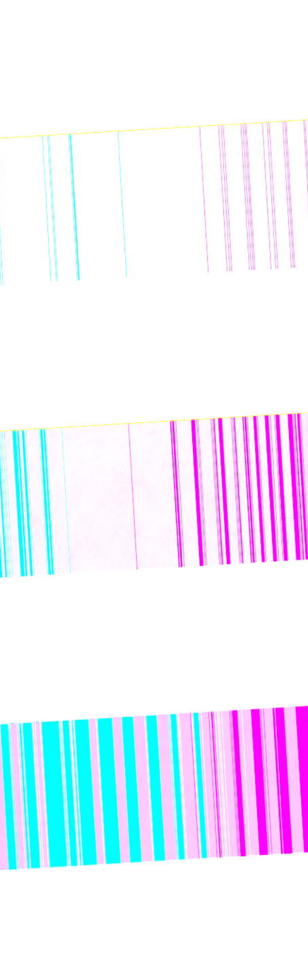

But how different is the conduct of those who are blessed by Providence with a religious education! Being early instructed concerning the obligations contracted by their baptism, the great end of their creation, and the principles of their religion in general; and moreover deeply impressed with the necessity of living according to the maxims of the gospel, in order to insure their salvation, they are generally disposed to set a high value on every opportunity of acquiring religious instruction. Beside, diligence in study holds such a distinguished rank among their important duties, that it renders the otherwise thorny path of learning a sweet and pleasing one to them. It seldom happens, that a few years, thus devoted to the pursuit of virtue and useful knowledge, fail in forming the minds of young persons to the love of both; their whole time being divided between religious duties and necessary relaxation, they contract an early habit of being always profitably occupied. They imbibe the spirit of sincere piety, which not only teaches them what their duties are, but how to place their greatest satisfaction in discharging those duties faithfully. They gradually correct their faults, and even practise virtue in such a manner as would do credit to more matured age. They almost forget that there are any other amusements or pleasures than those innocent enjoyments within their reach; and are so perfectly sensible of the utility of school restraint, that they generally anticipate their emancipation from it with the deepest regret.

Thus the good seed frequently produces such speedy fruits in young persons, as give the most encouraging hopes of their becoming models of virtue to society, the consolation and ornament of their families; and perhaps instrumental to the salvation of many by their good example.

Another of the many groundless objections made to religious education is, that its pleasing fruits are often nipped in the bud, and that some young persons, who received a very christian education, are observed to be as anxiously devoted to the world and its vanities, as those who know nothing of religion.

Unhappily there have been individuals whose conduct justified such remarks; but, considering the fatal influence of bad example, bad company, ridicule, and all the other temptations that assail young persons in society it is a wonderful proof of the effect of religious instruction, that such instances are few. Comparatively speaking, it is certain, that they are few—so few, as to leave it still an undeniable truth, that a good education is seldom so totally thrown away as that, sooner or later, its fruits do not appear. Those young persons who were religiously educated, yet whom false maxims, or pernicious example, had engaged to imitate the follies of worldlings, seldom persist in stifling the remorse caused in their hearts, by the opposition between their consciences and their conduct. They are carried away for a time, but often, through the mercy of God, and the bias their minds so early received, with no worse effect than to superadd the lessons of their own experience to those of early instruction. They were often told that the pleasures of virtue are the only real pleasures; that those of the world are empty and bitter; that the fulfilment of duty is the road to contentment, and that serving the world is purchasing insipid enjoyments at a very dear rate. They perceive, some sooner, some later, but almost all perceive at last, that those maxims are *truths*, and then it is that they recall and resolve to act on the salutary instructions of their youth. There have been some, it is true, who unfortunately persevered, even to the evening of life, in their ungrateful abuse of the graces conferred in a religious education; but even those have been known to prove on the bed of death, by their contrition and sincere return to their Creator, that the fear of God, which they had early imbibed, had not completely lost its influence, nor the virtuous impressions made on them by a good education had been entirely effaced. However, those are graces due to none, and least deserved by those who most presumptuously depend on them. The danger of abusing so great an advantage as a religious education, should ever be present to the minds of those who receive it, and stimulate them to acquire such a store of virtue in eir youth, as may strengthen them to resist the dangers they have to encounter in after-life. The allurements of the world are dangerous to all, but are particularly to be dreaded for females, who seldom possess sufficient firmness to resist example, and who frequently from their cradle manifest a love of the world, of extravagance and show, with a passion for pleasure and endless variety—dangerous propensities, that in some young persons appear quite destroyed, but afterwards prove to have been only dormant, from the absence of objects and occasions calculated to rouse them. It becomes their duty in particular, to *remember their Creator in the days of their youth before the time of affliction come;* to endeavour to correct the faults inherent in their characters; to profit of the blessings of a religious education; to guard against inapplication while at school, and to avoid, at their departure, inconstancy, in the virtuous habits they have acquired.

Those being the great evils which sometimes tend to prevent the good effects of the best education, the object of this work is to assist youth in guarding against them—to lead them early into the path of piety, and enable them to persevere in that path during life. The young persons for whom *The Ursuline Manual* is expressly intended, will perceive that it is nothing more than a collection of their ordinary Devotions, with the addition of such spiritual exercises as they may require on extraordinary occasions, which will prevent the necessity of multiplying Prayer Books. The preparation for approaching the Sacraments, in particular, is explicit and detailed; to give them all the instruction they require for the due performance of such solemn duties; and to impress them with a just idea of their importance. The other abridged instructions comprised in this volume will, it is hoped, refresh and invigorate the impressions already made, and from the brevity of their form be less easily forgotten than the more ample ones usually given on those important points.

As very few prayers enter into the system laid down for their conduct during the period of their education, for the purpose of leaving more leisure for attending to their studies and attaining the several ends for which they are placed at school, it becomes particularly incumbent on them to sanctify these studies, and not to allow whim or caprice to influence their conduct in the discharge or neglect of their school duties, lest the habits of sloth or indifference which they then indulge, may predispose their minds for much more serious omissions in the weighty avocations of after-life. Their principal efforts then should tend to the attainment of piety, and the acquiring of a certain solidity of character, which is founded on good sense, and directly opposite to the fickleness, affectation, and false timidity, which make many young ladies appear almost fools, whom nature did not intend for such.

Solid information and the improvement of their minds are the next objects to be kept in view. They should always recollect that, after the pleasures derived from virtue, those to be found in the pursuit of knowledge, are the purest and most worthy of a rational being. Study improves the memory, forms the judgment, and if diligently and judiciously pursued, will give them such resources in their own minds, as will render them in after-life independent of idle visiters and conversations, with other still more dangerous amusements which a vacuity of mind renders necessary to some young ladies. In labouring to cultivate their minds, they should endeavour to imitate those great ornaments of their sex, whose knowledge kept pace with their sanctity—such as St. Catharine of Alexandria, St. Catharine of Sienna, &c. The example of the former, in particular, who is the Patroness of many celebrated schools, should direct young persons in the pursuit of learning, and also in the use to be made of mental acquirements. From her humility, meekness, diffidence in herself, and contempt for all worldly learning, when compared with the most trifling improvement in virtue, they will perceive the folly of setting great value on their acquirements, and still more of making an ostentatious show of such resources in conversation or otherwise. That ridiculous method of shining would never be adopted by young ladies, could they be convinced that it produces an effect directly contrary to their intentions. In aiming at an exhibition of the extent of their knowledge, they frequently show only its limits—and, at all events, prove that their conceptions of science in general must be very narrow, when they so much overrate their own trifling acquirements.

The general vocation of christians is, to live in the world—to sanctify themselves in the world—and to do good in the world according to their abilities. Therefore young persons should not forget to form their manners, and to qualify themselves in every other respect for mixing in society. The manners of those who profess piety, contribute materially to render it attractive or repulsive in the eyes of the generality of persons who judge only by appearances. Gentleness, forbearance, condescension, deference for others, and forgetfulness of self, are the dictates of charity, which is genuine politeness, and therefore should be observable in every christian's exterior comportment. The elegant manners, and all the forms and ceremonies of refined society, should not be neglected, provided they do not degenerate into those extravagant compliments, which have neither sense nor sincerity. This polish is by no means incompatible with the spirit of religion, as is proved by the example of many great saints, who, though most accomplished in the eyes of the world, were not on that account less pleasing in the sight of God.

The period of leaving school is peculiarly critical, even for those young persons who had conducted themselves with most piety, and profited in every respect of the advantages they enjoyed in the course of their education. The liberty which then succeeds to restraint—and their intercourse with such a variety of characters, whose principles differ materially from those they have been accustomed to consider as the only safe guides for their conduct, sometimes effect a greater change in a few months, than would be expected after a lapse of years. St. Augustine says of himself, that, "having been recalled home from his studies at sixteen years of age, vices began to spring up in his heart like briers in a neglected ground, and that they multiplied, because there was no discreet hand to pluck them out." Those young persons who would be sorry to say the same from experience, and thus to lose the happy fruits of their early efforts in the service of God, ought to follow the advice of St. Francis of Sales, who counsels "a christian to enter the world with great fear, to live in it with great watchfulness, and to guard against the poisonous infection of its air, by the strong antidotes of serious reflection and devout prayer." They should seriously reflect, before they leave school, on the graces they received during their residence there, and dwell particularly on the fruits that will be expected from those graces. It is to give them leisure for those reflections, and to dispose their minds, by prayer, for profiting of them, that, in several religious seminaries, a short retreat is appointed for those who have finished their studies, and are about to return home. That retreat is a last and very great grace annexed to their religious education, of which they should endeavour to profit, by giving their undivided attention to the means prescribed for going through it fervently, and endeavouring particularly to draw from the reflections of those few days, three very necessary dispositions for persons who are on the eve of entering the world. First, a holy fear of its dangers; because those dangers will never be sufficiently guarded against, if they be not sincerely dreaded—secondly, the utmost diffidence in their own strength, knowing that the least of those dangers to which they are about to be exposed, would be sufficient to overturn their good purposes, if they are left to themselves—lastly, a lively and firm confidence in God, who is just as well able to preserve them in the world, as he was to save Lot from the fire of Sodom, and the Hebrew children from the corruption of Babylon.

With regard to the line of conduct which young persons should pursue after their return home, it should be the result of serious reflection on that positive declaration of our Lord, that *no one can serve two masters;* that is, no one can conciliate the idle, useless pursuits of too many persons in the world, with the service of God; therefore they must expect to hear, on all sides the maxims of the world, which are as corrupt and wicked as their author, the Prince of darkness, without being influenced by any of them so far as to depart from the maxims of the gospel, on which *they know* they are to be judged. In a word, they must make an open profession of piety, and act consistently with that profession—that is, they must give that good example which the world itself expects from those who are well instructed. For this end, it would be advisable for young persons to call to mind that short rule for attaining eternal salvation, which their Catechism points out from the Scripture, viz.: *to avoid evil and do good.* It is necessary to avoid evil, that is, sin, and all occasions of sin. It would be melancholy, indeed, if young persons left a seminary of piety, without that sincere horror of sin, which would urge them to avoid, with the utmost care, every thought, word, and action, evidently sinful; but the *occasions* of sin, unfortunately so numerous in the world, are much to be dreaded by youth, on account of their great inexperience, and consequent inability to detect the snares which are laid for them, or to discern the fatal end to which a flowery path so often leads. But however inexperienced they may be in many respects, they will require nothing more than the voice of conscience to decide that the following are dangerous *occasions of sin*, which every young lady should particularly resolve to avoid.

First, *idleness*, which the Scripture says *has taught much evil.* It is natural enough for young persons, immediately after leaving school, to indulge in a little relaxation from the strict order and regularity of system to which they had been accustomed: but it is a common artifice of the enemy to persuade them, that this relaxation may extend to their spiritual duties—that the Sacraments may be deferred, and whole days spent in absolute idleness. Those who listen to that suggestion, will soon experience its bad effects—a relish for idleness, and a disgust for occupation, will insensibly steal upon their hearts, and if they do not put a stop to the growing evil by early and punctual attention to their religious duties, and a speedy regulation of their time, they will soon feel the truth of St. Bernard's words, that "idleness is the sink of all temptations—the mother of folly—the death of the soul, and the receptacle of all evil."

The second occasion of sin to be avoided is, *bad company, and indiscriminate friendships.*—Bad company is so evidently injurious, that no young person, who fears God, should expose her salvation by voluntarily associating with any one whose morals are known to be questionable. St. Teresa says of her self, that a vain female cousin, and another young person, engaged in all the vanities of the world, with whom she associated in her youth, effected such a change in her principles and conduct, as to leave no trace of the virtuous impressions she had received in the convent where she was educated. If bad company had such influence on that great saint, who was distinguished from her early years by solid virtue, sound sense, and great abhorrence of the shadow of evil, how much more injurious will it prove to those young persons, whose natural character and dispositions render them less able to resist its influence? With respect to friendships, young persons are greatly exposed to contract them indiscreetly, being too often carried away by the external qualifications of those whom they choose for their friends. The Scripture says, *Be in peace with many, but let one of a thousand be your counsellor*—that is, your friend and confidant In fact, so many qualities are necessary on both sides to render a close intimacy, confidence, or strict friendship safe, or useful between young persons in the world, that the best resolutions a young lady could make, on this head, are, to be extremely circumspect in selecting any one as a friend—to adhere to the great precept of charity, which requires, that every one should be loved for God's sake—and to be exact in treating all with affability and condescension, but very few with familiarity and unreserve. She should never choose a friend who does not fear and serve God; since friendship, without that foundation, must be injurious; and lastly, she should always give less confidence to the best and most deserving friend, than she does to her parents. Those should be the first friends of young persons, their only entire confidants, as well as their directors and advisers in the choice of any others—without their advice, nothing should be undertaken, and from them nothing should be concealed.

The other occasions of sin to be avoided, are, *bad books*, *novels*, *theatrical amusements*, *&c.* These have unhappily injured many young persons, being well calculated to destroy the good inclinations received from nature, and all the effects of a virtuous education. Heretical books, or any others tending to weaken faith, or lessen respect for religion, are dangerous lectures, and expressly prohibited. Well-instructed persons sometimes are not as guarded as they should be in this respect, from excessive curiosity, or from secret presumption on the strength of their faith; which presumption has often been followed by dangerous temptations. Among bad books may be specially ranked the infidel productions of the last century, which no young lady should venture to open. Those works, such as the writings of a Voltaire, a Rousseau, a d'Alembert, &c., whose fascinating style has served to communicate their poison to thousands, are the real disgrace of libraries, though they unhappily hold a distinguished place in too many.

A learned and excellent author, speaking of novels and romances, says, that "such compositions are injurious both to morals and true literature; that they pervert and deprave the heart, poison the morals, and excite the passions, which it is the real business of a christian to restrain:—that they chill by degrees the fervour of pious inclinations, and banish from the mind all that was in it of solidity and virtue: in fine, that young persons in the habit of reading such lectures, soon retain no ardour but for those things which the world esteems and God abominates." These considerations should make all young persons very cautious in the choice of books, and lead them never to read any, without having first ascertained whether they be calculated for their perusal. However, it should be remembered, that a book is not to be considered bad, merely because it contains a few exceptionable passages. Those will occur in works which are otherwise excellent, and calculated to convey useful information. Such passages should always be passed over; but to reject every work in which they are to be found, would not only restrain reading within very narrow limits, but likewise tend to weaken the judgment, and create unfounded fears.

Plays and *Theatrical Amusements* may be counted among the most dangerous occasions of sin which young persons have to avoid in the world. They are sometimes a stumbling-block to their piety and good resolutions, because it is now too much the custom to employ advice, solicitations, and even authority, to overcome every reluctance on this head.

The opinion of the most learned and holy doctors of the church has, at all times, been in opposition to theatrical amusements. By St. Augustine they are styled "the pest of souls; the ruin of virtue and decorum:" and St. Chrysostom denominates them "the fuel of the passions, and the pomps of Satan, which christians solemnly renounce." Notwithstanding this, it is a melancholy truth, that there are persons now found, who are so insensible to the real interests of their daughters, sisters, and other female friends, as to authorize, and even procure their presence at such diversions. An eminent prelate of the present day, whose profound erudition and invaluable writings already rank him among the most zealous and efficient defenders of religion and morality, loudly condemns this practice. He expresses just astonishment at the inconsistency of those parents, who first, by a christian education, provide their children with the means of saving their souls, and afterwards expose them to the evident risk of being eternally lost, by permitting them to frequent stage representations. "Those parents," continues he, "deserve no pity, if their children ultimately disappoint their hopes; because they have to reproach themselves with industriously eradicating the early lessons of virtue and morality they had received, and implanting those of the world, the flesh, and the devil, by conducting them to the head school, where these lessons are taught, *viz.* the play-house." However, as it is in every one's power, aided by divine grace, to resist solicitations on this head, as well as every other temptation; their success, with respect to many young persons, must be attributed to want of resolution on their part. It is true, that curiosity to witness these exhibitions, as well as the desire and love of amusement, are quite natural to youth; so much so, that the best instructed young persons must rather ambition the merit of overcoming such inclinations, than the privilege of not feeling them. But, at the same time, they should remember, that this is a victory which the Almighty requires and consequently, a steady determination never to assist at theatrical amusements, should be one of their most particular resolutions on entering the world. They are not ignorant of the various and solid reasons which exist for making and keeping such a resolution. Among those the two following should be particularly impressed on their minds:

First, the risk they run, by frequenting the theatre, of losing what should be dearer to them than life itself, the grace of God, and the love of virtue; because, as St. Augustine observes, "it is at the theatre that the flesh and the devil assault the minds and hearts of young people, by every means calculated to instil the poison of vice; to enervate the soul, and flatter the passions, by a general and simultaneous movement of all the allurements and charms of the senses."

Secondly, the bad example which the appearance of a well-instructed Catholic would give in a playhouse, as likewise the scandal which it may occasion, by leading others to indulge without scruple in amusements, of which they before hesitated to partake.

It may not be amiss here to caution young persons against the arguments generally made use of in favour of theatrical amusements; that by examining at leisure the emptiness and insufficiency of those arguments, they may not afterwards be influenced by their apparent plausibility. Young persons, for example, must expect to be told, that going to plays is not sinful, because many excellent characters frequent the theatre without scruple. It is unfortunately too true, that this dangerous practice is *patronized*, though it can never be *authorized*, by some Catholics, from whom a different line of conduct should be expected; but that circumstance does not in the least diminish its danger or its guilt. If precedent were a sufficient excuse before God for any sin, what crime is there that may not be committed with impunity? Therefore, so far from being decided, in this respect, by the opinion and practice of others, young persons should act consistently with the principles which were early impressed on their minds; and though the example of all those whom, in other respects, they consider most worthy of their deference and imitation, were alleged as a motive for going to plays, they should always answer, as Bossuet did to Louis XIV. on a similar occasion: "Sire, there are *great examples* for going to the theatre, but *great reasons* for staying away."

Young persons will be told, in the next place, that they may safely frequent the theatre, because the stage has undergone considerable improvement; that it is no longer what it formerly was—and that good plays cannot injure any one. Allowing that there were such a wonder exhibited as a play *perfectly good* in itself, it is certain that it would be impossible to find one perfectly safe in all its appendages, such as scenery, dress, action, &c. Those circumstances alone constitute a great portion of the danger of the stage—they communicate a fatal interest to the most insipid plays, and an infallible poison to those which are in themselves less dangerous. On this account alone the theatre should always be dreaded and shunned, particularly by young females, who are much more exposed to be injured by such circumstances, than by the play itself. But, even independent of those circumstances, the fact cannot be concealed, that however purified the plays of the present day may be from the old leaven, yet the far greater number are full of immoral sentiments, and always turn on some passion, from whose contagious influence, it would indeed be difficult to guard the heart of any female who witnesses those representations.

A third argument adduced in favour of plays is, the experience of persons who affirm that they frequent the theatre without being in the least injured by that practice. Those who make that assertion, must get credit, either for great insincerity, or great blindness. A holy father defines the theatre to be "Satan's *own* field of battle, whereon those who expose themselves in the combat, must engage their enemy with every species of advantage on *his* side, which his infernal malice can devise;" and divines expressly declare, that a christian who frequents the theatre, can only avoid falling into sin, by an escape as wonderful as it is rare; consequently, those who produce their own experience, in contradiction to the decision of divines —in opposition to the opinion of the holy Fathers, and likewise to the testimony of many persons who frequented the theatre, only to regret that practice on their sincere conversion, give great reason to apprehend that they endeavour to deceive themselves as well as others; or else, that their souls having become already the victims of these dangerous amusements, are dead in sin, and on that account insensible to new wounds.

All that remains to be said on this subject, is, that young persons should earnestly beg of God to enable them to rise superior to all ridicule or solicitation on this head, and to act, on occasion of temptation, with that christian firmness, which God will reward, and the world itself must admire.

With regard to the various other dangers and temptations, which are almost inseparably attached to the necessity of living and conversing in the world, young persons, who sincerely endeavour to serve God, should consider them rather as motives for unbounded confidence in the protection of the Almighty, than for excessive fear. To abstain from those which it is in their power to avoid, is all that is required from them Those who fulfil that duty, may in every other circumstance confidently promise themselves the paternal and special protection of Providence; because the Scripture threatens destruction, not to those who are in danger, but to those who love it too well to avail themselves of the opportunities of escape within their reach. *Eccles.* iii. 27.

Beside *avoiding evil*, a second condition for salvation, pointed out to young persons by their catechism, is *to do good.* Every well-instructed christian is fully aware that to do good is a necessary condition for attaining life everlasting, consequently resolve on complying with the injunction; nevertheless, the determinations of many on this head are but vague resolutions, which eventually produce no solid effects There are others also who perform a great many works of supererogation, while in the mean time they neglect the essential duties of a christian, as well as those attached to their situations in life. It is consequently of extreme importance, that young persons should not confine themselves to a general resolution of keeping the commandments, but that they moreover determine to discharge their respective duties. A firm conviction, that fidelity to those duties is, in reality, the observance of the commandments, and a short road to all the perfection required from them as christians, should induce them to form distinct, precise, yet rational ideas concerning their nature and extent. Thereby they will be prevented from doing too little or too much; and also, saved from that constant fluctuation in opinion and practice, which is too evident in those who have no fixed principles for their direction, or whose conduct is governed by any other rule, rather than the maxims of christianity.

To form this distinct idea of her duties, and make her resolutions accordingly, a young person may class them all under three heads—those which relate to God —those which regard her neighbour—and those which she owes to herself.

The duties which relate to the immediate service of the Almighty are, a fervent and punctual discharge of spiritual exercises, such as morning and night prayers—daily examination of conscience—mature consideration on the truths of eternity, which is so necessary for keeping alive their influence in the heart—fervent and regular frequentation of the Sacraments, on which the life of the soul may be said to depend—likewise that regular attendance at sermons, and other offices of the church, which is requisite for public edification. Any remarks on the necessity of discharging those duties with fidelity and fervour, or any directions as to the method of doing so, would be quite superfluous here. These matters have been frequently touched on throughout this work, and in some places rather diffusely explained, with a view, not only to inspire young persons with a spirit of fervour and punctuality in the discharge of their daily exercise of devotion, but also to guard them against the false notions of many persons, whose devotion consists in spending the greater part of their time in long prayers, which cannot be done without prejudice to other essential duties, and without causing the service which the Almighty requires in one way, to interfere with that which he equally exacts in another—an effect which can never follow from a well-regulated, rational system of devotion. On this account, the young persons for whom this work is particularly intended, are recommended to persevere in those daily devotions to which they had been accustomed, without adding to or retrenching from their number. In the discharge of those exercises they should be punctual, avoiding most carefully that inconstancy so common in youth, which prompts them to shorten—to prolong—to put off, or to omit practices of piety, without any better motive for so doing than their particular humour, disposition of mind, or want of inclination. To insure this regularity as much as depends on them, the time for their prayers, daily considerations, and other devotional exercises, should be regulated; remembering, however, that maxim which was so often impressed on their minds, and is again so frequently repeated in the course of this work, that all private devotions should be subservient to the duties of their station; and that, whenever it happens that both cannot be discharged, the former duties should always be sacrificed to the latter, by which, in the sight of God, they will be substituted. Those involuntary interruptions and passing deviations from their spiritual duties, when occasioned only by obedience, charity, or necessary condescension, so far from being injurious, are most conducive to their advancement in solid virtue.

The duties of young persons towards their neighbour, may be divided into those they owe to their immediate family, and those due to society at large. Their manner of discharging the former in particular, will be the real test of their having derived from a religious education the fruits it is intended to produce. Those who are instructed need not be told that respect, obedience, tenderness, and grateful affection, are the duties they owe their parents, and that kindness and charity are due to equals; but very few seem impressed with the necessity of conducting themselves altogether in such a manner as would render them amiable, useful, and edifying in their family. Those who have not been instructed, or who abuse the benefit of instruction, so far as to be totally devoted to the follies of the world, think of nothing but amusement and show; consequently they lead a life as useless to their friends as it is to themselves. Agreeable enough among strangers, they are usually unamiable and dissatisfied at home, because their element is dissipation and folly.—Others, on the contrary, aim at pleasing and serving God; but they seem to forget that it is impossible to do so without fulfilling the duties they owe to their family. They are generally abroad, either employed in works of devotion, or in rendering services of charity and instruction to others which are perhaps more wanted, and would consequently be better bestowed at home. They spend in private devotion the time which they should devote to the general good, and even amusement of their family; and if their little regulations be interrupted by a service required from them—by a visiter to be received—or by any other active duty of their state which requires to be discharged, their embarrassment or dissatisfaction often appears, to the great disedification of their neighbour, and discredit of religion. The intention of those persons to gain heaven may be very good, but they evidently mistak the way; as our Lord expressly declares, when he says it is not those who say, *Lord, Lord, who shall enter into the kingdom of heaven, but those who do the will of my Father, who is in heaven.* The will of God, in this particular, most certainly is, that a young person, who has received the blessings of a religious education, should afterwards endeavour to promote his glory, by promoting the peace and advantage, both spiritual and temporal, of her family. She is bound to preserve its peace, and, of course, should most carefully avoid all that could tend to disturb general tranquillity and harmony. Impatience and fretfulness would be particularly scandalous in those who are perceived to know and fulfil in other respects the duties of a christian. "Those," says a learned spiritual writer, "whose hearts are filled with charity and goodness, are strangers to lowering and contracted looks: true virtue always increases the sweetness and gentleness of the mind, though this is attended with invincible constancy, and inflexible firmness in every point of indispensable duty. That devotion is defective, or rather false, which is accompanied with pride, obstinacy, or uncharitableness. Whatever makes us sour or morose, certainly makes us worse, and instead of begetting in us a nearer resemblance with our divine model, it gives a strong tincture of the temper of the devils." These words should be attentively considered by all young persons, particularly by those who are conscious of acting in such a manner as renders them not a bond of union among their friends, but a source of discord; whose unsubdued temper, unamiable manners, selfishness, and love of their own ease, disturb that domestic society, which it should be their care and ambition to enliven, and of which the advantages they received should make them the soul and the charm.

To promote the spiritual advantage of her friends is, also, another duty of a young person; but, in endeavouring to do so, she should recollect, that this is seldom effected by disputes about religious matters—those are always unbecoming in youth, and should be avoided with diffidence, as above their capacity and beyond their sphere: nor is much good, in general, done by incessant admonitions or uncalled-for advice. The eloquent and successful voice, which seldom fails to persuade, is good example; an even, unruffled temper; amiable, obliging manners; tender charity, which is always disposed to excuse the faults of others; a readiness to oblige, and to undertake even more than a part in domestic cares, and to sacrifice cheerfully self-gratification to the gratification of others. Any young person who acts in this manner, and who is, beside, careful to contribute to the improvement and instruction of her younger brothers and sisters, may truly be said to fulfil her duty to her family—she promotes, as far as could depend on an individual, its real interest, by inducing others to imitate those virtues which they so much admire in her, and by convincing them, in her own person, of a truth little credited in the world, because seldom exemplified, *viz.* that there is nothing so admirable, so engaging, so cheerful, so sociable, in a word, so truly amiable, as solid piety.

The obligations of a christian towards society at large, chiefly consist in giving good example, that is, by paying strict attention to all public duties of religion; by practically showing forth the principles of religion; and also by not hesitating, when authorized by prudence and necessity, to espouse the cause of religion; and to support, by word as well as by actions, the maxims of the gospel. Charity is also a great debt due to every one—it is a virtue which inclines young persons to banish every idea which may occur to the prejudice of those who act in a manner that, to well-instructed young persons, appears wrong, but which they should attribute to ignorance or inadvertence. Charity should also restrain youth from that ridicule, or those uncharitable remarks, which are, unfortunately, the life and common topic of conversation in the world. Young persons could not adopt a better, or more excellent rule on this subject, than the following, given by an enlightened guide of youth: "Say nothing of any person which would not bear to be repeated to that person—avoid a tone of authority and decision, it is unbecoming in young persons—pronounce with great caution on the merits or demerits of others—and be so reserved and moderate in expressing your own sentiments, as to make it difficult for others to judge for or against you."

Concerning the customs and fashions of the world, it should be remembered that a rational compliance with them is a kind of duty which those who mix in society owe to its members. There are some fashions, which the express rules of prudence and economy do not permit a christian to adopt, however great her means or expectations may be;—there are others, which the laws of propriety expressly condemn. The appearance which some young ladies make in ball-rooms and places of public resort, is highly offensive to common decency—repugnant to every principle of modesty and christian reserve. Their fashionable mode of dress, as it is called, or rather their absolute undress, tends to a far different end from that they probably propose. It renders them objects of ridicule to the generality, and of contempt and disgust in the eyes of those whose opinion deserves respect. Fashions, which even border on such a scandalous system, should of course be pointedly and publicly swerved from, and condemned by the practice of every young person who knows how to respect herself, independently of the respect due to religion. But as to the other customs of fashionable persons regarding dress, conformity with them may be either vanity or virtue, according to the motive which inclines to such compliance. One point is certain, that religion neither requires nor authorizes any singularity, or affected deviation from the common rules of society, respecting dress, in such points as are in themselves strictly innocent. Any young person, who conforms exteriorly to the fashions in those particulars, yet in her heart, like queen Esther, disclaims any worse motive than compliance with the formalities of her rank in life, may be more pleasing in the sight of God, than others who attempt to excuse their neglect in dress by alleging religion and contempt of the world as its motive, but who, in reality, make those virtues serve as a cloak for singularity and real indolence.

One of the chief duties which young persons have to discharge towards themselves, after they leave school, is a continuation of the same interest, and in some measure the same exertion for their own advantage, with which they should have pursued their studies. It happens, not unfrequently, that many who left school thoroughly instructed in the christian doctrine, possessing a tolerable fund of useful information, a taste for study, and a love for useful pursuits, after a few years retain scarce any of these advantages. This may be traced to the total neglect of their own improvement, which they think themselves authorized to indulge because they have left school. Instead of cultivating the seeds of virtue, which instruction had sown, and building on the foundation which their studies had laid, they scatter what they had gathered in the one way, and forget what they had learned in the other. This is a great injustice to themselves, which many have regretted after it had become irreparable: therefore it is very necessary that young persons should not imagine, on leaving school, that their education is finished, and that they are so firmly grounded in virtue, or science, as to dispense themselves from further exertions for the improvement of their hearts and minds :—on the contrary, though school-days are peculiarly those of study, yet youth is always a season for improvement; while that lasts, they should profit of their exemption from the cares which may await their more advanced years, and never fail, as far as circumstances permit, to devote some part of each day to study, which may be pursued with more interest and success, when persons are disengaged from the various other duties of school. Reading, in particular, which is one of the most rational and interesting of all occupations, should not be neglected, because, when well directed, and attended with perseverance and reflection, it is a most effectual means of enriching the mind, improving the judgment, and giving solidity to mental acquirements. Music, drawing, or those other ornamental acquirements which engross so much time, and are attended with considerable expense, cannot, except through necessity, be laid aside by any young lady without injustice to herself, or to those friends who spared no exertions to render her accomplished in every respect.

But, as *it will avail a man nothing, to gain the whole world, if he lose his own soul*, it follows, that the essential duty which all christians have to discharge towards themselves, consists in the attention they are bound to pay to the concerns of their souls. Those who are brought up with care, and who enjoy in their early years such continual assistance, advice instruction, and admonition, as make the practice of virtue easy, and leave them little more to do, than to correspond with the exertions of others, very often fail in this important point, and fall off considerably when their virtue begins to depend more on themselves, and they are obliged to walk as it were alone in the path of God's commandments. Like the young king Joas, who continued to love and serve God only while under the care of the high priest Joiada, such young persons persevere in the practice of virtue, so long as they are urged or encouraged to do so; but as soon as external help fails, their resolution begins to waver, and thereby they run an evident risk of soon falling. The best method of guarding against this danger, is to impress on their hearts those solid principles of the fear and love of God, which are the foundation of true virtue, and also to adopt the means necessary for promoting their own immediate sanctification, particularly the following: First, the advice of a director, which is necessary to all christians, but indispensably requisite for youth. "Be not without a guide," says St. Jerom, speaking to young persons, "lest you should mistake your road, and perish in your wandering, or go faster, or slower, than God requires." Secondly, spiritual reading: a great variety of spiritual books should be avoided, lest their multiplicity serve to prevent the maxims of any from making a due impression. The *New Testament*, the *Lives of the Saints*, the *Introduction to a devout Life*, the *Imitation of Christ*, the *Spiritual Combat*, the *Think Well On't*, and the *Characters of real Devotion*, are works from which young persons may undoubtedly draw the two great benefits to be derived from spiritual reading, *viz.* instruction in the maxims of virtue, and encouragement for reducing those maxims to practice: a more extensive spiritual library will be better timed, when their judgment and character are firmly and happily formed.

Thirdly, serious reflection on the great truths of religion. This is a precaution absolutely necessary for preventing the maxims of the gospel from being effaced in their early years by those of the world. Death—judgment—the shortness of time, and duration of eternity—the misery of sin, the vanity of the world—the death and passion of Jesus Christ—the merit and necessity of suffering—the spirit of christianity, and duties of a christian, should be assiduously considered by all young persons, and great care taken on their part to retain the counsels and instructions of their early years, and make use of them as occasions may require, for the direction of their conduct.

This work, though particularly designed for the use and instruction of young persons during their studies, and on that account adapted to their capacities in simplicity of style, and confined chiefly to their actual wants, as to the selection of prayers and spiritual exercises, will be found very useful in assisting the memory, and seconding the laudable efforts of those who sincerely desire to preserve in their hearts the spirit of piety. It is recommended to them in their progress through life, as a summary of the advice and instructions they had been accustomed to receive, and as a kind of mirror, in which they may at any time discern how far they have retained or lost the virtuous impressions of their early youth. Should this work fall into the hands of any persons who were educated and instructed according to the principles it inculcates, yet who are now conscious that their life in the world does not correspond with the early graces they received, it is most sincerely hoped, that it will not only serve to remind them of the blessings they received from God, and the ingratitude of abusing the early mercies of the Lord, but also assist them to trace back their steps, at least, to the virtues of their childhood; and enable them to regain their first fervour, and to preserve with more fidelity, during the remainder of their lives, that perfect knowledge of the obligations of a christian, and that determined, efficacious will to fulfil them, which are the two most precious fruits to be derived from a RELIGIOUS EDUCATION.

TABLE OF MOVABLE FEASTS.

Year of our Lord.	Dominical Letter.	Golden Number.	The Epact.	Septuagesima Sunday.	Ash Wednesday.	Easter Sunday.
1855	g	13	xij	Feb. 4	Feb. 21	April 8
1856	f e	14	xxviij	Jan. 30	Feb. 6	Mar. 23
1857	d	15	iv	Feb. 8	Feb. 25	April 12
1858	c	16	xv	Jan. 1	Feb. 17	April 4
1859	b	17	xxvj	Feb. 20	Mar. 9	April 24
1860	A g	18	vj	Feb. 5	Feb. 22	April 8
1861	f	19	xviij	Jan. 27	Feb. 13	Mar. 31
1862	e	1	*	Feb. 16	Mar. 5	April 20
1863	d	2	xj	Feb. 1	Feb. 18	April 5
1864	c b	3	xxij	Jan. 24	Feb. 10	Mar. 27
1865	A	4	iij	Feb. 12	Mar. 1	April 16
1866	g	5	xiv	Jan. 28	Feb. 14	April 1
1867	f	6	xxv	Feb. 17	Mar. 6	April 21
1868	e d	7	vj	Feb. 9	Feb. 26	April 12
1869	c	8	xvij	Jan. 24	Feb. 10	Mar. 28
1870	b	9	xxviij	Feb. 13	Mar. 2	April 17
1871	A	10	ix	Feb. 5	Feb. 22	April 9
1872	g f	11	xx	Jan. 28	Feb. 14	Mar. 31
1873	e	12	i	Feb. 9	Feb. 26	April 13
1874	d	13	xij	Feb. 1	Feb. 18	April 5
1875	c	14	xxiij	Jan. 24	Feb. 10	Mar. 28
1876	b A	15	iv	Feb. 13	Mar. 1	April 16
1877	g	16	xv	Jan. 28	Feb. 14	April 1
1878	f	17	xxvj	Feb. 17	Mar. 6	April 21
1879	e	18	vij	Feb. 9	Feb. 26	April 13
1880	d c	19	xviij	Jan. 25	Feb. 11	Mar. 28

TABLE OF MOVABLE FEASTS.

Year of our Lord.	Ascension-Day.	Whit-Sunday.	Corpus Christi.	Indiction.	Sundays after Pentecost.	First Sunday of Advent.
1855	May 17	May 27	June 7	13	26	Dec. 2
1856	May 1	May 11	May 22	14	28	Nov. 30
1857	May 21	May 31	June 11	15	25	Nov. 29
1858	May 13	May 23	June 3	1	26	Nov. 28
1859	June 2	June 12	June 23	2	23	Nov. 27
1860	May 17	May 27	June 7	3	26	Dec. 2
1861	May 9	May 19	May 30	4	27	Dec. 1
1862	May 29	June 8	June 19	5	24	Nov. 30
1863	May 14	May 24	June 4	6	26	Nov. 29
1864	May 5	May 15	May 26	7	27	Nov. 27
1865	May 25	June 4	June 15	8	25	Dec. 3
1866	May 10	May 20	May 31	9	27	Dec. 2
1867	May 30	June 9	June 20	10	24	Dec. 1
1868	May 21	May 31	June 11	11	25	Nov. 29
1869	May 6	May 16	May 27	12	27	Nov. 28
1870	May 26	June 5	May 16	13	25	Nov. 27
1871	May 18	May 28	June 8	14	26	Dec. 3
1872	May 9	May 19	May 30	15	27	Dec. 1
1873	May 22	June 1	June 12	1	25	Nov. 30
1874	May 14	May 24	June 4	2	26	Nov. 29
1875	May 6	May 16	May 27	3	27	Nov. 28
1876	May 25	June 4	June 15	4	25	Dec. 3
1877	May 10	May 20	May 31	5	27	Dec. 2
1878	May 30	June 9	June 20	6	24	Dec. 1
1879	May 22	June 1	June 12	7	25	Nov. 30
1880	May 6	May 16	May 27	8	27	Nov. 28

THE

ROMAN CALENDAR

JANUARY 31 Days.

1 CIRCUMCISION of our Lord.
2 The Octave of St. Stephen.
3 The Octave of St. John.
4 The Octave of the Holy Innocents.
5 The Vigil of the Epiphany. St. Telesphorus, P. M.
6 The EPIPHANY of our Lord, with an Octave.
7 St. Lucian, Priest and Martyr.
8 St. Severius, Bishop of Naples.
9 SS. Julian and Busilla, MM.
10 St. William, Duke of Aquitain, C.
11 St. Theodosius the Cenobiarch, Ab.
12 St. Tutiana, M.
13 The Octave of the Epiphany.
14 St. Hilary, B. C
15 St. Paul the first Hermit. St. Maurus, M.
16 St. Marcellus, P. M.
17 St. Anthony, Ab.
18 Chair of St. Peter at Rome. St. Prisca, V. M.
19 St. Canute, King of Denmark, M.
20 SS. Fabian and Sebastian, MM.
21 St. Agnes, V. M.
22 SS. Vincent and Anastasius, MM.
23 The Desponsation of the B. Virgin MARY.
24 St. Timothy, B. M.
25 The Conversion of St. Paul.
26 St. Polycarp, B. M.
27 St. John Chrysostom, B. C. D.
28 Commemoration of St. Agnes.
29 St. Francis de Sales B. C.

30 St. Martina, V. M.
31 St. Peter Nolasco, C. *Founder of the Order of our Blessed* Lady, *for the Redemption of Captives.*

☞ *The 2d Sunday after Epiphany—The Festival of the* Most Holy name of Jesus.

FEBRUARY 28 Days.

1 St. Bridget, Virgin, Patroness of Ireland.
2 The Purification of the B. V. M.
3 St. Blase, B. M.
4 St. Andrew Corsini, B. C.
5 St. Agatha, V. M.
6 St. Ignatius, B. M.
7 St. Romuald, Ab. *Founder of the Order of* Camaldoli.
8 St. John of Matha, C. *Founder of the Order of the* Trinitarians.
9 St. Marcellus, P. M.
10 St. Scholastica, V. M.
11 SS. Saturninus, and his Companions, M.
12 St. Meltius, Bishop of Antioch, C.
13 St. Catharine de Ricciis, V.
14 St. Valentine, M.
15 SS. Faustinus and Jovita, MM.
16 St. Onesimus, Bishop of Ephesus, and M.
17 St. Theodulus, M.
18 St. Simeon, B. M.
19 St. Mansuetus, Bishop of Milan.
20 St. Eucherius, B. C.
21 St. Severian, B. M.
22 The Chair of St. Peter at Antioch.
23 (*Vigil.*) St. Serenus, Gardener, M.
24 St. Mathias, Apostle.
25 St. Felix, P. C.
26 St. Alexander, Bishop of Alexandria.
27 St. Leander, Bishop of Seville, C.
28 St. Romanus, Ab.

☞ *In Leap Years February has 29 Days, and the* Feast of St. Mathias *is kept on the 25th.*

MARCH 31 Days.

1 St. Albinus, B. C.
2 St. Simplicius, P. C.
3 St. Cunegundis, V.
4 St. Casimir, Prince of Poland, C.
5 St. Phocas, M.
6 St. Victor and Comp. MM.
7 St. Thomas of Aquino, C. D.
8 St. Cataldus, B. C.

9 St. Frances, Widow.
10 The Forty Martyrs of Sebaste.
11 St. Eulogius, P. M.
12 St. Gregory the Great, P. C. D.
13 St. Euphrasia, V.
14 St. Matilda, Widow.
15 St. Longinus, M.
16 St. Abraham, Hermit.
17 St. PATRICK, B. C. and PATRON of Ireland.
18 St. Edward, King of England, M.
19 St. Joseph, C. Spouse of the B. V. M.
20 St. Cuthbert, B. C.
21 St. Benedict, Ab. *Patron of the Western Monks.*
22 St. Basil, P. M.
23 St. Taribius, Bishop of Lima.
24 St. Simeon, M.
25 THE ANNUNCIATION OF THE BLESSED VIRGIN MARY.
26 St. Ludger, B. C.
27 St. John, Hermit.
28 St. Guntram, King and C.
29 St. Cyrillus, Deacon and M.
30 St. John Climacus, Ab.
31 St. Balbina, V.

☞ ***On Friday in Passion Week, the Festival of** the* Seven Dolours *of* the BLESSED VIRGIN MARY.

APRIL 30 Days.

1 St. Hugh, B. C.
2 St. Francis of Paula C. *Founder of the Order of* MINIMS.
3 St. Richard, B.
4 St. Isidore, B. C.
5 St. Vincent Ferrer, C.
6 St. Celestin I., P. C.
7 St. Hegesippus, C.
8 St. Dionysius, Bishop of Corinth.
9 St. Mary of Cleophus, sister of B. V. M.
10 St. Macarius, Bishop of Antioch.
11 St. Leo the Great, P C. D.
12 St. Victor, M.
13 St. Hermenegild, M.
14 SS. Tiburtius, &c. MM.
15 SS. Basilissa and Anastasia, MM.
16 St. Lambert, M.
17 St. Anicetus, P. M.
18 St. Perfectus, P. M.
19 St. Timon, D. M.
20 St. Agnus, V.
21 St. Anselm, B. C.
22 SS. Soterus and Caius, PP. MM.
23 St. George, M.
24 St. Fidelis of Sigmarengen, M

25 St. Mark the Ev.
26 SS. Cletus and Marcellin, PP. MM.
27 St. John, Ab. C.
28 St Vitalis, M.
29 St. Peter, M.
30 St Catharine of Sienna, V.

MAY 31 Days.

1 SS. Philip and James, App.
2 St. Athanasius, B. C.
3 The Invention of the Holy Cross.
4 St. Monica, Widow.
5 St. Pius V., P. C.
6 St. John before the Latin Gate.
7 St. Stanislaus, B. M.
8 The Apparition of St. Michael.
9 St. Gregory Nazianzen, B. C.
10 St. Congall, Ab.
11 *B. Francis de Hyeronimo.*
12 SS. Nereus, &c. MM.
13 St. John the Silent, B. C.
14 St. Boniface, M.
15 St. Dympna, V. M.
16 St. John Nepomucen, M.
17 St Paschal Baylon, C.
18 St. Venantius, M.
19 St. Peter Celestine, P. C. *Founder of the Order of* CELESTINES.
20 St. Bernardin of Sienna, C.
21 St. Valens, B. M.
22 St. Basilicus, M.
23 St. Desiderius, B. M.
24 SS. Donatian and Rogatian, MM.
25 St. Gregory VII., P.C.
26 St. Philip Neri, C. *Founder of the Congregation of* ORATORIANS.
27 St. Mary Magdalen of Pazzi, V.
28 St. Germanus, B. C
29 St. Maximinus, B. C.
30 St. Felix, P. M.
31 St. Angela of Brescia, *Foundress of the* URSULINE ORDER, *devoted to the Instruction of young Girls, rich and poor.*

JUNE 30 Days

1 St. Pamphilus, P. M.
2 SS. Marcellinus, &c MM.
3 St. Clotildis, Queen of France.
4 St. Francis Caracciolo, C.
5 St. Boniface, B. M.
6 St. Norbert, B. C. *Founder of the Order of* PREMONSTRATENSIANS.
7 St. Robert, Ab.

8 St. Metardus, B. C.
9 SS. Primus and Felician, MM.
10 St. Margaret, Queen of Scotland, Widow.
11 St. Barnaby, Apostle.
12 St. John of Sahagun, C.
13 St. Anthony of Padua, C.
14 St. Basil the Great, B. C.
15 SS. Vitus, &c. MM.
16 *St. John Francis Regis, C.*
17 St. Avitus, P. C.
18 SS. Marcus and Marcellinus, MM.
19 St. Juliana a Falconieri, V. *Foundress of the Order of* MANTELLATÆ.
20 St. Sylverius, P. M.
21 *St. Aloysius, Gonzaga, C.*
22 St. Paulinus, B. C.
23 *Vigil. Fast.*
24 The Nativity of St. John the Baptist, with an Octave.
25 St. William, Ab. *Founder of the Congregation de* MONTE-VIRGINE.
26 SS. John and Paul, MM.
27 St. Cressent, B. M.
28 *Vigil. Fast.* St. Leo II. P. C
29 SS. Peter and Paul Apostles, with an Octave.
30 The Commemoration of St. Paul the Apostle.

JULY 31 Days.

1 The Octave of St. John the Baptist.
2 The Visitation of the B. V. M.
3 St. Fulogius, and his companions, MM
4 St. Flavian, Bishop of Antioch.
5 St. Athanasius, Deacon, M.
6 The Octave of SS. Peter and Paul.
7 St. Benedict the XI., P. C.
8 St. Kylian, B. M.
9 St. Cyrillus, Bishop of Gortyna, M.
10 The Seven Brethren, MM.
11 St. Pius I., P. M.
12 St. John Gualbert, Ab. *Founder of the Religious Order of* VALLIS UMBROSA.
13 St. Anacletus, P. M.
14 St. Bonaventure, B C. D.
15 St. Henry II. Emperor of Germany, C.
16 The Commemoration

4*

of the B. V. M. of Mount Carmel.
17 St. Alexius, C.
18 St. Camillus de Lellis, C. *Founder of the Order for serving the* SICK.
19 St. Vincent of Paulo, C. *Founder of the* LAZARITES, *or* FATHERS OF THE MISSION.
20 St. Jerom Emilian, C. *Founder of the* REGULAR CLERGY of SOMASCHA.
21 St. Praxedes, V.
22 St. Mary Magdalen.
23 St. Apollinaris, B. M.
24 (*Vigil.*) St. Christina, V. M.
25 St. James, Apostle.
26 St. Anne, Mother of the B. V. M.
27 St. Pantaleon, M.
28 SS. Naz. Celsus, and Victor, MM. and St. Innocent, P. C.
29 St. Martha, V.
30 SS. Abdon and Sennen, MM.
31 St. Ignatius of Loyola, C. *Founder of the Society of* JESUS.

AUGUST 31 Days.

1 St. Peter's Chains.
2 St. Stephen, P. M.
3 The finding of St. Stephen, Protomartyr.
4 St. Dominick, C *Founder of the Order of* FRIARS PREACHERS.
5 The Dedication of the Church of the B. V M. of Nives.
6 The Transfiguration of our Lord.
7 St. Cajetan, C. *Founder of the Order of* THEATINS.
8 SS. Cyriacus, Largus, and Smaragdus, MM.
9 (*Vigil.*) St. Romanus, M.
10 St. Laurence, M. with an Octave.
11 St. Tiburtius, M.
12 St. Clare, V. *Foundress of the Order of* POOR CLARES.
13 St. Hypolitus, M.
14 (*Vigil. Fast.*)
15 The ASSUMPTION of the B. V. M. with an Octave.
16 St. Hyacinth, C.
17 The Octave of St. Laurence.
18 St. Helen, Mother of Constantine the Great.
19 SS. Timothy, &c MM.
20 St. Bernard, Ab.
21 St. Jane Frances de Chantal, Widow.

22 The Octave of the Assumption.
23 (*Vigil.*) St. Philip Beniti, C.
24 St. Bartholomew, Ap.
25 St. Lewis IX. King of France, C.
26 St. Zephyrinus, P. M.
27 St. Joseph Calasanctius, *Founder of the poor Regular Clergy of the pious Schools of the* MOTHER OF GOD.
28 St. Augustine, B.C.D.
29 The Decollation of St. John the Baptist.
30 St. Fiaker, C.
31 St. Raymund Nonnatus, C.

SEPTEMBER 30 Days.

1 St. Rose of Lima, V.
2 St. Stephen, King of Hungary, C.
3 St. Simeon Stylites, C.
4 SS. Marcellus, &c. MM.
5 St. Laurence Justinian, B. C.
6 St. Onesiphorus, M.
7 St. Regina, V. M.
8 The Nativity of the B. V. M. with an Octave.
9 St. Gorgonius, M.
10 St. Nicholas of Tol n-tine, C.
11 St. Protus, M.
12 St. Eanswide, V. Abbess.
13 St. Eulogius, B. C.
14 The Exaltation of the Holy Cross.
15 The Octave of the Nativity of the B. V. M.
16 SS. Cornelius and Cyprian, BB. MM.
17 The Impression of the Sacred Stigmas of St. Francis.
18 St. Joseph of Cupertino, C.
19 SS. Januarius, B. and Companions, MM.
20 (*Vigil.*) St. Eustachius and Companions, MM.
21 St. Matthew, Apostle and Evang.
22 St. Thomas of Villa nova, B. C.
23 St. Linus, P. M., St. Thecla, V. M.
24 Feast of the B. V M. of the Redemption of Captives.
25 St. Cleolfrid, Ab
26 SS. Cyprian and Justina, MM.
27 SS. Cosmas and Damian, MM.
28 St. Wenceslas, M.
29 Dedication of St. Michael's Church.
30 St. Jerom, C.

☞ *Sunday within the Octave of the Nativity of the* B. V. M. the Festival of the Holy Name of the B. V. M.

On the third Sunday in September, the seven dolours of the Blessed Virgin.

OCTOBER 31 Days.

1 St. Remigius, B. C.
2 The Feast of the Guardian Angels.
3 St. Dionysius the Areopagite, B. M.
4 St. Francis of Assisium, C. *Founder of the Order of* FRANCISCANS.
5 SS. Placidus and Companions, MM.
6 St. Bruno, C. *Founder of the* CARTHUSIAN MONKS.
7 St. Mark, P. C. and SS. Sergius, &c. MM.
8 St. Bridget, Widow.
9 St. Denis, B. and Companions, MM.
10 St. Francis Borgia.
11 St. Germanus, B. M.
12 St. Walfrid, B. C.
13 St. Edward, King and Confessor.
14 St. Callistus, P. M.
15 St. Teresa, V. *Foundress of the Reformation of the* BAREFOOTED CARMELITES.
16 St. Gall, Ab.
17 St. Hedwiges, or Avoice, Duchess of Poland, Widow.
18 St. Luke, Evangelist.
19 St. Peter of Alcantara, C.
20 St. John Cantius, C.
21 SS. Ursula and Companions, VV. MM.—*St.* Ursula *is the special Patroness of the* URSULINE ORDER, *instituted by St.* Angela of Brescia, *in* 1532, *for the Instruction of young Girls, rich and poor.*
22 St. Mark, Bishop of Jerusalem, M.
23 St. Theodoret, M.
24 St. Raphael, Archangel.
25 SS. Chrysanthus and Daria, MM.
26 St. Evaristus, P. M.
27 (*Vigil.*)
28 SS. Simon and Jude Apostles.
29 St. Theodorus, Ab.
30 St. Marcellus, M.
31 (*Vigil. Fast.*) St Quintin, M.

☞ *The first Sunday of October*, the Festival of the Rosary of the B. V. M.

NOVEMBER 30 Days.

1 The FESTIVAL OF ALL SAINTS, with an Octave.
2 The Commemoration of the Faithful departed.
3 St. Malachy, Bishop of Armagh.
4 St. Charles Borromeo, B. C. *Patron of the Ursuline Schools.*
5 St. Elizabeth, Mother of St. John Baptist.
6 St. Leonard, Hermit.
7 St. Engelbert, B. M.
8 The Octave of all Saints.
9 The Dedication of the Church of our Saviour, called St. John of Lateran.
10 St. Andrew Avellino, C.
11 St. Martin of Tours, B. C.
12 St. Livin, B. M.
13 St. Stanislaus Kostka, C.
14 St. Laurence, Bishop of Dublin.
15 St. Gertrude, V.
16 St. Martin, P. M.
17 St. Gregory Thaumaturgus, B. C.
18 The Dedication of the Churches of SS. Peter and Paul, at Rome.
19 St. Elizabeth, of Hungary, Widow.
20 St. Felix of Valois, C. *Founder of the Order of* TRINITARIANS.
21 The Presentation of the B. V. M.
22 St. Cecilia, V. M.
23 St. Clement, P. M.
24 St. Columban, Ab.
25 St. Catharine, V. M.
26 St. John of the Cross.
27 St. Virgil, B. C.
28 St. Didacus, C.
29 (*Vigil.*) St. Saturninus, M.
30 St. Andrew, Apostle.

☞ *On the second Sunday in November*, the Feast of the Protection of the B. V. M.

DECEMBER 31 Days.

1 St. Eligius, B. C.
2 St. Bibiana, V. M.
3 St. Francis Xavier, C. *Apostle of the Indies.*
4 St. Peter Chrysologus, B. C., St. Barbara, V. M.
5 St. Sabbas, Ab.
6 St. Nicholas, B. C.
7 St. Ambrose, B. C. D.
8 The Immaculate Conception of the B. V M. with an Octave
9
10 St Melchiades, P. C

11 St. Damasus, P. C.
12 St. Synesius, M.
13 St. Lucy, V. M.
14 St. Spiridion, B. C.
15 The Octave of the Conception of the B. V. M.
16 St. Eusebius, B. M.
17 St. Olympias, Widow.
18 The Expectation of the B. V. M.
19 St. Nemesion, M.
20 (*Vigil.*) St. Philagonius, B. C.
21 St. Thomas, Apostle.
22 St. Ischyrion, M.
23 St. Servulus, C.
24 (*Fast.*) Vigil of the Nativity.
25 The NATIVITY OF OUR LORD.
26 St. Stephen, the first Martyr.
27 St. John, Apostle and Ev.
28 The Feast of the Holy Innocents, with an Octave.
29 St. Thomas of Canterbury, B. M.
30 The Office of the Sunday within the Octave of the Nativity.
31 St. Sylvester, P. C.

FEASTS AND FASTS

THROUGHOUT THE YEAR.

Holy Days on which there is a strict obligation to hear Mass, and refrain from servile works.

All Sundays in the year.
The Feast of the Circumcision of our Lord, Jan. 1
The Epiphany, Jan. 6.
The Annunciation, March 25
Ascension of our Lord.
Corpus Christi.
Assumption of the B. V. Mary, August 15.
Feast of All Saints, November 1.
Nativity of our Lord Jesus Christ, Dec. 25.

Fasting Days.

All days in Lent, except Sundays.

The Eve of Whitsuntide.

The Quarter-Tenses, or Ember days, that occur in the four seasons of the year.

The Vigil of the Assumption of the Blessed Virgin Mary, and of All Saints.

Every Friday in Advent, and Christmas Eve.

Days of Abstinence from Flesh Meat.

Every day in Lent, except when the use of meat is allowed by the Archbishop or Bishop of the diocess.

All Fridays in the year.

All Ember days and Vigils as above.

If a fasting day fall on a Sunday, the fast is kept on the Saturday before. If Christmas Day fall upon a Friday, neither fast nor abstinence is observed.

N. B.—The Catholic Church commands all her children to be present at the great Eucharistic Sacrifice which we call the Mass, and to rest from servile works on Sundays and holidays.

Secondly, To abstain from flesh on all the days of fasting and abstinence.

Thirdly, To confess their sins at least once a year

Fourthly, To receive the blessed sacrament at least once a year, during the Easter time.

The time for satisfying the Easter precept in the United States, is, in virtue of a late concession, from the first Sunday of Lent to Trinity Sunday, both inclusively.

AN

ABRIDGMENT

OF THE

CHRISTIAN DOCTRINE.

The Ten Commandments of God.—Exodus xx.

1. I AM the Lord thy God, who brought thee out of the land of Egypt, and out of the house of bondage. Thou shalt not have strange gods before me. Thou shalt not make to thyself a graven thing, nor the likeness of any thing that is in heaven above, or in the earth beneath, nor of those things that are in the waters under the earth. Thou shalt not adore them, nor serve *them:* I am the Lord thy God, mighty, jealous, visiting the iniquity of fathers upon their children unto the third and fourth generation of those that hate me; and showing mercy unto thousands of those that love me, and keep my commandments.

2. Thou shalt not take the name of the Lord thy God in vain; for the Lord will not hold him guiltless that shall take the name of the Lord his God in vain.

3. Remember that thou keep holy the Sabbath day. Six days shalt thou labour, and shalt do all thy works; but on the seventh day is the Sabbath of the Lord thy God: thou shalt do no work on it, thou, nor thy son, nor thy daughter, nor thy man servant, nor thy maid servant, nor thy beast, nor the stranger that is within thy gates. For in six days the Lord made heaven and earth, and the sea, and all things that are in them, and

rested on the seventh day; therefore, the Lord blessed the seventh day, and sanctified it.

4. Honour thy father and thy mother, that thou mayest be long-lived upon the land which the Lord thy God will give thee.

5. Thou shalt not kill.

6. Thou shalt not commit adultery.

7 Thou shalt not steal.

8. Thou shalt not bear false witness against thy neighbour.

9. Thou shalt not covet thy neighbour's wife.

10. Thou shalt not covet thy neighbour's house, nor his servant, nor his ox, nor his ass, nor any thing that is his.

The six Precepts of the Church.

1. To hear Mass on Sundays, and all holidays of obligation.

2. To fast and abstain on the days commanded.

3. To confess our sins at least once a year.

4. To receive the blessed Eucharist at Easter, or within the time appointed.

5. To contribute to the support of our pastors.

6. Not to solemnize marriage at the forbidden times; nor to marry persons within the forbidden degrees of kindred, or otherwise prohibited by the church; nor clandestinely.

Seven Sacraments.

Baptism . . . . . . *Matt.* xxviii. 19
Confirmation . . . . *Acts* viii. 17.
Eucharist . . . . *Matt.* xvi. 26.
Penance . . . . . *John* xx. 23.
Extreme Unction . . *James* v. 14.
Holy Orders . . . *Luke* xxii. 19
Matrimony . . . . . *Matt.* xix. 6.

The three Theological Virtues.

Faith—Hope—and Charity.

The four Cardinal Virtues

Prudence—Justice—Fortitude—and Temperance.

The seven Gifts of the Holy Ghost.—Isa. xi. 2, 3.

Wisdom,	Fortitude,	
Understanding,	Knowledge,	The fear of the Lord.
Counsel,	Piety, and	

The twelve Fruits of the Holy Ghost.

Charity,	Patience,	Benignity,	Modesty,
Joy,	Longanimity,	Mildness,	Continency, and
Peace,	Goodness,	Fidelity,	Chastity.

The spiritual Works of Mercy.

To give counsel to the doubtful.—To instruct the ignorant.—To admonish sinners.—To comfort the afflicted.—To forgive offences.—To bear patiently the troublesome.—To pray for the living and the dead.

The corporal Works of Mercy.

To feed the hungry.—To give drink to the thirsty. —To clothe the naked.—To harbour the harbourless. —To visit the sick.—To visit the imprisoned;—and, to bury the dead.

The eight Beatitudes.—Matt. v.

1. Blessed are the poor in spirit; for theirs is the kingdom of heaven.
2. Blessed are the meek; for they shall possess the land.
3. Blessed are they that mourn; for they shall be comforted.
4. Blessed are they that hunger and thirst after justice; for they shall be filled.
5. Blessed are the merciful; for they shall obtain mercy.
6. Blessed are the clean of heart; for they shall see God.

7. Blessed are the peace-makers; for they shall be called the children of God.

8. Blessed are they that suffer persecution for justice' sake, for theirs is the kingdom of heaven.

The seven deadly Sins, and the opposite Virtues

	Contrary Virtues	
Pride,		Humility,
Covetousness,		Liberality,
Lust,		Chastity,
Anger,		Meekness,
Gluttony,		Temperance,
Envy,		Brotherly love,
Sloth.		Diligence.

Sins against the Holy Ghost.

Presumption of God's mercy—Despair—Impugning the known truth—Envy at another's spiritual good—Obstinacy in sin—Final impenitence.

Sins crying to Heaven for Vengeance.

Wilful murder—The sin of Sodom—Oppression of the poor—Defrauding labourers of their wages.

Nine Ways of being accessary to another's Sin.

By counsel—By command—By consent—By provocation—By praise or flattery—By concealment—By partaking—By silence—By defence of the ill done.

Three eminent good Works.

Alms-deeds, or works of mercy—Prayer—and Fasting.

The Evangelical Counsels.

Voluntary poverty—Chastity—and Obedience

The four last things to be remembered

Death—Judgment—Hell—and Heaven.

Painted by Sir Joshua Reynolds.

MORNING PRAYER.

Published by Edward Dunigan, New-York.

Subjects for daily Meditation.

Remember, christian soul, that thou hast this day, and every day of thy life,

God to glorify,	Heaven to gain,
Jesus to imitate,	Eternity to prepare for,
The angels and saints to invoke,	Time to profit of,
	Neighbours to edify,
A soul to save,	The world to despise,
A body to mortify,	Devils to combat,
Sins to expiate,	Passions to subdue,
Virtues to acquire,	Death perhaps to suffer,
Hell to avoid,	And judgment to undergo.

Thou shalt love the Lord thy God with thy whole heart, and with thy whole soul, and with thy whole mind. This is the greatest and first commandment: and the second is like to this—Thou shalt love thy neighbour as thyself. On these two commandments dependeth the whole law and the prophets.—*St. Matt.* xxii.

MORNING EXERCISE.

It is of great consequence to the perfection of each day that it should be begun well. The first thoughts of a Christian in the morning are, as it were, those first-fruits of which the Almighty was always most jealous. Endeavour to contract the holy habit of raising your heart to the Almighty immediately on awaking, to implore his protection and holy grace, that the day which his infinite goodness now adds to your life may not add to your sins, but, on the contrary, increase your merits, and tend to his glory. It may be the last of your life—perhaps you may never see another morning, perhaps you may never have another day to glorify God, to imitate Jesus Christ, to expiate your sins, to avoid hell, to gain heaven, or to devote to any of the other important duties of a Christian, which this page presents to you as subjects for daily meditation. You are accustomed to repeat those subjects while you dress: endeavour to do so with such serious attention, that they may powerfully animate you not to throw away a single moment of the day you are commencing, and which may terminate by your being presented before the tribunal of divine justice. Let your first remembrance, then, be of God, your first action the sacred sign of the cross, and your first words an offering of your whole being to your Creator, in the following or any other form.

My God, I offer thee my heart, and most fervently beg of thee to take possession of my whole being. It is for thy love, O divine Jesus, that I now rise. Deign to accept of every thought, word, and action of this day; give them a blessing; preserve me from sin, and grant me the graces necessary to merit eternal life.

As soon as you are sufficiently dressed, say the following prayer kneeling,

O ETERNAL and adorable Trinity! Father, Son, and Holy Ghost! I adore, bless, and glorify thy infinite majesty. Prostrate in spirit at the foot of thy throne, I thank thee for all the blessings I ever received from thy pure, gratuitous mercy.—I particularly thank thee, for having granted me this day, to advance in thy fear and love. It may be my last; therefore, my God, I most earnestly beseech thee to enable me to avoid sin, and to employ every moment to thy greater glory, and the sanctification of my soul *Amen.*

As the ordinary, and most trivial duties of life can, according to the Apostle, be sanctified by an upright intention, take care to direct to the glory of God, even those actions, which too many young persons perform through vanity, or at best through custom. Besides thinking of God while you wash, dress, &c., say the following short prayers.

MY God, grant that all my thoughts, words, and actions, may be sanctified by a pure intention of pleasing thee alone.

O MY divine Saviour, may the tortures and humiliations of thy thorny crown sink deeply into my heart, that, strengthened by thy grace, I may never indulge vanity, or exceed that moderation which religion prescribes in the arrangement of dress

MAY the precious blood and water which issued from thy sacred side, O merciful Jesus cleanse my soul from every stain of sin.

O MY God, may the precious robe of innocence, which I received at baptism, be refreshed and purified by sincere repentance, and the saving merits of thy adorable Son, that at the awful moment of death I may exchange this vesture of dust for the bright garment of immortality. *Amen.*

When it becomes your duty to repeat the prayers aloud for the rest of your companions, do not say them precipitately, or, on the other hand, be unreasonably tedious, but take particular care to repeat them distinctly, reverentially, and altogether in such an edifying manner, as will prove your own interior attention to what you say, and also animate the devotion of those who hear you.

My Lord and my God! in union with all thy elect in heaven and on earth, I adore thee, I love thee, I praise and thank thee, for all the benefits of nature and grace, general and particular, which I have received from thy infinite goodness and liberality: principally for having created me to thy image and likeness, preserved me to this day, and given thy only begotten Son to suffer death for me on the cross, and to wash away my sins in his most precious blood. I thank thee for having called me to the true faith and religion of the holy Catholic and Apostolic Church—for having so often pardoned me my sins, and preserved me during this last night from a sudden death, and from all the other dangers which might have befallen me, had I not been protected by thy merciful and watchful Providence. Alas! my God, how shall I acknowledge all these favours? I, who am nothing, have nothing, and can do nothing, without thy gracious assistance. I wish I could make thee an offering of gratitude and love proportionate to thy benefits; but as thou knowest my poverty and weakness, I beseech thee to receive, as the only sacrifice of thanksgiving I have to offer, an oblation which I now make of my body, with all its senses; my soul, with all its faculties; my heart, with all its desires. I specially consecrate to thee, in union with the infinite merits of Jesus Christ, every thought, word, and action of this day; firmly purposing, with the assistance of thy grace, not to think, say, or do any thing, but what may tend to thy greater glory, and the sanctification of my soul. *Amen.*

V Blessed be the holy and undivided Trinity
R. Now and for evermore. *Amen.*

The Lord's Prayer.

Our Father, who art in heaven, hallowed be thy name; thy kingdom come; thy will be done on earth as it is in heaven. Give us this day our daily bread; and forgive us our trespasses, as we forgive them that trespass against us. And lead us not into temptation; but deliver us from evil. *Amen.*

The Angelical Salutation.

Hail Mary, full of grace, our Lord is with thee; blessed art thou amongst women, and blessed is the fruit of thy womb, Jesus. Holy Mary, Mother of God, pray for us sinners, now, and at the hour of our death. *Amen.*

The Apostles' Creed.

I believe in God, the Father Almighty, Creator of heaven and earth. And in Jesus Christ, his only Son our Lord, who was conceived by the Holy Ghost, born of the Virgin Mary; suffered under Pontius Pilate, was crucified, dead and buried; he descended into hell, the third day he rose again from the dead, he ascended into heaven, sitteth at the right hand of God the Father Almighty; from thence he shall come to judge the living and the dead. I believe in the Holy Ghost; the Holy Catholic Church; the communion of saints; the forgiveness of sins, the resurrection of the body, and life everlasting. *Amen.*

Confiteor.

I confess to Almighty God, to blessed Mary, ever Virgin, to blessed Michael the archangel, to blessed John the Baptist, to the holy apostles Peter and Paul, and to all the saints, that I have sinned exceedingly, in thought, word, and deed, *through my fault, through my fault, through my most grievous fault.*

Therefore I beseech the blessed Mary, ever Virgin the blessed Michael the archangel, the blessed John the Baptist, the holy apostles Peter and Paul, and all the saints, to pray to the Lord God for me.

May the Almighty God have mercy upon me, forgive me my sins, and bring me to everlasting life. *Amen.*

May the Almighty and Merciful Lord grant me pardon, absolution, and remission of all my sins. *Amen.*

V. Vouchsafe, O Lord, during this day,
R. To preserve me pure and without sin.
V. Have mercy on me, O Lord.
R. Have mercy on me, O Lord.
V. Lord, grant that thy mercy may be shown to me.
R. According to the hope I have placed in thee.
V. O Lord, hear my prayer.
R. And let my supplications come unto thee.

Let us pray.

Lord God all-powerful, who hast brought me safely to the beginning of this day, protect me by thy providence, that during the course of it I may not fall into sin, but that all my thoughts, words, and actions, being directed by thy holy grace, may tend to the accomplishment of thy divine will; that during this life, and the eternity of the life to come, I may, through thy divine assistance, be delivered and saved, O Saviour of the world! who livest and reignest one God world without end. *Amen*

O blessed Angel! to whose holy care I am committed by the supreme clemency, illuminate, defend, and govern me this day: preserve me particularly from sin, and watch over me at the awful moment of my death. *Amen.*

May the Lord bless and preserve me from all sin and danger; and may the souls of the faithful departed, through the mercy of God, rest in peace *Amen.*

O holy Mary, Mother of God, Queen of Angels and of men, I honour and reverence thee with all my heart, and I desire to do so as perfectly as thy divine Son would have thee honoured in heaven and on earth. O Mother of Mercy! I choose thee this day for my mother; look on me as thy child, and in thy goodness treat me as the object of thy tender mercy. O Mother of grace and mercy, refuge of sinners, may I, through thy powerful intercession, be delivered from all sin, and preserved from eternal death: protect me, bless me, obtain for me from thy divine Son Jesus, that I may be for ever his true and faithful servant, and do not abandon me, either now or at the hour of my death. *Amen.*

O great Saint! whose name I received in baptism grant me thy particular protection in every danger of soul and body; obtain for me the grace of fidelity to the obligations I contracted when, under thy patronage, I was admitted into the Church. And thou, O blessed citizen of heaven, whom I have this month chosen for my patron, obtain for me the virtue I stand most in need of, and above all, an ardent and solid love for Jesus my Saviour.

Holy Mary, Mother of God,
St. Joseph,
St. Patrick,
St. Augustine,
St. Charles,
St. Angela, *Pray for us.*

St. Ursula, and all your holy companions, *Pray for us.*
All you angels and saints of God, *Make intercession for us.*

An Act of Contrition.

O MY God! I am most heartily sorry for having offended thy divine Majesty; because I know that sin displeases thee, and that thou deservest to be sovereignly loved, adored, and faithfully served. I purpose firmly, with the help of thy holy grace, never more to offend thee deliberately, to do all that I can to atone for my sins, and to amend my life. *Amen*

An Act of Faith.

O MY God! I most firmly believe in thee, and in all that thou hast revealed to thy holy Catholic Church; because thou art truth itself, who canst neither deceive nor be deceived. *Amen.*

An Act of Hope.

O MY God! I most firmly hope in thee, because of all thy promises, and trust that thou wilt give me eternal life, and the graces necessary to obtain it, through the merits of my dear Lord and Saviour Jesus Christ. *Amen.*

An Act of Charity.

O MY God. I love thee more than all things, because thou art infinite in every perfection, and worthy of all my love: grant that I may daily increase in this divine love, that I may love my neighbour as myself, and prefer a thousand deaths to the loss of thee by any mortal sin. *Amen.*

Hail, holy Queen, Mother of Mercy! our life, our sweetness, and our hope.* To thee do we cry, poor banished children of Eve; to thee do we send up our sighs, mourning and weeping in this valley of tears. Turn then, most gracious Advocate, thine eyes of mercy towards us, and, after this our painful exile, show unto us that blessed fruit of thy womb, Jesus O clement! O pious! O sweet Virgin Mary!

V. Pray for us, O holy Mother of God.

R. That we may be made worthy of the promises of Christ.

* Jesus Christ alone can be strictly called the Life and Hope of Christians. Such expressions applied to the Blessed Virgin Mary, should be taken in a limited sense, relative to her quality of our Patroness and Advocate.

The Angelical Salutation.

V. The Angel of the Lord declared unto Mary.
R. And she conceived of the Holy Ghost.
Hail Mary, &c.
V. Behold the handmaid of the Lord.
R. May it be done unto me according to thy word
Hail Mary, &c.
V. And the Word was made flesh.
R. And dwelt among us.
Hail Mary, &c.
V. Pray for us, O holy Mother of God!
R. That we may be made worthy of the promises of Christ.

Let us pray.

Pour forth, we beseech thee, O Lord, thy grace into our hearts; that we, to whom the incarnation of Christ thy Son was made known by the message of an angel, may by his passion and cross be brought to the glory of his resurrection. Through the same Christ our Lord. *Amen.*

Instead of the *Angelus*, or *Angelical Salutation*, the *Regina Cœli*, or *Triumph, O Queen of Heaven*, is said from Easter to Trinity Sunday.

Triumph, O Queen of Heaven, to see, Alleluia,
The sacred Infant born of thee, Alleluia:
Spring up in glory from the tomb, Alleluia:
O by thy prayers prevent our doom, Alleluia.
V. Rejoice and be glad, O Virgin Mary! Alleluia.
R Because our Lord is truly risen, Alleluia.

Let us pray.

O God, who, by the resurrection of thy Son our Lord Jesus Christ, hast vouchsafed to gladden the world, grant, we beseech thee, that, by the intercession of the Virgin Mary, his Mother, we may receive the joys of eternal life. Through the same Jesus Christ our Lord. R. *Amen.*

A Prayer to be said by Children for their Parents.

O MERCIFUL God, who visitest the iniquities of parents on their children to the third and fourth generation, and showest mercy unto thousands of those who love thee and keep thy commandments; pour down thy blessings on my father and mother: reward, I beseech thee, O Lord, all their labours and tender solicitude for my welfare, by the remission of their sins and deliver them from the punishments which may remain due to them. Endue them with such fortitude, and resignation to thy divine will, as may enable them to bear patiently all the trials of this life: may thy heavenly grace make them fruitful in good works, and may they, like the holy patriarchs, enjoy the blessings of a long, happy, and peaceable life, and find in their children the consolation and support of their old age. May the precious inheritance of their virtues and welfare descend to their children; that through their wise counsels and good example, they and their offspring may be inseparably united in the enjoyment of eternal life, O Saviour of the world! who livest and reignest one God, world without end. *Amen.*

NIGHT PRAYERS.

I ADORE thee, O my God! I praise and thank thee, my sovereign Lord, and most liberal Benefactor, and invite all creatures in heaven and on earth to join with me, in glorifying thee for all the benefits of nature and grace, general and particular, which I have received from thy infinite goodness and liberality; particularly for my having been preserved to this moment, assisted by thy holy grace, and delivered by thy particular protection from the many evils which might have befallen me.

Alas! my God, how shall I acknowledge all these

favours; I, who am but an ungrateful creature, and who, though overpowered by thy benefits, cease not to offend thee: I most humbly beseech thee to enlighten my understanding that I may know my faults; touch my heart that I may sincerely detest them; and vouchsafe to strengthen my will, that I may atone for my sins and amend my life.

Examination of Conscience.

I SHOULD now examine, as seriously as if I were sure the Almighty would call me this night out of the world, whether I have offended God this day by thought, word, deed, or omission.

First, *with regard to God.*—Have I neglected, on awaking in the morning, to offer my heart to God? Have I said my morning prayers, or assisted at mass, with wilful distraction or irreverence; behaved disrespectfully in the chapel; taken the holy name of God in vain; or been totally forgetful of the divine presence during the course of the day?

Secondly, *with regard to my neighbour.*—Have I been wilfully disobedient; or indulged anger, impatience, ill-temper, hatred, jealousy, or desire of revenge?—Have I been guilty of rash judgments, detraction, or lies, or by any means been accessary to the sins of others?

Thirdly, *with regard to myself.*—Have I indulged pride or vanity; sinned, by thought, words, looks, or actions, contrary to purity; been guilty of sloth, neglected my improvement, or misemployed my time?

An Act of Contrition.

MY Lord and Creator, my divine Saviour and merciful Benefactor, who hast sacrificed thy life for my redemption, I am heartily sorry for all the sins I have this day committed against thy adorable Majesty. I sincerely detest every sin of my life, particularly those which displease thee most; and I detest them more for the injury they have done thee, than for the punishment they merit. Receive, O my divine Saviour! the efficacious contrition of thy own sacred heart, in atonement for the deficiency of my sorrow; and grant me, through thy sufferings and death, such sincere detestation of sin, that I may henceforward carefully avoid every occasion of offending thee, confess sincerely, and perform the penance enjoined me. *Amen*

V. Blessed be the holy and undivided Trinity.

R. Now and for evermore. *Amen.*

Repeat the *Our Father*, *Hail Mary*, the *Creed*, and *Confiteor*

Prostrate, before the closing of the day,
To thee, Creator of the world, we pray:
Shed round us, mid the darkness of the night,
Rays of thy mercy, clemency, and might.
Grant us in innocence and peace to sleep,
All sinful visions from our slumbers keep:
Let holy angels hover round our bed,
And guard us from the enemy we dread.
To Jesus, from a spotless Virgin sprung,
Be honour given, and praises ever sung;
Alike to God, th' Almighty Father, be,
And Holy Ghost, who reign eternally. *Amen.*

V. O Lord, save me whilst awake, and defend me whilst asleep.

R. That I may watch with Christ, and rest in peace.

V. Vouchsafe, O Lord, this night,

R. To preserve me pure and without sin.

V. Have mercy on me, O Lord.

R. Have mercy on me, O Lord.

V. O Lord, grant that thy mercy may be shown to me.

R. According to the hope I have placed in thee.

V. O Lord, hear my prayer.

R. And let my supplication come unto thee.

Let us pray.

Visit, I beseech thee, O Lord, this habitation, and drive far from it all the snares of the enemy. May thy holy angels dwell herein, to preserve me in peace and may thy holy benedictions always remain with me, through Christ our Lord. *Amen.*

O Angel of God! to whose holy care I am committed by the supreme clemency, illuminate, govern, and defend me this night from all sin and danger. *Amen.*

May the Lord all-powerful, the Father, the Son, and the Holy Ghost, watch over me, and preserve me from all evil. *Amen.*

An Act of Adoration.

My Lord, my God, and my Father, I adore thee, in union with all creatures in heaven and on earth, acknowledging thee for my God and sovereign Lord; and as I began this day by offering myself to thee, I desire to finish it, by consecrating anew to thy divine Majesty my body, my soul, my life, and all that I am: keep me this night under thy particular protection, and grant me the grace, that whilst my eyes are closed by sleep, my heart may be for ever awake to thy divine love, and that, after this transitory life, I may see and enjoy thee for ever in a happy eternity *Amen.*

O happy Mary! chosen to be
The Mother of grace and clemency;
Protect us now; and at the hour of death,
O bear to heaven our parting breath. *Amen*

Holy Mary, Mother of God,
St. Joseph,
St. Patrick,
St. Augustine,
St. Charles,
St. Angela,
St. Ursula, and all your holy companions,
Pray for us.

All you Angels and Saints of God, *Make intercession for us.*

An Act of Contrition.

O my God! I am most heartily sorry for having

offended thy divine Majesty, because I know sin displeases thee, and that thou deservest to be sovereignly loved, and faithfully served: I purpose firmly, with the help of thy holy grace, never more to offend thee deliberately, to do all that I can to atone for my sins, and to amend my life. *Amen.*

An Act of Faith.

O MY God! I most firmly believe in thee, and in all that thou hast revealed to thy holy Catholic Church; because thou art truth itself, who neither canst deceive nor be deceived. *Amen.*

An Act of Hope.

O MY God! I most firmly hope in thee, because of all thy promises; and trust that thou wilt give me eternal life, and all the graces necessary to obtain it: through the merits of my dear Lord and Saviour Jesus Christ. *Amen.*

An Act of Charity.

O MY God! I love thee more than all things, because thou art infinite in every perfection, and worthy of all my love: grant that I may daily increase in thy divine love; that I may love my neighbour as myself, and prefer a thousand deaths to the loss of thee by any mortal sin. *Amen.*

Repeat the *Hail, holy Queen,* also the *Angelical Salutation,* or *Triumph, O Queen of Heaven,* as before, pp. 59, 60.

The Seven Stations of our Lord's Passion.

1st, IN the Garden of Olives, where our divine Lord and Saviour Jesus Christ prayed three times to God his Father, was bathed in blood at the sight of our sins, was consoled by an angel, and taken by the Jews.

2d, In the house of Annas, father-in-law to Caiphas, where he was questioned on his doctrine and disciples, and received a blow from one of the servants of the high priest.

3d, At Caiphas's, where he was denied three time by St. Peter, and insulted and outraged all night.

4th, At Pilate's, where he was falsely accused by the Jews.

5th, At Herod's, where he was derided, clothed in a white garment, and mocked as a fool.

6th, At Pilate's, for the second time, where he was scourged at a pillar, crowned with thorns, Barabbas preferred to him, and condemned to the ignominious death of the cross.

7th, On Mount Calvary, whither he carried his cross, and was crucified for the redemption of all mankind.

Seven last Sayings of our divine Lord Jesus Christ on the Cross.

1st, In praying for his enemies: Father, forgive them, for they know not what they do.

2d, To the penitent thief: This day shalt thou be with me in paradise.

3d, To his Virgin Mother: Woman, behold thy son; and to St. John: Behold thy mother.

4th, I thirst, I thirst: and they gave him vinegar and gall to drink.

5th, My God, my God, why hast thou forsaken me?

6th, Into thy hands, O Lord, I recommend my spirit.

7th, All is consummated.

The Litany *of our* Lord Jesus Christ.

Lord, have mercy on us. Christ, have mercy on us. Lord, have mercy on us. Christ, hear us. Christ, graciously hear us.

God the Father of heaven,
God the Son, Redeemer of the world,
God the Holy Ghost,
Holy Trinity, one God,
Jesus, Son of the living God,
Jesus, Splendour of the Father,
Jesus, Brightness of eternal Light,

Have mercy on us.

Jesus, King of Glory,
Jesus, the Sun of Justice,
Jesus, Son of the Virgin Mary,
Jesus, whose name is called Wonderful,
Jesus, the mighty God,
Jesus, the Father of the world to come
Jesus, the Angel of the great council,
Jesus, most powerful,
Jesus, most patient,
Jesus, most obedient,
Jesus, meek and humble of heart,
Jesus, lover of chastity,
Jesus, our love,
Jesus, the God of peace,
Jesus, the Author of life,
Jesus, the example of all virtues,
Jesus, the zealous lover of souls,
Jesus, our God,
Jesus, the Father of the poor,
Jesus, the Treasure of the faithful,
Jesus, the good Shepherd,
Jesus, the true Light,
Jesus, the eternal Wisdom,
Jesus, the infinite Goodness,
Jesus, the Way, the Truth, and the Life
Jesus, the Joy of angels,
Jesus, the King of patriarchs,
Jesus, the Inspirer of prophets,
Jesus, the Master of the apostles,
Jesus, the Teacher of the evangelists,
Jesus, the Strength of martyrs,
Jesus, the Light of confessors,
Jesus, the Spouse of virgins,
Jesus, the Crown of all saints,

Have mercy on us.

Be merciful unto us. *Spare us, O Lord Jesus*
Be merciful unto us. *Hear us, O Lord Jesus.*
From all evil,
From all sin,
From thy wrath,

From the snares of the devil,
From the spirit of uncleanness,
From everlasting death,
From the neglect of thy holy inspirations,
Through the mystery of thy most holy incarnation,
Through thy nativity,
Through thy divine infancy,
Through thy sacred life,
Through thy labours and travails,
Through thy agony and bloody sweat,
Through thy cross and passion,
Through thy pains and torments,
Through thy death and burial,
Through thy glorious resurrection,
Through thy admirable ascension,
Through thy joys and glory,
In the day of judgment,
Lord Jesus, deliver us.

Lamb of God, who takest away the sins of the world,
Spare us, O Lord Jesus.
Lamb of God, who takest away the sins of the world,
Hear us, O Lord Jesus.
Lamb of God, who takest away the sins of the world,
Have mercy upon us, O Lord Jesus.
Christ Jesus hear us, Christ Jesus graciously hear us.

Let us pray.

O Lord Jesus Christ, who hast said, ask, and you shall receive; seek, and you shall find; knock, and it shall be opened unto you; grant, we beseech thee, to our most humble supplications, the gift of thy divine love, that we may ever love thee with our whole hearts, and never cease from praising and glorifying thy name. *Amen.*

O divine Redeemer, give us a perpetual fear and love of thy holy name, for thou never ceasest to direct and govern by thy grace those whom thou instructest in the solidity of thy love, who livest and reignest world without end. *Amen.*

O God, who hast appointed thy only begotten Son

he Saviour of Mankind, and hast commanded that he should be called Jesus; mercifully grant that we may enjoy in heaven the happy vision of him whose holy name we venerate upon earth; who, with thee and the Holy Ghost, liveth and reigneth, world without end. *Amen.*

A Prayer in honour of the Childhood of Jesus Christ.

O MOST amiable Jesus! who for my love and for my instruction didst vouchsafe to conceal thy eternal wisdom under the weakness and dependence of childhood, I most humbly thank thee for having shown me, in thy own sacred person, how I should sanctify my youth, and thereby draw a blessing on my future life; I beseech thee, O Lord, to penetrate my heart with thy fear and thy love, that I may profit of the example thou hast left me. Do not permit that a single day or hour of my life should be devoted to any other pursuit than thy service, the great and only end for which I came into the world. O adorable Jesus! since thou art pleased to ask for my heart, take it, I beseech thee, entirely and for ever; model it on thy own sacred heart; inflame it with thy love, and impress it with such a lively horror of sin as may never be weakened; infuse therein the virtues of thy holy youth, thy meekness, innocence, docility, and charity I desire to honour thy obedience to thy blessed Mother, by constant submission to my superiors. I offer up my prayers in union with thine; I unite my intentions in all I do to that pure and divine intention, which infinitely exalted even thy least actions whilst thou wert on earth. I particularly devote my studies, and all my exterior occupations, to honour thy laborious and humble employments during thy early age. O divine Jesus, take me, thy unworthy child, under thy protection; preserve me from the dangers and temptations of the world, which is thy enemy, and direct all my thoughts, words, desires, and actions, to thy greater glory. *Amen.*

A Litany in honour of the Child Jesus.

LORD have mercy on us.
Christ have mercy on us.
Lord have mercy on us.
Christ hear us.
Christ graciously hear us.
God the Father of heaven,
God the Son, Redeemer of the world,
God the Holy Ghost,
Holy Trinity, one God,
Child Jesus, Son of the living God,
Child Jesus, Son of the Virgin Mary,
Child Jesus, the Word made Flesh,
Child Jesus, image of the Godhead,
Child Jesus, splendour of eternal light,
Child Jesus, equal to thy eternal Father,
Child Jesus, glory of thy virgin Mother,
Child Jesus, first-born of all creatures,
Child Jesus, weeping in the manger,
Child Jesus, conqueror of tyrants,
Child Jesus, overthrower of idols,

Have mercy on us

Child Jesus, filled with zeal for the glory of thy Father,
Child Jesus, voluntary subject to thy blessed Mother,
Child Jesus, omnipotent in thy weakness,
Child Jesus, great in thy humility,
Child Jesus, fountain of graces,
Child Jesus, furnace of love,
Child Jesus, angel of the great council,
Child Jesus, root of the patriarchs,
Child Jesus, inspirer of the prophets,
Child Jesus, joy of the shepherds,
Child Jesus, star of Jacob,
Child Jesus, expectation of the eternal hills,
Child Jesus, the desired of all nations,
Child Jesus, the divine model of youth,
Child Jesus, the protector of children,
Child Jesus, the mighty—the admirable—the prince of peace,

Have mercy on us.

Be merciful unto us, *Spare us, O Lord Jesus.*
Be merciful unto us, *Hear us, O Lord Jesus.*
By thy ineffable incarnation,
By thy sacred birth,
By thy humility and piety,
By thy precious tears,
By thy painful circumcision,
By thy glorious manifestation,
By thy holy presentation,
By the labours, sufferings, and humiliations of thy childhood,
By thy tender love for youth,
Lord Jesus, deliver us.
Lamb of God, who taketh away the sins of the world, *Have mercy on us, O Lord Jesus.*
Lamb of God, &c. &c.
Lamb of God, &c. &c.

Let us pray.

Lord Jesus Christ, Son of the living God, who having been conceived by the Holy Ghost, wert pleased to be born in a stable; to be adored by the heavenly host; to be circumcised; manifested to the Gentiles; presented in the temple; carried into Egypt; brought back to Nazareth; to reveal in part thy eternal wisdom among the doctors at Jerusalem, and to pass thy holy childhood in subjection to thy blessed Mother and reputed Father; permit us little children to come to thee, and forbid us not, that by thy holy grace we may reverence the mysteries of thy sacred youth, with such sincere devotion, as to become conformable to thee in meekness, humility, docility, and charity, O divine Child, who, with the Father and the Holy Ghost, livest and reignest, one God, world without end. *Amen.*

A devout prayer of St. Bernard to the Blessed Virgin.

Remember, O most pious Virgin! that it has never been heard of in any age, that those who implored thy powerful protection were abandoned by thee. I therefore, O sacred Virgin, animated with the most lively confidence, cast myself at thy sacred feet, most earnestly beseeching thee to adopt me as thy child, to take care of my eternal salvation, and to watch over me at the hour of death. O do not, Mother of the Word Incarnate! despise my prayer, but graciously hear and obtain the grant of my petitions. *Amen.*

A Prayer before the Acts.

Give us, O Almighty and Eternal God! an increase of faith, hope, and charity; and that we may obtain what thou promisest, grant us to love and practise what thou commandest; through Jesus Christ our Lord. *Amen.*

An Act of Contrition.

O my God! I am most heartily sorry for all my sins; I detest them above all things, from the bottom of my heart, because they displease thee, my God, who art so deserving of all my love, for thy most amiable and adorable perfections. I firmly purpose, by thy holy grace, never more to offend thee deliberately; and by the same grace I will endeavour to atone for my sins. *Amen.*

An Act of Faith.

O my God! I most firmly believe that thou art one only God, Creator and Sovereign Lord of heaven and earth, infinitely great, and infinitely good. I most firmly believe that in thee, one only God, there are three Persons really distinct, the Father, the Son, and the Holy Ghost, who are all one and the same God: I most firmly believe that Jesus Christ, thy beloved Son, the second Person of the most adorable Trinity, was made man, and died on the cross to redeem and save us: that he arose the third day, that he ascended into heaven: that he will come again, at the end of the world, to judge all mankind; that he will reward the good with eternal happiness, and condemn the wicked to everlasting torments. I likewise most firmly believe, that out of his infinite love for us, he has left us, in the most adorable sacrament of our altar, his own most precious body and blood, his soul and divinity, for our spiritual food, and for our sacrifice ; and that he has left in his Church the power of forgiving sins. I believe these, and all other truths which the holy Roman Catholic Church proposes to our belief because it is thou, my God, who hast revealed them all, and thou art truth itself; thou neither canst deceive nor be deceived. In this faith, I desire to live, and in the same, by thy holy grace, I am most firmly resolved to die. *Amen.*

An Act of Hope.

O MY God! relying on thy almighty power, confiding in thy infinite goodness and mercy, and in thy sacred promises, I most firmly hope to receive the pardon of all my sins, and grace to serve thee faithfully in this life, that I may deserve to enjoy thee for ever in the next: through my Lord and Saviour Jesus Christ. *Amen.*

An Act of Charity.

O MY God! I love thee with my whole heart and soul; I love thee above all things, for thy most amiable perfections, and I love my neighbour for thy sake: grant that I may daily increase in this divine love, and prefer a thousand deaths to the loss of it by any mortal sin. *Amen.*

An Act of Divine Love and Oblation

O MY God and my All! I most ardently desire, by every breath I draw, by every thought, word, and action, by every movement of body and soul, to tell thee a thousand and a thousand times, that I love thee more than my life, or any thing in the world, and that I consecrate myself to thee, renewing my baptismal vows, together with the promises and resolutions of my life past. I offer thee also all the homage, love, joy, praise, thanks, and adoration, of the church militant, triumphant, and suffering; all that it has offered, or will offer to thee to the end of time; all the love, complacency, and delights thou possessest in thy divine essence, one God and three Persons; all the homage my beloved Jesus renders thee in the adorable sacrament of the altar; and all the masses that are now celebrating, that I may be a victim immolated with each, to thy honour and glory, without will, wish, or desire, but those solely of pleasing thee, loving thee, living for thee, and dying for thee. I am thine, O my God, make me so entirely and eternally. Above all, take my heart, fill it with thy love, extirpate from it all other affections, and make of it a burning furnace of pure flames of thy most ardent love for ever and ever. *Amen.*

May the most just, elevated, and amiable will of God be accomplished in all things: may it be praised and glorified for ever. *Amen.*

On the Means of Sanctifying Study.

As your studies are at present among your chief duties, and occupy the greatest portion of your time, it is of considerable importance that you use your utmost endeavours to sanctify them, by directing those pursuits to the glory of God and your own spiritual advantage; otherwise, what will it avail you at the hour of death, to have studied with the greatest diligence, or the greatest success, since whatever is not done for God is lost for eternity; whereas, on the contrary, the most trifling among your school duties, if offered to Him, and discharged for his love, is rendered meritorious, and inserted in the book of life. You should be convinced, that profane studies tend to great good or great evil, according as they are differently pursued; therefore be careful to adopt the right plan, and to lay up for yourself a treasure of merit, by the very means which so many young persons either neglect entirely, or pervert to bad purposes.

To sanctify your studies, you should observe three things: First, You should look on them as next in importance to your spiritual duties; since submission to the will of God, obedience to your parents, and justice to yourself, require that you do all in your power to acquire that useful knowledge which, next to virtue, is the most desirable of all acquisitions: consequently, loss of time, idleness, or sloth, should appear to you, as they really are, great faults.

Secondly, You should take the greatest care to purify your intention in studying. Your primary intention in all your studies should be to accomplish God's holy will, to please his divine Majesty, and to obey your parents, as likewise those who hold their place. Pride, vanity, a desire to excel others, or to attract admiration are mo tives which reason and religion should teach you to despise and renounce.

Thirdly, You should join prayer with study. On this head, nothing can be more applicable to your present circumstances, than the advice of St. Vincent Ferrer to young persons employed in studious pursuits: "If you desire," says he, "to study with advantage, let devotion accompany your studies: consult God more than your books, and ask him with humility to make you understand what you read and learn. Interrupt your application by short ejaculatory prayers: never begin or end your studies but by prayer: science is a gift of the Father of Lights; do not, therefore, consider it as the fruit of your own intellect or industry." It is unnecessary to add any thing to this most excellent admonition: attend to it, and you will soon perceive the benefit that will result, learning and virtue will mutually assist each other, your efforts will be more successful, for God's particular blessing will not be refused to such studies as are pursued in a Christian manner. Be careful to accompany interiorly the following offering of your studies, which is made aloud in your class, and to renew through, out the day, by frequent aspirations, the sentiments it contains.

Prayer.

I OFFER, O my God! in union with the adorable actions and sufferings of Jesus Christ during his mortal life, the duties I am now going to perform for thy love, and in obedience to thy most holy will. I most humbly beg thy divine blessing, and the light of thy holy Spirit, that all my studies, and various duties, may tend to thy greater glory and my eternal salvation; as likewise to the service and edification of my neighbour. *Amen.*

On the holy Sacrifice of the Mass.

To assist devoutly and reverently at the adorable sacrifice of the Altar, is the greatest act of religion that man can perform; it is that which most glorifies God, and which most promotes our own eternal interests. Yet it is a melancholy truth, that an opportunity of assisting at mass is so little valued, that the generality of persons confine themselves to hearing Mass on Sundays and holidays, because on those days they are commanded to assist at the divine mysteries; and even at masses of precept, many are present with sinful distractions and disedifying indevotion.

You may unfortunately witness such conduct hereafter; but if you ever imitate it you will be highly culpable, because you cannot, as some may, plead by way of excuse, the want of instructions, or early impressions of respect and devotion towards the august and adorable sacrifice of our altars. You should therefore recollect, that at all times the most edifying piety and recollection, in assisting at these tremendous mysteries, will be expected from you, as the fruits of the knowledge you will be known to have acquired of your duty in this respect, and also as the fruits of the happiness you now enjoy in assisting daily at this divine sacrifice. It is therefore of the utmost consequence, that you now endeavour to conceive an exalted idea of the excellency and efficacy of the Mass, as likewise a deep sense of the happiness of assisting at this august sacrifice. Those dispositions will be best acquired by fervour and reverence in hearing Mass now, since the habit of doing so daily and devoutly in your youth, must tend to draw down a blessing on your present and future life. To give solidity and permanency to your devotion in discharging one of the most solemn duties of our holy religion, you should be careful to retain the explanation you received of the types, figures, and ceremonies of the Mass: a knowledge of them, though not absolutely necessary, is at least extremely conducive to devotion, since the most trivial action, ceremony, or even ornament used at Mass, is not without mysterious signification. But you should particularly impress on your mind three points—

1st. The nature and efficacy of the Mass.

2dly, The ends for which it is offered.

3dly, The dispositions in which you should be, and the method you should observe to assist worthily at the holy sacrifice.

First, As to the nature of the sacrifice of the Mass, you know from your catechism, that "*a sacrifice*," in general, "*is that first and most necessary act of religion, by which we acknowledge God's supreme dominion over us, and our total dependence on him.*" It consists in the oblation of a victim by a lawful minister, and in a change being made in that victim, to acknowledge the supreme dominion of God over all his creatures.—In the Mass, Jesus Christ is the Victim—the Priest makes an oblation of this Victim to the Eternal Father, on behalf of all men; and, finally, it undergoes a change, which shows forth the death of our Redeemer, by the apparent separation of the body from the blood, and the consumption of both by the priest. This most adorable sacrifice is the *pure offering* which is made to God *in every place, from the rising of the sun, even to the going down*, according to the prophecy of Malachy, (i. 11.) It is the same in substance with the sacrifice of the cross, because the Priest and the Victim are the same; the difference is only in the manner of offering. Jesus on the cross offered himself a bleeding victim to the justice of God for our redemption—Jesus on the altar offers himself an unbloody victim, to glorify God and sanctify us, by applying to our souls the merits of his passion and death.

Secondly, The ends for which Mass is offered: those ends are four:—

1st, To acknowledge the sovereign dominion of the Almighty.

2d, To thank him for his benefits.

3d, To atone for our sins and those of the world.

4th, To implore the blessings and graces of which we stand in need.

In the old law there was a separate sacrifice instituted for each of those ends; but in the Mass all are included, because it fully answers every end for which sacrifice is offered to God.

The Mass is a *holocaust*, or sacrifice of adoration, in which Jesus offers himself to his eternal Father wholly and entirely, rendering to him such homage as is due to the Almighty; and which enables us also to acknowledge the majesty and dominion of God in a manner worthy of the Divinity, which it would otherwise be impossible for any creature to do.

It is a sacrifice of thanksgiving, and one fully adequate to acknowledge worthily all the blessings and graces, general and particular, which the Almighty bestowed on the world.

It is a victim of *expiation*, of such value as would suffice to atone for all the iniquities of millions of worlds, and that in a superabundant manner.

Lastly, It is a sacrifice of *impetration*, that is to say, it is offered to implore from God all the graces, blessings, and assistance, spiritual or corporal, general or particular, which we desire for ourselves and others.

This is the nature, and these are the ends of that adorable Sacrifice, "*which*," as your Catechism says, "*was reserved for the New Law, to fulfil the figures of the Old Law, and to give religion its full perfection.*"—"Ah!" cries a great servant of God, speaking on this subject, "how much is it to be wished that we knew the value of the treasure in our possession! happy, infinitely happy are Christians, if they but feel their happiness! What a source of blessings would this sacrifice be to them! What graces would they draw from it for body and soul, for time and eternity!" It is almost impossible to reflect on the infinite love which Jesus manifests, in thus permitting himself to be offered in sacrifice as often as we wish, without endeavouring to correspond with his love, and manifesting, to the best of our power the most unbounded gratitude for so great a blessing as we possess in this adorable mystery. This you can most effectually do by carefully avoiding sin, which is the great obstacle to your sharing in the blessings and graces that are daily and hourly bestowed on the world, through and by this great sacrifice: also by resolving to hear mass every day, and never to let sloth, indifference, or any other such cause, deprive you of the inestimable advantages annexed to so holy a practice.—There are, it is true, cases in which duties of obligation may interfere to prevent your assisting at Mass on week days. Such, however, will rarely occur, if the morning be profited of for discharging a duty so well calculated to draw down a blessing on the day. These cases need not be pointed out; you are sufficiently instructed to discern them, and also to know, that when you are absent from Mass on week days, *only* to perform the more manifest will of God elsewhere, you lose nothing before God, who, in all cases, and under all circumstances, requires the discharge of duty before the gratification of private devotion.

Thirdly, The dispositions with which you should hear Mass, regard your interior sentiments and exterior comportment; as is evident from your Catechism, which directs you to assist at this divine sacrifice "*with great recollection and piety; and with every mark of outward respect and devotion.*" You should therefore always endeavour to assist at Mass with lively faith, contrition, and confidence in the mercy of God; those virtues are the most proper disposition for hearing mass, as well as the natural fruits of that great sacrifice.

Faith is necessary, because without it you would not be enabled to penetrate the wonders which pass before your eyes on the altar.—*Contrition* for sin is naturally to be expected from every one who considers in the Mass a lively representation and renewal of the Sacrifice of the Cross, which was offered for its expiation;—and *Confidence* in the infinite mercy of God, is a disposition at all times calculated to obtain great favours from the divine goodness, but it is particularly so at Mass. Endeavour always to excite this sentiment in your heart, when you assist at this august sacrifice, by considering the greatness and infinite value of the victim you then offer to God. Had you been at the foot of the Cross when Jesus Christ immolated himself in torments for your sake.

would you have hesitated in asking *any favour?* Would you have thought any grace *too great* to hope for, or any sin too great to be forgiven, if you represented your necessities to a God who was expiring for your sake, and, in such propitious moments, implored mercy through his sacred passion and death? Be firmly convinced that your confidence in God should be equally lively whenever you hear Mass, for you have the very same grounds for hope. It is the same God who offers himself for you—it is the same unbounded love that causes him to do so; his sacred blood and infinite merits plead your cause just as efficaciously on the altar as they did on Mount Calvary, where, *with a loud cry and tears*, as St. Paul expresses it, he implored mercy and salvation for all sinners, and amongst them for you. Think of the penitent thief, whose unbounded confidence in the merits of a Redeemer obtained for him the greatest of all possible graces—perfect conversion and eternal happiness. Ask for any thing, and every thing you desire; ask with confidence, and you shall receive: for, in presenting Jesus Christ to his eternal Father, you will always be sure of giving more than you implore. It will serve to animate your devotion in hearing Mass, to offer it up each time for some particular intention; such as, to obtain the grace to conquer some fault; to acquire some virtue; for the conversion of some sinner; for those that are in the agonies of death; or for the suffering souls in purgatory; but, in particular, be careful to offer it, especially on days of obligation, for the four ends of the sacrifice, which you will find comprised in the short offering prefixed to the Ordinary of the Mass.

As to the profound respect, recollection, silence, and guard over the senses, which are the *exterior* dispositions, or rather, that which forms the comportment required for assisting at Mass, it would appear sufficient to have faith not to fail in them. "When you behold," as St. Chrysostom says, "the Lord him self laying the Victim on the Altar, and offered, and the priest attending, and praying over the sacrifice, purpled with his precious blood—when you consider, that what is then done is far more awful, more astonishing, more extraordinary, than when fire, falling from heaven, consumed the sacrifice of Elias, you cannot, without inexcusable presumption and impiety, be guilty of exterior disrespect at Mass." Yet, unfortunately, such impiety is not very unusual. The ministers of God may now, with too much truth, repeat the words of the same holy Doctor: "I see," says he, "persons behave disrespectfully, and without due attention in the Church. Can any impiety be found equal to this? At worldly assemblies every thing is regulated and carried on without confusion; and here, in the company of angels, you talk and laugh! Should we be surprised, if thunder fell from heaven, to punish such impiety?" Reflect on those expressions, which are not too strong for the subject, and consider also, that persons who act in this manner renew, as far as depends on them, the insults, mockery, and derision, which were so great an aggravation to the sufferings of Jesus Christ on the cross. This consideration alone should impress you with a lasting horror of the scandalous custom of conversing, laughing, and saluting in the chapel, and even during the tremendous Sacrifice: a custom which you should carefully guard against, in defiance of human respect, or the politeness which is often alleged as an excuse for returning salutes, or replying to inquiries in the chapel. Such politeness is not less disedifying than misplaced.

The method to be observed in hearing Mass may vary according to each person's devotion: it is in itself of less consequence than all the rest; because those whose hearts are penetrated with the dispositions here pointed out, cannot fail to hear Mass well whatever method they adopt. However, as young persons should not give themselves much latitude in so solemn a duty as this, you should generally speaking, in hearing Mass, follow the directions of your Catechism, which says, that the best manner of hearing Mass, is to "*offer it with the priest—to meditate on Christ's sufferings—and to go to communion*;" that is, either to follow the priest, which you can do by using the Ordinary of the Mass; or else, to occupy yourself entirely in commemorating the sufferings of Christ, for which also you have a method in this book. In either case, when you do not communicate sacramentally, you should not neglect making a spiritual communion.

Spiritual communion is a most holy and profitable devotion, calculated for all times, but particularly for the time of the Mass. It consists in ardently desiring to receive the adorable Eucharist, and in uniting the heart with God. It is made by an act of faith in the real presence of Christ in the holy Eucharist, an act of hope in his mercy, an act of love for his infinite perfections, and an act of desire to enjoy the happiness of sacramental communion. The best method you can adopt, would be to endeavour to excite sentiments of these virtues in your heart, while the priest communicates; uniting your heart to God as fervently as you can, and conversing with him interiorly, just as you would do if you had actually received the holy communion. Do this in whatever terms devotion may suggest: but whenever you want a form for the purpose, the prayer for spiritual communion, to be found in each of the following methods for hearing Mass, will answer extremely well.

A Prayer before Mass.

O MY GOD! I most humbly beg of thee to grant me the necessary dispositions for assisting devoutly at the adorable sacrifice which I am about to present to thy divine Majesty, in union with Jesus Christ thy beloved Son, and with thy whole Church. I offer this Mass as a *holocaust*, to acknowledge thy absolute dominion over me, and all creatures; as a sacrifice of *thanksgiving* for all thy benefits; as a sacrifice of *expiation* for my sins, and those of all creatures, living and dead; and as a sacrifice of *impetration*, to implore for myself and all mankind the graces and blessings, spiritual and temporal, of which we stand most in need. I unite my heart to the dispositions which animate the heart of Jesus while he offers himself on the altar, and to those of the blessed Virgin when she stood at the foot of the cross. O my divine Jesus! grant that, like those who witnessed thy death on Mount Calvary, I may depart from this sanctuary penetrated with compassion for thy sufferings, and with sorrow for my sins, by which they were caused; as likewise with a firm resolution rather to die than to offend thee wilfully henceforward. *Amen.*

While the Priest sprinkles Holy Water *before* SOLEMN MASS *on* Sundays, *the following* ANTHEMS *are sung.*

Ant. ASPERGES me, Domine, hyssopo, et mundabor: lavabis me, et super nivem dealbabor.	*Anth.* THOU wilt sprinkle me, O Lord! with hyssop, and I shall be cleansed: thou wilt wash me, and I shall be made whiter than snow.
Ps. Miserere mei, Deus, secundum magnam misericordiam tuam.	Ps. Have mercy on me, O God, according to thy great mercy.
V. Gloria Patri, &c.	V. Glory be to the Father, &c.
Ant Asperges me, &c.	*Anth.* Thou wilt sprinkle me, &c.

The Priest having returned to the foot of the Altar, says,

V. Ostende nobis, Domine, misericordiam tuam.	V. Show us, O Lord, thy mercy.
R. Et salutare tuum da nobis.	R. And grant us thy salvation.

V. Domine, exaudi orationem meam.
R. Et clamor meus ad te veniat.
V Dominus vobiscum.
R. Et cum spiritu tuo.

V. O Lord, hear my prayer.
R. And let my cry come unto thee.
V. May the Lord be with you.
R. And with thy spirit.

The Prayer, Exaudi.

Hear us, O holy Lord, Almighty Father, eternal God! and vouchsafe to send thy holy angel from heaven to guard, cherish, protect, visit, and defend all that are assembled in this place: through Jesus Christ our Lord. *Amen.*

From EASTER *to* WHIT SUNDAY, *inclusively, instead of the foregoing* Ant. Asperges, &c. *the following is sung, and* Alleluias *are added to the* Versicles *and* Responsaries, &c.

ANTHEM.

Vidi aquam egredientem de templo a latere dextro, Alleluia: et omnes ad quos pervenit aqua ista, salvi facti sunt et dicent, Alleluia.
Ps. Confitemini Domino, quoniam bonus: quoniam in sæculum misericordia ejus. Gloria.

I saw water flowing from the right side of the temple, Alleluia: and all to whom that water came were saved, and they shall say, Alleluia.
Ps. Praise the Lord. because he is good: because his mercy endureth for ever. Glory, &c.

A Prayer said before Mass in the United States of America.

We pray thee, O Almighty and eternal God, who, through Jesus Christ, has revealed thy glory to all nations to preserve the works of thy mercy; that thy church, being spread through the whole world, may continue with unchanging faith, in the confession of thy name.

We pray thee, who alone art good and holy to endow with heavenly knowledge, sincere zeal, and sanctity of life, our chief bishop, N. N. the vicar of our Lord Jesus Christ, in the government of his church; our own bishop, N. N. [*or, if he be not consecrated,* "our bishop elect;"] all other bishops, prelates, and pastors of the church, and especially those who are appointed to exercise among us the functions of the holy ministry, and conduct the people into the ways of salvation.

We pray thee, O God of might, wisdom, and justice, through whom authority is rightly administered, laws are enacted, and judgment decreed, assist, with thy Holy Spirit of counsel and fortitude, the President of these United States; that his administration may be conducted in righteousness, and be eminently useful to thy people over whom he presides, by encouraging due respect for virtue and religion; by a faithful execution of the laws in justice and mercy; and by restraining vice and immorality.—Let the light of thy divine wisdom direct the deliberations of congress, and shine forth in all their proceedings and laws framed for our rule and government; so that they may tend to the preservation of peace, the promotion of national happiness, the increase of industry, sobriety, and useful knowledge, and may perpetuate to us the blessings of equal liberty.

We pray for his excellency, the governor of this state, for the members of assembly, for all judges, magistrates, and other officers, who are appointed to guard our political welfare; that they may be enabled by thy powerful protection, to discharge the duties of their respective stations with honesty and ability.

We recommend, likewise, to thy unbounded mercy, all our brethren and fellow-citizens, throughout the United States, that they may be blessed in the knowledge, and sanctified in the observance of thy most holy law: that they may be preserved in union, and in that peace which the world cannot give; and after enjoying the blessings of this life, be admitted to those which are eternal.

Finally, we pray thee, O Lord of mercy, to remember the souls of thy servants departed, who are gone before us, with the sign of faith, and repose in the sleep of peace; the souls of our parents, relations, and friends; of those who, when living, were members of this congregation; and particularly of such as are lately deceased; of all benefactors, who, by their donations or legacies to this church, witnessed their zeal for the decency of divine worship, and proved their claim to our grateful and charitable remembrance. To these, O Lord, and to all that rest in Christ, grant, we beseech thee, a place of refreshment, light, and everlasting peace—through the same Jesus Christ our Lord and Saviour. *Amen.*

THE ORDINARY OF THE MASS.

✠

In Nomine Patris, et Filii, et Spiritus Sancti. Amen.	In the name of the Father, and of the Son, &c. Amen.
Ant. Introibo ad altare Dei.	*Anth.* I will go unto the altar of God.
R. Ad Deum, qui lætificat juventutem meam.	R. To God, who rejoiceth my youth.

Psalm xlii.

Judica me, Deus, et discerne causam meam de gente non sancta: ab homine iniquo et doloso erue me.	Judge me, O God, and distinguish my cause from the nation that is not holy: from the unjust and deceitful man deliver me.

R. Quia tu es, Deus, fortitudo mea, quare me repulisti, et quare tristis incedo dum affligit me inimicus?

R. Since thou, O God, art my strength, why hast thou rejected me; and why do I go sorrowful whilst the enemy afflicteth me?

P. Emitte lucem tuam et veritatem tuam: ipsa me deduxerunt, et adduxerunt in Montem sanctum tuum, et in Tabernacula tua.

P. Send forth thy Light and thy Truth; they have conducted and brought me unto the holy Mount, and into thy Tabernacle.

R. Et introibo ad altare Dei: ad Deum qui lætificat juventutem meam.

R. And I will go unto the altar of God: to God who rejoiceth my youth.

P. Confitebor tibi in cithara, Deus, Deus meus: quare tristis es, anima mea? et quare conturbas me?

P. I will praise thee on the harp, O God, my God: why art thou sorrowful, O my soul? and why dost thou disturb me?

R. Spera in Deo, quoniam adhuc confitebor illi: salutare vultus mei, et Deus meus.

R. Hope in God, for him will I still praise: he is my God, and the Saviour I look for.

P. Gloria Patri, et Filio, et Spiritui Sancto.

P. Glory be to the Father, and to the Son, &c.

R. Sicut erat in principio, et nunc, et semper, et in sæcula sæculorum. *Amen.*

R. As it was in the beginning, is now, and ever shall be, world without end. *Amen.*

P. Introibo ad altare Dei.

P. I will go unto the altar of God.

R. Ad Deum qui lætificat juventutem meam.

P. Adjutorium nostrum in nomine Domini.

R. Qui fecit cœlum et terram.

P. Confiteor Deo omnipotenti, &c.

R. Misereatur tui omnipotens Deus, et dimissis peccatis tuis, perducat te ad vitam æternam.

P. Amen.

R. Confiteor Deo omnipotenti, beatæ Mariæ semper Virgini, beato Michaeli Archangelo, beato Joanni Baptistæ, sanctis Apostolis Petro et Paulo, omnibus Sanctis, et tibi Pater, quia peccavi nimis cogitatione, verbo et opere, mea culpa, mea culpa, mea maxima culpa. Ideo precor beatam Mariam semper Virginem, beatum Michaelum Archangelum, beatum Joannem Baptistam, sanctos Apostolos Pe-

R. To God who rejoiceth my youth.

P. Our help is in the name of the Lord.

R. Who made heaven and earth.

P. I confess to Almighty God, &c.

R. May Almighty God be merciful to thee, and, forgiving thee thy sins, bring thee to everlasting life.

P. Amen.

R. I confess to Almighty God, to the blessed Mary, ever a Virgin, blessed Michael the Archangel, blessed John Baptist, the holy Apostles Peter and Paul, to all the saints, and to you, Father, that I have sinned exceedingly in thought, word, and deed, through my fault, through my fault, through my most grievous fault. Therefore I beseech the blessed Mary, ever a Virgin blessed Michael the

trum et Paulum, omnes Sanctos, et te, Pater, orare pro me ad Dominum Deum nostrum.	Archangel, blessed John Baptist, the holy Apostles Peter and Paul, and all the saints, and you, O Father, to pray to the Lord our God for me.
P. Misereatur vestri omnipotens Deus, et dimissis peccatis vestris, perducat vos ad vitam æternam.	P. May Almighty God be merciful unto you, and, forgiving you your sins, bring you to life everlasting.
R. Amen.	R. Amen.
P. Indulgentiam, absolutionem, et remissionem peccatorum nostrorum, tribuat nobis omnipotens et misericors Dominus.	P. May the Almighty and most merciful Lord grant us pardon, absolution, and remission of our sins.
R. Amen.	R. Amen.
P. Deus, tu conversus vivificabis nos.	P. O God, thou being turned towards us, wilt enliven us.
R. Et plebs tua lætabitur in te.	R. And thy people will rejoice in thee.
P. Ostende nobis, Domine, misericordiam tuam.	P. Show us, O Lord thy mercy.
R. Et salutare tuum da nobis.	R. And grant us thy salvation.
P. Domine, exaudi orationem meam.	P. O Lord, hear my prayer.
R. Et clamor meus ad te veniat.	R. And let my cry come unto thee.

P. Dominus vobiscum. — P. The Lord be with you.

R. Et cum spiritu tuo. — R. And with thy spirit.

The Priest, going to the Altar, says,

Take away from us our iniquities, we beseech thee, O Lord, that we may be worthy to enter with pure minds into the Holy of Holies: through, &c. Amen.

Bowing down, he says,

We beseech thee, O Lord, by the merits of thy saints, whose relics are here, and of all the saints, that thou wouldst vouchsafe to forgive me all my sins. Amen.

Whilst he reads the Introit, *say,*

Let the name of the Lord be blessed both now and for ever. From the rising to the setting of the sun all praise is due to the name of the Lord. Who is like the Lord our God, who dwells on high, and looks on all that is humble both in heaven and earth. Glory be to the Father, &c.

P. Kyrie eleison. R. Kyrie eleison. P. Kyrie eleison. *Lord have mercy upon us.* [R. Christe eleison. P. Christe eleison. R. Christe eleison. *Christ have mercy upon us.* [P. Kyrie eleison. R. Kyrie eleison. P. Kyrie eleison. *Lord have mercy upon us.*

GLORIA IN EXCELSIS.

Gloria in excelsis Deo, et in terra pax hominibus bonæ volun- — Glory be to God on high, and on earth peace to men of good will.

tatis. Laudamus te; benedicimus te; adoramus te; glorificamus te. Gratias agimus tibi propter magnam gloriam tuam, Domine Deus, Rex cœlestis, Deus Pater Omnipotens. Domine Fili unigenite Jesu Christe. Domine Deus, Agnus Dei, Filius Patris. Qui tollis peccata mundi, miserere nobis. Qui tollis peccata mundi, suscipe deprecationem nostram. Qui sedes ad dexteram Patris, miserere nobis. Quoniam tu solus sanctus. Tu solus Dominus. Tu solus altissimus, Jesu Christe, cum Sancto Spiritu, in gloria Dei Patris. Amen.

We praise thee, we bless thee; we adore thee; we glorify thee. We give thee thanks for thy great glory, O Lord God, heavenly King, God the Father Almighty. O Lord Jesus Christ, the only begotten Son. O Lord God, Lamb of God, Son of the Father, who takest away the sins of the world, have mercy on us. Who takest away the sins of the world, receive our prayers. Who sittest at the right hand of the Father, have mercy on us. For thou only art holy. Thou only art the Lord. Thou only, O Jesus Christ, together with the Holy Ghost, art most high in the glory of God the Father. Amen.

The Priest, turning towards the People, salutes them, saying,

P. Dominus vobiscum.

R. Et cum spiritu tuo.

P. The Lord be with you.

R. And with thy spirit.

At the Collects,

We humbly beseech thee, O Almighty and eternal God, mercifully to give ear to the prayers of thy servant, which he offers to thee in the name of thy Church, and on behalf of us thy people: accept them to the honour of thy name, and the good of our souls, and grant us all those blessings which may contribute to our salvation: through, &c. Amen.

At the Epistle,

Be thou, O Lord, eternally praised and blessed, for having communicated thy Spirit to the holy prophets and apostles, disclosing to them admirable secrets, redounding to thy glory and our great good. We firmly believe their word, because it is thine. Give us, we beseech thee, the happiness to understand their instructions, and so conform our lives thereto, that at the hour of death we may merit to be received by thee into the mansions of eternal bliss.

At the end of the Epistle, *the Clerk answers,*

Deo gratias. Thanks be to God

During the Gradual *or* Tract,

How wonderful, O Lord, is thy name through the whole earth. I will bless the Lord at all times; his praise shall be ever in my mouth. Be thou my God and protector; in thee alone I put my trust; O let me never be confounded.

Before the Gospel,

Cleanse my heart and my lips, O Almighty God, who didst cleanse the lips of the prophet

Isaiah with a burning coal: and vouchsafe, through thy gracious mercy, so to purify me, that I may worthily attend to thy holy gospel: through Christ our Lord. Amen.

May the Lord be in my heart, and on my lips, that I may worthily, and in a becoming manner, attend to his gospel. Amen.

P. Dominus vobiscum.

P. The Lord be with you.

R. Et cum spiritu tuo.

R. And with thy spirit.

P. Sequentia, (vel initium,) sancti Evangelii secundum, &c.

P. The continuation (or the beginning) of the holy Gospel according to, &c.

R. Gloria tibi, Domine.

R. Glory be to thee, O Lord.

During the Gospel,

Be thou ever adored and praised, O Lord, who not content to instruct us by thy prophets and apostles, hast even vouchsafed to speak to us by thy only Son our Saviour Jesus Christ, commanding us by a voice from heaven to hear him: grant us, merciful God, the grace to profit by his divine and heavenly doctrine. All that is written of thee, divine Jesus, in thy gospel, is truth itself; manifesting infinite wisdom in thy actions; power and goodness in thy miracles; light and instruction in thy maxims. With thee, sacred Redeemer, are the words of eternal life; to whom shall we go but to thee, eternal Fountain of Truth? I firmly believe, O God, all thou teachest; give me only grace to practise what thou commandest, and command what thou pleasest.

At the end of the Gospel, *answer*,

R. Laus tibi, Christe. — R. Praise be to thee, O Christ.

Then add with the Priest, in a low Voice

May our sins be blotted out by the words of the Gospel.

THE NICENE CREED.

CREDO in unum Deum, Patrem omnipotentem, factorem cœli et terræ, visibilium omnium et invisibilium.

I BELIEVE in one God, the Father Almighty, Maker of heaven and earth, and of all things visible and invisible.

Et in unum Dominum Jesum Christum Filium Dei unigenitum; et ex Patre natum ante omnia sæcula. Deum de Deo; Lumen de Lumine; Deum verum de Deo vero; genitum non factum; consubstantialem Patri, per quem omnia facta sunt. Qui propter nos homines, et propter nostram salutem, descendit de cœlis, et incarnatus est de Spiritu Sancto, ex Maria Virgine, ET HOMO FACTUS EST.* Cru-

And in one Lord Jesus Christ, the only begotten Son of God; and born of the Father before all ages. God of God; Light of Light; true God of true God; begotten not made; consubstantial to the Father, by whom all things were made. Who for us men, and for our salvation, came down from heaven, and became incarnate of the Holy Ghost of the Virgin Mary. AND WAS MADE MAN.*

* At these words all kneel

Crucifixus etiam pro nobis sub Pontio Pilato, passus et sepultus est. Et resurrexit tertia die secundum Scripturas. Et ascendit in cœlum, sedet ad dexteram Patris. Et iterum venturus est cum gloria judicare vivos et mortuos : cujus regni non erit finis.

He was crucified also for us, suffered under Pontius Pilate, and was buried. And the third day he rose again according to the Scriptures. And ascended into heaven, sitteth at the right hand of the Father, and he is to come again with glory to judge both the living and the dead, of whose kingdom there shall be no end.

Et in Spiritum Sanctum, Dominum et vivificantem, qui ex Patre Filioque procedit: qui cum Patre et Filio simul adoratur, et conglorificatur : qui locutus est per prophetas. Et unam sanctam Catholicam et Apostolicam Ecclesiam. Confiteor unum Baptisma in remissionem peccatorum. Et expecto resurrectionem mortuorem, et vitam venturi sæculi. Amen.

And in the Holy Ghost, the Lord and Giver of Life, who proceedeth from the Father and the Son: who, together with the Father and the Son, is adored and glorified: who spoke by the prophets. And one holy Catholic and Apostolic Church. I confess one baptism for the remission of sins. And I expect the resurrection of the dead, and the life of the world to come. Amen.

P. Dominus vobiscum.	P. The Lord be with you.
R. Et cum spiritu tuo.	R. And with thy spirit.
Oremus.	*Let us pray.*

At the Offertory,

O my God, I sincerely offer myself and all I have to thee, to do and suffer whatever thou commandest or permittest. Receive my offering, and cleanse me from my sins, that through the infinite merits of the Victim about to be presented to thy divine Majesty, I may become acceptable in thy sight.

OBLATION *of the* HOST.

Accept, O holy Father, Almighty and Eternal God, this unspotted Host, which I thy unworthy servant offer unto thee, my living and true God, for my innumerable sins, offences, and negligences, and for all here present: as also for all faithful Christians, both living and dead; that it may avail both me and them unto life everlasting. Amen.

When the Priest pours the Wine and Water into the Chalice,

O God, who in creating human nature, hast wonderfully dignified it, and still more wonderfully reformed it, grant that, by the mystery of this Water and Wine, we may be made partakers of his divine nature, who vouchsafed to become partaker of our human nature, namely, Jesus Christ our Lord, thy Son, who with thee, in the unity of, &c. Amen.

Oblation *of the* Chalice.

We offer unto thee, O Lord, the chalice of salvation, beseeching thy clemency, that it may ascend before thy divine Majesty as a sweet odour, for our salvation, and for that of the whole world. Amen.

When the Priest bows before the Altar,

Accept us, O Lord, in the spirit of humility and contrition of heart, and grant, that the sacrifice which we offer this day in thy sight, may be pleasing to thee, O Lord God.

When he blesses the Bread and Wine,

Come, O almighty and eternal God, the sanctifier, and bless this sacrifice, prepared for the glory of thy holy name.

Washing his Fingers, he says, Ps. xxv. 6.

I will wash my hands amongst the innocent, and will compass thy altar, O Lord.

That I may hear the voice of thy praise: and tell all thy wondrous works.

The beauty of thy house I have loved, O Lord and the place where thy glory dwelleth.

Take not away my soul with the wicked; nor my life with bloody men.

In whose hands are iniquities; their right hand is filled with gifts.

But I have walked in my innocence: redeem me, [illegible] have mercy on me.

[illegible] has stood in the direct way; in the ch[illegible] will bless thee, O Lord.

G[illegible] the Father, &c.

Bowing before the Altar, he says,

Receive, O holy Trinity, this oblation which we make to thee, in memory of the Passion, Resurrection, and Ascension of our Lord Jesus Christ, and in honour of the blessed Mary ever a Virgin, the blessed John Baptist, the holy Apostles Peter and Paul, and of all the Saints, that it may be available to their honour and our salvation; and may they vouchsafe to intercede for us in heaven, whose memory we celebrate on earth. Through the same Christ our Lord. Amen.

Turning towards the People, he says,

Orate fratres, ut meum ac vestrum sacrificium acceptabile fiat apud Deum Patrem omnipotentem.	Brethren, pray that my sacrifice and yours may be acceptable to God the Father Almighty.
R. Suscipiat Dominus sacrificium de manibus tuis, ad laudem et gloriam nominis sui, ad utilitatem quoque nostram, totiusque Ecclesiæ suæ sanctæ.	R. May the Lord receive the sacrifice from thy hands, to the praise and glory of his name, and to our benefit, and that of his holy Church.

At the Secret Prayer *or* Prayers,

Mercifully hear our prayers, O Lord, and graciously accept this oblation, which we thy servants present to thee; that as we offer it to the honour of thy name, so it may be to us here a means of obtaining thy grace, and hereafter eternal happiness. Through, &c.

P. Per omnia sæcula sæculorum.	P. World without end.

R. Amen.	R. Amen.
P. Dominus vobiscum. R. Et cum spiritu tuo. P. Sursum corda. R. Habemus ad Dominum. P. Gratias agamus Domino Deo nostro. R. Dignum et justum est.	P. The Lord be with you. R. And with thy spirit. P. Lift up your hearts. R. We have lifted them up to the Lord. P. Let us give thanks to our Lord God. R. It is meet and just.

The common Preface.

It is truly meet and just, right and available to salvation, that we should always and in all places, give thanks to thee, O holy Lord, Father Almighty, eternal God. Through Christ our Lord: by whom the angels praise thy majesty, the dominations adore it, the powers tremble before it, the heavenly virtues, and blessed seraphim, with common jubilee, glorify it. Together with whom we beseech thee, that we may be admitted to join our humble voices, saying:

Holy, holy, holy, Lord God of Sabaoth. Heaven and earth are full of thy glory. Hosanna in the highest. Blessed is he that comes in the name of the Lord. Hosanna in the highest.

THE CANON OF THE MASS.

We therefore humbly pray and beseech thee, most merciful Father, through Jesus Christ thy Son our Lord, that thou wouldst vouchsafe to accept and bless these gifts, these presents, these holy unspotted sacrifices, which in the first place we offer thee for thy holy Catholic Church, to which vouchsafe to grant peace; as also to preserve, unite, and govern it throughout the world: together with thy servant N. our Pope, N. our Bishop, as also all orthodox believers and professors of the Catholic and Apostolic Faith.

COMMEMORATION OF THE LIVING.

Be mindful, O Lord, of thy servants, men and women, N. and N.

He prays silently for those he intends to pray for

And of all here present, whose faith and devotion is known unto thee, for whom we offer, or who offer up to thee, this sacrifice of praise for themselves, their families, and friends: for the redemption of their souls, for the health and salvation they hope for, and for which they now pay their vows to thee, the eternal, living, and true God.

COMMUNICATING with, and honouring in the first place, the memory of the ever-glorious Virgin Mary, Mother of our Lord and God Jesus Christ: as also of the blessed Apostles and Martyrs, Peter and Paul, Andrew, James, John, Thomas, James, Philip, Bartholomew, Matthew, Simon and Thaddeus, Linus, Cletus, Clement, Xystus, Cornelius, Cyprian, Lawrence, Chrysogonus, John and Paul, Cosmas and Damian, and of all thy Saints; by whose merits and prayers grant that we may be always defended by the help of thy protection. Through the same Christ our Lord. Amen.

Spreading his Hands over the Oblation, he says,

We therefore beseech thee, O Lord, graciously to accept this oblation of our servitude, as also of thy whole family; dispose our days in thy peace, preserve us from eternal damnation, and rank us in the number of thine elect. Through Christ our Lord. Amen.

Which oblation do thou, O God, vouchsafe in all respects to bless, approve, ratify, and accept; that it may be made for us the body and blood of thy most beloved Son Jesus Christ our Lord.

Who the day before he suffered, took bread into his holy and venerable hands, and with his eyes lifted up towards heaven, giving thanks to thee, Almighty God, his Father; he blessed it, brake it, and gave it to his disciples, saying: Take and eat ye all of this, FOR THIS IS MY BODY.

At the Elevation.

While the Priest pronounces the words of Consecration, do you contemplate in silence the wonders that pass before you. Your God, your Saviour, and your Judge, descends on the altar; hail his sacred presence by the most lively sentiments of respect, confidence, and love.

O Victim of Salvation! Eternal King! Incarnate Word! sacrificed for me, and all mankind! Precious body of the Son of God! Sacred flesh, torn with nails, pierced with a lance, and bleeding on a cross, for us poor sinners! Amazing goodness! infinite love! O let that tender love plead now on my behalf: let all my iniquities be here [illegible], and my name be written in the Book of life. I believe in thee; I hope in thee; I love thee. To thee be honour, praise, glory, and benediction, for ever and ever Amen.

O sacred Blood, flowing from the wounds of Jesus Christ, and washing away the sins of the world! cleanse, sanctify, and preserve my soul, that nothing may ever separate me from thee. Behold, O eternal Father, thy only begotten Son, and look upon the face of thy Christ, in whom thou art well pleased. Hear the voice of his Blood, crying out to thee, not for vengeance, but for mercy and pardon. Accept this divine oblation, and through the infinite merits of all the sufferings that Jesus endured on the cross for our salvation, be pleased to look upon us, and upon all thy people, with an eye of mercy.

We most humbly beseech thee, Almighty God, command these things to be carried by the hands of thy holy angels, to thy altar on high, in the sight of thy divine Majesty, that as many as shall partake of the most sacred body and blood of thy Son at this altar may be filled with every heavenly grace and blessing. Through the same Christ our Lord. Amen.

Commemoration of the Dead.

Be mindful also, O Lord, of thy servants N. and N., who are gone before us with the sign of Faith, and rest in the sleep of peace.

Here particular mention is made of such of the Dead as are to be prayed for.

To these, O Lord, and to all that sleep in Christ, grant, we beseech thee, a place of refreshment, light, and peace, through the same Christ our Lord. Amen.

Here, striking his breast, the Priest says,

Also to us sinners, thy servants, confiding in the multitude of thy mercies, vouchsafe to grant some part and fellowship with thy holy apostles and martyrs; with John, Stephen, Matthias, Barnabas, Ignatius, Alexander, Marcellinus, Peter, Felicitas, Perpetua, Agatha, Lucy, Agnes, Cecily, Anastatia, and with all thy saints: into whose company we beseech thee to admit us, not in consideration of our merit, but of thy own gratuitous pardon. Through Christ our Lord.

By whom, O Lord, thou dost always create, sanctify, enliven, bless, and give us all these good things. By him, and with him, and in him, is to thee, God the Father Almighty, in the unity of the Holy Ghost, all honour and glory.

P. Per omnia sæcula sæculorum.

P. For ever and ever.

R. Amen.

R. Amen.

Oremus.

Præceptis salutaribus moniti, et divina institutione formati, audemus dicere:

Let us pray.

Being instructed by thy saving precepts, and following thy divine directions, we presume to say:

Pater noster, qui es in cœlis, sanctificetur nomen tuum; adveniat regnum tuum: fiat voluntas tua, sicut in cœlo, et in terra. Panem nostrum quotidianum, da

Our Father, who art in heaven: hallowed be thy name: thy kingdom come: thy will be done on earth, as it is in heaven. Give us this day our daily bread: and

nobis, hodie: et dimitte nobis debita nostra, sicut et nos dimittimus debitoribus nostris. Et ne nos inducas in tentationem.

forgive us our trespasses, as we forgive them that trespass against us. And lead us not into temptation.

R. Sed libera nos a malo.

R. But deliver us from evil.

P. Amen.

P. Amen.

Deliver us, we beseech thee, O Lord, from all evils, past, present, and to come: and by the intercession of the blessed and ever glorious Virgin Mary, Mother of God, and of the holy apostles Peter and Paul, and of Andrew, and of all the saints, mercifully grant peace in our days: that through the assistance of thy mercy we may be always free from sin, and secure from all disturbance. Through the same Jesus Christ, thy Son our Lord, who with thee and the Holy Ghost liveth and reigneth, God.

P. Per omnia sæcula sæculorum.

P. World without end.

R. Amen.

R. Amen.

P. Pax Domini sit semper vobiscum.

P. May the peace of the Lord be always with you.

R. Et cum spiritu tuo.

R. And with thy spirit.

At his breaking and putting part of the Host into the Chalice, say, May this mixture, and consecration of the body and blood of our Lord Jesus Christ, be to us that receive it effectual to eternal life. Amen.

Then bowing and striking his Breast, he says,

Agnus Dei, qui tollis peccata mundi, miserere nobis.	Lamb of God, who takest away the sins of the world, have mercy upon us.
Agnus Dei, qui tollis peccata mundi, miserere nobis.	Lamb of God, who takest away the sins of the world, have mercy upon us.
Agnus Dei, qui tollis peccata mundi, dona nobis pacem.	Lamb of God, who takest away the sins of the world, give us peace.

In Masses for the DEAD, *he says twice,* Give them rest; *and lastly,* Eternal rest. *The following Prayer is also omitted.*

Lord Jesus Christ, who saidst to thy apostles, I leave you my peace, regard not my sins, but the faith of thy Church; and grant her that peace and unity which is agreeable to thy will: who livest. Amen.

Lord Jesus Christ, Son of the living God, who, according to the will of thy Father, through the co-operation of the Holy Ghost, hast, by thy death, given life to the world: deliver me by this thy most sacred body and blood from all my iniquities, and from all evils: make me always adhere to thy commandments, and never suffer me to be separated from thee: who livest and reignest with God, the Father, in the unity of, &c. Amen.

Let not the participation of thy body, O Lord Jesus Christ, which I, though unworthy, presume [illegible] turn to my judgment and condemna[illegible] through thy mercy, may it be a safeguard and remedy both of soul and body. Who with God the Father, in the unity of the Holy Ghost, livest and reignest one God, for ever and ever. Amen.

Taking the Host in his Hands, he says,

I will take the bread of heaven, and call upon the name of the Lord.

Striking his Breast, he repeats three times,

Lord, I am not worthy that thou shouldst enter under my roof: say but the word, and my soul shall be healed.

On receiving the sacred Species, he says,

May the body of our Lord Jesus Christ preserve my soul to life everlasting. Amen.

Taking the Chalice in his Hand, he says,

What return shall I make the Lord for all he has given to me? I will take the chalice of salvation, and call upon the name of the Lord. Praising I will call upon the Lord, and shall be saved from my enemies.

Receiving the Blood of our Saviour, he says,

May the blood of our Lord Jesus Christ preserve my soul to everlasting life. Amen.

During the Ablutions *and* Post Communion, *make a Spiritual Communion, as follows.*

O my divine Saviour! I fervently adore thee in this sacred and venerable sacrament, I love thee with all the affections of my heart, and I hope with confidence in that infinite goodness which induces thee to remain among us. O that I could this moment enjoy the happiness of really communicating! O that I could this day receive that precious body which was once sacrificed for my love, and that adorable blood which flowed from thy sacred veins to wash away the sins of the world! But, alas! I am most unworthy of so great a favour. I do not deserve to receive thee, O God of all sanctity! Yet I ardently desire to do so, and I humbly conjure thee to accept this desire, and to give thyself to me by the influence of thy all-powerful grace. Come, O my God! my only Good! come to me, for I now offer thee my whole heart, most ardently desiring that it should belong to thee for whose love it was created, and whose love can alone make it truly happy. I now consecrate and present to thee all my thoughts, words, and actions, from this moment to the happy day of my next communion, in union with thy infinite merits, and as a preparation for that great happiness. O my God, I already look forward to it with joy, and I beg of thee most earnestly to grant me such purity of heart, and such fervent dispositions in approaching to thy holy table, that each communion may produce in my soul an increase of thy fear and love, and strengthen me to perform the exalted duties of a true Christian, in whatever situation of life thy providence shall hereafter place me.

P. Dominus vobiscum.	P. The Lord be with you.
R. Et cum spiritu tuo.	R. And with thy spirit.
P. Ite, missa est,	P. Go, you are dis

(*vel*) Benedicamus Domino.	missed, (*or*) Let us bless the Lord.
R. Deo gratias.	R. Thanks be to God.

In Masses for the Dead.

P. Requiescant in pace.	P. May they rest in peace.
R. Amen.	R. Amen.

Bowing before the Altar, the Priest says,

Let the performance of my homage be pleasing to thee, O holy Trinity: and grant that the sacrifice which I, though unworthy, have offered in presence of thy Majesty, may be acceptable to thee, and through thy mercy be a propitiation for me, and all those for whom it has been offered Through, &c. Amen.

Turning towards the People, he gives them his Blessing, saying,

May Almighty God the Father, Son, and Holy Ghost, bless you. Amen.

P. Dominus vobiscum.	P. Our Lord be with you.
R. Et cum spiritu tuo.	R. And with thy spirit.
P. Initium sancti Evangelii secundum Joannem.	P. The beginning of the Gospel according to St. John.
R. Gloria tibi, Domine.	R. Glory be to thee, O Lord.

In the beginning was the Word, and the Word was with God, and God was the Word: the same was in the beginning with God. All things were made by him, and without him was made nothing that was made: in him was life, and the life was the light of men: and the light shineth in darkness, and the darkness did not comprehend it.

There was a man sent from God, whose name was John. This man came for a witness, to give testimony of the light, that all men might believe through him. He was not the light, but came to give testimony of the light. He was the true light which enlighteneth every man that cometh into this world.

He was in the world, and the world was made by him, and the world knew him not. He came unto his own, and his own received him not. But as many as received him, to them he gave power to become the sons of God: to those that believe in his name, who are born, not of blood, nor of the will of the flesh, nor of the will of man, but of God: AND THE WORD WAS MADE FLESH, and dwelt among us: and we saw his glory, as it were the glory of the only begotten of the Father, full of grace and truth.

R. Deo gratias. R. Thanks be to God.

A METHOD OF FOLLOWING MASS,

WHEN OFFERED FOR THE DEAD.

A Prayer before Mass.

O ETERNAL God! who, besides the general precepts of charity, hast commanded a particular respect to be shown to parents, kindred, and benefactors, and by the institution of the Sacrifice of the Mass, has left us the means of testifying our love and gratitude towards them even after death, vouchsafe that the mass I this day offer in union with thy minister, for the souls of N. and N., may shorten their sufferings, if they be still detained in the purifying flames of purgatory.

As there may be many of my friends, relatives or ancestors, tormented in these intense flames who were the instruments of thy Providence, in bestowing on me existence, education, and innumerable other blessings, grant that I may be the means of obtaining for them a speedy release from their excessive sufferings, and a free admittance to thy eternal joys: through Jesus Christ our Lord. *Amen.*

At the beginning of Mass.

O ALMIGHTY God! with whom the spirits of the just live, and in whose holy custody are deposited the souls of all that depart hence in an inferior degree of grace, and are therefore detained in a state of suffering; as we bless thee for the saints already admitted into thy glory, so we humbly offer up our prayers for the afflicted souls who continually sigh after the day of their deliverance.

If among them be the souls of those for whom we this day petition, vouchsafe to pardon their sins, that they may behold thee, and in thy glorious light eternally rejoice. Through Jesus Christ our Lord. *Amen.*

Introit. Psalm lxiv

GRANT them, O Lord, eternal rest, and let perpetual light shine on them. *Ps.* A hymn becometh thee, O Lord, in Sion, and a vow shall be paid thee in Jerusalem: hear my prayer, all flesh shall come to thee. Grant them, &c. *to Ps.*

Lord, have mercy on us.
Christ, have mercy on us.
Lord, have mercy on us. } Each repeated three times.

Collect.

O God! the Creator and Redeemer of all the faithful, give to the souls of thy servants departed the remission of their sins; that through the help of pious supplications, they may obtain the pardon they have always desired. Who livest, &c.

Lesson. Rev. xiv. 13.

In those days: I heard a voice from heaven, saying to me: Write: Blessed are the dead, who die in the Lord. From henceforth now, saith the Spirit, that they may rest from their labours: for their works follow them.

Gradual.

Eternal rest grant to them, and may perpetual light shine on them. V. *Ps.* cxi. The just shall be in everlasting remembrance: he shall not fear the evil hearing.

Tract.

Release, O Lord! the souls of all the faithful departed, from the bonds of their sins. V. And by the assistance of thy grace, may they escape the sentence of condemnation. V. And enjoy the bliss of eternal light.

The Sequence *for the* Dead.

The day of wrath, that dreadful day,	Dies, iræ, dies illa,
Shall the whole world in ashes lay,	Solvet sæclum in favilla
As David and the Sybil say.	Teste David cum Sybilla.
What horror must invade the mind,	Quantus tremor est futurus,
When the approaching Judge shall find	Quando Judex est venturus,
Few venial faults in all mankind.	Cuncta stricte discussurus!
The last loud trumpet's wond'rous sound	Tuba mirum spargens sonum
Shall through the rending tombs rebound,	Per sepulchra regionum,
And wake the nations under ground.	Coget omnes ante thronum,
Nature and death shall with surprise	Mors stupebit, et natura,
Behold the trembling sinner rise,	Cum resurget creatura.
To view his Judge with conscious eyes.	Judicanti responsura.
Then shall, with universal fear,	Liber scriptus proferetur,
The seven-sealed judgment book appear,	In quo totum continetur,
To scan the whole of life's career.	Unde mundus judicetur,
The Judge ascends his awful throne,	Judex ergo cum sedebit,
Each secret sin shall here be known.	Quidquid latet, apparebit:
All must with shame confess their own	Nil inultum remanebit.

Ah, wretched! what shall I then say,	Quid sum, miser! tunc dicturus,
What patron find, my fears t'allay,	Quem patronum rogaturus,
When even the just shall dread that day?	Cum vix justus sit securus?
Thou mighty, formidable King!	Rex tremendæ majestatis!
Of mercy unexhausted spring!	Qui salvandos salvas gratis,
Save me! O save! and comfort bring.	Salva me fons pietatis.
Remember what my ransom cost;	Recordare Jesu pie
Let not my dear-bought soul be lost,	Quod sum causa tuæ viæ,
In storms of guilty terrors tost.	Ne me perdas illa die.
In search of me why feel such pain;	Quærens me, sedisti lassus:
Why on thy cross such pangs sustain,	Redemisti, crucem passus:
If now those sufferings must be vain?	Tantus labor non sit cassus.
Avenging Judge, whom all obey,	Juste Judex ultionis,
Cancel my debt, too great to pay,	Donum fac remissionis
Before the sad accounting day.	Ante diem rationis.
O'erwhelmed, oppressed with doubts and fears,	Ingemisco tanquam reus:
Their load my soul in anguish bears:	Culpa rubet vultus meus:
I sigh, I weep—accept my tears.	Supplicanti parce, Deus.
Thou, who wert moved at Mary's grief,	Qui Mariam absolvisti,

Who didst absolve the dying thief,
Dost bid me hope, O grant relief.
Reject not my unworthy prayer,
Preserve me from the dangerous snare,
Which death and gaping hell prepare.
Give my immortal soul a place
Among thy chosen right-hand race,
The sons of God and heirs of grace.
From that insatiate abyss,
Where flames devour and serpents hiss,
Deliver me, and raise to bliss.
Prostrate my contrite heart I rend,
My God, my father, and my friend,
Do not forsake me in the end.
Well may they curse their second birth,
Who rise to a surviving death.
Thou great Creator of mankind,
Let all thy faithful mercy find Amen.

Et latronem exaudisti,
Mihi quoque spem dedisti.
Preces meæ non sunt dignæ:
Sed tu bonus fac benigne
Ne perenni cremer igne.
Inter oves locum præta,
Et ab hædis me sequestra,
Statuens in parte dextra.
Confutatis maledictis,
Flammis acribus addictis,
Voca me cum benedictis.
Oro supplex et acclinis,
Cor contritum quasi cinis,
Gere curam mei finis.
Lacrymosa dies illa!
Qua resurget ex favilla
Judicandus homo reus.
Huic ergo parce Deus:
Pie Jesu Domine, dona eis requiem. Amen.

Gospel. John vi. 51, 55.

AT that time: Jesus said to the multitude of he Jews: I am the living bread, which came down from heaven. If any man eat of this bread, he shall live for ever: and the bread that I will give is my flesh for the life of the world. The Jews therefore strove among themselves, saying: How can this man give us his flesh to eat? Then Jesus said to them: Amen, Amen, I say unto you, except you eat the flesh of the Son of Man, and drink his blood, you shall not have life in you. He that eateth my flesh, and drinketh my blood, hath everlasting life: and I will raise him up in the last day.

Offertory.

LORD JESUS CHRIST, King of Glory! deliver the souls of all the faithful departed from the flames of hell, and from the deep pit. Deliver them from the lion's mouth, lest hell swallow them, lest they fall into darkness; and let the standard-bearer, St. Michael, bring them into the holy light. * Which thou promisedst of old to Abraham and his posterity. V. We offer thee, O Lord, a sacrifice of praise and prayers: accept them on behalf of the souls we commemorate this day, and let them pass from death to life. *Which thou, &c. *to* V.

At the Oblation, and subsequent Prayers.

O GOD! what victim can better appease thy justice, than that which we are going to offer in this unbloody renewal of the sacrifice of the cross? As that divine oblation disarmed the wrath, and induced thee to revoke the sentence of condemnation pronounced against mankind, so mercifully grant, that this adorable sacrifice may atone for the sins and imperfections of those souls for whom it is offered; that being released from the flames by which they are surrounded, they may be received into thy kingdom, and through the passion and death of our divine Redeemer, pass into eternal joys.

O all-bountiful Jesus! who art the propitiation for the living and the dead, what thanks are due to thee for having left us this divine sacrifice, and for having thus rendered it available to the souls of the faithful departed; mercifully grant, that they for whom it is offered this day, being released from suffering, may shortly prove powerful advocates for us in heaven, who now intercede for them on earth. Amen.

Psalm cxxix *paraphrased.*

From the depths have I cried to thee, O Lord, Lord hear my voice.—Sensible of my own nothingness and unworthiness, I raise my voice to thee, O King of glory, and entreat thee to listen favourably to the prayer of thy servant.

Let thine ears be attentive to the voice of my petition.—Despise not the work of thy hands, reject not the humble efforts of thy unworthy servant on behalf of those suffering souls, who now burn with the most inflamed desire of being united to thee.

If thou wilt observe iniquities, O Lord, Lord who will sustain it?—If thou wilt consider the multitude of my offences; if thou wilt view me in the terror of thy justice, I must flee from this Altar, and, instead of trying to plead the cause of others, endeavour to hide myself from thy wrath.

For with thee there is merciful forgiveness, and by reason of thy law I have waited for thee, O Lord.—Let thy mercy, O God, interpose now between me and thy justice, and having purified my soul in the blood of the spotless victim now offered for the living and the dead, may my prayers find a gracious acceptance in thy sight.

My soul hath relied on his word, my soul hath hoped in the Lord.—Covered with the precious merits of my divine Saviour, and sheltering myself under the standard of the cross, the source of all our hope, I claim the release of those suffering souls who know that their Redeemer liveth, and whose only hope rests on his sacred passion and death.

From the morning watch even until night, let Israel hope in the Lord.—Night and day shall I continue my supplications, O God of Israel; be not deaf to my cries, and reject not the voice of my mourning.

Because with the Lord there is mercy, and with Him plentiful redemption.—Let that mercy, O my God, which thou delightest to exercise, be applied to those whose greatest torment is the absence of thy sweet and adorable presence. Jesus Christ, a willing victim on this new Calvary, pleads powerfully for the perfect remission of every stain that now separates them from thee.

And He will redeem Israel from all its iniquities.—Jesus Christ the just, now become an object of malediction for the sins of his people, claims for those departed objects of our solicitude, that gracious pardon announced by the prophet to repentant Israel; his sacred merits we presume to offer in atonement for the residue of human frailty.

Secret.

Look down favourably, we beseech thee, O Lord! on the sacrifice we offer for the souls of thy servants: that as thou wast pleased to bestow on them the merit of Christian faith, thou wouldst also grant them its abundant reward. Through, &c.

At the Preface.

It is truly meet and charitable, it is a holy and wholesome thought, that we address thee, O Lord God omnipotent! on behalf of those who have departed this life, that thou wouldst grant them a place of rest and eternal happiness. O Jesus! who dying for mankind, arose again glorious and immortal from the dead; who ascended into heaven, triumphed over death, and led captivity captive; who art to descend again in great power and majesty to judge the living and the dead, we humbly address thee in favour of the souls recommended this day to thy mercy; give them a share in those eternal joys *which the eye hath not seen, the ear hath not heard, nor hath it entered the heart of man to conceive,* (1 Cor. xi. 9.) There, amidst the elect and celestial choirs, let them proclaim, Holy, Holy, Holy, is the Lord God of Sabaoth; the heavens and the earth are full of thy glory. Hosanna to him who is on high.

Blessed is he who cometh in the name of the Lord. Hosanna in the highest.

At the Canon.

We recommend to thee, O Lord! the souls of thy servants N. N., and as, in mercy to them. thou didst become man, so now vouchsafe to admit them into the number of the blessed. Remember, O Lord! that the souls for whom we pray are thy creatures, not made by strange gods, but by thee, the only true and living God, for there is no other God but thee; none that can work wonders like unto thine.

Let their souls find comfort and mercy in thy sight, and remember not their former sins, nor any of those faults they may have fallen into through human frailty, or the violence of temptation; for though they sinned, they still retained a true faith in thee, O holy Trinity, Father, Son, and Holy Ghost, and a lively zeal for thy honour; they faithfully adored, and died in favour with thee, O divine Lord, as well as in peace and charity with all mankind.

Remember not, O Lord! we beseech thee, the sins and ignorance of their youth, but according to thy great mercy, be mindful of them in thy glory. May the heavens be now opened to receive them. May the Archangel St. Michael, chief of the heavenly host, conduct them. May the holy angels of God meet and accompany them into the city of the heavenly Jerusalem. May blessed Peter the Apostle, to whom were given the keys of the kingdom of heaven, receive them. May holy Paul the Apostle, who was a vessel of election, help them. May St. John, the beloved Disciple, to whom God revealed the secrets of heaven, intercede for them. May all the holy Apostles, to whom was given the power of binding and loosing, pray for them. May all the blessed and chosen servants of God intercede for them, that being delivered from present confinement and suffering, they may be admitted into the kingdom of heaven, through the assistance and merits of our Lord and Saviour Jesus Christ. Who livest, &c.

And now, all-powerful God! at this awful moment, when, by the words of consecration, thy divine Son is actually present, I offer up to thee this same beloved Son, who died for mankind. I humbly entreat thee, through the infinite merits of his death, to show compassion and mercy to the souls for whose repose the holy sacrifice is this day offered.

At the Elevation of the Host.

Hail! most blessed Jesus! eternal Son of the Most High God! O deign to be merciful to those for whom we pray; thou who didst expire on the cross for their sakes, give rest to their souls.—To whom shall we apply, but to thee? Thou hast the words of eternal life, by which thou canst shorten their sufferings, and give them eternal rest.

At the Elevation of the Chalice.

Hail! sacred blood! that flowed for the sins of the world; wash away whatever stains may render thy servants unfit to be admitted into heaven. O good and merciful God! look on the face of thy Christ, in whom thou art always well pleased, and permit the souls for which he suffered to rest eternally in thy divine presence.

After the Elevation.

Lord Jesus Christ! we earnestly entreat thee, by thy bitter agony and prayer in the garden, to become an advocate with thy eternal Father, on behalf of thy servants N. N. Lay before him, we conjure thee, all those drops of blood which, in thy anguish of spirit, flowed from thy sacred body, and offer them as a sacrifice of atonement, that thereby the souls of N. N. may be discharged from all the punishment still inflicted by divine justice on the guilt of sin.

Lord Jesus! who wast pleased to suffer death on the cross for the redemption of mankind, we humbly beseech thee to offer up all that anguish and pain which thou didst endure, especially at the moment of thy death, on behalf of thy servants, that thy precious merits may be accepted for the repose of their souls, as superabundant atonement for that punishment which may still remain due for sin.

Lord Jesus Christ, who so loved us as to become man for our salvation, we beseech thee to represent to the Eternal Father thy infinite charity and goodness on behalf of thy servants, N. N.; plead their cause, that by such powerful mediation they may be freed from unspeakable pains, and find the gates of life open to receive them.

O Lord, grant them to partake now of the fruits of thy holy incarnation, of thy bitter passion, of thy glorious resurrection and admirable ascension: grant that they may be sensible of the effects of this holy sacrifice, and of all the prayers which are offered to thee by the whole Church. Remember, O compassionate Jesus! that thy sacred arms were stretched forth on the cross; that in the excess of thy torments, thou didst cry out to thy eternal Father, commending thy spirit to him; have compassion now, we beseech thee, on the souls of thy servants, N. N., who in a state of suffering expect relief from thee; receive them into thy arms; give them shelter in thy adorable heart from all molestation, till the anger of God pass over. Into thy hands, we commend their spirits; despise not, we beseech thee, those souls, which are the work of thy hands, created and redeemed by thee. O divine Jesus! vouchsafe to look on them with eyes of mercy and compassion; and grant them comfort, peace, and eternal rest.

By that love which brought thee from heaven, and by the infinite merits of thy death, have compassion on the souls of thy servants N. N.; satisfy for all their sins, failings, and defects; let them now experience the multitude of thy tender mercies; make them sensible of the excess of thy goodness; and since they can do nothing to mitigate the pains of purgatory, speak thou for them, we beseech thee; thou, who art the eternal Word, and to whom the Father can refuse nothing.

Repeat the LORD'S PRAYER *with the Priest, after which say:*

O DIVINE LORD! whose adorable heart ardently sighs for the happiness of thy banished children, we humbly beseech thee to remember the souls of thy servants for whom we pray; command them, we conjure thee, to be received by thy holy angels, and conveyed to the abodes of rest and peace. *Amen.*

At the Agnus Dei.

LAMB of God, who takest away the sins of the world, grant them rest.—Lamb of God, who takest away the sins of the world, grant them rest.—Lamb of God, who takest away the sins of the world, grant them everlasting rest.

From the Agnus Dei to the Communion.

O ETERNAL GOD! behold here on this altar, as was once on the cross, thy dear and only Son, the beloved Object of thy complacency. Behold this adorable Victim, who, to appease thy anger, sacrifices his own precious body and blood; that body, which was torn with stripes, and covered with wounds; and that blood, which was shed to wash away the sins of the world. He immolates himself with the same excess of mercy and love, as he did on Mount Calvary. O let not this sacred blood be shed in vain, but grant that its infinite merits may be applied to the souls of thy suffering servants, and give them admittance to thy presence, that they may bless and praise thee for ever and ever. Ah, my God! thou knowest that the flames which surround them are not more active than their ardent desire to behold thee.

When shall these souls be united to thee, O God? When shall they see thee in the land of the living? Till then, they sigh and bewail their banishment, desiring continually to enjoy thy divine presence—to be admitted into thy eternal kingdom. Alas! while myriads of blessed spirits see, love, and enjoy thee incessantly; while they are inebriated with the plenty of thy house, the souls of these thy servants are perhaps burning in flames, plunged in darkness, and far removed from the light of heaven. O! thou, who art infinite in mercy! be not deaf to my supplications for their speedy relief. O blessed Angels and Saints! vouchsafe to join me in making intercession for N. N., and obtain for them admittance into your happy society. As the hart pants after the fountain of living waters, so do these souls thirst after thee, O God! the inexhaustible source of eternal and ineffable joys. Thou knowest the longing sighs of these suffering souls, O infinitely bountiful and compassionate Father! and thou alone canst terminate their banishment. Thou canst open that spring of living water, for which they so ardently thirst; thou canst fill their hungry souls with good things, and bestow on them the inheritance purchased by the blood of a dying Saviour. Draw aside then the veil which hides thy amiable countenance; for what do these souls desire, but to contemplate, praise, and love thee, their Sovereign Good, for all eternity.

At the Communion.

I MOST ardently desire, O my adorable Saviour, that thou wouldst honour this day the dwelling of my heart by thy divine presence. With what confidence could I then implore rest and eternal peace for the suffering souls of purgatory whom thou lovest, though thy justice forces thee to banish them for a time from their heavenly inheritance. Look nevertheless, O merciful Redeemer, on the work of thy hands; hasten the happy hour of their deliverance, and grant that, partaking spiritually of the merits of thy august sacrifice, I may submissively accept, and patiently bear all that is disagreeable and painful to inclination, and thus avert a long separation from thee after the close of my mortal life. *Amen.*

Postcommunion.

GRANT, we beseech thee, O Lord! that our humble prayers on behalf of the souls of thy servants, both men and women, may be profitable to them; so that thou mayest deliver them from all the punishment due to their sins, and make them partakers of the redemption thou hast purchased for them. Who livest, &c.

After Dominus vobiscum, *the Priest says,* May they rest in peace. R. *Amen.*

At the last Gospel.

MAY now the bright company of angels meet your souls, O departed servants of the Lord may the crowd of apostles receive you; may the triumphant army of glorious martyrs conduct you; and may a happy rest be your portion in the company of the patriarchs. May Jesus Christ appear to you with a mild and cheerful countenance, and give you a place among those who are to be in his presence for ever.

May your God arise, and put your enemies to flight. Let them vanish like smoke, and as wax before the fire, so let them perish. May all the reprobate of hell be filled with confusion and shame; but let the just and elect rejoice and be happy in the presence of God, and may you be of that blessed number. May Christ Jesus himself rescue you from torments, who lovingly died for you. May the eternal Son of the living God place you in his garden of Paradise, and may he, the true Shepherd, own you for those of his flock; may he liberate you from confinement, and place you at his right hand in the inheritance of his elect. We pray that it may be your happy lot to behold your Redeemer face to face; to be for ever in his presence, in the vision of that truth which is the joy of the blessed; and thus placed among those happy spirits, may you be for ever replenished with heavenly sweetness. *Amen.*

A Prayer after Mass.

AND now, O God! having recommended to thy mercy the souls of thy departed servants, grant we may ever remember that we are most certainly to follow them. Give us grace to prepare for our last hour by a good life, that so death, however sudden it may be, may not find us unworthy of admittance into eternal glory. Open likewise the eyes, and soften the hearts of those who have the misfortune of being at variance with thee; inspire them, we humbly beseech thee, with a true sense of their dreadful danger that by a timely consideration of the uncertainty of life, and the certainty of death, they may be sincerely converted, and obtaining pardon for their sins in this life, be happy with thee for ever in the next. *Amen.*

A DEVOUT METHOD OF HEARING MASS

CONFORMABLY TO

THE MYSTERIES OF THE PASSION.

It is the common opinion of the Saints, that among all the exercises of piety, none is so pleasing to God, and so profitable to our souls, as frequent reflection on the sufferings of Jesus Christ, and a continual effort on our part to commemorate and honour his sacred passion and death. Respect, justice, love, and, above all, gratitude, oblige us to this, and should concur to make the sufferings of our divine Redeemer the most ordinary and familiar reflection of our lives. Our own interest should likewise urge us to adopt this holy practice, since it is considered by the saints a short and secure road to perfection. St. Bonaventure says, that "he who devoutly applies himself to meditate upon the life and death of Jesus, finds there all he requires, and needs not seek any thing out of Jesus Christ."

As one of the most perfect methods of assisting at Mass, is to meditate devoutly on the Passion of Christ, so the best means of honouring that Sacred Passion is to hear Mass for that end; for, in this adorable Sacrifice, which St. F. de Sales justly styles "the centre of religion, the heart of devotion, and the soul of piety," we are furnished with an offering of thanksgiving for our redemption, proportioned to the benefit; and also with a motive for daily increasing in gratitude for such blessings, as eternity itself will not appear too long to acknowledge.

A Prayer before Mass.

O divine Jesus! sacred Victim, immolated for the redemption of mankind! I earnestly beseech thee that I may assist at this adorable sacrifice with the most lively faith, animated hope, unbounded gratitude, and tender love. Permit me to follow thee in spirit through the different stages of thy sacred passion, and give me an abundant share of that infinite charity which induced thee to suffer such excessive torments for my sake.

With the daughters of Sion, who met thee carrying thy cross, and thy blessed Mother, who saw thee expire for our salvation, I desire to compassionate thy sufferings, and to detest sin, as the only sovereign evil. I offer this divine sacrifice, to commemorate in a special manner thy dolorous passion, and to obtain through its efficacious merits the grace of true and sincere devotion towards thy life-giving sufferings and death.

At the Beginning of Mass.

The priest going from the sacristy to the altar, represents Jesus Christ retiring from the Cenacle to the garden of Gethsemani Unite your sentiments with the divine dispositions of the Son of God, and dispose yourself by sincere repentance to assist worthily at the great sacrifice about to be offered.

O Divine Lord! in the multitude of thy mercies I will enter thy house, and adore thee in thy holy temple. Though my sins are multiplied beyond number, yet I will appeal to thy unbounded mercies, which far exceed my malice, or the extent of my ingratitude. I will confide in the sufferings of my Redeemer, and hope, through his infinite merits, to find grace and salvation. O dear Jesus! thou who hast washed me heretofore in the laver of baptism, wash me yet more from my iniquity, and cleanse me from my sin: sprinkle me with thy blood, and I shall be cleansed; wash me and I shall be made whiter than snow.

At the Introit.

When the priest bows and kisses the altar, contemplate our divine Lord prostrate before his heavenly Father, loaded with the sins of mankind, and bathed in blood through excess of sorrow. Reflect on the anguish which the treacherous kiss of Judas caused our divine Redeemer.

O Good Jesus! I fervently bless thee, for all thou hast done and suffered for my salvation Give me grace to weep over those sins which drew streams of blood from thy sacred veins. I desire to commemorate with the most lively and humble contrition, thy agony in the garden, and I firmly resolve to detest my sins to the latest moment of my life. Pierce my soul with grief, for having repaid thy goodness with ingratitude, and let me frequently cry out with the humble publican: O God! be merciful to me a sinner May those bonds which confined thy sacred hands, burst the fetters of my sins, and restore me to the sweet liberty of thy children. I cast myself at thy sacred feet, and conjure thee to strengthen me by thy all-powerful grace, that under every trial and affliction I may submit cheerfully to the decrees of thy adorable Providence, and never cease to bless thy holy name.

At the Kyrie eleison and Gloria in excelsis.

The *Kyrie eleison* is repeated three times to honour the adorable Trinity; it may also serve to remind you of the denials of St Peter, and to excite the deepest regret for your much more frequent denials of so good a master. At the *Gloria in excelsis*, reflect on the miraculous conversions which signalized the public life of Jesus Christ, and beg that one benign glance may convert and penetrate your soul, as it did that of St. Peter.

O MY God! have mercy on me, according to thy great mercy: pardon me, who have so often had the misfortune of denying thee, by a life altogether opposite to thy sacred maxims. Look on me, divine Jesus, with that compassion and tenderness which the sight of misery always excited in thy most amiable heart. Purify me, as thou didst thy penitent apostle, that I may worthily unite with thy Church in celebrating the wonderful work of man's redemption. O how fervently should I join in thy praises, most amiable Jesus! How ardently should I sing, Glory be to God on high, glory be to that adorable Being, who, forgetful of his own glory, underwent for my sake such prodigious humiliations! O my sovereign King! my divine and adorable Model! since thou wert pleased to descend so low as my frai nature, grant that I may place all my glory honour, and happiness, in sharing thy humiliations, and carrying thy cross.

At the Epistle and Gospel.

When the priest goes from the middle of the altar to the *Epistle* side, and thence to the *Gospel* side, represent to yourself the eternal Son of God, dragged about to the different tribunals of Annas, Caiphas, Pilate, and Herod; and when you stand to hear the Gospel, remember that it is the word of Him, who alone has the words of eternal life; of Him, who came from heaven to instruct you, and who, for your sake, confirmed his doctrine by shedding his precious blood.

O Eternal God! unerring Truth! whose sacred word I am so happy as to hear, penetrate my heart by the influence of thy grace, that I may not hear it to my eternal reprobation, like the Jews who so long and so fruitlessly listened to thy sacred maxims. O spotless Lamb of God! while thy judges proclaim thee an impostor, I rise without fear or shame to declare in the face of heaven and earth, that I believe thee to be Christ, the Son of the living God, and that I most unreservedly assent to all and every article proposed by thy holy Church to my belief. But, O divine Lord! give me grace to profess my faith by my actions as well as by my words. Have mercy on all who are involved in the dreadful night of infidelity · may the light of thy grace shine upon them, and so penetrate their hearts, that they may embrace the truth, and be united to the communion of thy holy Church.

At the Offertory.

When the priest unveils the chalice, and offers the bread and wine, contemplate your merciful Redeemer, stripped of his garments, bound to a pillar, and cruelly scourged; offer yourself, in union with the sacrifice he then offered of his precious blood, and which he renews on the altar.

Adorable Jesus! when I reflect on the torments thou didst endure when fastened to the pillar, I begin to conceive the enormity of sin, and the immense extent of thy eternal love. I behold in thy wounds the greatness of my ingratitude and the depth of the misery to which I am reduced. But, O Lord! how happy am I, in being able to present thee, at this moment, a victim of thanksgiving and atonement, fully proportioned, or rather far exceeding, the magnitude of my obligation, and the multitude of my crimes. I offer thee the streams of blood that flowed from thy sacred body during thy ignominious scourging, and also the bread and wine which is now presented to thy divine Majesty. Accept, in union with this precious oblation, my body and soul, my thoughts, words, desires, affections, and sufferings; in fine, my whole being, that henceforward I may be entirely thine by the bonds of ardent charity.

At the Lavabo and Orate Fratres.

When the priest washes his hands, call to mind the testimony which Pilate gave to the innocence of Jesus Christ; and at the *Orate fratres* adore your Saviour, exhibited to the people as a mock king. Prostrate yourself in spirit before your Sovereign Lord, and pour out at his sacred feet the grateful effusions of your compassion and love.

O most adorable blood! which flowed as a remedy for all human woes, I beseech thee to wash, purify, and sanctify my sinful soul, that I may, with a pure and upright conscience, assist at these awful mysteries. I cannot, O my God! presume to wash my hands among the innocent, for alas! I have been long since excluded from the happy few who never offended thee; but, at least, I can claim a privilege not reserved to the innocent alone, but mercifully granted even to the most guilty. I can wash my hands, my heart, my soul, in thy precious blood. I can cast myself on thy divine mercy, with a firm resolution, rather to die, than to offend thee during the remainder of my life. O King of my soul! I acknowledge thee for my sole and sovereign Lord. O Jesus! I implore, by the sorrow and agony of heart thou didst endure when Barabbas was preferred to thee, that thou wouldst preserve me from ever preferring any created object to thy friendship and favour. By thy ignominious clothing with a purple garment, I entreat thee to give me a garment of justice, when I shall appear before thy dread tribunal, and I fervently conjure thee, that through thy infinite mercy and the merits of thy thorny crown I may hereafter obtain a crown of immortal glory.

At the Preface

The priest praying some time in secret before the *Preface*, represents and commemorates the admirable silence observed by Jesus Christ in the course of his sacred passion. Do you now address your divine Lord in the secret of your heart; represent to him all your spiritual necessities; implore an application of his infinite merits to the wounds of your soul, and when the priest raises his voice to recite the Preface, do you redouble your fervour, and join in spirit with the Church militant, triumphant, and suffering, in praising and magnifying that divine Lamb who was slain for the health and life of his own creatures.

O DIVINE Searcher of Hearts! from whom nothing is hidden, since thou desirest so ardently to establish thy reign in my soul, permit me to represent to thee its miseries, and all the obstacles which unfortunately oppose the sweet empire of thy love in my heart. O Lord, thou needest not my representations, to discern my wants. I am too insensible, to feel my miseries as I ought—too weak, to call loudly on thy mercy—too guilty, to deserve being heard Let my silence then speak, O most merciful Saviour! let my multiplied miseries plead on my behalf. Thou wilt not be deaf to their eloquent supplications: and surely, my God! thou needest but consult thy own sacred heart, and that infinite love which brings thee daily on our altars, to find motives for granting pardon and mercy to the most unworthy of thy creatures. O blessed spirits of neaven! holy and happy saints of God! who, in the mirror of his adorable sanctity, behold the enormity of sin, supply for me, who am unworthy to join with the Church in celebrating his praises and magnifying his goodness.

At the Canon.

Let the low and solemn voice in which the *Canon* is read, re mind you of that mourning and consternation which amazed and silenced all nature at the sufferings of Jesus Christ; and when the priest spreads his hands over the oblation, making the sign of the cross, call to mind the torments our divine Redeemer endured when fastened to the cross.

O MY God! when I reflect on the number and enormity of my sins, I am sensible that I have no claim to a share in those precious graces which thou hast died to purchase for thy creatures; but when I contemplate that cross on which thou didst agonize—when I turn my eyes on this altar, this new Calvary, on which thou art about to descend, and again offer thyself for my salvation, I feel convinced that thou wilt always be to me a Jesus, a Saviour. Accept, therefore, of my whole being, in union with the sacred oblation I am about to offer. Purify my sinful soul in those streams of blood which gushed from thy adorable wounds, and which will soon flow on this altar. Grant to us all, through its efficacious merits, the grace to practise what thy holy law commands, and to avoid what it prohibits. Extend the blessings of peace and unity to thy Church; repentance and pardon to all sinners; comfort to the sick, the dying, and the afflicted; in a word, mercy and eternal happiness to all, since for all, O divine Victim! thou didst shed thy adorable and saving blood. I particularly implore thy precious graces, O my God, for those for whom I am bound to pray—those who have recommended themselves to my prayers—who pray for me, or who, at this moment, may specially want thy divine assistance. O may this adorable and august sacrifice be received by thy Divine Majesty as was the victim which Christ offered in his own person on the altar of the cross.

At the Elevation.

At the *Elevation* of the sacred host and chalice, reflect on the pangs which Jesus endured, when, lifted up between heaven and earth, his precious blood flowed abundantly for the remission of your sins, for the conversion of the world, and of his greatest enemies. Let the first-fruit of his Cross and Passion, applied to the penitent thief on the cross, encourage you to recur confidently to his mercies, and to hope that his infinite love will one day assign you likewise a place in Paradise.

Hail, O King of Glory! Prince of Peace! and Saviour of the World! Hail, O immaculate Victim! sacrificed for me and all mankind on the altar of the cross. I bless thee, I adore thee, I love thee, O divine Jesus! and I ardently invite the whole universe to join in praising and blessing thy holy name. O bleeding and adorable Victim of my sins! why have I not the faith, the love, the anguish which penetrated the hearts of those who beheld thy sacred blood flow from thy precious wounds? Hear, O eternal God! the voice of this blood, which cries loudly, not for vengeance, but for pardon and mercy. O! let it plead powerfully on my behalf; let it blot out my sins, cleanse every stain from my soul, and render me pure and pleasing in thy sight.

After the Elevation.

BEHOLD, O almighty and all-gracious God! thy Son Jesus, in whom thou art well pleased. Look upon the face of thy Christ and my Saviour, here present; look upon this spotless Lamb, this adorable victim, this pure holocaust of obedience, humbled to the ignominious death of the cross. Behold in him what may move thee to look upon us with an eye of mercy and compassion. He is our High Priest, sprinkled with his own blood. Receive the sacrifice he has offered for us, in consideration of the honour and homage that are due to thy sovereign goodness from me and all creatures. Extend, O compassionate Creator! its efficacious virtue to the souls of the faithful departed, and grant them rest and life everlasting, particularly to N. N.: deign to mitigate their punishment, and translate them to that place of glory for which they are destined. Thou didst once promise that, looking on the rainbow, thou wouldst remember the covenant made between thee and the Patriarch Noah (*Gen.* ix.): canst thou then look on the blood of thy beloved Son Jesus, offered to thee in sacrifice, without rememcering the great covenant of the New Law, sealed and confirmed with the effusion of his sacred blood?

O dearest Jesus! why cannot I love thee as thy goodness deserves? The more thou hast humbled thyself for my sake, the more I am bound to love thee, and spend my life in thy service. Remember thou hast purchased my soul at a dear rate; O let not thy blood be lost or shed in vain, but receive me into the number of thy elect. I detest my sins, which were the cause of thy sufferings; alas! they were the nails that pierced thy hands and feet, and fastened thee to an ignominious cross. O who will give sorrow to my heart, and a fountain of tears to my eyes, that I may bewail them in the bitterness of my soul all the days of my life, and thus, at the hour of death, be entitled to hear those consolatory words addressed to the penitent thief: *This day shalt thou be with me in paradise.* I acknowledge, that I do not deserve to be ranked among the number of thy children; yet, in obedience to thy precept, and with profound veneration for thy sacred words, I will presume to say that heavenly prayer which thou hast taught me: *Our Father, &c.*

At the Agnus Dei.

When the priest says the *Agnus Dei,* reflect on the miraculous change of heart wrought in the Centurion and other witnesses of the death of Jesus Christ, and be careful, as far as it depends on you, not to depart from this new Calvary without participating in their holy dispositions.

O INNOCENT Lamb of God! who takest away the sins of the world, have mercy on me, for thy peculiar and distinguishing property is infinite mercy. Give to my heart the sorrow and repentance of those who mourned thy cruel death, and teach me, like them, to place all my hopes in thee, and to love and seek thee as my only sovereign good. I most humbly beseech thee, by all the anguish thou didst endure during the course of thy passion, especially at the separation of thy sacred soul from thy body, that thou wouldst have mercy and compassion on me, when I shall be on the point of appearing before thy dread tribunal. Let thy passion and death then interpose between my soul and the rigours of thy justice. Ah! while I yet sojourn in this valley of tears, let the remembrance of thy bitter draught of vinegar and gall preserve me from delighting in the false pleasures of this world, and let thy burning thirst upon the cross make me thirst only after the enjoyment of thy presence. May the recollection of thy saving death penetrate my soul with such lively gratitude, that from this moment I may place all my happiness in loving and serving thee, my only joy and sovereign felicity.

At the Communion.

The *Priest's Communion* represents the burial of Jesus Christ's sacred body when it was taken from the cross; and the covering of the chalice is a figure of the sepulchre shut up, and covered with a stone. This is the time peculiarly adapted to invite our Lord by a spiritual communion to repose in your heart, and to honour it frequently by his sacramental presence, or habitually by the influence of his holy grace.

O my God! how can I reflect on the happiness of those who approach worthily to the holy Eucharist, without ardently desiring to enjoy the like blessing? how can I assist at this adorable sacrifice, without regretting the sins and miseries which justly deter me from receiving thee sacramentally! I am not worthy, O infinite purity, to lodge thee in my heart; I am not worthy to share in the happiness of those who now enjoy thy sacramental presence. But, Lord! though I cannot unite myself to thee really, yet I am not forbidden to do so in spirit and desire. I believe most firmly that thou art present in this sacred host; I hope in that infinite mercy which detains thee therein; and I ardently love and desire to receive thee, notwithstanding my unworthiness. I unite in the adoration, love, humility, and fervour of all who this day received thee throughout the universe, with the most perfect dispositions; and I earnestly beg of thee, by that tender love which induces thee to give thyself to thy creatures, to accept of every thought, word, and action, from this to my next communion, as so many acts of love, desire, and preparation to receive thee; and I earnestly conjure thee to crown all thy blessings by the inestimable grace of a worthy communion at the hour of my death.

At the last Collects.

The *last Collects* represent the apparitions and instructions of Jesus Christ to his Apostles and Disciples after his resurrection; and the *Priest's Blessing* denotes that parting benediction given by our divine Lord, when ascending into heaven. Remember, when the last Gospel is reading at the left side of the altar, that Jesus Christ did not come to call the just but sinners to repentance, and that his infinite mercy is thus daily renewing on our altars the Sacrifice of the Cross, should animate even the most guilty to recur with confidence to his infinite goodness and abundant merits.

O BLESSED Redeemer! who coming forth from the grave didst rise triumphant over death, I praise and glorify thee for all thy mercies, and in particular for having conversed so long with thy apostles, and confirmed them in that saving faith, which they were destined to transmit to succeeding ages. O! how shall I thank thee for the inestimable advantage of having beheld thee sacrificed on this altar, and for having thereby participated in the abundant merits of thy passion and death. Let me not depart from this sanctuary without those sentiments of piety, and that spiritual strength for the amendment of my life, which may be always drawn from this adorable sacrifice. Pardon, O Lord! my distractions and irreverences. Engrave on my heart the remembrance of thy sufferings, that I may henceforward glory only in Jesus Christ, and in him crucified. Teach me to follow thy divine example, that rising with thee to a new life, I may, through thy powerful grace, advance daily and hourly in virtue, and at length attain to the unlimited and eternal enjoyment of thee, my God and my All! in the kingdom of thy glory. *Amen.*

ON THE SACRAMENT OF PENANCE.

The Sacrament of Penance, which the Saints term "the second plank after shipwreck," is one of the greatest blessings we derive from the sufferings and death of Jesus Christ. But as its efficacy chiefly depends on the dispositions of those who approach the holy tribunal, of course preparation for Confession becomes one of the most serious duties of a Christian. That rigid justice, which so severely punished one mortal sin in the angels, and which rigorously inflicted on the eternal Son of God all the penalties due to man's offences, will not assuredly remit the real guilt of sin in those who only carelessly comply with the external form of Confession, without taking the necessary pains to excite in their souls the dispositions which so holy an action requires. Those who are so happy as to have been early instructed in the method of preparing for Confession, should be particularly grateful to God for so great a blessing, and endeavour, by exact compliance with all they know to be necessary, to draw from this Sacrament the graces which it infallibly bestows on those who receive it with due dispositions.

One of the best rules which can be followed with respect to Confession, is to approach the sacred tribunal each time as if it were to be the last. What would be your dispositions, if you were actually stretched on your death-bed, and about to prepare for a confession which you knew would be followed by that tremendous judgment which has caused the greatest saints to tremble? How earnestly would you, in that situation, implore light to see the state of your soul!—how seriously would you endeavour to discover all your sins!—how bitterly would you deplore having ever offended so good a God!—how sincere and exact would be your accusations, and how firmly would you resolve, not only to avoid sin, but to repair, as far as possible, every injury you had occasioned, and expiate every offence of which you were guilty! Do now what you would then do; for the Confession you are about to make may be your last; and even though you may have many opportunities of recurring to the Tribunal of Penance, yet be convinced, that at the hour of death there could not be a more serious subject of remorse, than multiplied, but careless Confessions. On the other hand, no tongue can describe the consolation and peace of those who have been wise enough to settle their accounts with God in time, and who did not put off to a season of sickness, anxiety, and mental as well as bodily weakness, the awful task of preparing for eternity. It is in your power now to purchase this hap piness for yourself, by seriously attending to the five following requisites for a good Confession:—1st, Serious examination of conscience.—2d, Sorrow for sin.—3d, A determined resolution never more to offend God, and to avoid the occasions of sin.—4th, A candid, humble confession to an approved priest.—5th, A sincere desire and intention to satisfy God's justice, and your neighbour's also, if injured in reputation or property.

Place yourself in the presence of God, by a lively act of faith, and firm conviction that his all-seeing eye penetrates to the bottom of your heart. Endeavour to conceive the importance of acquitting yourself well of so serious a duty as Confession, and consider how grateful you should be to God for granting you an opportunity which is denied to so many sinners, of regaining his grace and friendship.

A Prayer to beg of God the grace to make a good Confession.

O MY God! and most liberal Benefactor! how can I present myself before thee, loaded as I am with sin, and above all debased by the crime of ingratitude for thy innumerable mercies! But thou art my Creator, thou knowest the miseries of my soul; thou seest how often I have abused the greatest graces, how unworthy I am of thy favours; yet notwithstanding, thou still desirest not the death of me a wretched sinner, but rather that I be converted and live. If thou didst not ardently love me, thou wouldst not now invite me to return to thee, nor offer me a pardon I have so little deserved. O my good God! since I could not conceive the desire of regaining thy friendship without thy grace, vouchsafe to finish thy own work, and to assist me in preparing for this confession. Teach me to conceive and tremble at the danger in which I have been too often, of eternal separation from thee O let the misery of those unhappy souls, to whom repentance is now impossible, yet who once had the same advantages I enjoy, awaken me to all the exertions necessary for making a good confession, and do not permit that my negligence or insensibility should frustrate the designs of thy infinite mercy.

Beg the Light of the Holy Ghost to discover your Sins.

O MY God! I am firmly convinced, that however sincerely I may desire to discover all my offences, yet, that I am absolutely incapable of discerning even the least of my sins, without the assistance of thy holy Spirit. O Judge of the living and the dead! before whom I must appear one day, to give an account of all my thoughts, words, actions, and omissions, from my coming to the use of reason to the last instant of my life, give me, I entreat of thee, that light and grace without which I can do nothing. O divine Spirit of Light and Truth! descend into my heart, and grant me one ray of that light which will enlighten my soul at the moment of her departure from this world. Alas! I shall then see all my sins in their true colours, when it will be too late to detest and renounce them; but now is *the acceptable time, the day of salvation*, every moment of which is precious: this life is that season of mercy in which thou hast promised to receive and pardon a repenting sinner. O! do not then refuse me thy divine assistance, now that the knowledge of myself can lead to my perfect conversion. Discover to me all that displeases thee in my heart; let nothing escape the exact scrutiny I am about to make, that I may thoroughly know myself, and then, by an humble, candid, contrite accusation, make myself known to thy minister

---

AN EXAMINATION OF CONSCIENCE.

To fulfil your duty with regard to examination of conscience, you should, as St. Augustine says, establish within your own heart a tribunal, and there taking for the rule of your judgment the Gospel of Jesus Christ, and the principles of Christianity laid down by its divine Founder, judge yourself with the same impartial justice as you would an indifferent person, or rather with all the rigour with which you would act towards a declared enemy; for, in fact, we have no greater enemy than ourselves in all that regards our eternal interests.

Examine your conscience carefully on all the sins you have fallen into since your last confession, and also on any fault you may have committed in making it. Take sufficient time for this important inquiry; for it is a certainty, that every sin forgotten through criminal carelessness, will always remain against us before God, and consequently prevent the pardon of the rest of our sins. But, though our examination for confession should be made with the greatest exactness, yet scrupulous anxiety should be carefully avoided, as God requires no more than moral care and application, such as every rational person would give to any affair in which he earnestly wished to succeed.—The different heads to be examined on, are the Sins committed relative to the Sacraments—the ten Commandments of God—the six Precepts of the Church—the seven deadly sins—the duties of our State of Life—our predominant Passion—and, lastly, with respect to each sin, the number of times it has been committed, as nearly as we can recollect, and any circumstance which may materially alter its nature, or increase or diminish its malice.

An Examination for Young Persons.

Respecting the Sacraments.—Have you confessed or communicated without sufficient preparation?

Respecting the Commandments.—1st Commandment.—Did you neglect on awaking to make an offering of your heart to God? Did you omit your morning prayers, or discharge any other spiritual duty with wilful distraction? Have you assisted at the spiritual lecture or instructions without the respect and attention due to the word of God? Have you passed the day in total forgetfuness of God's holy presence?

2d Commandment.—Did you take the holy name of God in vain?

3d Commandment.—Were you wilfully distracted during Mass, particularly on a day of obligation? Did you laugh, talk, look about, or behave in any other way disrespectful in the chapel?

4th Commandment.—Have you been disobedient to your mistresses, who now hold the place of your parents? Did you ridicule or disregard their advice, murmur at or intentionally slight their orders or regulations? Did you fail in the attention you owe to the instructions of your masters, and to those of every other person concerned in your education?

5th Commandment.—Have you given way to anger, impatience, hatred, jealousy, or desire of revenge? Have you been guilty of injurious words, or did you refuse to apologize or forgive? Have you, by bad example, bad advice, or by any means, been accessary to the sins of others? Have you, by ridicule, by opposition, by teasing, or by any other way whatever, deterred others from acting uprightly? Have you been guilty of intemperance, or in any way intentionally injured your health? Have you neglected to relieve the poor according to your ability?

6th and 10th Commandments.—Have you sinned by words, actions, looks, thoughts, or desires contrary to purity?

7th and 9th Commandments.—Have you been guilty of theft, or wantonly destroyed what did not belong to you?

8th Commandment.—Have you been guilty of rash judgments, detraction, or lies? Have you, by talebearing, or in any other way, given occasion to quarrels, disunion, or any other breach of charity? Have you spoken of the faults of others, or listened voluntarily to any uncharitable conversations? Have you deliberately entertained or manifested feelings of dislike towards any one? Have you given any one pain by unkind or cutting remarks? Have you exposed your companions to impatience, or the commission of any fault, by acting in a manner which you supposed capable of producing these bad effects?

Respecting the seven deadly Sins.—Have you been guilty of pride or vanity in thoughts, words, or actions? Have you given way to sloth, or indulged habitual indolence in the discharge of your duties?

Respecting your present Duties.—Have you neglected your improvement, wilfully misspent your time, or, through obstinacy, contempt, or repugnance to restraint, transgressed the rules established for preserving order and regularity? and have you, by this example, or by ridicule, been the cause of others acting in like manner?

An Examination for a general Confession.

Sins committed relative to the Sacraments.—Did you neglect confessing and communicating at Easter? Did you, through carelessness, forget a mortal sin in confession?—Have you ever told a lie in confession or concealed a mortal sin through fear, shame, or any other motive?

[All confessions and communions which follow such concealments are sacrilegious, and must be repeated.]

Did you accuse yourself of your sins in such terms as would disguise them? or were you negligent in expressing the circumstances, motives, persons, or consequences, which increased the malice, or altered the nature of the sin?—Did you confess with an intention of committing the same sins again?—Have you wilfully neglected performing your penance?—Did you refuse or neglect complying with the injunctions of your director? such as quitting the occasions of sin, becoming reconciled to your enemies, or repair ing any injustice done to your neighbour, in character or property; such conditions being essentially necessary for the validity of absolution.—Were you in the habit of making the advice of your director the subject of ridicule?—Did you quit your ordinary confessor from the sole motive of having more liberty to indulge your slothful and sinful habits under the direction of a stranger?—Have you received any sacrament, particularly the blessed Eucharist, in the dreadful state of mortal sin?—Have you presumed to approach the holy communion after breaking your fast, or without sufficient preparation?—Did you communicate through custom, through hypocrisy, human respect, or any other such criminal motive?

First Commandment.

[This commandment is transgressed by all sins against faith, hope, charity, and the virtue of religion.]

Sins against Faith.—Have you been ignorant of such things as are essentially necessary for salvation; such as the principal mysteries, the Creed, Lord's Prayer, Commandments of God and the Church, the Sacraments, and necessary dispositions for approaching them worthily, particularly the blessed Eucharist and Penance?—Did this ignorance proceed from your own fault, such as your not having studied the Catechism; not having attended instructions, or behaved at so serious a duty without respect or attention; talking, laughing, causing others to do so, or not making any effort to retain instructions, or learn prayers?—Have you wilfully doubted any article of faith, or examined divine mysteries with idle curiosity?—Did you deny any article of faith, or did you expose your faith to the danger of being weakened, or even lost, by reading infidel or heretical books?—Did you enter churches or meeting-houses, or assist at the sermons, baptisms, marriages, or religious ceremonies of persons of other persuasions?—Did you question the authority of the Church to institute festivals or fasts, or use the words of the Holy Scripture in jest, or without due respect?—Did you hold intercourse with persons publicly excommunicated?—Were you guilty of superstition, by consulting fortune-tellers, giving credit to dreams, or using charms for the recovery of health or things lost?

Sins against Hope.—Did you despair of salvation, or of the forgiveness of your sins; or, on the contrary, did you sin by presumption; continuing to offend God because of his mercy and patience?—Were your resolutions of amendment grounded on a presumptuous idea of your own strength, forgetting that all our sufficiency is from God?—Did you murmur against divine Providence, or repine under trials, such as the loss of friends, property, &c.?

Sins against Charity, or the Love of God.—Have you loved any creature as much or more than God; or has any inordinate attachment caused you to offend God?—Did you take pleasure, either in offending God yourself, or seeing others commit sin?—Did you pass whole days without thinking of God, resisting his inspirations, daily receiving his blessings without gratitude or thanksgiving?—Were you habitually negligent and slothful in his divine service?

Sins against the Virtue of Religion.—Did you habitually neglect, on awaking in the morning, to offer your heart to God, and direct your intention to him in all your actions?—Did you omit your morning or night prayers, or neglect your daily examination of conscience, and other religious duties?—Were those serious omissions habitual, or were they under such circumstances as would give bad example or disedification?—Were you wilfully distracted at prayer?—Did you assist at the holy sacrifice of the Mass with distraction or irreverence?—Specify if it was at a Mass of obligation.—Did you behave with irreverence in the chapel: laugh, talk, gaze about, loll in a disrespectful posture, or occasion those sins in others?

—Did you frequent the temple of the Almighty through sinful motives, such as to exhibit dress or new fashions, to see others, or to be seen?—Have you profaned or disrespected holy things; such as the sacred vessels or relics; turned into ridicule the ceremonies of the Church, or any thing whatsoever relative to the word of God, or his holy service?—Have you spoken disrespectfully of the saints, or ridiculed their actions?—Have you ridiculed clergymen, or persons consecrated to God?—Did you dissuade any one from performing good works of any description such as hearing Mass, praying, giving alms, &c.?

Second Commandment.

[This commandment forbids cursing, swearing, irreverence to the holy name of God, his saints, and holy things in general.]

Did you break any vow, or solemn promise made to God?—Did you make a rash vow?

[Every vow is rash and irreligious, which is made without mature deliberation, and the advice and express consent of a director.]

Did you take an unnecessary oath; or swear contrary to truth, doubting, or not caring whether the matter were true or false?—Have you been the cause of others cursing or swearing, or did you neglect preventing swearing when in your power to do so?—Have you taken such rash oaths as could not be kept without sin; such as to swear to be revenged?—Did you commit a double crime, by keeping as well as making such an oath?—Have you been in the habit of taking the holy name of God in vain, or using any other holy expression lightly or disrespectfully?—Did you imprecate any evil on yourself or others?

Third Commandment.

[The duties required by this commandment relate principally to the sanctification of the Lord's Day, the hearing of Mass, &c. The chief sins against it are servile work, and profane employments on the Sabbath.]

Have you lost Mass on Sundays or holidays of obligation, or on those days heard only a part of Mass?

—Did you, by rising late, spending too much time in dressing, or going on a journey without having heard Mass, expose yourself to the danger of sinning against this commandment?—Have you been the occasion of others losing Mass, either by preventing their assisting at it in person, or by talking to, or otherwise distracting them during a considerable part of the holy sacrifice?—Did you neglect making servants, children, or others under your care assist regularly at Mass on Sundays and holidays?—Did you so occupy those in your employment, as to prevent their hearing Mass; or did you occasion trades-people to work on Sundays or holidays to satisfy your vanity, or for any other insufficient cause?—Have you neglected to sanctify the Lord's day, by devoting the greater part of it to prayer, spiritual reading, giving or receiving instructions, and other spiritual and holy works?

[Remember, that the Precept of hearing Mass on a Sunday may be dispensed with by sickness and other just causes; whereas the command of sanctifying the Lord's Day is in all circumstances indispensable.]

Fourth Commandment.

[This commandment points out the reciprocal duties of parents, children, masters, servants, apprentices, and in general all those subject to, or governing others. But, as this book is intended principally for young persons, the following examination is confined to the duties of children towards parents. It is only to be observed, that as, while young persons are at school, the duty, respect, and obedience due to parents, are transferred to masters and mistresses, likewise to aunts, uncles, or guardians, while under their care, or to any other person whosoever appointed by God to govern them; of course, what would be sinful with regard to parents, becomes sinful with regard to those who hold their place.]

Have you disobeyed your parents; and was it accompanied with obstinacy?—Have you been deficient in the love, respect, deference, tenderness, and gratitude, so justly due to parents; or have you nourished hatred, aversion, or contempt for them; did you wish their death, or desire them any other injury?—From what motive?—Have you, by misconduct, or any other means, occasioned your parents to be guilty of passion, or any other sin? Have you joined with your brothers, sisters, or any other persons, in opposing parents, in contradicting them, or counteracting their will?—Have you given them pain by rude or disrespectful answers, ill-tempered looks, stubbornness, self-will, or opposition to their desires?—Did you ridicule their advice, or receive their admonition or correction with sullenness or ill-humour?—Have you impatiently borne the defects and infirmities of your parents, particularly in sickness or old age?—Have you been guilty of suspicions, rash judgments, exaggerations, or inventions to their disadvantage?—Did you communicate those uncharitable and undutiful ideas to your brothers, sisters, or others; and did you thereby lessen their confidence, affection, and duty? —Have you neglected to procure for your parents every corporal and spiritual assistance in your power, particularly in their last illness?—Have you neglected praying, and procuring prayers for them; or did you fail to execute their last will, and comply with their dying wishes?—Have you ill-treated your brothers, or sisters, or caused dissensions in your family? mention what injury was occasioned by such conduct. —With respect to ecclesiastical superiors, such as your director, parish priest, &c., have you disobeyed them, disregarded their counsel, presumed to question their just regulations, ridiculed them, or in any other manner deviated from the respect due to their sacred character?—Have you, on occasions of difference of opinion between ecclesiastics, presumed to censure one side or the other? those matters being quite out of the sphere of seculars.—Have you ill-treated or abused servants; spoken to them in a harsh, commanding, or haughty manner, or given them bad example?—Have you encouraged them in the common habit of tale-bearing; or made use of them as instruments to gratify your curiosity, vanity, or any other passion?—Have you accused them on suspicion, or by tale-bearing; or in any other way occasioned servants to lose their place, or sustain any other injury

—Have you been inconsiderate towards them while sick; or overpowered them with occupations, so as to leave them no leisure for religious duties?—Have you neglected to instruct or procure them instructions?

[This duty, though properly belonging to the heads of families, should, if neglected, be discharged by those who, from having received a christian education themselves, are best qualified to impart instruction to others.]

Fifth Commandment.

[This commandment, which forbids taking away the life of the body by wilful murder, and of the soul by scandal, or causing any one to fall into mortal sin; also quarrelling, revenge, bad example, hatred, includes the principal duties prescribed by the great precept of fraternal charity, or loving our neighbour as ourselves.]

Did you desire your own death or that of others; from what motive?—Did you injure your health by concealing any serious malady through pride or love of amusement?—Did you witness, encourage, or become any way instrumental to the crime of duelling, fighting, or dissension?—Were you guilty of quarrelling and fighting?—Did you take revenge for any injury, or desire an opportunity of doing so?—Did you indulge sentiments of hatred, revenge, aversion, ill-will, or contempt; or did you beat, strike, or hurt any one, through passion, or any other bad motive?—Have you been at variance with your neighbour; for what length of time?—Was this scandalous conduct public or observable?—Have you, after a seeming reconciliation, still nourished coldness, and refrained from the accustomed testimonies of charity?—Have you caused the spiritual death of your neighbour, by occasioning the commission of a mortal sin, which is called the crime of scandal?—Have you in conversation, or by any other means, taught others the evil of which they were ignorant; to how many?—Were they younger than you; or were they brothers, sisters, or others to whom you particularly owed good example?—What was the evil?—Did you intend that sin should be committed?—Have you acted sinfully in the presence of others?—What was the action?—Did it produce the evil consequence of others following your example?—Did you command, consent to or defend an evil action?—Did you participate in an evil action by assistance, by silence, by connivance, by not correcting or preventing it when in your power, or by not manifesting it to those who could do so?—Did you excite vanity in others, by flattery, or over-rating the trifling advantages of body or mind?—Have you neglected to relieve the poor according to your ability; or, when unable to give alms, have you spoken to them harshly or contemptuously?

[The precept of *giving alms* becomes of obligation from the moment we arrive at the use of reason.]

Sixth and Ninth Commandments.

[These two commandments may be examined together: the ninth forbidding in thought what the sixth forbids in conduct. Remember, that all the commandments may be transgressed in thought as well as in action; but in none is the danger of mortal sin so great, as in any deliberate transgression of the sixth and ninth commandments, whether in thought, word, action, or desire.]

Have you been guilty of any action contrary to purity?—Have you wilfully transgressed the rules of modesty, in dressing, undressing, or in any other way?—Were those faults committed in the presence of others, or were you negligent in those respects even when alone?—Have you acted with levity, or were you so far forgetful of reserve and modesty, as to permit others to act towards you with unbecoming freedom?—Have you had any dangerous sinful conversation?—How many were concerned?

[In general, all such conversations as young persons would not hold in the presence of parents, mistresses, or those they respect, may be suspected, at least, as unworthy the presence of God.]

Have you contracted any intimacies, or nourished attachments for those whose society you found to be injurious, or who were in any respect disapproved of by your parents or superiors?—Did you, through vanity or any other motive, transgress the rules of modesty in dress?—Have you sung or listened to im modest songs ?—Have you read, circulated, or listened to bad books?—Have you privately written or received such letters as are disapproved of by your parents or mistresses ?—Have you looked at immodest pictures or any other improper object?

[Those who feel their consciences charged with any sin, or even doubt of sin, on those commandments, should be careful to accuse themselves of whatever may be sinful, and submit their doubts to the judgment of their director.]

Seventh and Tenth Commandments.

[These commandments, like the sixth and ninth, may be examined together, and for the same reasons ; the tenth forbidding in thought what the seventh forbids in action ; that is, every species of injustice to our neighbour in property, whether in action or desire.]

Have you stolen any thing whatsoever ?—How much, or how often ?—Did you cause others to steal, or have you shared in or concealed stolen goods ?—Have you, by theft, or in any other way, considerably injured any one in property ?—Have you taken any thing from your parents, or given any thing out of their house without their consent, to servants or others ?—Have you neglected complying with the indispensable obligation of restoring what you stole when in your power to do so ?—Have you lost, through carelessness or negligence, any article which you undertook to keep for others ?—What was the value ? You are bound to make restitution.—Have you cheated in buying, selling, at cards, or in any other way ?—Have you purchased stolen goods, or bought of children, servants, or others who had no right to sell ?—Have you passed forged notes or false money, knowing them to be such ?—Have you contracted debts, without the intention or the means of paying them ?—Have you neglected paying, as soon as possible, dress-makers, milliners, and such trades-people as you may have had to deal with, thereby subjecting them to the loss of time, and other inconveniences attendant on incessant solicitations ?—Have you been guilty of extravagance, and unnecessary expense in dress, for self-gratification, vanity, or any such bad motive?—Have you injured the property of others, or did you retain articles only lent?—Have you appropriated any thing found? If the owner be not discovered, the article or its value should be given to the poor.—Have you desired the property of others, or wished them a reverse of fortune, that you may gain thereby?

Eighth Commandment.

[This commandment forbids all false testimonies, rash judgments, lies, and in general every word or action injurious to the reputation of your neighbour, or contrary to religion and truth.]

Have you borne false testimony against your neighbour; that is, have you reported a falsehood of any person?—What was the nature of such report?—What was your motive in making it, and what injury resulted?—Have you been guilty of rash judgments, or evil suspicions?—Did you disclose such sinful ideas?

[In this, as well as every other matter concerning charity, the persons injured, such as parents, ecclesiastics, superiors, etc., the nature of the faults imputed to them, as, whether in a matter mortally or venially sinful, materially alter the nature of the sin, and of course should be specified.]

Have you told lies to the prejudice of your neighbour, in which consists the sin of calumny? In this case you are obliged to restore his good name, by retracting the calumny.—Have you been guilty of other falsehoods, such as lies of excuse, boasting, or vanity? were those habitual?—Have you caused others to tell lies, or persisted yourself in falsehoods?—Have you, to support one untruth, told many others?—Have you contracted a habit of equivocation or exaggeration?—Have you been guilty of detraction, publishing the faults of your neighbour, making them the subject of your conversation or ridicule?—Have you listened to detraction; taken pleasure therein, or not prevented it when in your power to do so?—Have you, by curious questions, caused others to commit the sin of detraction?—Have you broken promises, or betrayed the secrets of others?—Was it in a matter of consequence, and did it occasion any injury?—Have you opened letters, read wills, or other secret papers? from what motive?

[Every sin against charity, whether by detraction, rash judgment, suspicion, ill-natured reports, or insinuation, want of kindness, or forbearance, is a transgression of this commandment, and a violation of the clear and positive rule of charity, which points out every one's duty on this head, *viz. to act, speak, and even think of others, as we wish they should think, act, and speak of us.*]

The PRECEPTS *of the* CHURCH.

[The first precept of the Church, *viz. to hear Mass on Sundays and Holidays*, has been examined in going over the third commandment. The second precept obliges all those to *fast* who have attained the age of twenty-one, and to *abstinence* all who have attained the use of reason.]

Have you broken the fast or abstinence ordained by the Church?—Have you, when considered by a physician incapable of fasting or abstinence, neglected to ask permission from your pastor to eat meat?—Have you caused others to break the fast or abstinence commanded by the Church?—When dispensations were necessary, have you eaten fish and meat the same day, or eaten meat more than once a day, or in mixed company, when it could be avoided?—Have you eaten eggs on any day on which they are forbidden, or taken any thing made up with eggs?

Every person should inquire into the ordinances of the diocess in which she lives, and act conformably thereto; some Bishops forbidding, others allowing the use of eggs, etc., on certain days.

The third precept of the Church obliges *to confess our sins at least once a year.*—Have you, since your first confession, passed a year without approaching the Sacrament of Penance.

The fourth precept of the Church obliges *to receive the blessed Eucharist at Easter*, or within the time appointed for discharging that duty; also to communicate in our parish chapel.—Have you, since your first communion, neglected complying with this precept?

The fifth precept, which obliges *to contribute to the support of our Clergy*, regards principally the heads of families; therefore it is passed over in an examination prepared only for young persons; they, however, should be early impressed with a just sense of an obligation which is much stricter than is generally imagined.

The sixth precept of the Church *forbids the solemnization of marriage within forbidden degrees of kindred, clandestinely*, or *within forbidden times*; that is, from Ash-Wednesday to Low-Sunday inclusively, and from the first Sunday of Advent to Twelfth-day inclusively.

The Seven Deadly *or* Capital Sins.

Pride.—Have you deliberately entertained thoughts of pride, or over-rated any little interior or exterior advantages you may possess?—Have you sought the esteem and applause of creatures, indulged uneasiness or discontent when those have been withheld; or have you given way to excessive discouragement when told your faults, or for any other cause?—Did you entertain feelings of contempt for others, in consequence of defects either mental or corporal, or any other cause whatsoever?—Have you been self-conceited, full of confidence in your own opinion or judgment, contemning that of others, neglecting to ask, or refusing to receive advice, foolishly imagining you were capable of guiding yourself?—Have you, through pride, refused to acknowledge your faults, to ask pardon for them, or to make any necessary reparation?—Have you spoken in a proud, haughty, self-sufficient, over-bearing manner?—Have you boasted of having acted wrong on any occasion, such as showing obstinacy to superiors, or refusing to apologize; was this before companions, or other persons likely to be injured by such example?—Have you performed your actions through pride, vanity, or human respect?—Have you aimed at a display of talents or personal advantages, solely to attract notice and admiration?—Have you yielded to vanity on account of dress, accomplishments, riches, or any other such unimportant advantages?—Have you sinned by ambition, inordinately desiring honours, riches, rank, or any species of worldly grandeur?—Have you, in the pursuit of learning and other acquirements, exerted yourself solely from motives of vanity, jealousy, or to rival your companions?—On the other hand, have you neglected to cultivate your talents, because they were not of the first order?—Have you sinned by hypocrisy, affecting piety, or discharging your religious duties with more exactness before others than when unobserved?—Have you hypocritically concealed real vices under the appearance of virtue?

There are various other ways of sinning by Pride, not included in the foregoing examination. Those who feel that this vice predominates in their conduct, should examine into the motives of even their best actions or good works, as it often happens that those very undertakings, which appear to have God for their object, are frequently pursued only because they attract the esteem and admiration of the world. Such persons should spare no pains in endeavouring to correct a vice which may destroy the merit of the most useful and well-regulated life; for Pride, beside being the vice of the thoughtless, of the ignorant, the cowardly, and the narrow-minded, is, according to St. Chrysostom, "that crafty thief, who steals those riches which are beyond the reach of robbers; it is a canker, which destroys and corrupts those treasures which moth nor rust cannot consume; it is the vice, which snatches from millions an eternal recompense for their temporary labours; it is the successful engine of the devil, who by pride and vain-glory effects the ruin of souls, whose virtues render them otherwise superior to all his stratagems"

Covetousness or *Avarice*, the second deadly sin has been examined in going over the seventh and tenth commandments.

Lust, or *Luxury*, the third deadly sin, has been already examined under the sixth and ninth commandments.

Anger, the fourth deadly sin, is committed by passion.

Have you been in a passion?—How often?—Before how many persons?—What were the effects of this temporary madness?—Have you given way to impatience, crossness, peevishness, fretfulness, ill-humour, or discontent?—Have you manifested impatience and want of resignation in pain and sickness; refused to submit to remedies, and thereby given great and unnecessary trouble to servants and other attendants?—Have you made indisposition a plea for indulging ill-humour, perverseness, and emancipation from all sort of restraint?—Have you indulged an imperious, irritable, dissatisfied turn of mind, thus troubling not only your own peace, but that of every one connected with you?—Have you endeavoured to irritate others, or did you take delight in teasing or calling them names?

Gluttony, the fifth deadly sin is committed by eating or drinking to excess.

Have you transgressed on this point?—Did any bad consequences follow, such as sickness, &c.?—Have you eaten what you knew would injure your health?—Have you sought any inordinate gratification of appetite?—Have you indulged discontent concerning diet?—Have you publicly or privately murmured on this subject, or have you been difficult to be pleased in your diet; not reflecting, that thousands want what you refuse and despise?

Envy, the sixth deadly sin, is committed by repining at the prosperity of our neighbour, or indulging any sinful, ill-natured satisfaction at his misfortune.

Have you repined, grieved at, or endeavoured to lessen the prosperity of others?—Have you been dejected, because you considered yourself surpassed by others in amiable qualities, talents, or even personal advantages?—What were the consequences?—Has your jealousy or envy caused you to endeavour to lessen the reputation of others, or have you rejoiced at hearing them undervalued, or spoken ill of?—Have you indulged jealousy at the affection or preference shown to brothers, sisters, or companions?—Have you, on this account, rejoiced at their punishment or disappointment, or have you joined others in endeavouring to mortify them?

Sloth, the seventh deadly sin, is committed by indulging a certain laziness of mind and body, which prevents the fervent discharge of every duty.

Have you indulged a slothful, indolent disposition, without making the necessary efforts to correct it?—Has this habit of sloth influenced you with regard to your spiritual duties, so far as to cause you to neglect them, or to discharge them with tepidity and disgust? —Have you studied your ease, shunning every inconvenience, never curbing your inclinations, caprices, or humours, solely on account of the difficulty attendant on self-restraint?—Have you lost your time, spending whole hours in absolute idleness, or what is much the same, frittering them away in idle, worldly conversations, reading silly books, or such unprofitable occupations?—Have you given trouble to your parents or other superiors, by never taking any pains yourself in the care of your person, clothes, and every thing else left to your charge?

It remains for you now to examine, whether you feel so great a tendency to any one vice in particular, as to influence your ideas, feelings, and conduct. This is what is called the *predominant passion*, which all Christians should endeavour to discover and combat. The sketch of the chief predominant passions, transferred to the end of this Work, will assist in this examination. It is not, however, by any means necessary to go through it, except for general confessions, or any other occasion when it may be found useful.

The foregoing examination, written only for young persons, will be found insufficient by others more advanced in years, and engaged in situations of life which severally include duties not adverted to here. It is, then, recommended to all those who may use this examination, to take into consideration their age, circumstances, and the duties of their different stations in life.

OF CONTRITION

Having by a diligent and prudent Examination of your Conscience, endeavoured to discover all the sins you have been guilty of since your last Confession, you may pass to the second part of your preparation for the Sacrament of Penance, by endeavouring to excite in your heart the deepest contrition.

This is not only the most difficult, but also the most essential requisite for a good Confession. It is a condition of reconciliation with God, from which nothing can dispense. Such circumstances as the loss of speech, or the want of a Clergyman, evidently dispense from the obligation of Confession. Sudden death, which often leaves no time for the performance of the penance enjoined, exempts from satisfaction, at least in this life. But nothing can dispense from contrition; without that, no sin ever was or ever will be pardoned; whereas, on the contrary, one sincere act of unfeigned contrition suffices to induce the Almighty to blot out the most grievous crimes.

Contrition, as the word imports, is a sorrow for sin, with which the heart is so deeply penetrated, as to be as it were *broken;* a sorrow, which necessarily includes a hatred and sincere detestation of sin. It proceeds from perfect love of God. It is the heartfelt regret of a child, who bitterly laments the misfortune of having offended a beloved parent, whose displeasure he fears more than death, and whom he loves infinitely more than life. Such was the sorrow of the prodigal son, when he exclaimed: *O my Father, I have sinned against heaven and before thee,* Luke xv. 18. An act of this kind of sorrow, properly called *Contrition,* justifies a sinner the instant it is produced; thus was Magdalen purified from all her sins, because her tears of contrition flowed from a heart penetrated with the most perfect charity. Contrition, nevertheless, however perfect it may be, does not dispense with the obligation of recurring to the Sacrament of Penance, or ardently desiring to do so, if deprived of an opportunity.

The second kind of sorrow for sin is called *Attrition*, and is much inferior to Contrition, both in its causes and in its effects. It is the regret of a slave, who returns to a master whose chastisement he fears, or of a child, who regrets having forfeited a claim to the possessions of his father. It is generally produced either by a sense of the baseness of sin in itself, or, more commonly, by a fear of hell, or the loss of heaven. If attrition be accompanied by a hope of pardon, if it exclude the will of sinning again, it is an impulse of the Holy Ghost, and a gift of God, which disposes the sinner for the happiness of perfect reconciliation with God in the tribunal of penance.

Sorrow for sin, whether perfect or imperfect; that is, *Contrition*, or *Attrition*, must have the six following qualities: First, it must be *interior;* that is, it must dwell in the heart, not on the lips, and consist in an inward, sincere feeling of sorrow, not in empty expressions of regret, which, of themselves, are of no avail before Him who sees the heart. Witness Saul and David: the former, when reproached for his crimes by the Prophet, acknowledges his guilt with all the appearance of sorrow; nevertheless, he dies a reprobate. David is also reproached by God's prophet with far more grievous transgressions; he, in like manner, confesses his crimes, which are fully remitted by God. Whence this difference? From the difference between their sorrow;—that of Saul was merely exterior; that of David was interior, and therefore efficacious.

Secondly, Contrition must be *supernatural;* that is, produced by motives of faith; such as regret for having offended a God infinitely amiable, infinitely good to us; a God who alone can render us either eternally happy, or eternally miserable: motives which are merely natural or temporal, such as the loss of health, fortune, reputation, or the shame and confusion which sin entails, though they are ample subjects of bitter regret, are in themselves absolutely insufficient to recover God's friendship, as is proved in the case of Antiochus, who vainly implored pardon for his sins, because his sorrow for them, though very lively, was solely produced by the pangs with which the Almighty punished him.

Thirdly, Contrition must be *sovereign ;* that is, it must be superior to, and greater than, every other sorrow; for, as we should prefer our salvation to all that is most dear to us on earth, not excepting our very life: consequently our sorrow for having offended God, and for having forfeited our right to the kingdom of heaven, should be greater than for any other loss whatsoever. By sovereign sorrow, however, is not meant *sensible* sorrow, such as would be felt for the loss of a parent, or a dear friend; the word *sovereign* here only signifies that we should consider sin the sovereign evil, that is, the first and greatest of all evils; for, though the loss of the friendship and goods of this world, in general, affects our senses much more than the loss of eternal goods, yet, in the bottom of our soul, our sorrow for having sinned must outweigh every other.

Fourthly, Contrition must be *universal ;* that is, it must extend to every sin you have committed. Thus, to cherish the least attachment to any of your sins, though you should feel the sincerest regret for all the rest, would render you incapable of pardon. For, as St. Gregory says, what will it avail a sinner, to regret the sin of anger, if he be intent on revenge?—Of what use will it be to you, to regret and renounce lies, injustice, or any other crime, if you persevere in uncharitable dislike to your neighbour, or do not detest from your heart your proud and imperious conduct towards others? In such cases, your contrition would not suffice, because it would not be *universal.*

Fifthly, Contrition must be accompanied with a firm

resolution of never deliberately relapsing into sin. This resolution should be *sincere;* that is, it should include a firm determination to avoid carefully not only sin but every occasion of sin. It should be an absolute *resolution*, not the conditional resolution of those who say, they would sin again if there were no hell. It must be *courageous;* that is, it must lead the sinner to burst all sinful engagements or attachments, however strong they may be. It must be *universal;* that is, your resolution must not be confined to any particular sin, but must extend to all the faults you may have been in the habit of committing, or may be exposed to commit hereafter. Lastly, it must be *efficacious*, *constant*, and founded, not on a presumptuous confidence in our own strength, but on an humble dependence and firm reliance on the assistance of God. This description of resolution, so very different from the vague purposes of amendment, which satisfy too many in preparing for confession, is so indispensably necessary to true contrition, that the sorrow which does not include it, cannot be any thing better than gross illusion or hypocrisy.

The sixth and last quality of Contrition is, a willingness and determination to accept and perform any penance which may be imposed in the tribunal of Confession, to repair, to the best of your power, the injuries done your neighbour in his property or reputation, and also to suffer in the spirit of penance the painful consequences which often follow from sin. This was the disposition of the prodigal son, when he willingly consented to be ranked among the servants of his father; and also of Zacheus, who resolved to give half his goods to the poor, and to return four times as much to those whom he had wronged.

Such should be the qualities of true Contrition, that excellent disposition of heart, which St. Cyprian esteems ' the best sacrifice a mortal creature can offer to his Creator." "That disposition which," St. Ambrose says, "opens heaven, closes hell, cures all the diseases of the soul, repairs all spiritual ruin, and serves as a sponge to efface all iniquities." That disposition, which is so pleasing, so acceptable to God, that he never has rejected, nor ever will reject a contrite heart; a disposition which may be conceived and produced in a moment; for neither the shortness of time, nor the extremity of the last hour, hinders the pardon of a penitent sinner. Finally, Contrition is so profitable, that it not only obtains pardon for all past offences, but gains a future crown of eternal glory. This indispensable disposition for a good Confession, must be a special gift from God, his powerful grace alone can penetrate the soul with that sincere sorrow, which, as St. Augustine says "so changes the heart, as to embitter those things which once appeared sweet, and to change into subjects of real anguish, torment, and affliction, those objects which heretofore delighted the sinner."

The first step you should take, for acquiring true Contrition, is to beg of God most earnestly to dispose your heart for conceiving that lively and sincere sorrow he requires from you. "Those only," says St. Ambrose, "on whom Jesus deigns to look, can detest their sins." Peter denies his Divine Master, and weeps not, because the Lord had not looked on him—he repeats his ungrateful denial, nor does he yet weep, because the penetrating glance of Jesus had not pierced his soul. But Peter a third time denies his Lord; Jesus then looks on him, and immediately this penitent Apostle weeps most bitterly. Do you then earnestly beseech of Jesus to look on you, to dispose your heart for conceiving all the sorrow required from you, and to give you himself, that precious gift of sincere Contrition, which you cannot procure of yourself, which he alone can bestow, and without which you can never be absolved.

A Prayer to beg of God the grace of sincere Contrition.

I HAVE now, O my God! aided by thy grace, endeavoured to discover the number of my transgressions, and have examined, to the best of my power, the state of my conscience. But, alas! O Judge of the living and the dead! how far different is my judgment from thine!—How many offences are still perhaps hidden from my view, though perfectly known to thee! But, my God! as I am persuaded it is not so much a knowledge of their number, as sorrow for their deformity, that thou requirest, I now earnestly implore of thee to give me that lively, sincere, efficacious contrition, which I know is a necessary condition of my pardon. My heart was formed by thee, thou alone canst change it; it is in thy hands, and though most ungrateful, most insensible, it is not too obdurate for thee to penetrate and soften. One drop of thy adorable blood, one of those precious tears which my offences drew from thy eyes, would suffice to produce in my soul the most lively contrition. Ah! look on me, Eternal Light! and my understanding will be enlightened to conceive the enormity of sin; touch my heart, and it will be broken with sorrow for having ever offended thee. Convert me, and I shall be converted; for my destruction, my misery, and my misfortune, is from myself, but my salvation must come from thee, O my most merciful Father! from thee, whom I have so ungratefully abandoned, and so grievously offended.

Motives for exciting Contrition.

THOUGH contrition must be produced in the heart by the special aid of God's grace, yet that does not dispense sinners from making, on their part, every effort to excite in their souls the most lively sorrow For this purpose, after begging of God the grace of contrition, you should next do what lies in your power, by seriously and deliberately meditating on the following motives, which your Catechism recommends, as most calculated for exciting sentiments of sincere contrition. Consider, first, the nature of sin itself, and endeavour to conceive, if possible, an adequate idea of its hateful deformity. This is a point on which Christians in general are not only blinded, but even infatuated. Those who would grieve over the death of a friend, give a mortal wound to their own souls without a feeling of sorrow. Thousands who would scorn to be subject to a fellow-creature, and detest a mean action, according to the world, enslave themselves willingly to the devil, and are guilty of the basest acts of treachery towards God, without an emotion of shame or regret.—Why? Because nothing is so rare as a just idea of sin, nothing so difficult as to find a person who considers an offence against God in its proper light; that is, who considers sin as the greatest misfortune, disgrace, and humiliation; the only real evil that can be endured. This is a truth so certain, that were all the scourges of heaven, sickness, hunger, thirst, famine, plague, humiliations, poverty—in a word, every species of torment the mind can conceive or the body endure, collected on one side, and a single mortal sin opposed on the other, the misfortune of committing that sin would as far exceed all the other calamities, as the heavens are elevated above the earth. O! if sinners were thoroughly persuaded of this truth, what tears of contrition would deluge the universe! what groans and sighs of repentance would be heard on all sides! But do you, who have enjoyed the blessings of early instruction, conceive better than others less favoured, the horrid act you committed when you sinned? You would think it madness to harbour a leper in your house, lest you should catch his disgusting disease; yet by yielding to one single temptation, you opened, not your house, but your heart, to a monster. whose loathsome and abominable deformity would strike you with deadly horror, were it visible; a monster, who robbed you in an instant of the greatest treasure you possessed, your Creator's friendship;—who cruelly despoiled you of the lovely ornament of sanctifying grace, and of all the merit you may have acquired in the whole course of your life; who shamefully degraded you from the glorious dignity of a child of God, and covered your soul with so frightful a leprosy, as would strike you dead with horror, if you could but see the melancholy, hideous figure into which you were transformed. O sin! dreadful misfortune! only real evil! can the soul thou hast miserably degraded feel it difficult to detest, to renounce thee for ever!

Consider, in the second place, that by sin you have been mad enough to expose yourself to endure the intolerable and eternal pains of hell, and to dwell for ever in that infernal abyss, an object of anger and indignation to God—of scorn and insult to the devils—and of hatred and horror to yourself. Descend in spirit into that lake of fire and brimstone, which will eternally blaze, without ever being extinguished, and contemplate the wretched fate of those, whom the just vengeance of God cut off in the midst of their mad career. Behold them surrounded, penetrated, consumed with fire; trampled on by hideous demons, whose temptations they unfortunately listened to during life; cursing and detesting the day that gave them birth, and vainly calling on death to terminate those insufferable woes, which are never to have an end. Consider, that even the least of their torments is so aggravated by the importunate idea of Eternity, as to be rendered insupportably agonizing, and then ask yourself how it is possible, that those who believe in hell, should dare to sin; or how those who have sinned, and deserved hell, should be insensible to the greatness of their misfortune? O great God! whose justice is not exercised until thy mercy has been slighted, pierce my heart with thy fear, that I may tremble at thy judgments. O! let the torrents of burning tears which the damned will for ever shed, teach me that sin alone is a just subject of tears and regret—let that sting of remorse, that worm of conscience, which gnaws them to the soul, and which will never die, teach me to listen now and during my whole life to the salutary admonitions and remorse of my conscience. Let their bitter, violent sorrow for the abuse of thy graces, urge me to profit of those yet within my reach, and teach me to detest, from the bottom of my heart, not only all my past sins, but even the shadow of sin in future, since I know that there is no fault, however small, which may not lead to a mortal offence, and thereby to hell; and that there are few among the damned who did not descend into the dreary, dismal dungeon of woes by the fatal neglect of slight faults.

Consider, thirdly, beside the awful risk you have run of being condemned to hell, you have also forfeited by sin your claim to the kingdom of heaven; that blessed city, whose walls, as the holy scripture describes them, are of precious stones, whose streets are of pure and transparent gold, watered with the river of Life flowing from the throne of God;—that city, whose dazzling splendour knows no night—from which pain, sickness, grief, privations, and every description of sufferings, however trivial, are eternally banished, and whose blessed inhabitants, crowned with wreaths of immortal glory, and shining far brighter than the sun, magnify and adore their munificent Benefactor, in one uninterrupted transport of love. For happiness like this you were created; you were placed on earth to merit heaven; you were born and instructed in the true faith; thus, placed in the road to heaven, the sacred character of baptism gave you an undoubted claim to that blessed abode. Your desires were generally left unsatisfied, that disappointment may force you to sigh after heaven; and your pleasures and pursuits often embittered, that you may learn to undervalue temporal delights, and labour to merit those of heaven. But what have you done, by committing one mortal sin? You, in a manner, renounced an eternity of bliss—you blotted out your own name from the book of life—you excluded yourself from the seat of eternal delights—you closed the gates of heaven against your own soul. For contemptible pleasures, momentary enjoyments, which were never free from bitterness, you sacrificed, you willingly relinquished immortal blessings, everlasting treasures. If Esau was overwhelmed with anguish for having relinquished his birthright; if he *roared out*, as the scripture says, with great anguish, what should be your sorrow, for having forfeited a place in the kingdom of your Father—for having abandoned the society of the saints, those friends of God, who once had the same temptations you have to endure, but who were faithful to the end, and thereby received the crown of life.—Endeavour to detest your criminal indifference to your own eternal interests, and fervently thank God, for having still left abundant means within your reach, of regaining your birthright, and opening once more, by sincere contrition, those gates to bliss which your sins had closed.

The fourth motive for contrition is, *the thought of having offended a God infinitely good to us.* This motive should be particularly dwelt on, because the sorrow produced by gratitude is certainly much more perfect than that which springs from fear, or the privation of any benefit. Beside, this motive seldom fails to excite feelings of sincere sorrow. The double recollection of innumerable benefits received from God, and innumerable offences committed against God, is so just a motive of regret, that no heart which is not completely hardened could be insensible to it. Endeavour, then, to recall to your remembrance the principal benefits you have received from that God, who, amongst other marks of his tenderness, thought of you even before you existed; who caused you to be born in the true faith, and brought you safely to the waters of baptism, in preference to so many others more deserving. Ask yourself, who was it watched over you while you were a weak infant, and inspired others with the tenderness which induced them to do for you what you were unable to do for yourself?—Who provided you with tender parents and friends, of which others more deserving are left destitute?—Who gave you the means of attaining religious instruction, as likewise a liberal and Christian education?—Why were you not born among those savage tribes, who live and die without ever hearing the name of their Creator?—Who gives you, daily and hourly, all the temporal blessings you enjoy, food, clothing, lodging?—Why are you not like thousands who are poor, abandoned, shivering with cold, and deprived of all the common necessaries of life?—But principally, and particularly, who has so often pardoned you your sins, and waited your repentance until now?—Why were you not cut off the first time you were so unfortunate as to sin?—Why are you not burning this moment with the damned in hell, many of whom offended God less than you have done?—Who is it that inspires you with a desire of returning to God, and provides you with an opportunity of confessing your sins, which any one of the damned would give ten thousand worlds to purchase? These inquiries, which may be considerably lengthened, will prove to you that God has been indeed infinitely good to you. Nevertheless, it is this God of infinite goodness you have outraged by sin; it is this divine and liberal Benefactor, whose benefits you have not only received with indifference, but often perverted into occasions of sin. Ah! would you not blush at such base ingratitude towards a fellow-creature who had served you thus?—Has not gratitude often urged you to exertions for them which you never made for God? —Should not the benefits of your Creator, contrasted with such insensibility and repeated transgressions, be a powerful motive for contrition during the remainder of your life?

The fifth motive for detesting sin is, *because it offends a God infinitely good in himself.* This motive, which is no other than the perfect love of God, produces that pure and disinterested sorrow, which is properly called *contrition.* Generally speaking, sinners are much less affected by this motive than by all the rest: the sorrow it excites may more justly be termed the fruits and recompense of conversion, than its primary cause. Should you feel little impressed with this pure motive, be at least humbled and astonisned at your insensibility. Recollect that nothing is more natural than to admire what is beautiful, and to love what is amiable. The greatest savage would refrain from injuring an innocent, beautiful, engaging child, because there is something in beauty, virtue, and innocence, which engages love and admiration for themselves alone. Why, then, should you feel so insensible to the adorable perfections, sacred attributes, and enchanting beauty of that divine Being, whose most perfect works and greatest saints are but a faint image of himself? This proceeds chiefly from your having formed no conception of what God is in himself. It is true, that a clear view of his divine perfections is reserved for heaven; but there is an inferior knowledge of God, which may be acquired upon earth, chiefly by two means: the first, by endeavouring habitually so to trace all perfection to God, as to admire the beauty of God alone in all that is admirable, and to love the goodness of God in all that is amiable; but the second, and most essential, is to avoid even the least deliberate sin, and thereby merit those pure lights, which discovered to the saints such perfections in God, as caused some of them to weep their whole lives over one venial offence. The day will come when you will think as they did; but, in the mean time, endeavour to animate your faith, and profit of their experience Ask the blessed in heaven, what it is that constitutes their bliss, and they will reply, that their paradise is the possession, the view, the enjoyment of God. Descend once more into the abyss of hell, and you will learn from the damned, that their chief punishment is, not the fire that consumes them; not the devils who torment them; nor the eternal darkness which surrounds them; but that their hell is truly the loss of God—the eternal loss of that transporting Beauty, that immense ocean of every perfection, which they see as he is since they quitted this life. What, then, must God be in himself? How transporting must that Beauty be, which enraptures the Saints, and even attracts the very reprobate, in spite of themselves! How inexpressibly amiable must that infinite Goodness be, whom it is sufficient to have seen once, or even imperfectly conceived an idea of, to love without measure! If you could form even a slight conception of that eternal *Sun of Justice*, how soon would you exclaim, with the model of penitents, St. Augustine: "Too late have I known thee, O infinite Beauty!" Your detestation of sin would be proportioned to your love for God, whom it offends; and though there were no hell to punish your transgressions, nor a heaven to reward your services, you would still flee from the shadow of sin, and bitterly lament having committed a single imperfection, because it offends a God infinitely good in himself.

The sixth and last motive recommended by your Catechism for exciting Contrition, is, *to reflect on the sufferings and death of Jesus Christ.* You may, whenever you feel inclined, confine yourself to this consideration alone in exciting yourself to sorrow; it is better calculated than any other to touch the heart, and to give weight to all the motives on which you have already meditated. Place yourself, with the greatest humility and recollection, at the foot of the Cross, and consider the torments of mind and body which Jesus endures; consider this adorable Victim covered with wounds, his sacred head crowned with thorns, his divine eyes closed with agony and streaming in tears; his hands and feet pierced, and his whole body resting on those nails, whereby his wounds are every instant enlarged; his most amiable heart tortured by the ingratitude of those whom he had worked miracles to relieve and convert. This affecting spectacle would no doubt penetrate your soul with horror, compassion, and anguish, if, with a lively faith, you viewed the work of your sins in the sufferings of your Redeemer. Ah! if you beheld a parent, a friend, even an indifferent person, expiring of a broken heart, caused by the pain and misery your faults had occasioned, what would be your feelings? But should that parent or friend unexpectedly recover from the extremity of death, and again experience from you the same treatment as before, would you not acknowledge yourself, and be looked on by all the world as a monster of the basest ingratitude? This is precisely the light in which you should now view yourself. You have caused the death of your true parent—your sins, more than his cruel enemies, fastened him to the cross;—your pride covered a God with humiliation; your impatience under the slightest contradictions, exposed this meek Lamb to the most insulting outrages; your vanity and attachment to the vain amusements of the world, crowned his divine head with thorns;—your ingratitude and insensibility pierced his heart;—your selfish search after every gratification, deprived him even of a cup of cold water in the agonies of death. You know that sin caused his death, and yet you have repeatedly sinned;—you have crucified again the Son of God; that is, you have, as far as is in your power, renewed the sufferings of Jesus Christ, by renewing their cause. Have you ever considered this truth? Reflect seriously on it now, and that you may conceive that sincere detestation of your sins which is the foundation of solid conversion, recall to your mind once more the other motives of lively sorrow on which you have already reflected. One glance at the Cross of Jesus Christ should suffice to remind you of them all, for it clearly proves the horror and filthiness of sin, since the blood of a God alone could efface its stain. It shows you the danger of sin, since, notwithstanding the effusion of that blood, sin still condemns millions to hell, rekindles the flames which Jesus died to extinguish, transforms his infinite love into inexorable justice, and despoils so many thousands of that kingdom of glory, so dearly purchased for them. It plainly proves the ingratitude of sin, which does not blush to offend anew a God so good to man, as to die for his redemption; and lastly, it proves the abominable malice of sin, which has urged sinners to offend a God who must be infinitely good in himself to suffer so much for those whose reprobation could not, for an instant, diminish his beatitude. Such reflections as these must make an impression on any heart which is not absolutely hardened.

After you have sincerely weighed these motives for sincere sorrow, you should endeavour to produce acts of lively and sincere contrition. As those should proceed much more from your heart than your lips, they will be best made in your own words. You would do well, however, if leisure permit, to repeat fervently the following acts, because they express the dispositions for justification required by the holy Council of Trent, which says, that "those who would obtain the grace of justification, must, 1st, have faith; 2d, they must fear the justice of God; 3d, must hope for mercy through Jesus Christ; 4th, must begin to love God; 5th, must hate sin; 6th, must sincerely resolve to change their lives, and keep the commandments."

An Act of Contrition.

O God of infinite holiness! in whose sight sin is always abominable, what an object of horror must I now appear before thee, defiled as I am with innumerable offences. I acknowledge my transgressions, O Lord! I feel that I am not worthy to appear in thy presence, or to call on that adorable name, which I do not deserve to pronounce. I have offended thee more grievously than many who are now plunged in the eternal fire of hell. I have abused thy graces, trampled on thy blood, ungratefully turned thy benefits against thyself, and neglected opportunities of salvation which will never return. Ah! if I had treated my fellow-creatures with half the ingratitude I have shown thee, my good God, I would despair of their forgiveness; but, though most unworthy either to ask or obtain thy pardon, I do not despair of being once more received into thy grace and friendship. I know that I cannot trust too confidently in thy mercies; I know that my multiplied sins are few, when contrasted with thy abundant merits, and that thou never canst reject an humble and contrite heart. I cast myself, with all my sins and miseries, at the foot of thy Cross, where no sinner was ever condemned who implored thy pardon with humility and sorrow. I embrace thy feet with the penitent Magdalen, and I ardently wish that, like her, I could love thee as much as I have offended. Ah! do not refuse me that pardon, which I desire more ardently than any other blessing I could possibly enjoy. Take compassion on me, O my God and my Father! for to whom can I have recourse but to thee? If thou reject me, who will receive me? Or who could pardon such sins as mine, if not thou, O infinite Mercy? I have already been loaded with too many favours, to doubt of thy willingness to receive thy prodigal, repentant child. I never should have thought of returning to thee, if thou hadst not called me thyself: I never could detest my sins as sincerely as I do, if thy grace had not touched my heart. Thou seest that heart, O great God! and thou knowest that it is filled with the most lively sorrow. I do, my merciful Redeemer! detest my sins from the bottom o my heart. I sincerely detest sin in general, because it is thy enemy. I detest most sincerely all the sins of my life, particularly those which have displeased thee most, those which are hidden from my view, and those I am going to accuse myself of in this confession. I now look on those offences as the greatest misfortunes of my life, and heartily regret them, because they have made me hateful in thy sight, exposed me to the dreadful misfortune of being eternally separated from thee, and excluded me from the kingdom of heaven. I detest them, because they have offended my most merciful and liberal Benefactor, and because they fastened thy most adorable body to the Cross. But, my God, these are not my only motives for sincerely detesting my sins : if there were neither heaven nor hell ; if I never received, nor ever could hope for a benefit from thee, still I would abhor all sin, and heartily regret having had the misfortune of committing so great an evil, because it offends thee, O infinite, adorable Perfection! who can never be sufficiently loved for thyself alone. O why did I not always think as I now do? Why was I so miserable, so blind, as to listen rather to the suggestions of the devil, than to thy divine inspirations? Why were the best days of my life spent in exasperating my Creator? At least, may I now for ever forsake that sinful, useless course I have too long pursued ; may sin always appear to me, as it now does, more dreadful than hell itself; and the least temptation to offend thee, more frightful than death. O let every hour of my life henceforward increase my sorrow for all my offences, and strengthen my firm resolution to prefer a thousand deaths to the unspeakable misfortune of committing one deliberate sin.

Resolution of Amendment.

If your heart be really penetrated with the sentiments you have expre[illegible]ed in the foregoing Act of Contrition, it will not [illegible] necessary to suggest the obligation you are under of forming serious resolutions for the amendment of your life. This resolution of never sinning again, is so essential to Contrition, that, without it, there can be no real sorrow It is, nevertheless, a point on which many persons fail; the greater number contenting themselves with a sort of general intention of doing better in future, an intention which costs nothing; which often is only in imagination; which, at best, is very weak and indeterminate. As this defect of a firm, decided purpose of amendment, and the want of foreseeing and resolving against habitual faults, is the great cause of so many fruitless Confessions, you should be particularly careful in making your resolutions. Remember that those resolutions should be *firm*, *distinct*, and *humble*.—They should be *firm;* that is, they should be steadily established on the following solid reflections, *viz.* That your salvation is the only really important concern you have on earth; that however young you may be now, the hour of death will at last arrive, when most certainly every other pursuit, beside the service of God, will appear nothing but folly. If you lose your soul, all is lost, and lost for eternity; that however difficult you may find it to correct your faults, or to overcome your passions, there is no alternative; they must be encountered; if not, the loss of your soul will be the unhappy but certain consequence. You will of course perceive the obligation of firmly resolving, in occasions of temptation, to resist, no matter what you may feel, and to say to yourself, as St. Gregory did to a great monarch, who required some condescension which conscience forbad: "If I had two souls, I might sacrifice one to please the world and gratify myself; but as I have but one, I am firmly resolved to save it."

Secondly, Your resolutions should be *distinct;* that is, you must, besic a firm general determination of changing your life, eflect on the particular faults you are accustomed to commit, and then resolve particularly against them. Call to mind also the duties you have been most in the habit of neglecting, that you may determine, in the presence of God, to comply with them in future.—For example, if you have been in the very bad custom of omitting your morning and night prayers, or your daily examination of conscience, you must resolve to acquit yourself of these duties punctually in future. If you have lost your time, or neglected the duties of your state, your resolution must be to prefer these essential duties to every pursuit, and even so distribute your time, as to insure their fulfilment at stated hours. If you have been idle, or neglected your employments, you should resolve, not only to avoid such conduct in future, but even to make up for lost time by double diligence. In a word, the slothful should resolve to become active and diligent; the perverse and ungovernable, gentle and docile; the peevish and fretful, patient and mild; the proud and vain, humble and diffident; the insincere should resolve to avoid the shadow of a lie, and to make candour their favourite virtue, &c.

Thirdly, Your resolution should be *humble;* for to fulfil such resolutions is in reality more difficult than it generally appears. Young persons, in particular, so seldom reflect on their own weakness, that they are always ready to say with St. Peter: *Though all should be scandalized in thee, I never will be scandalized:* but, as may be expected, those presumptuous resolutions are generally followed by a relapse. Do you then take special care, when forming your resolutions, to distrust yourself, and place all your confidence in God, without whom you can do nothing, but with whose powerful assistance all things are possible When you have made all the resolutions you judge necessary, and that as firmly, distinctly, and humbly as you are able, place them in the hands of God, in the sacred heart of Jesus, and under the protection of his most blessed mother.

Prayer.

DIVINE Jesus! whose holy grace has opened my eyes to the miserable and sinful state of my soul who has penetrated my heart with sorrow for my offences, it is in thy presence I now most solemnly resolve to begin a new life, and endeavour to become, from this very moment, what I shall certainly wish to have been at the hour of my death. I resolve to adopt all the means I know to be necessary for preserving thy grace, and persevering in virtue. I resolve to discharge my spiritual duties with the utmost fidelity, to employ my time carefully, and in the manner that thou requirest, since I must account for every moment of it to thee. I resolve to strive particularly against those faults I am most accustomed to commit, and to avoid those dangerous occasions which have hitherto led me into sin. These are my firm resolutions, O my God! but I tremble when I consider my former inconstancy and my present weakness. I do not deserve those graces I have so often abused; but notwithstanding, since thou knowest I can do nothing without thee, I humbly hope thou wilt give me the grace and strength necessary for persevering in thy love, and keeping most faithfully the resolutions I now make. Preserve me, O Lord, from presumptuous confidence in my own strength, for that alone would cause my fall. Alas! there are many now in hell, who at some period of their mortal life felt more fervour, more sorrow for sin, and made more firm purpose of amendment than I do; I also may deserve to be abandoned by thee. My God and only hope! leave me not to myself—accept my resolutions, but do thou give them efficacy; permit me to place them in thy hands, in thy sacred heart, and under the protection of thy blessed Mother, and my good Angel; that thus my weakness may be powerfully assisted, and that I may be preserved from the misfortune of a relapse into sin.

As all the Contrition you could feel, or all the sorrow which ever filled the hearts of the greatest penitents, would of itself be insufficient to atone for your sins, you should always recollect to build your hopes of pardon on the merits of your Redeemer and to unite your sentiments of contrition to the bitter anguish and efficacious sorrow which Jesus Christ was pleased to endure for your offences, particularly in the Garden of Olives. Enter there in spirit, and behold, in the person of your Saviour, a perfect model of what a true penitent should be, and offer up all his merits and sufferings to supply for the deficiencies of your sorrow, and other dispositions This may be done in the following form.

Prayer.

O DIVINE Lord! I am fully sensible that it is the greatest of all misfortunes to offend thy divine Majesty, and that no misery can exceed that which is attached to the violation of thy law; therefore I again declare, that I abhor my sins, and return to thee with my whole heart. But, O my God! when I consider that one single offence is a just and sufficient cause for eternal tears—when I reflect on the bitter regrets which the saints felt for a venial sin, and then compare my grievous offences with my imperfect sorrow, I am justly alarmed at my great insensibility. O! why is not my sorrow as great as my offences!—why cannot I grieve for them even unto death, and collect in my heart all the contrition that was ever felt by the greatest penitents, that thus it may truly be broken with sorrow, and incapable of enjoying any other satisfaction than that which is found in unceasing regret! But since those holy dispositions are graces to which I have no claim, I beseech of thee, O divine Lord! to accept my desires, and to supply from the treasure of thy infinite merits all the deficiencies in my Preparation for this Confession. Accept on my behalf, O adorable Jesus! the clear view thou hadst of all my sins in the Garden of Olives, to supply for my imperfect knowledge of them, or any defect in my examination. I offer up thy sighs, thy tears, thy fainting, thy bloody sweat, and the bitter anguish which penetrated thy amiable heart, to supply for the weakness of my contrition. I offer thee thy merciful resolution of dying for the expiation of sin, to atone for any deficiency thou mayest discern in my determination never more to offend thee, and to perform all the actions of my life in the spirit of contrition and penance. O adorable Heart of Jesus! which was sorrowful even unto death for those very sins I am about to accuse myself of; which was wounded on the Cross, and thus rendered the refuge of sinners, I call on thee now with all the earnestness, humility, and confidence I am capable of, and entreat of thee, by thy infinite love for sinners, to remember all I cost thee, and to apply to my soul abundantly the infinite merits of thy humiliations, sufferings, and anguish.

OF CONFESSION.

With respect to the acknowledgment of your sins in the sacred Tribunal of Penance, observe, that it should have four qualities:—First, it should be *sincere;* that is, each sin should be declared openly, fully, and candidly, such as we conceive it to be in the sight of God. All equivocal expressions, tending to disguise the real state of the conscience, should be carefully avoided: any inclination to reserve in this sacred tribunal, where the *Searcher of Hearts* is the invisible Judge, should be sovereignly dreaded, as the most dangerous artifice of the devil, who thereby ruins many whom he could not otherwise destroy. It is easy enough to deceive a Confessor, but impossible to deceive the Almighty, who presides in the tribunal to pardon or condemn, according to the dispositions of the heart, which he clearly discerns. In vain does a Confessor absolve, while the Almighty condemns —in vain does he hope to open for you the gates of heaven, which your insincerity has doubly barred—in vain does the minister of God desire you to depart in peace, when the Almighty already punishes your concealment by that sting of remorse, which occasions far more pain than could the most humiliating accusation. How intolerable the anguish of the reflections which must always follow from one insincere confession! "I am now at enmity with God—I am a hypocrite—I have lied to the Holy Ghost himself --all my confessions since this last bad one, and all my communions are, without doubt, sacrilegious :— whatever good works I may have since done are ineffectual, and this very sin must be confessed some time or other :—I must necessarily go back through all this duplicity—I must accuse myself, not only of the sin concealed, but must declare that I concealed it; and must also declare my several crimes since that one, though I have already confessed them to other clergymen." Is it not then much better to arm ourselves at once with a firm resolution to shake off this galling load; to submit with generosity to a short, a private humiliation, so inadequate to the greatness of our offences, and so abundantly productive of comfort? We shall then have nothing to fear; the past need no more be examined: calmness and humble confidence shall then abide in our hearts, and a good conscience be our delight hereafter. Penitents would always act with the utmost sincerity at Confession, if they were accustomed to consider the sacred tribunal as a place so awful, so holy, as that nothing human should enter there. Beside, confessors should not be viewed in any other light than as the ministers of God, and as holding the place of Jesus Christ. The Spirit of God, with which they are filled, moves them to compassion and tenderness. They are too well acquainted with human frailty, to be surprised at any accusation, be it ever so grievous, nor could you tell them any thing with which they were not before acquainted. They know how prone all are to sin, and how averse from accusing themselves in Confession. They will therefore be rather struck with admiration at the humble avowal of crimes, than shocked at the sinner's weakness. Beside, the Seal of Confession is inviolable—no power on earth can authorize the least breach of it without the penitent's free expressed consent.

Secondly, your Accusation in Confession should be *entire ;* that is, you must declare all your mortal sins, as far as you can remember; for if, after a careful examination of your conscience, some sin still escape your memory, the sin forgotten is pardoned with the rest, with an obligation, however, of declaring it at the next Confession. But if this forgetfulness be the effect of negligence in your examination, the sin forgotten, or any other is not pardoned, and the whole confession becomes null and sacrilegious. Beside declaring all your mortal sins, the number of times each has been committed must be specified : for example, it is not sufficient to say, "I have disobeyed my parents," or, "I have told lies," when perhaps disobedience and lying were habitual, or at least happened several times. It should be specified whether a sin were habitual, and how often in the day, week, or month, it has been committed ; adding the words *more* or *less*, when not quite certain ; neither should you puzzle or disturb yourself on this head, for it is not so much an effort of memory, or an exact computation, that is required from you, as a sincere intention of stating the number of your offences as nearly as you can ; avoiding in this instance, as in every other, all scrupulosity and anxiety. You should also specify the circumstances which change the nature of a sin : for example, unnecessary swearing is sinful, but to swear contrary to truth is *perjury ;* to swear against God, is *blasphemy ;* to swear against ourselves, is *imprecation ;* consequently it would not suffice to say, "I have sworn, or been in the habit of swearing;" the nature of the oaths must be specified. You are obliged likewise to mention all circumstances which aggravate a sin: for example, to steal a crown is a sin, but to steal ten crowns is a much greater offence; to steal from a rich man is also a sin, but to steal from a poor man is infinitely greater. In a word, whenever your own character, obligations, situation in life, or those of your accomplices, give a peculiar enormity to the crime, or in any respect increase its malignity, you are obliged to specify all those aggravating circumstances, as well as the degree of deliberation with which you sinned, the scandal or bad effects occasioned.

Thirdly, your Confession must be *humble;* you should be so covered with confusion for your sins, as not to relate them as you would relate matters of little importance. Acknowledge your faults with the humility of the Publican in the Gospel, who sought not to diminish the confusion he conceived was due to his crimes. Let your accusation also be *prudent;* never mention the names of accomplices, except in cases of absolute necessity, which are very rare: content yourself with mentioning your own sins, without adding those of others, or seeking to throw the blame on others, like Eve, who cast the blame of her crime on the serpent, and Adam, who accused Eve.

Your Confession, lastly, should be *simple;* that is, you should confine yourself to the declaration of your sins, or any matters relating to conscience, without running into superfluous, round-about details, or trivial circumstances, unnecessary to the explanation of your sins, and tending to intrude on the precious time of a confessor, as also to take off, on your part, from the devotion which should accompany so solemn a duty. It will help much to simplicity and clearness in your confession, if you observe, both in your examination and accusation, the order which has been before pointed out.

Should you be detained any time by the confessions of others, take particular care to avoid distraction. As to the scandalous and irreligious custom of conversing at confessionals, either to remark or complain of the length of time taken up by others, or for any other purpose whatever, it cannot be too much condemned, and you will be particularly culpable if you follow bad example in this respect; thus proving your total forgetfulness of the instructions you have received, and the method you have been so long accustomed to in approaching the sacraments. What can be more contrary to the true spirit of repentance, than such levity and insensibility to the misfortune of having offended a God who sees the heart, and is about to pronounce sentence according to your dispositions?

Immediately before you enter the confessional, renew your sorrow, as well as your good resolutions, and endeavour to enliven your faith, love, and confidence, by the following or any other short prayer:

Prayer.

O adorable Jesus! the invisible High Priest of our souls! who, in the excess of thy love, hast instituted this consolatory sacrament of pardon and mercy, it is before thee I am going to present myself; it is thy divine authority which I reverence in the person of thy minister. O compassionate Physician of our souls! who didst not refuse to heal with thy own divine hands those lepers whose horrid malady was a figure of sin, I am going to approach to thee, convinced that thou wilt and canst make me clean. O! let me be so happy as to find mercy and pardon; let no evil disposition of mine be an obstacle to thy merciful designs on my soul. O omnipotent Jesus! what is impossible to me, is infinitely easy to thee—change then my heart, show me so clearly what sin is, and what it deserves, that I may cheerfully accept the pain and humiliation which I may feel in avowing my offences. Let thy divine Spirit be in my heart, and on my lips, that my confession may be sincere, entire, humble, and penitent.

Mother of God! Mother of Mercy! and Refuge of Sinners! intercede for me now, that this Confession I am going to make, may not render me more guilty, but may obtain for me the remission of my sins, and grace to avoid them in future.

Holy Angel, to whose care I am committed, do not leave me, now that I so particularly require your charitable assistance. Watch over me, while I declare my sins in the sacred tribunal; preserve me from temptation, and intercede for me with our common Lord and Master, that his holy grace and the words of his minister may sink deep into my heart, and tend to the perfect and lasting change of my life.

On entering the confessional, place yourself in spirit at the feet of Jesus Christ: begin by making the sign of the Cross, saying, "Bless me, Father for I have sinned." When the Priest has said, "May the Lord be in your heart and on your lips, that you may sincerely and candidly declare all your sins, in the name of the Father, and of the Son, and of the Holy Ghost, Amen," say the Confiteor as follows:

"I confess to the Almighty God, to the Blessed Virgin Mary, to the blessed Michael the Archangel, to the blessed St. John the Baptist, to the holy Apostles St. Peter and St. Paul, to all the saints in heaven, and to you, my father, that I have sinned exceedingly in thought, word, and deed; through my fault, through my fault, through my most grievous fault." At these words you should bow your head, and penitently strike your breast; then say how long it is since your last confession,—secondly, whether you were absolved, and have communicated:—and thirdly, whether you performed your penance. Then begin your Confession, by accusing yourself of any sin which might have been forgotten in your last confession, or any faults committed in approaching that sacrament. After which proceed to the accusation of your other sins, beginning by those which you feel most repugnance to mention, as this act of humility and generosity is likely to draw down a blessing from God on the rest of your Confession; you need only preface the first sin with the words, *I accuse myself*.

When you have accused yourself of all your sins, and submitted any doubts on your mind to the opinion of your director, conclude your Confession, not by saying, "I have no more," as is the ignorant custom of many persons, but in the following form:—"For these, and all the sins of my life, I am most heartily sorry, humbly beg pardon of God, and penance and absolution of you, my father:" then immediately bowing your head, finish the Confiteor as follows:—"Therefore I beseech the blessed Virgin Mary, the blessed Michael the Archangel, the blessed St. John the Baptist, the holy Apostles St. Peter and St. Paul, all the saints in heaven, and you, my father, to pray to God for me." The Priest then says: "May the Almighty God be merciful to you, forgive you your sins, and bring you to everlasting life. May the almighty and merciful Lord grant you pardon, absolution, and full remission of all your sins."

If your confessor judge proper to defer absolution, it would be extremely wrong in you to repine, as a delay is frequently expedient, and, in many cases, absolutely necessary: for example, should you unfortunately appear habitually addicted to any mortal sin—unwilling to repair the injuries you have done your neighbour in his property or reputation—habitually inattentive to your duties of obligation—ignorant of the principal mysteries of religion—slothful in examining your conscience—or little penetrated with sorrow for your sins. Under such circumstances, and numberless others, a Priest could not give you absolution without committing sin.—On the contrary, if you be found disposed for absolution, your director will give you penance, which you should receive in the spirit of humility; but if it appear to you impracticable, or such as may notably interfere with your other duties, you may respectfully represent your difficulties. He will then give you notice, that he is about to absolve you. While this sentence of mercy is pronouncing, bow your head in the most respectful manner; imagine yourself at the foot of the Cross, and that the precious Blood of Jesus Christ blots out all your sins. Renew your sorrow for having offended so good a God, and beg of his divine Majesty, that you may rather die than ever offend him by any wilful offence. In these pious sentiments receive the absolution, which is given in the following form:—"May our Lord Jesus Christ absolve thee from every bond of excommunication and interdict, as far as I have power, and thou hast need. I therefore do absolve thee from all thy sins, in the name of the Father, and of the Son, and of the Holy Ghost. Amen.

"May the passion of our Lord Jesus Christ, the merits of the blessed Virgin Mary, and of all the Saints; may whatever good thou shalt do, or whatever evil thou shalt suffer, be to thee unto the remission of thy sins, the increase of grace, and the recompense of life everlasting. Amen."

When you leave the confessional, do not disturb your mind by examining whether you have confessed well, or have forgotten any of your sins, but rest assured, that if you made your Confession with sincerity and the other requisite dispositions, you are, according to the express decision of the Council of Trent, fully absolved from every sin which you may have omitted through forgetfulness, even though it were mortal.—Retire with recollection and respec to some quiet place, and there, indulging for some time the feelings of gratitude and joy which should animate your heart, return most sincere thanks to your merciful and indulgent Father. In doing so, you need not immediately confine yourself to any particular form of prayer; you cannot fail to rejoice, if you have any conception of the greatness of the blessing you have received, in being reconciled to God; the uneasiness and remorse you experienced under the weight of your sins, must make you value the peace and delight of a good conscience, so that you cannot want words to express your gratitude. What would you say to a parent, whom you had grievously offended, but who had at length forgiven and forgotten your unnatural ingratitude?—How would you thank a friend, who had not only delivered you from death, but had even sacrificed his own life for your ransom? God is that parent, who has just pardoned you; he is that friend, who has redeemed you from eternal death;—thank him then, with all your heart and soul, and afterwards devoutly repeat the following acts.

Prayers after Confession.

O God of infinite goodness! who hast shown such mercy to a miserable sinner! O most indulgent Father! who hast received once more thy prodigal child, how shall I thank thee? how shall I testify the joy and gratitude that fill my heart? O that I could worthily thank thee, my good God! and acknowledge as I ought, that infinite mercy which *forgiveth all* my *iniquities*, which *healeth all* my *diseases*. Ps. cii. 3 O! that I could now be heard all over the world, I would publish to all sinners, that thou art a God *compassionate and merciful*, who *wilt not always be angry, nor threaten for ever*. Ibid. 8, 9. I would invite all who ever had the misfortune of offending thee, to return with their whole hearts, that they may enjoy with me the bliss of having been received into thy grace and favour. Thou wouldst receive them no less mercifully than thou receivedst me; *for as a father hath compassion on his children, so hath the Lord compassion on them that fear him.* Ibid. 13. My God, thou hast broken the bonds of my sins; thou hast blotted out, with thy own precious blood, the sentence of eternal death which stood against me; thou hast snatched me almost from the brink of hell, and delivered me from the power of the devil, who has now no claim to my soul: *as far as the east is from the west, so far hast* thou *removed* my *iniquities from me,* (Ib. 12.) and by the mouth of thy minister thou hast desired the most unworthy of all sinners to "*Go in peace.*" O divine Jesus! I have obeyed thy command, my heart rejoices, my soul is truly at peace, because I hope I am no longer thy enemy; because thou hast received me with mercy and forgiveness, and satisfied the first and only desire of my heart. But, Lord! hast thou not said, that those to whom much has been forgiven, should love thee much? To whom hast thou ever remitted such ingratitude as mine?—who had ever so little claim on thy compassion, yet, at the same time, who ever experienced more of thy mercy and goodness? O! let me then love thee, at least, more than those who offended thee less, and to whom less was remitted; let me love thee unceasingly, and sincerely begin, from this happy day, to serve thee alone, and love thee above created things. O most bountiful Redeemer! so worthy of my whole heart, though thou hast mercifully forgiven me, yet I will never pardon myself;—though I firmly trust thou hast forgotten my iniquities, yet I will never forget them, but grieve over them to the last moment of my life. The more mercy and tenderness I have experienced from thee, the more reason I have to deplore my misfortune in having ever offended so good a God. This day shall be the beginning of my perfect conversion—from this moment forward, the recollection of my past ingratitude and thy ineffable goodness shall be ever present to my mind, and, with the assistance of thy grace, shall be a double motive for detesting sin, and faithfully observing my resolutions, which I fervently renew, and once more present to thy divine Majesty. Do not refuse to receive, O my God! the remainder of my life. I am heartily sorry for the years I have misspent; they have gone down as a shadow; they have passed away without fruit; but as I cannot recall them, I will at least think of them in the bitterness of my soul. O! let the ardour with which I pursued a life of sin, be in future applied to thy service, that where sin hath abounded, thy divine grace may be still more abundant. Let the change in my conduct be visible to all, and may I henceforward edify more than I have hitherto scandalized.

O DIVINE Lord! vouchsafe graciously to remember thy holy thoughts from all eternity, and chiefly that tender design of becoming man for the redemption of the world. Pardon me, through the merits of these, all my vain and evil imaginations, as well as the bad thoughts I may have excited in others.

O most compassionate Jesus! I, a wretched sinner, dare to present thee all the words of salvation which have fallen from thy sacred lips, and which others have uttered, or shall hereafter utter to the glory of thy name; and I earnestly beseech thee, through these expressions, full of glory to God, and peace to men, to forgive whatever I have said offensive to thy divine Majesty, or what others, through my means, may have sinfully uttered.

O most amiable Lord Jesus Christ! remember all thy good works thou hast performed for our salvation, and through their infinite merits graciously pardon my reiterated offences against thy holy law. Mercifully direct all my thoughts, words, and actions to thy greater glory, and regulate them by the model of thy own blessed life.

O Jesus Christ, Saviour of the world! who invitest the sinner to return to thee, kindly receiving, refreshing, and consoling him; remember, that with thy precious blood thou wert pleased to redeem my sinful soul; to thy sacred wounds I therefore flee for refuge; and as in thy mercy thou didst pray for thy enemies, and sacrifice thy life for thy tormentors, vouchsafe to impart to me the benefits of thy sacred death and passion. Grant that I may never again crucify thee by any wilful offence, but, sincerely grieving for the past, and resolutely striving against present temptations, I may fervently persevere to the end in thy love and service. Into thy hands I commend my whole being. O Jesus, Son of David! have mercy on me.

O holy Virgin, and all ye Saints and Angels, bless and extol the Lord for his infinite mercies; beg of him to accept the confession I have made, to supply, through his goodness, for all its deficiencies, and graciously to confirm in heaven the sentence of absolution which has been pronounced upon me on earth.

OF SATISFACTION.

Before you leave the chapel, perform, if possible, with the greatest devotion, or at least as soon as you conveniently can, the penance imposed on you in confession. This leads to *Satisfaction*, the third part of the Sacrament of Penance.

Satisfaction, as your Catechism tells you, is the performance of the prayers and other good works enjoined by the Priest to whom you confess, as a penance for your sins. It is likewise the reparation which you owe to God, or your neighbour, for the injuries done by your offences. To satisfy for sin, is to do or to suffer something in atonement for it. All sin must be expiated by penance, either in this life or in the next, except when remitted by acts of perfect charity, or in baptism, where alone sin is forgiven without any obligation of penance. But after a Christian has ungratefully abused this first grace, and offends his Creator anew, it is just, that though he is pardoned in the Sacrament of Penance, yet, that God should require some satisfaction; lest, as St. Chrysostom says, we become more criminal by impunity. It is for this reason that Penance is imposed in the Tribunal of Confession, where Absolution remits the eternal punishment due to sin, but does not dispense from the penalties which must be suffered either here or hereafter. But, as the minister of Jesus Christ in the Tribunal of Penance, imitates rather the mercy than the justice of God in his judgment of sinners, he does not always, particularly towards youth, impose such severe penance as would authorize a penitent to look on it as a sufficient satisfaction for sin. A great deal is left to your own fervour, therefore you should never forget that your sacramental penance, though perfectly sufficient for the integrity of the sacrament, is not always adequate to the satisfaction due to God; —*that* satisfaction must be proportioned to the number and enormity of the offences committed. This circumstance would urge many to embrace a life of fervour and penance, if they had any idea of the rigorous penalties which God adjudges to a single transgression. Of this you may form some idea from the example of David, who by a sin of vanity, which was not in appearance very grievous, and which beside had been previously pardoned, was nevertheless punished by the loss of seventy thousand of his subjects. You may also conceive what proportionable satisfaction for sin is, by the severe penances of the primitive ages, and still more by the dreadful torments of purgatory, which far exceed all the pains that could be endured in this world, and which are reserved for those sinners whose offences have been remitted, but not sufficiently satisfied for in this life. Whence you can perceive how great is the error of those who never think of doing, or suffering any thing in satisfaction for their sins; or who, at most, content them selves with the Penance enjoined in Confession; not reflecting that the infinite justice of God, which so often visibly inflicted such severe punishments on repentant and pardoned sinners, will not be satisfied with a few prayers or good works, as a reparation for so much anger and pride—so much continued negligence in spiritual duties—so many lies—disobedience—ill temper—loss of time, &c., &c. Sin is always the same, always equally hateful to God, always equally deserving of punishment proportioned to its enormity. When once it is committed, it must not only be pardoned, but likewise fully atoned for, before a soul can enter heaven. Therefore, if you be wise, you will faithfully follow the advice of St. Augustine, who counsels sinners to prevent the punishment of God by punishing themselves. Never look upon your sins as atoned for, because they have been confessed; though, on the other hand, the pain and humiliation of confessing our sins are often accepted by God as a great part of the punishment due to sin, particularly with regard to those who have great difficulties in confessing, and great courage in overcoming those difficulties. Be careful to endeavour to satisfy for your sins, and lessen the immense debt you have contracted, by embracing for this end every means within your reach; among which means, the chief are, regular and fervent recourse to the Sacraments, as the principal channels through which the merits of Jesus Christ are applied to our souls—great devotion to, and confidence in the death and passion of our divine Redeemer, and the holy custom of uniting not only your sacramental penance to his sufferings and infinite merits, but also every thought, word, and action of your life, performing all in the spirit of penance.—Great patience and humility in afflictions and crosses, is also an excellent and efficacious mode of satisfying for sin: you should receive those which Providence sends you, not only with patience, but even with gratitude, such as you would feel towards any person who furnished you with money to pay a debt which you could not otherwise discharge. If the pains and afflictions of this life were viewed in that true light, how many would escape the intolerable pains of purgatory, where they will find, that an hour's suffering there is more intolerable than years of penance here; and also, that years of suffering there are less meritorious than an hour's voluntary penance in this world.

You should likewise be particularly fervent in your endeavours to gain all the Indulgences held forth by the Church to her children, and comply faithfully with the conditions under which they are granted.

OF INDULGENCES.

An *Indulgence*, as your Catechism explains it, is releasing from the temporal punishment due to sin after the guilt is remitted in the Sacrament of Penance.

In the primitive ages, when the penitential canons were in force, that is, when canonical penances were imposed on sinners, those penances, in cases of persecution, or extraordinary fervour on the part of the penitent, were remitted or changed for some less painful work, and that remission or exchange was called an *Indulgence*.

An Indulgence, therefore, is not a pardon for sin, because sin must be remitted before an Indulgence can be gained.—It is not leave to commit sin, as is said by some who know nothing of its nature, for no power on earth could give that permission—but it is a releasing of the temporal punishments which remain due to sin already pardoned. Those temporal punishments God inflicts on sinners, whose crimes he has forgiven, in the same manner as a good parent punishes a child to give him a horror of his fault, and prevent his relapsing again into the same. This punishment, which remains due to sinners whose crimes have been forgiven, is suffered either in this world by sickness, pains of mind or body, loss of goods, or voluntary penances; or else in the next world by the fire of purgatory; and it is from the necessity of that atonement that an Indulgence dispenses.

There are two kinds of Indulgences, *viz.* a Plenary Indulgence, and a partial, or limited Indulgence.

A Plenary Indulgence, duly gained, is a full and entire remission of all the temporal punishment due to sin.—The most celebrated Plenary Indulgence is a *Jubilee*, so called from the Old Law, which decreed a general release from debts, bondage, and other grievances. This Plenary Indulgence was in early times granted every hundredth year; it was afterwards confined to every fiftieth, and is now granted every twenty-fifth year, and also on any other important occasion, such as the accession of a new Pope to St. Peter's Chair.

A partial Indulgence, such as of ten years, or a hundred days, or forty days, dispenses from as much of the temporal punishment due to sin, as would be remitted by ten years, a hundred days, or forty days of the canonical penances formerly imposed on sinners. So that a person who, for example, gains an Indulgence of seven years, is released from as much punishment due to his transgressions, as he would be if he had performed a course of seven years' canonical penance.

There are certain dispositions and particular conditions required for the gaining of every Indulgence whether it be plenary or partial.—The essential disposition is, being in the state of grace; and the conditions usually prescribed by the Church are, a good confession and communion, with a certain number of prayers for the following intentions :—1st, The exaltation and prosperity of the holy Catholic Church. 2dly, The extirpation of heresy, and the conversion of sinners. 3dly, Union among Christian Kings and Princes.

You have in this book a method of offering your communion for the gaining of an Indulgence; and as to the prayers to be said for that purpose, five Paters and Aves, with the Creed, the Psalm Miserere, or the Acts of Faith, Hope, and Charity, are those which are usually said, if there be no particular prayers specified.

A Method of offering the Penance enjoined in Confession.

Accustom yourself to direct your intention before you recite your sacramental Penance, fervently uniting it to the sufferings and merits of Christ. This may be done by the following or any other short

Prayer.

O my God and my Creator! I offer thee the penance I am about to perform; it was thou who imposed it on me by the ministry of my confessor, and I desire to perform it with the utmost contrition, devotion, and humility. But, Lord! since thou well knowest it is inadequate to my sins, and that any thing I could do would be incapable of blotting out the least of my offences, permit me to unite this penance, as well as all the actions, pains, and sufferings of my life, which I now offer in the spirit of penance, to the bitter sufferings of my Redeemer; to the great sacrifice of expiation which Jesus offered on Mount Calvary for my sins; also to the merits of the Blessed Virgin, to the penance and sufferings of all the saints and all the just, that thereby the deficiencies of my imperfect satisfaction may be abundantly supplied for.

When you have finished your Thanksgiving after Confession, and said your penance, call to mind for a moment, before you leave the chapel, those words which Jesus Christ addressed to the infirm man to the Probatica, whom he had miraculously cured: *Behold, thou art made whole—sin no more, lest some worse thing happen to thee*, St. John, v. 14. Consider these words as addressed to yourself, now that, through the mercy of God, you have reason to hope you are healed;—take care that you sin no more, lest you may never again receive so many graces; or that the worst of all misfortunes befall you, in the privation of the opportunity, or even of the desire of returning to God anew: then, indeed, as the Gospel says, would your latter state be worse than the former.—If your communion has been deferred by your director, let it be your first and principal care to comply with any conditions required from you for absolution; such as amendment of life, correction of any bad habit, reconciliation with your neighbour, &c. But if you have been permitted to communicate, endeavour most earnestly to prepare for worthily receiving that adorable sacrament which will fortify you in your good resolutions, infuse abundant grace into your soul, and best insure your perseverance in virtue.

OF FIRST COMMUNION.

From the moment you were old enough to understand what is meant by the adorable Eucharist, you should look forward with a holy impatience to your first Communion, and never pass a day without humbly and fervently begging the Almighty to prepare you for that happiness. Each time that you see your elder companions communicate, you should make a spiritual communion, by an act of Faith in the adorable Eucharist, an act of hope, of love, and ardent desire to communicate yourself; looking on those who enjoy such a happiness as objects of that holy envy which is very allowable and innocent, since the angels themselves would envy a Christian the felicity and honour of receiving the Almighty, if it were possible for them to desire any thing they do not possess.

If these were your dispositions with regard to the holy Communion, so long as your extreme youth, ignorance of the Christian Doctrine, or any other cause, deferred your first Communion, you need not be told to rejoice from your heart, now that you have been chosen to prepare for that most solemn duty; you will naturally feel delighted at the prospect of soon enjoying the happiness you so much desired Your first care should be to make your most humble and grateful thanksgivings to God. There is reason to hope that it is He who has selected you for his temple, since that choice was not made without consulting his Divine Majesty, and imploring the light of his Holy Spirit by prayer. But that sentiment which should predominate over all others on this occasion, is a holy fear of the awful duty for which you are now going to prepare, and a deep sense of its great responsibility. This disposition is of the utmost importance, so much so, that the first Communion is always deferred until children are old enough *to discern the body of the Lord;* that is, as your Catechism says, until they are of an age to understand what the blessed Eucharist is; how they should prepare to receive it worthily; the terrible misfortune of an unworthy Communion, and the risk those run who prepare negligently for an action of such importance, that thereby they may learn to tremble at their own weakness, to trust unreservedly in God's grace, and at the same time to leave nothing in their own power undone for rendering themselves less unworthy of the happiness of communicating. You have now attained that age, and you do not, it is hoped, resemble many children, who are more delighted at the thoughts of making their first Communion, than impressed with the necessity of sparing no exertion to make it well. But as so much depends on this sentiment of holy fear, which should spring from the prospect of having to perform so soon the most solemn and awful of all duties, you should most earnestly beg of God to enlighten your understanding, and penetrate your heart, that you may know and feel what you are about, and never be so thoughtless as to prepare lightly for a Sacrament, which no created being could dare to receive, had not the command proceeded from God himself. Endeavour likewise to conceive a just notion of this great work, by reflecting seriously that your first Communion is without comparison the most important action you will ever have to perform. This is the action on which perhaps your eternal salvation or misery depends, because nothing more directly leads a soul to heaven or to hell, than the good or bad use of this Sacrament; now, *that* is often decided by the first Communion. Those who are so happy as to make it worthily, begin well, and receive in the first visit of their Saviour abundant graces and special assistance for persevering in his holy service; whereas those who are so truly unfortunate as to profane the precious body and blood of Jesus Christ the very first time they receive it, make at once rapid strides in guilt—they become old in sin, while they are yet children; their hearts are hardened; their after life is too often depraved; their end unfortunate, and their eternity miserable:—all which may be traced to the crime of an unworthy first Communion. How many perhaps of the blessed in heaven owe their happiness to the care, the fervour, and purity of heart with which they approached, for the first time, the holy communion! how many of the damned in hell would now be reigning with God, if in their early youth they had not drawn down the divine vengeance on themselves by an unworthy communion! These considerations should animate you to enter with all the fervour, good-will, and steadiness you are capable of, on the six weeks' preparation you are required to make for this most important duty. That time will appear short indeed, when you reflect on the great work you have to prepare for, *viz.* nothing less than the reception of the Almighty himself, the same God for whose coming the world was four thousand years sighing, and whom the blessed Virgin, though exempt from the smallest stain, prepared to receive in her sacred womb by years of retirement and prayer. You cannot therefore be too careful in banishing from your mind every other concern beside your Communion, which is now for you the *one thing necessary*. Recollect that you are provided, by God's particular providence, with every possible means for acquiring the essential dispositions for a worthy Communion. If you were situated like many other children, who are as deserving as you, and yet are deprived of the advantages you enjoy, you would be obliged in conscience to seek after instruction—to study your religion and your obligations, and to spare no pains for acquiring a sufficient knowledge of the Christian Doctrine, before you could presume to make your first Communion. Left to yourself, how much difficulty would you perhaps find in learning all you are bound to know! How great a risk would you run in approaching the holy Communion, ignorant of half the happiness, or half the obligations of those who receive that adorable Sacrament! But God, who specially loves you, has spared you all that difficulty, and put it almost out of your power to profane the Sacrament through *ignorance*;—you have not to seek for instruction; God has sought after you, to bestow on you that favour, and not only that, but the blessing likewise of good advice, good example, and spiritual assistance of every kind; consequently any defect of dispositions would be much more criminal and more ungrateful in you, than in those who make their first Communion without half, or perhaps any of the advantages you enjoy. In a word, it will be solely and entirely your own fault, if you do not make your first Communion with the two essential dispositions required for that solemn duty.—Those dispositions are,

First, To be fully instructed in your religion; and

Secondly, To be in the state of grace.

You cannot fail to acquire both these dispositions if you go through in the proper spirit the preparation appointed for first Communion. That preparation, which consists in the daily instructions on the Christian Doctrine, given to those who are preparing for first Communion—in the general confession they are required to make—the three visits daily to the blessed sacrament appointed for them—and lastly the spiritual retreat, will be useful to each individual only inasmuch as she endeavours to enter into the spirit of those regulations; because all the exertions of others for your good, will be unavailing without your own efforts. Your duty, then, during the time set apart for the preparation for your first Communion, is,

First, to attend to the instructions you receive with the reverence and respect which are due to the word of God—as also with application and fear, considering the account you will have to render of so great a grace, and with a serious desire of profiting of all you hear, and reducing it to practice.

Secondly, you must carefully watch over your conduct, not only to avoid the least wilful transgression, but likewise to correct any faults which may have been pointed out to you as obstacles to God's grace. Redouble your attention to prayer; be extremely diligent, gentle, and docile; and do not fail to give that general edification which is so justly expected from those who are preparing for their first Communion.

Thirdly, when you are making your general confession, endeavour to give your whole mind and heart to that great work, and go through it with that application, seriousness, contrition, and sincerity which would mark this important action were it to be your last; thereby you will morally insure the third disposition for a good Communion, and repair any defects which may have been in your past confessions; those made in early youth being often unhappily defective in some essential point, such as want of sufficient examination, sincere contrition, firm resolution of amendment, or full and entire accusation.

Lastly, when you enter into the retreat which is appointed for the three days immediately preceding the festival on which you are to communicate, you should renew all your joy at the near approach of the happiest day of your life, and consider that a vast deal depends on spending those last three days with great fervour. The six preceding weeks were devoted, five of them to a course of instructions that you may acquire the first disposition for a good communion, *viz.* a competent knowledge of the Christian doctrine—and the sixth week was employed in making a general confession to insure your communicating with the second and most essential disposition for doing so worthily, *viz.* purity of heart. But it is intended that during the time of your retreat you should prepare for receiving absolution in perfect dispositions of contrition, and firm purpose of amendment, as likewise to excite those sentiments of lively faith, firm hope, sincere love, profound humility, and ardent desire to communicate, which are the ornaments with which Jesus Christ will expect to find your heart adorned. For this purpose you should, during your retreat, aim at what is called the spirit of retreat; that is, endeavour to keep your thoughts and your heart fixed on the great work you are about, and which should interest you more, the nearer it approaches. Take particular care not to frustrate the end proposed in separating you from your companions, by indulging in dissipation or talkativeness, even with the few who are in retreat with you, and preparing for the same solemn act. When permitted to converse together, you should usually speak of God, of the happiness you expect, and thereby mutually animate each other. Do not forget, that it is very easy to be dissipated and distracted with a few companions, or even with one; consequently, that the essential of retreat is to keep your heart united to God, and likewise that it will be almost impossible, at your age, to gain any thing like interior recollection, if you do not keep a guard over yourself exteriorly, and carefully observe the rules of silence, laid down for the few days of your retreat.

If you observe these recommendations during your preparation for your first communion, you will do all in your power towards disposing yourself for the first entrance of your Creator into your bosom, and render it truly the happiest and most salutary event of your life. But as your doing so depends particularly on the special grace of God, who alone can make you desire what is good, and strengthen you to accomplish it, your general practice, from the moment you are chosen for communion, should be to implore the divine assistance to make it worthily. This you can do, by constantly raising your heart to God in the course of the day, and by acquitting yourself with great devotion of the three visits to the Blessed Sacrament appointed for each day. At the

1st. Recite the Hymn of the Holy Ghost, and the Acts of Faith, Hope, and Charity. At the

2d, Say the Litany of Jesus, the following Prayer, and a Hail, holy Queen, for the conversion of sinners. At the

3d visit, say the Litany of the Blessed Virgin, a Pater and Ave for the souls in purgatory, and the short Act of Consecration to the sacred Heart of Jesus.

A Prayer to be said while preparing for first Communion.

O Divine Jesus! who during thy mortal life didst receive children with the tenderness of a father and didst command that they should not be forbidden to approach thy sacred person, I see that thou art in the holy Eucharist the same God of goodness and mercy since thou now invitest me not only to approach thee, but to receive thy adorable body and blood. I am transported with joy, when I think that the happy day I have so long desired is now approaching; my heart is filled with gratitude and astonishment at the thought that thou wilt really bestow on me, who am nothing but a weak child, and a great sinner, the most precious of all thy gifts. But yet, O eternal Majesty! this prospect ought to make me fear as much as rejoice. What should become of me, if I were to receive thee unworthily? How many have had that terrible misfortune, who were not so young, so weak, or so imperfect as I am! Alas! that day which I have looked forward to as the happiest of my life, may become the most unfortunate of all. Ah, Lord! is it I who am the person who should betray thee? I, whom thou hast loved so much, and so particularly loaded with favours! Could I be so hardened, as to repay all thy mercies by profaning thy sacred body and blood, on thy first solemn entrance under my roof? No, my good God! with the assistance of thy grace I will never do that. Though I ardently long for my first communion—though I prefer the happiness and honour of receiving thee, to all the pleasures and dignities that could be enjoyed on earth, yet I entreat thee, with the utmost sincerity, rather to take me out of life, than permit that I should live to communicate unworthily. I depend on thee alone, not on my own efforts, for avoiding so great a misfortune, and also for acquiring all the dispositions necessary for receiving thee worthily. I thank thee from my heart, for the religious advantages which I enjoy, and which are now more necessary and more valuable to me than ever. I beg of thee, by that precious blood which purchased them for me, to give me grace to profit of them all to the utmost of my ability. Enlighten my understanding, that I may comprehend the instructions I receive; strengthen my memory, that I may retain them; and above all, penetrate my heart with thy fear and love, that the sacred seed of thy word may sink so deeply into my heart, as to produce a hundred-fold. I ask the same favours for all my companions, who are preparing with me for the happiness of communicating: grant most mercifully, that we may all receive thy adorable body and blood with hearts purified by a good confession from every stain of sin, and animated with a lively faith, firm hope, ardent love, sincere humility, and with every other fervent disposition thou requirest from us, that thereby our first communion may be to us a happy pledge of our eternal union with thee in heaven. *Amen.*

Instructions and Devotions for Communion.

As you have been so happy as to be early impressed with the sentiments of profound veneration and respect due to the most adorable of all mysteries, and fully instructed in all that is necessary to be known concerning the holy Eucharist, it is not necessary to tell you, that a diligent, fervent preparation should precede the holy communion. However, as early impressions are quickly effaced, if they be not occasionally renewed, you are most earnestly recommended, at each of your communions, to endeavour to revive in your soul the same sentiments with which you were penetrated the first time you were admitted to the holy table—the same value for the honour of communicating—the same ardent desire of that happiness—the same holy fear of profaning the most sacred of all mysteries; or rather, to leave nothing undone which may render your heart, at each communion, more pure, more ardent, and more humble than the preceding, and thereby each time less unworthy of the presence of Jesus Christ. The blessed Aloysius of Gonzaga, whom the Church holds forth to youth as a striking example that the most exalted sanctity is perfectly attainable in the tenderest years, may be said to owe his angelical life on earth, and his actual fellowship with the angels in heaven, to his ardent devotion to the holy communion, to his fervent exactness in preparing for that awful duty, and to the abundant fruits which he consequently drew from a participation of this divine sacrament. His whole life may be said to have been devoted to the adorable Eucharist; for, having merited by the most unsullied innocence, ardent piety, and faithful discharge of duty, the privilege of weekly communion, while yet very young, he invariably employed the first three days of the week in thanksgiving for communion, and the three last in preparing for so great a benefit. How happy would you be, if you persevered to the end of your life in imitating such example.

You are, no doubt, convinced that one communion is the most precious benefit which man can receive, or even God himself bestow. You also know, that to communicate is the most holy, the most awful, and infinitely the most important action of your life; you should, therefore, be careful to act conformably to that belief, otherwise your being instructed in what you ought to do, would render you much more guilty than others. You should accustom yourself to look upon every enjoyment and advantage in this world as mere trifles, when compared with the honour and happiness of receiving your Creator in the holy Communion; and all occupations and pursuits as folly, when they interfere with the great duty of preparing for so solemn an action.

Preparation for the holy Communion is of two kinds, viz. *remote* and *immediate.*—You should endeavour most earnestly to acquit yourself of both, because the graces received in the holy Communion are propor tioned to the dispositions of those who communicate. If, for example, you draw water from a fountain in a vessel that is small, and at the same time half filled with other things, you will of course receive much less water, than if you took a larger vessel completely emptied. So it is with those who communicate; if they approach the adorable Eucharist with a heart free indeed from mortal sin, but at the same time contracted and choked up by attachment to the world, by many venial faults and wilful imperfections, and totally divested of that ardent piety, purity of heart, and devotion, which induces the Almighty to enrich his creatures with abundant blessing, it is clear that the graces they receive will be few, and that those who make many such communions will not advance as far in virtue, as a person better disposed would by once receiving the bread of life.

Remote Preparation for the holy Communion, consists in that habitual care which all persons should take to lead a christian, regular, holy life, and to keep their conscience free, not only from mortal sin, which is the great obstacle to a worthy communion, but also from that fatal attachment to any venial sin, which is the obstacle to a profitable communion. This remote preparation, properly speaking, should extend from one communion to another—each reception of the holy Eucharist should be a preparation for the following, and thanksgiving for the foregoing communion. You should communicate at stated periods, once a month, once a fortnight, or oftener, according to the advice of your director. In proportion as the happy days of communion draw near, your longing desires to be united to your God should increase; your thoughts, affections, and actions, even the most indifferent, should be directed as a preparation for your approaching happiness; above all, your watchfulness over yourself, and endeavours to correct your habitual failings, should redouble. Thus would remote preparation for the holy Eucharist conduce to the sanctification of your whole life, and each communion become a perfect preparation for your viaticum, or las reception of the precious body and blood of Jesus Christ.

Immediate Preparation for Communion consists, as your Catechism points out, " in being in the state of grace, penetrated with a lively faith, animated with a firm hope, and inflamed with an ardent charity." If you have done every thing in your power to make your confession according to the method you have been taught, and with all the dispositions which have been so fully explained; if you sincerely detest, not only grievous sins, but every venial offence of your life, and generally every spot and stain which may be an obstacle to the grace you hope to receive, you may trust in the mercy of your Creator, that you have acquired the first immediate dispositions for a good and fervent communion. This disposition consists in sanctifying grace, and that purity of heart which Jesus Christ recommends to all communicants, by washing the feet of his Apostles before he administered to them his adorable body, though he had expressly assured them that they were clean; that is, exempt from every grievous sin. But remember, that if you expected the visit of any person whom you loved and highly respected, you would not be content with preparing a perfectly clean chamber for his reception, you would also endeavour to ornament it as much as possible; consequently, you should not be satisfied with having cast out the filth of sin from that heart in which God himself is so soon to lodge; you should endeavour to adorn and beautify it to the utmost extent of your ability. The ornaments of the soul are virtues: one single act of love, of contrition, of humility, one victory over any particular failing, sinful inclination, or passion, exalts and advances a soul more in the sight of God, than all the brilliant achievements of the greatest conquerors; and also, is more effectual in preparing a soul for communion than many long prayers, which often proceed only from the lips Be therefore particularly careful, when preparing for communion, to profit of every little opportunity of overcoming yourself; such as, being silent when you are inclined to speak impatiently; bearing with the little trials which the tempers or inclinations of others may occasion; behaving with gentleness and forbearance, when spoken to unkindly; endeavouring to oblige every one, particularly those who may have disobliged you; being strictly obedient and docile to your superiors, and uniformly exact to all the rules of your school, offering up your studies, and the salutary restraints you are under, as a preparation for communion; conquering your own will, and cheerfully yielding to that of others; avoiding the least appearance of ill temper, even in looks, and taking care o bear all the little inconveniences you may have to suffer from cold, heat, or fatigue, without those idle, superfluous complaints which are so common, yet which never diminish the evil. These little acts of virtue are the gems with which Jesus desires to find your heart ornamented. If you be on your guard, you will find innumerable occasions for thus proving your desire to receive worthily a God who does so much for you, and who has prepared, in the holy Communion, so great and precious a recompense for the sacrifices you may have to offer him when he enters your heart.

The immediate preparation should commence at least three days before your communion; that is, you should spend those three days as retired as the duties of your state of life will permit; but at all events, in a spirit of recollection, in watchfulness over yourself, and in the practice of those acts of virtue alluded to, which are consistent with all circumstances and conditions. You should likewise discharge your spiritual duties most fervently, particularly your meditations, for which the following considerations are arranged. If you require any instructions as to the method of meditation, you will find sufficient in the explanation of that holy exercise to be found in this book. But though you ought to prepare for communion as fervently as if every thing depended on yourself, yet you should be firmly persuaded that all your own efforts however fervent they may be, could never dispose your soul for a worthy communion; *that* must be chiefly the work of God, who will not refuse to do for you, if you humbly and constantly implore it, all that he knows to be beyond your ability. A very enlightened spiritual writer observes on this subject, that "if a great monarch were to condescend to lodge with a poor widow, he would not expect that she should provide him with accommodations suited to his rank—he would know her poverty, and therefore would send the officers of his household to prepare all things necessary." Let one of your chief petitions to God be that he, in like manner, would deign to prepare his own dwelling in your soul; that as he knows your poverty and weakness, he himself would supply for all your deficiencies, and send forth his Holy Spirit into your heart; that he would also employ the ministry of his holy angels to assist you, and by their intercession make all things ready for the reception of so great and good a King. For this intention, say devoutly, on the three days preceding your communion, the following Prayer, and beg the same grace frequently by short aspirations, which you know may be made in the most distracting occupations.

A Prayer to be said for three Days before Communion.

O ADORABLE Jesus! who hast left us the precious treasure of thy sacred body and blood, to be the food and life of our souls, discover to me the extent of the happiness I hope to enjoy in a few days, by receiving thee in the holy Eucharist. I am soon to approach thy sanctuary, to sit at thy table, and be honoured with the actual presence of that Omnipotent Being, before whom the angels themselves tremble. O my

God! I rejoice at the prospect of so great a blessing I ardently desire to receive thee, and adore thee in the centre of my soul. I earnestly beg thy powerful grace, that my sins may not be an obstacle to the blessings which always follow from a worthy communion. O merciful Jesus! thou seest my heart, thou knowest that I would prefer all the miseries of this world, and even a thousand deaths, to the misfortune of receiving thee unworthily. Thou art too merciful, too good to permit that I should commit that evil which I sincerely dread; therefore I firmly trust in thee, and now place my whole heart and soul in thy divine hands, that thou mayest thyself prepare the abode thou art so soon to enter. I desire that every moment, from this to the happy day of my communion, may be spent in the fervent exercise of all the virtues that should adorn thy sanctuary; particularly lively faith in this adorable mystery, firm hope, ardent love, sincere contrition, and an earnest desire to be united to thee. Give me, I conjure thee, light to discover my sins, and grace to detest and sincerely confess them; that the merits of thy precious blood being applied to my soul in the tribunal of penance, I may approach to thee, clothed with the wedding garment of innocence, and receive, in the holy communion, those graces necessary for persevering in thy service to the end of my life. *Amen.*

MEDITATIONS

FOR THE THREE DAYS BEFORE COMMUNION

First Day.

On the opposite Dispositions of Communicants.

The preparatory Acts for Meditation will be found in the course of this Work, as pointed out by the Index.

I. *Point.*—Consider seriously, that the adorable Eucharist is denominated by the Church, *a source of* *death to the wicked*,* because this bread of life, though the source and fountain of life itself, can as little strengthen those who are spiritually dead in mortal sin, as food could strengthen a dead body. Such souls, far from participating in the divine treasures contained in the holy Eucharist, defile themselves with the guilt of the most horrible of all sacrileges; they insult the Almighty himself—attack and profane the adorable humanity of Jesus Christ—they trample on the blood of the new covenant—and, to crown all their misfortunes, they, as the Apostle says, *eat and drink their own damnation.* Ponder well the import of those awful words;—consider, that like the Jews, who consented that the blood of Jesus should fall on them to their destruction, unworthy communicants ratify themselves the sentence of their condemnation —a sentence which they, as it were, write on their own hearts—a sentence, which begins to be in some measure executed, even in this life, for the justice of God often abandons the profaners of his adorable body to such obduracy and insensibility, that they at length sink into a species of spiritual lethargy:—after having braved the greatest of all dangers, they seem to fear no other, and they thoughtlessly run on from sin to sin, until at length the time for repentance and mercy is over. Trace these dreadful evils to their source, and you will find them all to originate in mortal sin, that sovereign evil, without which there would be no evil;—that great and only obstacle to the designs of Jesus in the institution of the adorable Eucharist—that fatal source of the sacrileges which have ever been committed against the most holy of all mysteries. Endeavour to conceive a lively horror of mortal sin—a sincere conviction that it is the greatest of all evils, the most dreadful of all misfortunes. If your heart be deeply impressed with these sentiments, they will prove your greatest security against

* Mors est malis.—*Lauda Sion*, Hymn for Corpus Christi.

incurring the guilt of sacrilege. Divine Jesus! penetrate my heart with so great a horror of sin, that I may dread nothing so much as becoming thy enemy by any mortal offence, and that I may tremble at the very idea of profaning thy most sacred body and blood.

II. *Point.*—Consider, secondly, that, next to the misfortune of unworthily communicating, there can be few states more dangerous, than that of persons who approach the adorable Eucharist with wilful tepidity, negligence, and indevotion. For this there are three solid reasons, which you should seriously consider. First, such communicants are deprived by their own faults of almost all the graces annexed to the holy Eucharist, and thus run an evident risk of drawing little, if any, profit from Communion. Secondly, they contract a fatal habit of approaching the sacrament of infinite love in a careless and lukewarm manner, and are thereby in imminent danger of soon committing sacrilege. Thirdly, nothing is more common than illusion on this important matter; for many, whose tepid and negligent dispositions appear to themselves nothing worse than venial sin, are really guilty, in the eyes of God, of that criminal indolence and sloth which is a grievous offence. In the same manner as sacrilegious communions proceed from a want of sufficient horror of mortal sin; so are fruitless, tepid communions, caused by the little care which Christians take to avoid venial sin. Instead of looking on a deliberate, though slight offence of God, as a real evil, and a great misfortune, they commit faults without number or remorse. Though they do not abandon at once the holy habit of approaching regularly the sacrament of our altars, yet they appear as careless about the correction of their faults, as if they never were to communicate;—they discharge their spiritual duties carelessly—and continue heaping one fault on another, until they lose all remorse for what they term only slight faults. Such persons evince their habitual sloth, dissipation, and tepidity, in preparing for Communion. A confession, which they intend should include all mortal sin, and a few vocal prayers, comprise the whole of their preparation for the most solemn of all duties. The God of all sanctity is then introduced into a soul defiled with innumerable stains. The God of infinite love enters a heart, which, as he himself declares, he rejects and abominates, because it is tepid, and neither hot nor cold. Such Communions, as may be expected, are fruitless, or rather they are too often fruitful in great evils, and are almost a certain road to sacrilege. O how much should they be dreaded!

III. *Point.*—Consider, thirdly, that if an unworthy Communion is the most dreadful of all misfortunes, and a tepid or negligent Communion the greatest of all dangers; so also is a worthy Communion the most precious and glorious advantage that a creature can enjoy. Next to the clear view and full possession of God in heaven, there can be no happiness so great as that of communicating. If our faith were lively, we should be so convinced of this truth, that the prospect of a communion would fill us with transports of joy:—we would long for the happy day which was to unite us to Jesus Christ, and be so completely occupied with the expectation of such a blessing, as to become almost insensible to all other enjoyments. To produce those sentiments in your heart, you need but reflect on a few of the advantages of a good Communion. Consider, that this most holy Sacrament increases and preserves grace, which is the life of the soul; it enlightens the mind with the brightest light, inflames the heart with the sacred fire of charity; it points out and makes us love our duties; it strengthens us to fulfil them; it moderates the violence of passion, and it penetrates the soul with such sweet and holy peace, as must be felt to be understood. To say all in one word, a worthy Communion unites us so intimately to God, and procures for us such an abundant infusion of his gifts and graces, as caused a father of the Church to say, that "a single Communion would suffice to make a saint." Consider these truths seriously. Reflect with holy transport on the glory and happiness within your reach. Convinced of the infinite excellence of the adorable Sacrament which you are preparing to receive, banish all other cares, that you may devoutly dispose yourself for that wonderful union with God, which was never granted to angels. But as this work is far beyond your power, beg earnestly of that God of love, whom you are about to receive, to give you such ardent desires of enjoying the happiness of worthy communion, as will urge you to remove every obstacle to so great a blessing. O my good God! if I really felt how delightful it is to be united to thee, how soon would I despise every other pleasure, and sigh after thee alone for whom alone I was created. Thou knowest that I desire at least to receive thee worthily; deign then to penetrate my soul with respect and love, that I may so fervently prepare for thy heavenly visit, as never to find death in the fountain of life.

SECOND DAY.

The Passion of our Lord Jesus Christ applied to the Holy Communion.

I. *Point.*—CONSIDER, first, that when Jesus Christ instituted at his last Supper the adorable Sacrament of his Body and Blood, he commanded his Apostles, and in their persons all creatures, to call to mind his Passion and Death as often as they communicated. Such a command ought not to have been necessary;—gratitude for the benefit of redemption—love for the God who died for us—compassion for his excessive sufferings—contrition for the share we had in occasioning them, are all motives which should make the sufferings of Christ a subject familiar to our thoughts, and impress on the mind and heart of every

Christian a lively image of Jesus crucified. But our divine Redeemer well knew the frailty and ingratitude of man; he knew, that the greater number would seldom, if ever, call to mind his sufferings, and therefore he left them not only a precious and striking memorial of his Passion in the holy Eucharist, but also a command to think on him, on his infinite love and suffering, in receiving his adorable Body. *Do this in remembrance of me.* Luke xxii. 19. Endeavour now to comply most fervently with this command of your divine Redeemer. Place yourself in spirit at the foot of the cross, and consider how much it cost your Redeemer to purchase for you the happiness of communicating. Far from being admitted to the honour and advantage of sacramental union with God, you would have been condemned to eternal separation from him, if Jesus had not died to save you. Your approaching happiness is then the purchase of your Redeemer's sufferings—the adorable body you are going to receive as your spiritual food, is the same which was exposed to insult, contempt, and misery, during three and thirty years; scourged at a pillar, crowned with thorns, and at length ignominiously nailed to the cross. Ah! if those excessive torments had made a deep impression on our hearts, how differently should we feel disposed in approaching that adorable sacrament, wherein the memory of his passion is renewed! Beg of Jesus himself, with the greatest earnestness, to give you the dispositions he requires. O my crucified Saviour! thou didst suffer such torments for my salvation, as would separately have caused thy death, if a miracle did not preserve thy life to endure still more. Why have I been so ungrateful as to forget all thou hast done for my sinful soul? Vouchsafe, O divine Jesus! to enter my heart, notwithstanding its unworthiness; that I may not only learn to die to myself, by reflecting on thy sufferings, but also live to thee, by the efficacy of thy adorable body.

II. *Point.*—Consider your divine Saviour prostrate on the earth, in the Garden of Gethsemani, fainting with grief, and exhausted with a bloody sweat, occasioned by excessive interior anguish, at the view of the sins of all mankind; particularly the ingratitude of those who are loaded with his mercies—the pride and vanity of those who are early instructed in the divine truths of his holy gospel—the tepidity, sloth, and indifference of those from whom he has a right to expect the most ardent love;—in a word, the foresight he had of the abuse of his graces, and the little fruit that many, even among his most favoured servants, would draw from his sacred passion and death. This was truly the chalice which Jesus dreaded to drink, and which made his sacred heart sorrowful even unto death, as we may easily conceive by our own experience, since we feel that an unkind, ungrateful action of a friend, would grieve us more than many injuries heaped on us by an enemy. Consider now, that among all the benefits Jesus Christ bestowed on the world, none is so precious, or so peculiarly the fruit of his sacred passion, as the holy Eucharist; consequently, those who draw little or no profit from that fountain of grace, and who feel little love, gratitude, and respect for so astonishing a mark of God's tenderness, are certainly those who should reproach themselves with having contributed most to the interior sufferings of Jesus Christ. Reflect seriously on yourself, and beg of God to enlighten your mind, that you may see whether you be not of this number. You cannot doubt of your being among those whom he has most loved and favoured;—early instruction, particular graces, spiritual assistance, and a thousand other marks of his tenderness, prove to you that Jesus thought of you in the height of his sufferings, and destined for you a particular share in the fruits and merits of his sacred passion. What use have you made of those special blessings? Have you been more grateful, from having been more favoured? Has the knowledge of your duty caused you to discharge it better? What profit have you drawn from your communions? Where are the faults you have corrected, or the virtues you have acquired, after so many times receiving the Almighty himself? Ask your own conscience these questions; it is better you should do so now, than defer so necessary an examination to that tribunal of justice where we must all appear, to account for that precious blood, which our sins and his infinite love caused Jesus to shed in the course of his sacred Passion.

III. *Point.*—Consider, seriously, that after Jesus had been in an agony three hours; after he had proved the efficacy of his sacred Blood, by the wonderful conversion of a great criminal, and expressed his ardent thirst for the conversion of all men, he expired. Then the earth shook to its centre; from which you should learn how much cause sinners have to dread the rigorous justice of God, who did not spare his only begotten Son. The rocks were rent, to show you that your heart should be broken with sorrow at the recollection of your Redeemer's sufferings, even though it were as cold and as hard as marble. The opening of the sepulchres, and resurrection of the dead, admonish you, that if you would participate in the fruit of our Redeemer's Passion and Death by a worthy Communion, you must open the sepulchre of your conscience, and cast out all the dead works of iniquity by a candid and contrite confession. Reflect particularly, that the sepulchre in which Jesus would have his most precious body laid, was new, no person having been laid there before; (*St. John* xix.) therefore, the soul which prepares to become the repository of the same precious body, should be renovated by contrition, and a firm resolution of leading a new life, and banish all that could disturb the reign of Jesus Christ in her heart. Are these your dispositions? Have the foregoing reflections animated you to renounce all such vain pleasures as may unfortunately lead you to crucify again the Son of God?—This is the moment to form those salutary resolutions, if you have hitherto neglected doing so. Penetrated with that holy fear of the judgments of God, and that firm confidence in his mercy, which the sufferings of Christ should naturally inspire, examine your heart at the foot of the cross, and see all that so great an example demands from you. Do not the excessive torments of Jesus reproach you with immortification and self-seeking? Does not the hard bed of the cross condemn your attachment to your own ease, and your horror of the least inconvenience? Can you reflect on such divine patience, meekness, and charity, without detesting your fretful, uncharitable conduct towards your fellow-creatures, your irritable and untractable temper? The silence of Jesus is a miracle of meekness—have you imitated it, when undeservedly or even justly reproved? The first words of our divine Redeemer on the cross, are a prayer for his executioners—is it thus you return good for evil; or rather, are you not perhaps actually criminal in the eyes of God, by anger, contempt, coolness, or want of charity towards your neighbour? Such is the examination you should make at the foot of the cross; for certain it is, that your crucified Lord is the model on which you will finally be judged. The day will come when a crucifix for the last time will be presented to you. To those who have endeavoured to avoid sin, which crucified their Lord, and to imitate the virtues which the cross teaches, the sight of that affecting object in the last awful ceremony, will be a source of the greatest consolation and confidence. To some, it cannot be otherwise than an anticipated condemnation. It is in your power now to choose either: perhaps on the resolutions which you make in this very meditation, and the fruits of amendment you draw from it, depends your eternal salvation. Resolve, then, generously to make a friend of Him, who will one day be your judge, and henceforward never to look on a crucifix without thinking of your obligation to imitate the virtues of your crucified Lord. O my merciful Redeemer! prostrate in spirit at the foot of thy cross, I thank thee for all thou hast done and suffered for my salvation. I beg of thee, by the efficacy of thy precious blood, to soften the obduracy of my heart, to enlighten my mind, and to strengthen my will, that I may faithfully accomplish all that thou requirest.

THIRD DAY.

On the chief Virtues which should adorn a Communicant.

I. *Point.*—Consider that the holy Eucharist is called a mystery of faith, and that faith is perhaps the most necessary virtue for a good Communion; because without faith, we should discover nothing more than ordinary food in the bread of life. In this sacred mystery all is obscure, beyond the reach of our understanding, and imperceptible to our senses;—we see nothing, feel nothing, taste nothing but common bread—we hear nothing extraordinary, so that it is the voice and light of faith alone, which, as the Church says, *supplies the defect of the senses,** and firmly persuades us that the adorable Eucharist is not bread, though it appears so to us, but the living, glorious, immortal body of Jesus Christ. Ah! how grateful should you be for that precious gift of faith, by which you are enabled to penetrate the veils that conceal the Almighty from our view! With what astonishment and delight should you be penetrated now that faith assures you that your God, your

* Præstet fides supplementum
Sensuum defectui.
Pange lingua, or Hymn for Benediction

Creator, will so soon be your guest! With what profound humility, reverence, and awe, should you await the visit of that divine Being who drew the world out of nothing by his infinite power, who rules it by his wisdom, and who could in an instant destroy it by one act of his will! He it is, whom I am going to receive: yes, I firmly believe it, because Jesus Christ, the infallible truth, has said, *this is my body*. But has my faith all the requisites for enabling me to make a good and fervent Communion? Beside being firm, is it lively, active, supported by good works; or rather, does it bear any resemblance to that fruitless and dead faith, of which the Apostle speaks—to the faith of many nominal Christians, whose belief and conduct are in direct opposition? O Lord! from thee I received my faith, even before I was capable of feeling the value of that precious gift: to thee I must now owe its increase: give it, I beseech thee, all the animation and efficacy thou requirest.

II. *Point.*—Consider that there is no sacrament so calculated to excite the most tender and unbounded confidence in God as the holy Eucharist. It is the precious pledge of eternal life; the greatest of God's gifts; therefore He, who is bountiful enough to give such a blessing, cannot refuse any favour, since all others are less than that which is offered to us in one Communion. O consolatory thought! O solid foundation for hope and confidence! To-morrow I shall receive my God; to-morrow that compassionate Saviour will visit me, whose mortal life was a series of mercies—who never refused to pardon a repentant sinner—who received all who approached his sacred person—who deigned, with his own divine hands, to touch and heal the lepers themselves, and to whom no one was ever known to apply in vain. He is more anxious to grant me favours, than I could be to receive them. Ah! if the poor of this world could become rich, by only relying with confidence on the liberality of a powerful benefactor—if the sick had a certainty of receiving health, by resigning themselves to the care of a physician—if the afflicted could be consoled by confiding in a friend, who would be found indigent, weak, or dejected, throughout the world? But the liberality or kindness of creatures is always limited and insufficient, whereas that of the Almighty has no bounds, except those limits which we ourselves too often put to it by distrust. He will have mercy on us *according to our hope* in him, as the prophet says. O my God! how true it is, that *the man is blessed who hopes in thee;* since that soul cannot want any thing, who confidently expects all from thee. O! since I am going to receive the greatest gift thou canst bestow, why should I not firmly trust that thou wilt strengthen my weakness, inflame my insensibility, and give me, by this Communion, the grace to do all that is necessary for obtaining the effect of thy promises, since hope without good works is no better than presumption. Yes, my God, I hope for all this, and hoping in thee, I can never be confounded.

III. *Point.*—Consider why did Jesus Christ resolve to remain on our altars to the end of time, in a state of degradation and obscurity? Because he loves you too much, to leave you an orphan. Why does he conceal his adorable majesty, his divinity, and even his humanity, in this sacrament? It is, as St. Bernard says, "that the excess of his love alone may appear, and that the splendour of his glory may not deter you from approaching him with confidence." Why will this divine victim of love descend from heaven to-morrow, and renew the oblation of himself on our altars? To give you in his precious body and blood the most amazing proof of his tenderness, and to afford you by his actual presence a favourable opportunity of asking and receiving whatever you desire, *that your joy may be complete.* All this is so certain, that you may truly say with the Apostle, *He has loved me, and delivered himself for me*

Were I alone to be redeemed, he would have died for my sake; and were I alone to communicate, he would descend from heaven to become my nourishment. O infinite love! O mystery of charity! how little art thou understood by those who are the objects of thy tenderness! how little impression has the infinite love of God made on the hearts of his creatures! Consider seriously, whether you be not amongst the number. Are you not perhaps at this moment unmoved by the love Jesus manifests in choosing you to become his temple? Search into the cause of your insensibility—is it not your neglect of that serious meditation on the benefits of God, in which, as the Prophet says, *the fire of charity is enkindled?* Are not your affections, which should belong to God, thrown away on creatures, which are the work of his hands? If so, it is not surprising that you are a stranger to that ardent love which animated the saints, and enabled them to do so much for the divine honour. Beg of that God of love who came to *cast fire upon earth*, to give you that sincere, generous, ardent love, which you cannot have without his assistance. O adorable Benefactor of my soul! I now feel that I was made to love thee, and that my heart can never find true rest but in thee. "O eternal Beauty! too late have I known thee! O infinite goodness! too late have I loved thee." Ah! my good God! thou didst form my heart, thou alone canst inflame its affections. I beg of thee, by all the love thou hast ever felt for man; and in particular, by that infinite charity which invites me to approach thy altars, that thou wouldst give me as the fruit of this meditation, the most lively and ardent charity. I resolve most seriously, to endeavour on my part to obtain that most precious gift, by making henceforward frequent acts of thy love—by performing all my actions through a motive of love—by detesting and avoiding, for thy love, all that displeases thee. Give efficacy, O Lord! to these resolutions, for on thee alone I depend; thou art the God in whom I firmly believe; thou art the foundation of my hope, and the only worthy object of my love.

Immediate Preparation for Communion.

FROM the evening before the day on which you intend to communicate, you should retire from all that could distract your mind; and as far as your situation and duty permit, observe more than ordinary silence and recollection.

Endeavour to excite the fervour of devotion by frequent aspirations; such as, O divine Lord, prepare me to receive thee. Come, Lord, and do not delay. *As the hart panteth after the fountains of water, so my soul panteth after thee, O my God.* Ps. xii. 1.

Immediately on your awaking in the morning, call to mind the happiness you expect; and to animate your fervour, imagine your Angel Guardian says to you, as an Angel formerly did to the Prophet Elias, *arise* and *eat*, 3 Kings xix. 5. When you are dressing, think with holy fear of that man who dared to present himself at the marriage feast without a nuptial garment. Beg of God, as you are accustomed to do every morning, but with more than ordinary fervour, not only to restore to you the garment of innocence which you lost, but also to clothe you with the wedding-robe of charity, that you may be less unworthy to appear before his divine Majesty. When you have entered the chapel, which you should take care to do at least half an hour before the holy sacrifice commences, imagine that your heavenly Father comes out to meet you, as the Gospel represents the father of the prodigal child to have done; and endeavour to conceive the same sentiments of humility, contrition, and confidence, which filled the breast of that penitent. Then occupy yourself until Mass begins, either in praying mentally, without any set form of words, or in repeating, rather with your heart than with your lips the following acts.

Prayers before Communion.

An offering of the holy Communion.

O divine Lord! I offer thee the communion I am about to make, in union with the superabundant merits of Jesus Christ thy beloved Son, and the infinite love of his adorable heart. In union with the merits of the blessed Virgin, and the ardent love of her sacred heart; in union with the merits and love of those happy souls who enjoy thy glorious vision in heaven, and of the just who still live upon earth. O my God! I earnestly desire to approach to thee in this adorable sacrament, with that lively faith, that profound humility, that tender confidence, that pure conscience and ardent love, with which so many holy souls are inflamed, in partaking of this sacred banquet; accept at least my desire, and supply by thy mercy all my deficiencies. I offer my Communion, and the adorable Sacrifice at which I am going to assist, to render thee the honour and glory which are due to thy infinite Majesty; to satisfy thy justice, which I have irritated by my sins; to thank thee for the innumerable benefits which I have received from thy liberality, and to obtain from thy infinite mercy the graces which are necessary for me, particularly the grace to subdue my predominant passion, and to acquire the virtue in which I am most deficient, but especially the grace of a happy death.

I likewise offer my Communion, O merciful Father! in memory of the Passion and Death of thy dear Son, my divine Redeemer, to enter into his views and designs, to accomplish his most holy will, to love him with more ardour and perfection; to participate in the merits of his labours and sufferings; to acquire his spirit; to imitate his virtues; to model my life on his; and to make to his adorable heart a public reparation for all the sacrilegious communions, irreverences, and profanations, which are committed against him in this august sacrament of his love. I offer it, O God of unbounded liberality! to thank thee for all the graces thou hast bestowed on mankind, particularly for all those thou hast conferred on thy blessed Mother, as likewise on the Angels and the Saints, especially on my Angel Guardian and holy Patron. I offer it likewise for the triumph of our holy religion the exaltation of the Catholic Church, the conversion of infidels, heretics, schismatics, and all those who are in the unhappy state of mortal sin; also for the necessities of my relatives, friends, associates, benefactors, and enemies; for the perseverance of the just, the comfort of the afflicted, and the deliverance of the suffering souls in purgatory. In a word, for all those for whom I am obliged to pray; and I desire to enter into all the intentions requisite for gaining the indulgences which are held forth by the Church to worthy communicants.

An Act of Faith.

THOU hast declared, O eternal Truth! that thou art really present under these lowly elements, which present nothing more to my senses than mere material bread! I believe it most firmly, and require no other assurance than thy own divine words. Yes, I openly confess that it is thou thyself I am going to receive; thou who, born for my sake in a stable, wert pleased to die for me on a cross; and who, glorious in heaven, art still concealed under these mysterious veils. I do not desire to behold thee; for were I to touch thy wounds, and, like St. Thomas, examine thy sacred side, I could not exclaim with more confidence than I now do, thou art *my Lord and my God*, John xx. 28 Wert thou to speak to me from this very tabernacle, thy voice would affect me less than that which resounds in thy gospel: though my senses tell me the contrary, I submit them entirely to the obedience of faith; and were I to die a thousand deaths in testimony of this truth, I remain immovable in this declaration: *Thou art really a God hidden, a God Saviour* Isa. xx. *I believe, Lord; help thou my unbelief* Mark ix. 23.

An Act of Fear.

PERHAPS, O Lord! I am so unfortunate as to be guilty of some hidden sins, which may be an obstacle to the graces thou desirest to bestow on me? Perhaps, like Judas, I may give thee the kiss of peace to-day, and to-morrow betray thee? Instead of coming to me as to a faithful disciple, perhaps thou approachest me with horror and indignation, as to a concealed enemy? How can I answer for the exactness of my confession, the fervour of my contrition, or the sincerity of my resolutions? Is it not custom, or human respect, that brings me at present to the foot of thy altar? In renouncing my faults, have I not spared some favourite though secret passion? Like thy disciples, with the most heartfelt anguish, I ask thee, "Is it I, O Lord?" But Judas, who was to perpetrate the most abominable treachery, proposed the same question. Is not my anxiety, as his was, only false and apparent? I am terrified, O my God, at the thought, and it is to thyself I have recourse, to preserve me from so shocking a profanation. Is it I, O Lord, is it I who will be guilty of sacrilege? No, thou wilt never permit it; for thou seest that I would not willingly incur this guilt, and that there is nothing I dread more than so great a misfortune. After having been as diligent as I could, I will now rest entirely on thy infinite mercy. *Depart from me, O Lord, because I am a sinful creature*, Luke v. *Have courage child, thy sins are forgiven thee*, Matt. ix.

An Act of Contrition.

AH, my God! I am not so happy as to possess an innocent and pure heart: this thou alone canst create it must be the work of thy all-powerful grace. Alas

I have no trace of that precious innocence which makes some happy souls so acceptable in thy sight, but at least I hope that my heart is truly contrite and humble, and as such that thou wilt not despise it, nor reject the tender of its affections. O my God! I sovereignly detest my sins, because they are displeasing to thy divine Majesty; they are always in my sight, and the bitterness of my regret serves as a continual punishment for my rebellion against thy holy law. Look, O Lord! on the face of thy Christ, thy only beloved Son, in whom thou art well pleased; remember the labours of his penitential life, the bitterness of his sacred passion, the anguish of his ignominious death. I offer thee his infinite and superabundant merits, that thou mayest mercifully pardon my crimes, and take not vengeance of my manifold offences. Ah! divine Jesus! why cannot I participate in that mortal anguish which overwhelmed thy soul in the Garden of Olives, when thou didst present thyself to thy Eternal Father as a victim of atonement to his offended justice? I unite my feeble sorrow to thine, and firmly resolve, with thy divine assistance, to do every thing in my power to prevent future relapses, and to suffer every affliction in expiation of my former transgressions. Remove from me, O Lord, all dangerous occasions of sin, and assist me with thy powerful grace; should my passions at any time rebel against thy holy law, shorten my days if necessary, and prevent by my death the only evil I dread, that of offending thee mortally. But, I do not merely detest the grievous offences of my sinful life, I abhor every thing that could have displeased thee in the slightest degree, or that could have impeded the course of thy grace; for thou art infinitely deserving of all my love, and of the utmost fidelity in thy service. I hope thou hast already cleansed my soul from the stain of sin in the sacrament of penance, but I desire to become still purer in thy sight; vouchsafe then to *wash me yet more from my iniquity, and cleanse me from my sin. Create a clean heart in me, O God and renew a right spirit within my bowels*, Ps. l.

An Act of Hope.

Thou comest to me, O my divine Redeemer! thou seekest to become my guest, and to abide in the inmost recesses of my soul. What may I not expect from thy excessive goodness and unbounded liberality? I present myself before thee with all the confidence which thy tenderness inspires. I come on thy gracious invitation, and confidently hope that thou wilt enlighten, comfort, and strengthen me; for art thou not, O divine Lord! the master of my heart? and when shall that heart be more absolutely under the influence of thy grace, than when thou shalt have taken possession of it by thy sacramental presence?

An Act of Humility.

Who am I, O God of glory and majesty! who am I, that thou shouldst deign even to look on my unworthiness? Whence am I honoured with this unspeakable favour, that my Lord and my God should come in person to visit me? How shall I, a sinner, a worm of the earth, a mere contemptible nothing, venture to approach the God of all sanctity? How shall I presume to eat the bread of angels? Ah, Lord! I do not deserve this mark of thy predilection, this additional proof of thy tenderness and love. The consideration of thy exalted greatness and my profound misery, penetrates me with awe and confusion. I have not words to express the sentiments of my heart. With the utmost sincerity, I can only declare the extent of my unworthiness, and admire that infinite goodness which induces thee to stoop to the lowest and basest of thy creatures. O compassionate Lord! thou knowest all my wants, and thou art desirous to relieve them: for this purpose thou hast expressly invited me to approach thy altar, and to become a guest at thy sacred table. Behold, I come on thy invitation; I present myself before thee with all my necessities and miseries, acknowledging that I am but dust and ashes, and infinitely unworthy that thou shouldst enter under my roof. *Whence is this to me?* Luke xi. *What is man,* O Lord, *that thou art mindful of him, or the son of man that thou shouldst visit him?* Ps. viii

An Act of Desire.

O MY God, my joy, my life, my treasure! hasten the moment which my heart desires. Come, O amiable Jesus! come and delay no longer. Come, to purify, sanctify, and inflame my soul. When shall I have the happiness to be truly thine? When, O infinite Charity! shall I live only by thee and for thee? Come, and work this miracle of mercy, in giving thyself wholly and entirely to thy unworthy creature. O my sovereign Beatitude! disengage from this moment my heart from the slavery of its passions and vices; adorn it with thy virtues, and extinguish in it every other desire but that of loving and pleasing thy divine Majesty. Let others sigh after the false enjoyments of this life; for my part, nothing, without thee, in heaven or on earth, shall ever content the desires which thou thyself hast excited; for what have I in heaven, and besides thee, what do I desire on earth? Let me see thee, love thee, seek thee alone, O God of my heart, my consolation, my life, my happiness, and my all!

An Act of Love.

O DIVINE JESUS! the God of my heart and the life of my soul! as the hart pants after the fountains of water, so does my soul pant after thee, the fountain of life, and the ocean of all good. I am overjoyed at the happy tidings, that I am to go into the house of the Lord; or rather, that our Lord is to come and take up his abode under my roof. O happy moments! when shall I be admitted to the embraces of the living God? O! come, divine Jesus! and take full possession of my heart for ever. I offer it to thee without reserve, and I desire to consecrate it to thee eternally. I love thee with my whole heart and soul, at least I desire to love thee sovereignly and entirely: nothing less than infinite love could induce thee to visit thy unworthy creature. O! teach me to make a suitable return of love, and to serve thee faithfully during the remainder of my life.

A METHOD OF HEARING MASS

BEFORE COMMUNION.

From the Beginning of Mass to the Gloria in ex celsis.

To hear Mass with fruit, and to obtain from that adorable Sacrifice abundant treasures of grace, there is no method more efficacious than to unite ourselves with Jesus Christ, who is at once our Priest, Mediator, and Victim. Separated from him, we are nothing; but even in the eyes of God himself we are truly great by and with his beloved Son. United thus with Jesus Christ, covered as it were with his merits, present yourself before the throne of mercy, saying:

Divine Jesus! Mediator of the New Testament! who didst ascend *into heaven, to appear in the presence of God for us*, (Heb. ix. 24.) yet daily descendest on our altars, to renew that sacrifice by which we were all redeemed, mercifully penetrate my heart with a just sense of the happiness and the advantage of assisting at a sacrifice, by which I can abundantly satisfy the justice of God, honour his divine Majesty, acknowledge his infinite mercies, and obtain the graces necessary for serving him on earth and enjoying him in heaven. Permit me, O divine Jesus! to ascend this new Calvary with thee, that my whole soul may do homage to the greatness of thy majesty; that my heart, with all its affections, may acknowledge thy infinite love; that my memory may dwell on the admirable mysteries here renewed; and that the sacrifice of my whole being may accompany that which thou art about to offer. Alas! I am unworthy to join with thy minister in adoring thee; I can neither feel the extent of thy blessings, nor acknowledge them as I ardently desire to do; but, O Lord! be thou with me, that by thee, and with thee, I may worthily assist at these tremendous mysteries

From the Gloria in excelsis *to the* Epistle.

At the *Gloria in excelsis* you may devoutly join in the prayer of the Church, and at the *Dominus vobiscum* and following prayers, imagine you behold Jesus Christ himself turning, as he did to Magdalen, with the consolatory assurance of your sins having been remitted.

O Saviour of my soul! how sweet is the hope, that thou hast absolved me from my transgressions; that thy sacred blood has washed them away; and that thou art about to seal my pardon by the most precious gift thou canst possibly bestow. O divine Lord! let this encouraging hope be realized; say to my soul, that thou art her salvation. With the fervent penitent of the gospel, I cast myself at thy sacred feet; let me hear with her, from thy own adorable lips, the consolatory sentence of peace and mercy; let me experience with her, the conviction that thou hast accepted my repentance, and granted me pardon. Alas! I well know that I have neither her humility nor her contrition, her fervour nor her love to offer; but, O my God! I venture to say, that my hopes are established on still surer grounds than would be those virtues, were I happy enough to possess them. If many sins were pardoned her, because *she* loved thee much, still greater crimes will be remitted to me, because *thou* hast infinitely loved me, a wretched creature. O adorable Jesus! in thy love and mercy I firmly trust; deign then to do for me what is altogether above my strength and capacity; purify my soul, and prepare it for the reception of thy life-giving sacrament.

At the Epistle *and* Gospel.

I BELIEVE, O my God! every article proposed by the holy Catholic Church to my belief; and through thy grace I am disposed to die, rather than relinquish the precious gift of faith, which elevates me to the adoption of the Sons of God, and makes me heir and joint-heir with Jesus Christ. *Rom.* viii. 15, 17. I believe; O divine Lord! penetrate my heart and soul with the entire import of these short but comprehensive words, and let them produce one of those prodigies of grace and conversion, which so often followed from similar confessions. I believe all thou hast revealed, without exception or reserve; for *thou hast the words of eternal life*, and thou art likewise *the way* and *the truth*. St. John xix. 6. On thy unerring word I also most firmly believe that thou art really present in the august sacrament of which I am about to participate. O what miracles are contained in this sacred and ever adorable mystery! Incomprehensible as they are, I believe them all; I adore thy omnipotence, which is a sufficient pledge of their possibility; and thy boundless love proves to me, in an endearing manner, that they are real. Were my faith as animated as I hope it is sincere, my heart would be inflamed at the near approach of its heavenly guest, and every movement of my body and soul would be a transport of gratitude and ardent love. Come, then, O Lord! thou art the God in whom I firmly believe. Come, for thou art the support and term of my hope, and thou art, by excellence, the adorable object of my most fervent love. Come, enliven and increase in my soul the divine virtues infused therein on my admission into the bosom of thy Church. Come, and purify my baptismal robe, that I may present myself before thee with a nuptial garment, and may not deserve to be excluded from the marriage feast.

At the Offertory.

While the minister of God disposes the bread and wine for the sacrifice, dispose your heart for participating in its abundant fruits.

Receive, O Lord, this spotless host, which thy minister offers thee in the name of thy Church. Receive, eternal Majesty! this oblation of bread and wine, which will soon become the body and blood of Jesus Christ, who, to render thee in the name of weak mortals the adoration thou meritest, vouchsafed to clothe himself with our miseries—to become susceptible of death, and to immolate himself daily on our altars as the precious victim of our salvation. O omnipotent Lord! behold me at thy feet loaded with miseries, and charged with innumerable debts, which would overwhelm me, were I not provided by thyself with a treasure of infinite value to acknowledge thy mercies, to satisfy thy justice, and to obtain for myself and others the graces thou desirest to bestow. Animated with the most lively confidence in the merits of my Redeemer, I offer thee once more his sufferings and death; and I make this offering for the great ends for which he instituted this adorable mystery.—I offer thee this sacred Victim to adore thee as my God, to testify my love for thee, my sovereign Benefactor! to thank thee for the blessings thou hast bestowed on all mankind; to implore thy mercy on behalf of all those in a dreadful state of mortal sin, and to obtain the deliverance of the suffering souls in purgatory To this offering I unite an unreserved oblation of my whole being, and I desire to do so with the most generous and ardent love. I conjure thee, O my God! by the perfect oblation of my divine Saviour on the altar of the cross, to pardon my past ingratitude, and to grant me the inestimable grace of preservation from all mortal sin. But, O my sovereign Benefactor! how shall I thank thee for the precious gift of thy body and blood which thus enables me to satisfy my obligation! This gift, which the homage of angels and men would be insufficient to acknowledge, can only be repaid by itself. I then offer thee my Redeemer himself, as a sacrifice of praise, and *pay my vows to thee*, (Ps. cxv. 18.) in union with him in whom from all eternity thou wert well pleased.

At the Preface.

During the prayer which serves as a preliminary to the Canon, or main action of the sacrifice, endeavour to animate your devotion, and prepare with great fervour to adore your Redeemer when he shall have descended on the altar.

Permit not, O Lord! that my mind should wander from the consideration of the adorable mysteries now celebrating on this altar. Enlighten my understanding, inflame and animate every affection of my heart, that I may be attentive to these miracles of mercy and love. O give me to understand *the breadth, and length, and height, and depth* (Ephes. iii. 18.) of that love which will soon veil thy glories under the humiliating forms of bread and wine! O that my heart were penetrated with ardent love, that I might be enabled to acknowledge less unworthily thy infinite greatness and boundless mercies. Prostrate in spirit before that throne of glory where the cherubim and seraphim, with all the heavenly host, adore thy awful Majesty, I conjure thee to receive my homage, in union with the transports of admiration and love with which they incessantly proclaim that thou art Holy, Holy, Holy, and that *the Lamb which was slain is worthy to receive power, and divinity, and wisdom, and strength, and honour, and glory, and benediction*, for ever and ever. Amen. Apoc v 12.

From the Canon *to the* Elevation.

Ah! my God, why do I not sigh for thy coming on this altar, with as much ardour as did the ancient patriarchs and prophets; with as much pure desire as thy blessed Mother, the first and most perfect adorer of thy sacred humanity. I offer thee my heart, soul, mind, strength, desires, and affections, in union with the admirable dispositions of thy saints; but particularly in union with the love and devotion of that incomparable Virgin, in whose pure soul, prepared by thy divine spirit, and adorned with the treasures of thy grace, thou didst delight to dwell. I offer thee, to atone for my coldness and tepidity, her sacred heart, with all the love with which it ever was, and for all eternity will be animated. I offer thee her heavenly contemplations, her purity, profound humility, and sufferings at the foot of the cross; beseeching thee, through her intercession, to pardon the iniquities of her unworthy servant.

And thou, O most sacred Virgin! obtain for me a share in the holy dispositions that adorned thy soul from the moment of thy immaculate conception; since I am also destined for the residence and sanctuary of a God. O assured refuge of sinners! I address thee with the most lively confidence, beseeching thee to obtain that I may be worthily replenished with him who was born of thee—with him who is *the desire and expectation of all nations.*

At the Consecration.

The moments which immediately precede the descent of our divine Lord on our altars, and the entrance of the same God into our hearts, are certainly those in which our souls should be penetrated with the most lively sentiments of humility, adoration, love and gratitude.

Therefore, while all heaven attends in admiration and reverential awe to the adorable mysteries now celebrating on earth, do you profoundly humble yourself before God, and with lively faith, animated hope, and ardent love, lay all your miseries and sins on the altar; that being washed away by the tide of that precious blood which will soon flow thereon, they may be no obstacle to the grace of a worthy communion.

O Jesus! *brightness of eternal light, unspotted mirror of God's Majesty!* (Wisd. vii. 26.) my sovereign Life, and only Good! thou art He whom I have so long, so ardently desired! He whom I acknowledge for *my Lord and my God,* and who alone art worthy of the homage and adoration of men and angels. O Monarch of heaven and earth! mighty in word and work! Luke xxiv. 19. *Verily thou art a hidden God, the God of Israel, the Saviour;* (Isa. xlv. 15.) but the shades which conceal thy majesty are those of the tenderest love.

O divine Jesus! thou art now glorified by the homages of numberless angels who invisibly assist at these sacred mysteries. O how should their adorations and love confound and humble me, since it is not for them, but for me, that thou art hidden and degraded on the altar! O holy angels! blessed spirits! love and adore the Almighty for me, and redouble your ardours to supply for my insufficiency.

From the Elevation *to the* Pater noster.

Now that your Saviour himself is present on the altar, endeavour to profit of so favourable an opportunity for exposing all your wants and miseries to him, who desires nothing more ardently than to remedy them.

O ADORABLE Jesus! the happy moment is fast approaching, when that sacred body which was immolated on the cross will abide in my heart, and that precious blood, which was shed with so much anguish for my ransom, will be really and truly applied as a sovereign remedy to my soul. My God! is it possible that thou, whom the heavens cannot contain, will confine thy greatness within the narrow limits of my heart; that thou, before whom the angels themselves are not pure, will unite thyself to a soul like mine, disfigured and defiled with innumerable crimes! O Lord, with the most sincere conviction of my wretchedness, I protest with the centurion, that I am *not worthy thou shouldst enter under my roof.* St. Matt. viii. 8. Shall I then say with St. Peter: *Depart from me, O Lord, for I am a sinful creature?* St. Luke v. 8 Shall I depart from this sanctuary, which I am unworthy to enter, and relinquish that happiness, for which my soul sighs, but which I shall never merit! Ah! no, my divine Saviour! I will not leave thee for to whom should I go, but to thee? Hast thou not invited *all that labour and are heavy laden* (St. Matt. ix. 28.) to approach thee? Therefore, notwithstanding the miseries of my soul, I come, perfectly convinced that *if thou wilt, thou canst make me clean.* St. Matt. viii. 2. I am weak, but thou wilt be my sovereign strength; I am poor, but thou wilt adorn my soul with the riches of thy grace: thou wilt destroy my pride, by the force of thy profound humiliations in the centre of my soul! thou wilt warm my tepidity, by the fire which thou camest on earth to enkindle; (St. Luke xii. 49.) thou wilt communicate to me thy divinity itself, that I may not live, but that thou mayest live in me. Come, then, O my God! *the desire of the everlasting hills,* (Gen. ix. 26.) the friend of sinners, the comfort of the afflicted, *the hope of all the ends of the earth,* (Ps. lxiv. 6.) come into my house, and let salvation enter with thee; (St. Luke xix. 9.) come, that my soul, united with thee, may magnify its Lord, and my spirit rejoice in God, my Saviour. *Ibid.* i. 46, 47.

From the Pater noster *to the* Agnus Dei.

At the *Pater noster* you should devoutly repeat that sacred prayer, in which all others are contained, and rejoice in reflecting, that you are authorized by Christ himself to address the Almighty as your Father. Trusting, therefore, in the tenderness of his paternal heart, beg of him to nourish you this day with the true bread of his children.

O FATHER of my soul, who residest in the highest heavens, and yet attendest to the wants of thy children on earth, behold thy prodigal but repentant child, who returns to thee penetrated with regret for ever having sought to shake off that yoke, which thou thyself hast pronounced to be *sweet* and *light.* St. Matt. xi. 30. Pardon me, O my divine Benefactor! for thou knowest the clay of which I am formed; thou rememberest that I am but dust. Ps. c. 11, 14. Forget my criminal abuse of thy mercies, for the sake of Him in whose name I dare to address thee as my Father, my Friend, and only happiness. O give me thy divine spirit, that spirit of love and adoption, which will cause me to have recourse to thee in all my necessities. Give me a docile, obedient, and submissive heart, that thy supremely just and adorable will may be the rule of all my actions. But above all, O divine Lord! give me *the bread of life*, the food of immortality; give me thy divine Son! give me him in whom thou wert always well pleased, (St. Matt. iii. 17.) that being instructed by *thy wisdom* and *thy word*, I may never deviate from the respect and love due from a child to the best and most indulgent of fathers.

From the Agnus Dei *to the* Communion.

The interval between the *Agnus Dei* and the time for communicating, should be spent in fervent acts of confidence and love, to enliven your hope in Him who comes to take away your offences

LAMB of God, who takest away the sins of the world! let me not be excluded from a share in thy universal mercies. Cleanse and purify my soul; adorn it, I entreat thee, with those virtues which will render me less unworthy of participating in the food of angels.

O adorable Jesus! I am, it is true, wretched and unworthy; but hast thou not denominated thyself the *Father of the poor*; and shall not that endearing title encourage me to recur to thee, as to my Father, and the best of friends? Yes, my God, I will go to thee, for thou well knowest, that had I the heavens and the earth at my disposal, I would sacrifice all, rather than forego the happiness I am now going to enjoy. *What have I in heaven, and beside thee what do I desire upon earth? Thou art the God of my heart, and the God that is my portion for ever.* Ps. lxxii. 25, 26.

O amiable Virgin! thou who art styled by excellence *Blessed among women*, show thyself now my tender mother and powerful advocate; obtain for me the grace to receive with faith, purity, fervour, and humility, the divine object of thy ardent love

Blessed spirits! you who unceasingly attend, love, and adore the Almighty Being I am about to receive, intercede for me at this awful moment, and supply by your ardent charity for the tender devotion with which I would wish to receive my Redeemer under my roof.

At the Confiteor.

Reflect for some moments, in the bitterness of your soul, on the offences which render you unworthy of receiving the God of all holiness. Humbly acknowledging and sincerely detesting them, join in the *Confiteor*, and endeavour, in the spirit of humility and repentance, to cleanse your soul still more from every stain of sin or imperfection.

O DIVINE REDEEMER of my soul! into thy sacred heart I cast all my offences; they are not more numerous than thy mercies, nor can they equal the tenderness of that love which invites me to receive thee.

O Jesus! veiled as thou art, I acknowledge thee for my *Lord and my God;* I adore thee with all the powers of my soul, and I fervently love thee with my whole heart.

From the Communion *to the* End of Mass.

After having become the living temple of the Divinity, you should remain for some moments prostrate as it were at the sacred feet of your divine Lord. Penetrated with the profound adoration and respect which should result from the presence of the Almighty, produce occasional short acts of faith, hope, gratitude, and principally of love. This may be done in any terms your devotion may suggest, or else by the following prayers.

O DIVINE LORD! thou hast at length satisfied the earnest desires of my heart. I possess thee, I embrace thee; O make me entirely thine.

O Jesus! thou who constitutest the happiness of the blessed! is it possible that thou art at this moment present in my heart! Yes, I firmly believe that I possess thee, with all the treasure of thy merits.

O most sacred Virgin! who so long bore and so fervently loved the God I now possess, praise and magnify his goodness. Offer him for me those joys which filled thy pure soul at the moment of his incarnation in thy sacred womb, and assist me to make some return for his unbounded mercies.

Remember, O divine Lord! that one visit from thee would suffice to sanctity the greatest sinner: permit not then that I should receive thee in vain: let not thy precious blood fall on my heart, without producing therein the fruits of virtue thou hast so long expected. O take me out of life this moment, rather than permit me to relapse into sin.

Adorable Lord of heaven and earth! thou beholdest in my heart thy beloved Son; he is all mine; his abundant merits belong to me at this moment. I offer them to thee, O my God! and in return I ask for the most ardent love, sincere humility, and above all, the grace never to offend thee by any mortal sin.

Devout Prayers after Communion.

I RETURN thee my most fervent thanks, O amiable Jesus! for the blessing I now enjoy; I praise and glorify thee with all my soul, for the numberless favours I have received from thy goodness and liberality. I adore thee now reposing in my breast, O my God, and my All! a thousand times welcome! O most gracious Lord Jesus Christ! how sweet, mild, and merciful, art thou to all those who invoke thee: for when I had no being, thou didst create me; when I was thy enemy, thou camest from heaven to redeem me; and because without thee I was helpless, thou hast given me thy sacraments, with numberless graces, to fortify my weakness, and facilitate my salvation; but to crown all thy favours, thou givest me thy own body and blood for the nourishment of my soul. Thou shouldst retire from me, because I am a sinful creature,—dust and ashes,—the destined food of worms; —yet thou comest expressly to visit me and take possession of my whole soul O Lord, my

God, how wonderful is thy name throughout the earth! What return shall I make to the Lord for all he has given to me? O that thou wouldst fill my lips with praises, that all the days of my life I may sing forth thy glory, and celebrate thy wonderful works.

Bless my God for me, O ye Angels and Saints; thank my Lord for me; love my Jesus for me; and sing forth his praises to supply for my deficiency. O Beauty ever ancient and ever new! Too late have I known thee, too late have I loved thee. When shall the time come, that, disgusted with all earthly things, I shall seek my happiness in thee alone, and find rest to my soul? O heavenly manna! O adorable sacrament! O inestimable pledge of God's love to mankind! O standing memorial of Christ's passion and death! O inexhaustible fountain of divine grace! O boundless mercy! O divine charity! O sacred fire ever burning and never decaying! Hail, O merciful Jesus! my only happiness and delight! the joy of my soul, and my portion for ever! May my soul be sensible of thy adorable presence, and may I taste how sovereignly sweet thou art in the sacrament of thy love. Purify my heart, O divine Lord! from the dross of all earthly affections; enable me to curb my vicious inclinations, and to withstand the dangerous attacks of my infernal enemy—deign to bestow on me those virtues that will render me pleasing in thy sight, particularly ardent charity, profound humility, heroic patience, and perfect obedience. O! may I prove the extent of my gratitude by the most constant fidelity in thy service, and may I rather die than ever again offend thee by any mortal sin.

O that I could have the happiness of seeing thee loved and faithfully served by all creatures. Vouchsafe to let the light of thy countenance shine upon those who are in the darkness of infidelity; and dispel their errors, that they may embrace the truth, and faithfully practise all it requires. Grant peace and union to all Christian Princes, and preserve us from the dreadful scourges of war, famine, and pestilence Convert all those who are in the unhappy state of mortal sin, and reconcile those who are at variance. Have mercy on my parents, friends, benefactors, and enemies, and mercifully grant them all the graces they stand in need of. Reform all abuses, and remove all scandals from thy Church. Comfort all that are under any affliction, sickness, or violence of pain. Support those who are under temptation; protect such as are in danger; and grant the grace of a happy death to all those who are in their last agony. Extend thy mercy likewise to the souls of all the faithful departed, and mercifully admit them to the enjoyment of thy eternal glory. Grant to us all relief in our respective necessities, remission of all our sins, the grace of final perseverance, and life everlasting. *Amen.*

An Act of Adoration.

UNDER these sacred veils, where thy love for man conceals the splendour of thy Majesty, I most humbly adore thee, O Almighty God. The grandeur of the heavens is as nothing in thy sight; they shall perish, but thou shalt remain for ever! The earth thou hast poised in thy hand, the ocean is before thee but as a drop of water; all nature bends and trembles in thy presence. How then shall I extol thee, immortal King of Angels! What homage can I give, proportioned to thy greatness! Thou art the perfect image of thy eternal Father's substance! thou art the splendour of his glory! Thou art his powerful word, supporting all things; thee he hath seated at his right hand. Thy throne, O God, is for ever and ever; a sceptre of justice is the sceptre of thy reign. I bow before thy sacred Majesty; I acknowledge, with the sincerest gratitude, that thou art my Redeemer, my Creator and the supreme Arbiter of my eternal destiny. I desire to humble myself as profoundly for thy sake, as thou art humbled for my love in the centre of my soul; and to consecrate to the glory of thy name the whole extent of my being.

An Act of Oblation.

When I reflect, O my God! on the innumerable blessings and favours thou hast heaped on me, from the first moment of my existence to the present hour, I am penetrated with confusion; and my heart, overpowered with gratitude and love, is unable to express what I feel. I am surrounded on all sides with thy benefits: it is thou thyself who lovest and servest me in the creatures that minister to my wants: those to whom I am indebted for my existence, and who give me such proofs of their tenderness, are but the instruments of thy providence, and the channel of thy mercies on my behalf. Thou art not only the God of the Universe, thou art also, in a special manner, a God to me; so interested art thou in all that concerns my welfare, that thy attention seems to be fixed on me alone. Thou hast given me all that I am, and even all that thou art thyself. I can call thee, with as much reason as David could, *the God of my salvation and my mercy;* my refuge and my support; my treasure and my inheritance. What do I say? Dost thou not deign at present to become my nourishment, to incorporate thyself with my very substance, that I may know the extent of thy love, and possess within my breast a pledge of eternal life? How great, then, will be my ingratitude, if henceforward I do not endeavour, to the utmost of my ability, to correspond with this infinite love, this marked predilection! O my God! may I never be unmindful of thy favours—may my right hand be forgotten, and my tongue cleave to my mouth. if ever I neglect to extol thy mercies! But how shall I, a wretched, miserable creature, make thee a suitable return for all thou hast done for me? In myself I have nothing; but do I not possess, in the invaluable gift I have just received, an adequate thanksgiving—an offering worthy of thy supreme greatness? Accept then, O omnipotent Lord, the uninterrupted praise and thanksgivings which thy dear Son offered thee from the moment of his incarnation to the close of his mortal life; particularly at the institution of this sacrament, when fully sensible of our weakness, and of the infinite value of the benefits then bestowed, he raised his eyes to thee, O omnipotent Father! and in our name gave thanks. The sacrifice of my whole being is not worthy to be presented to thee; but in offering thee to thyself, I look on my debts as abundantly discharged. May thy infinite mercies be for ever exalted, for having given me so excellent a means of repaying, in some manner, all the obligations I have contracted towards thy justice as well as thy mercy.

A METHOD OF HEARING MASS

AFTER COMMUNION.

At the Commencement of the Mass.

Having received from your divine Redeemer the most convincing proof of love which God could bestow on his creature, endeavour to testify the lively gratitude which should penetrate your soul. For this purpose you could do nothing better, or more acceptable to God, than to assist anew at the adorable sacrifice; thus offering to the Almighty the only victim of thanksgiving proportioned to the benefit you have received.

O DIVINE JESUS! I possess thee now; thou thyself, omnipotent as thou art, can give me nothing more estimable, more precious. O my God! how canst thou possibly endure thy present habitation, far more wretched than the stable in which thou wert born?—how canst thou remain with a soul so ungrateful, so tepid, and, even at this moment, so little penetrated with a sense of thy divine presence? O

God! *how hast thou multiplied thy mercies* in favour of thy least deserving creature! Should not the profusion of thy benefits terrify me, when I consider my poverty, misery, and inability to acknowledge or repay them? Yet, on the other hand, O divine Benefactor of my soul! when was I ever so rich as at present? Convinced, then, of my personal indigence, yet filled with gratitude for the dignity to which I am raised by the union I have contracted with my Redeemer, I will again offer thee, O King of heaven and earth! a victim of thanksgiving proportioned to thy gifts; I will offer thee *a host of praise*, immolated not only on this altar, but in the midst of my heart.

And thou, O Jesus! *sweet and mild, and plenteous in mercy*, (Ps. xxxv.) give ear to my earnest petition; let me be now so closely united to thee, that I may become one with thee; create within me that humble, meek, and fervent heart, which will make me pleasing and acceptable in thy sight; let thy divine presence fill my soul with consolation and peace, and let thy mercies be now upon me. *according to the hope I have placed in thee.*

At the Gloria in excelsis.

You may fervently repeat the *Gloria in excelsis*, a prayer most acceptable to the Divinity, inviting both angels and men to give glory to God, not only on high, but also residing within your breast.

O God of my soul! worthy and adorable object of the praise and benediction of all creatures! permit me to *sing to thee a new canticle*, because in my favour thou *hast done wonderful things*. (Ps. xcvii. 1.) Permit me to bless thy adorable name, because thou art good, and *thy mercy endureth for ever*. In union with him who is *the splendour of thy glory, and the figure of thy substance*, (Heb. i. 3.) I praise thee, I bless thee, I adore thee, and rejoice in all that glory, that felicity, which is essential to thyself, and which the ingratitude of thy creatures can never lessen. Why cannot I extol thy goodness with lips purified as were those of thy Prophet? Why cannot I, O Jesus! residing in my heart! burn with the ardours which consumed the heavenly spirits who first sung the praises of thy hidden majesty? More ardent, though infinitely less favoured than I am, they proclaimed with joy the blessings thou wert come to scatter on earth. O that I had the hearts, the voices of men and angels, to thank thee for those with which thy coming this day has enriched me. O King of Peace! reign in my soul, and let thy dominion be absolute over all its powers, affections, desires, and movements. Let my perverse inclinations become submissive to the orders of thy amiable providence, that I may have no will but thine, no pursuit but that of pleasing thee; and no desire but that of enjoying thee eternally.

At the Gospel.

Imagine you hear the voice of the Eternal Father, saying: *This is my beloved Son, hear ye him*, St. Matt. xvii. 5. Listen with docility, not only to the maxims contained in the Gospel, but also to the words of eternal life, which Christ himself will speak to your heart. Not content with instructing you by his prophets and apostles, he has come this day in person to teach and enlighten you.

O ETERNAL TRUTH! how happy are those who listen to thy divine inspirations, who hide thy words in their hearts, that they may never sin against thee. (Ps. cxviii. 11.) *O that my ways may be* henceforth *directed to keep thy justifications.* (Ibid. ver. 5.) O that I may this day learn from thy own lips, that true life consists in knowing and loving thee alone. Eternal wisdom, proceeding out of the mouth of the Most High! my heart is at this moment thy throne and thy possession; teach me to practise the virtues of humility, charity, and obedience. But, alas divine Jesus! I deserve not thy heavenly lessons, I am unworthy that thou shouldst speak to my soul, for I have often transgressed thy law, trampled on thy graces and slighted thy inspirations. I have gone astray from thee like a sheep that was lost; but, O charita ble Pastor! seek thy servant, because, amid all my wanderings, I have never forgotten thy commandments; (*Ibid.* ver. 176.) I have never ceased to acknowledge thee for my God, my Redeemer, my heavenly Guide. O had I fled from sin with the horror it is calculated to inspire—had I valued as I ought, the graces which were purchased for me by thy precious blood, how near should I be to thee at this moment; how pleasing would my soul be in thy sight, how dear would it be to thy merciful heart! O my God! the hope and salvation of those who trust in thee! enlighten my darkness, *that I may know thy testimonies, for I have inclined my heart to keep them for ever.* (Ibid.)

At the Offertory.

Call to mind the transports of gratitude which filled the soul of Zacheus on receiving into his house *the Salvation of Israel;* persuaded that you are much more favoured than he was, endeavour to imitate his spirit of sacrifice, and take care not to be outdone by a publican in gratitude and fervour.

O ADORABLE JESUS! how insensible should I be to my own eternal and temporal welfare, did I refuse my heart to thee, for whom it was created, and who alone can satisfy its desires! Yet, my God! in offering thee all that I have, what do I present?—A soul, redeemed indeed by thy precious blood, but stained with such sins as should render it hateful in thy sight; an ungrateful heart, which thou hast repeatedly demanded, but which I have so long refused. O my God! canst thou accept now a gift which thy mercy alone could have caused thee to require? Yes, divine Jesus! thou wilt now accept my offering, for I present it to thee, not as *my* heart, but as *thy* sanctuary: not single, but incorporated with thee by as strict a union as a God can contract with his creature. O most merciful Lord! do thou crown all thy mercies, by bestowing on me that humble, contrite heart, which is the only offering thou desirest to receive from thy creatures. O divine Lord! assisted by that grace which I have this day abundantly received, I now make thee a free oblation of my whole being, which I am determined never more to reclaim.

At the Preface.

Enter into the spirit of the Church, and, in union with the minister of God, offer to the King of Heaven the hymns of praise which will extol his greatness and bless his mercies for all eternity

O KING of heaven and earth! thou art he, whose greatness and whose majesty no created intelligence can ever comprehend, and whose amiable perfections no human heart can ever sufficiently love! how then shall I presume to appear before thee? how shall I pronounce that sacred name I am so unworthy to utter? Yet, my God, permit me, for the sake of the adorable Victim I have received, to offer thee my most fervent adoration, in union with the angels who surround this altar; or rather, in union with the acceptable adorations of my divine Redeemer, the Holy of Holies, the Lord of Angels!

By thee, *O great High Priest, who hath penetrated the heavens*, (Heb. iv. 14.) I can join worthily in the praises which resound in the heavenly Jerusalem! Thou art come to me this day in the name of the Lord. Blessed for ever be that infinite mercy which is come to pardon me; blessed be that love, which is come to inflame me; blessed be that liberality, which is come to enrich me. O Son of David! Son of the Most High God! may never-ending Hosannas celebrate thy mercies heaped on me; and may I, through thy infinite goodness, one day join in the praise which will ascend before thy throne for all eternity.

At the Canon.

At this solemn part of the Mass, let the consideration of the love which the Almighty has this day manifested towards you, animate you not only with gratitude towards your divine Benefactor, but also with a lively interest in the temporal and eternal welfare of all your fellow-creatures. Pray fervently for all whether friends or enemies; since Jesus Christ loves all, and did not refuse to lay down his life for them.

O DIVINE JESUS! the Redeemer of all mankind! who art come to save even those who were lost! whose adorable blood was shed for many to the remission of sins! deign to listen to the prayers I now offer, not for myself alone, but for the great family of mankind whose Creator, Lord, and Sovereign Master thou art:—permit me to offer my supplications for the peace and prosperity of that Holy, Catholic, and Apostolic Church, which was founded on thy unerring word, established by thy miracles, enriched by thy merits, and peopled by thy saints;—of that Church, whose unworthy child I am, in whose bosom, through thy grace, I resolve to live and to die;—that Church, which has this day imparted to me her most precious treasure, in giving me the adorable body and blood of her heavenly Spouse.

O my God! bless, sanctify, and protect the Pope, thy representative on earth; have mercy on the Bishops, Priests, and all who labour in thy vineyard; animate them with zeal for the salvation of souls, who are the purchase of thy blood; give them prudence, perseverance, humility, and patience; inflame their hearts with that ardent zeal which consumed thy holy Apostles. Render their lives as holy as the law they inculcate; make them all according to thy own divine heart, and let their light so shine before men, that they, seeing their good works, may glorify their Father who is in heaven, (St. *Matt.* v. 16.) O my God! *I seek not that which is profitable to myself, but to many, that they may be saved*; (1 Cor. x. 33.) therefore I most earnestly conjure thee to show forth the riches of thy infinite mercy, by pardoning those who are in the dreadful state of mortal sin. Thou art the Lamb that *was slain, and hast* thou not *redeemed us to God in thy blood, out of every tribe, and tongue, and people, and nation, and hast made us to our God a*

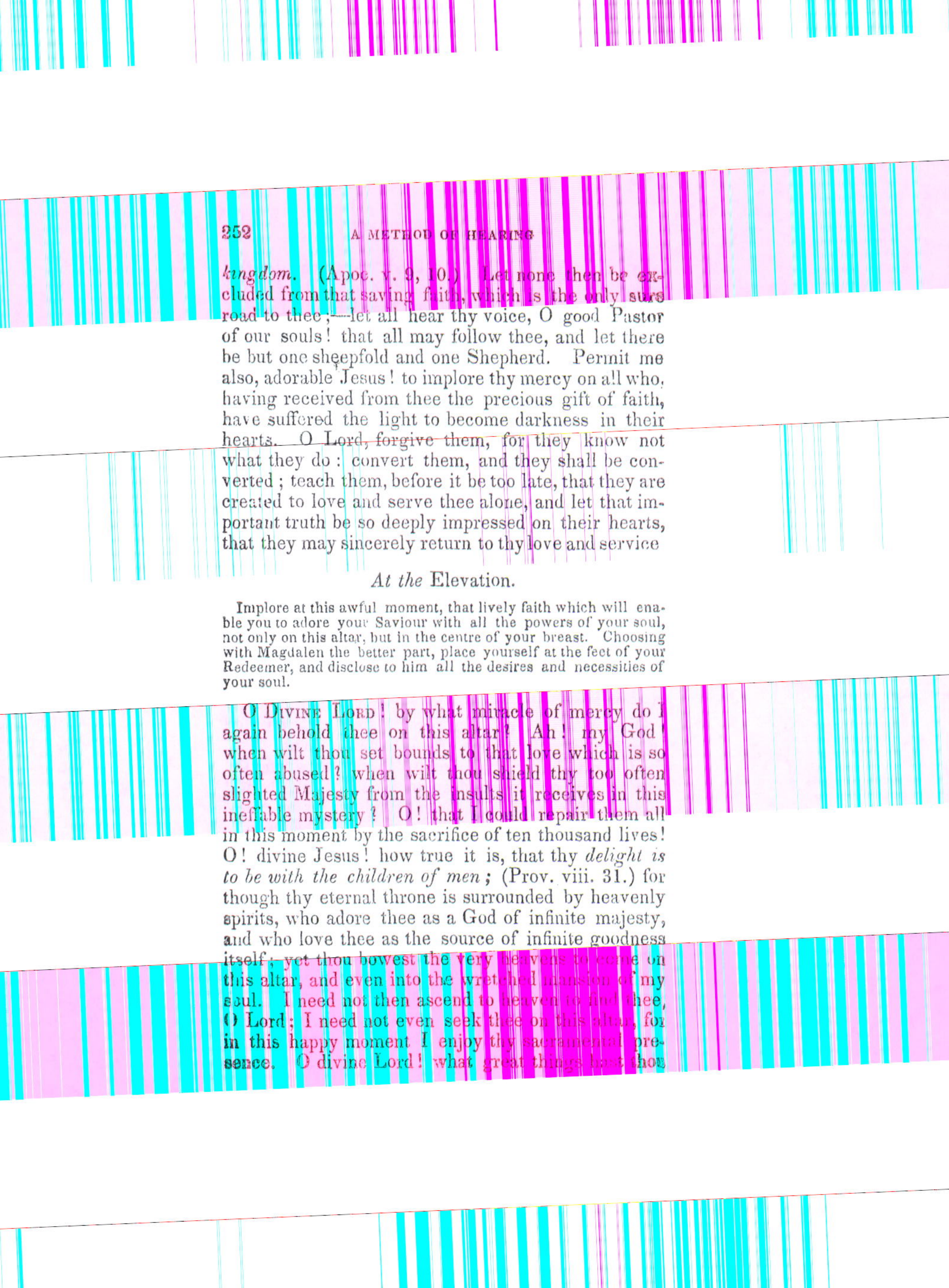

kingdom. (Apoc. v. 9, 10.) Let none then be excluded from that saving faith, which is the only sure road to thee;—let all hear thy voice, O good Pastor of our souls! that all may follow thee, and let there be but one sheepfold and one Shepherd. Permit me also, adorable Jesus! to implore thy mercy on all who, having received from thee the precious gift of faith, have suffered the light to become darkness in their hearts. O Lord, forgive them, for they know not what they do: convert them, and they shall be converted; teach them, before it be too late, that they are created to love and serve thee alone, and let that important truth be so deeply impressed on their hearts, that they may sincerely return to thy love and service

At the Elevation.

Implore at this awful moment, that lively faith which will enable you to adore your Saviour with all the powers of your soul, not only on this altar, but in the centre of your breast. Choosing with Magdalen the better part, place yourself at the feet of your Redeemer, and disclose to him all the desires and necessities of your soul.

O Divine Lord! by what miracle of mercy do I again behold thee on this altar? Ah! my God! when wilt thou set bounds to that love which is so often abused? when wilt thou shield thy too often slighted Majesty from the insults it receives in this ineffable mystery? O! that I could repair them all in this moment by the sacrifice of ten thousand lives! O! divine Jesus! how true it is, that thy *delight is to be with the children of men*; (Prov. viii. 31.) for though thy eternal throne is surrounded by heavenly spirits, who adore thee as a God of infinite majesty, and who love thee as the source of infinite goodness itself; yet thou bowest the very heavens to come on this altar, and even into the wretched mansion of my soul. I need not then ascend to heaven to find thee, O Lord; I need not even seek thee on this altar, for in this happy moment I enjoy thy sacramental presence. O divine Lord! what great things hast thou done in my soul! But, my God! what can be the reason that I am so little sensible of thy adorable presence? How is it possible that I conceal fire in my bosom, and yet do not burn? (*Prov.* vii. 27.) Why am I so slothful and tepid, when I possess in my soul the principle of life? Alas! how little return of gratitude hast thou ever met in my heart!—but, my God, what can resist thee? Hast thou not often triumphed over hearts equal even in malice to mine? Do, then, I conjure thee, that for which thou art come; transform me into thyself, and let me experience the effect of the petition thou didst deign to make on our behalf, *viz.* that we should be one with thee, as thou and thy heavenly Father art one, (St *John* xvii. 21.)

At the second Memento.

It is a holy and wholesome thought to pray for the dead, that they may be loosed from their sins; (2 Mac. xii. 46.) therefore endeavour to accelerate the bliss of those who are destined to love and praise God for eternity, and who will abundantly repay, before the throne of the Most High, the charitable interest of their intercessors on earth.

O Almighty God! the resurrection and the life! he that believeth in thee, even though he were dead, shall certainly live, and enjoy in thy kingdom the true liberty of the children of God. Look then, I beseech thee, with compassion and mercy on those suffering souls who have always believed and confessed thy name. O sovereign Lord! remember that they were *the work of thy own hands;* (Job x. 3.) created in thy power, redeemed in thy mercy, preserved in thy goodness, and formed to thy adorable image. Ah! why then hidest thou thy adorable face from those who have been dear to thy sacred heart, and who long to behold and enjoy thee, their sovereign Beatitude? Accept, O eternal God! in their favour, the adorable Victim, who now offers himself to thee on this altar, and whom I likewise possess in the centre of my soul. Apply to them also, O Lord, the indulgence which thy Church this day holds forth in thy name to worthy communicants, and let not my imperfect dispositions be an obstacle to the exercise of thy mercy on their behalf. In consideration of thy beloved Son, cease to remember their iniquities, and take no further revenge of their sins. I particularly implore thy mercy, O Lord! for my parents, friends, and benefactors; for all those who are most abandoned; for those to whose sufferings I may have been accessary; for all who, during life, were most devoted to the adorable sacrament of thy love, and also for those who were the fervent clients of thy blessed mother. O almighty Lord! transport them into thy bosom, where they shall be replenished with the goods of thy house; confirm them in thy sight for ever, that they may joyfully sing a hymn to thee in Sion, and pay to thee a vow in Jerusalem. (*Ps.* lxiv. 1.)

At the Pater noster.

After repeating with the Priest the *Pater noster*, call to mind the indulgence which the prodigal son experienced from his father on his sincere return, and acknowledge with gratitude, that the tenderness of his good parent has been infinitely surpassed in your favour by your heavenly Father.

Almighty Lord! how shall I presume to address thee as my Father, since by my abuse of thy mercies I have forfeited the title of thy child? O my God! I acknowledge that I have squandered thy graces, that I have been deaf to thy voice, and have abandoned thee, my only good. I have sinned against heaven and before thee, and were I treated as I deserve, I should be for ever excluded from that kingdom which I was created to enjoy. Yet notwithstanding all, I will not despair, for I possess in my soul the sweet pledge of my forgiveness;—thou canst not behold me without looking at the same time on the face of that dear Son, whose delight, while on earth, and whose food it was to do thy will. But, O my God! hast thou not already anticipated my conversion? Didst thou not see from afar, by facilitating to me the means of return to thy arms? Didst thou not clothe me in the tribunal of thy mercy with the robe of innocence? And this very day hast thou not fed me with the heavenly banquet, which is only prepared for the children of thy kingdom? Why didst thou load me with mercies, often denied to those whom thou hast always with thee, and who have never disobeyed thee in any thing? Ah! it is because I was lost, and thou hast found me, because I was dead, and by thy all-reviving grace I am now reanimated. O complete thy mercies, infinite goodness: *restore unto me the joy of thy salvation;* (Ps. i. 14.) restore unto me that peace and happiness I once enjoyed in thy service. I am not worthy to be called thy child, but I entreat thee once more, in the name of thy beloved Son, to receive me among the last of those who are happy enough to love and serve thee.

At the Domine non sum dignus.

You should have been sincerely persuaded, with the centurion that you were unworthy to receive under your roof the Lord o Glory, but since, overlooking your misery, he has not disdained to visit you in person, beseech of him, who is meek and humble of heart, to destroy every vice in your soul, particularly that *pride*, which *is the beginning of all sin.* (Eccles. x. 15.)

Divine Jesus! I was not worthy to receive thee—I am unworthy to possess thee—and I acknowledge myself infinitely undeserving of thy stay in my sinful heart. O may the love and humility of this thy minister, and of all those happy souls who are at this moment about to receive thee in any part of the world, supply for the little preparation thou hast found in my heart; and may their thanksgiving and lively gratitude offer thee such homage as thou canst never expect to receive from me. My God! since thou hast condescended to enter under my roof; since hou hast come in person to heal my soul, when one word would have sufficed, leave me not without effecting the cure for which thou art come; depart not, until thou hast planted on the ruins of my pride and vanity the divine virtues of humility and meekness, so strongly inculcated by thy divine example Teach me, I beseech thee, to walk in thy footsteps, make choice of my heart, to model it after thine, and to adorn it with the solid virtues of charity, patience, compassion for the poor and afflicted, a lively horror of sin, and all that offends thy divine Majesty.

At the Blessing *and* last Gospel.

At the Priest's blessing, most fervently implore the parting benediction of your divine Guest, that it may remain as a memorial and a preservative of the graces you have this day received.

My God, thou shalt never leave me until thou bless me—until thou givest me that efficacious benediction which will be the safeguard of thy graces. That the world may know I sincerely love thee, and have had the happiness of receiving thee, I will follow thee, and serve thee faithfully to the last moment of my life; but yet, my God! with what diffidence should I make these promises! How often have I promised to be faithful to thy law, and yet on occasions of trial, how repeatedly have I transgressed! Thou hast given me thy precious body and blood, yet I have ungratefully refused thee the most trifling sacrifices. Thus have I hitherto acted, and what I once did, I may and certainly shall do again, if not supported by thy powerful grace. Yet, notwithstanding my experience of past weakness, I do again promise to keep thy commandments, to love thee and serve thee with all my heart and soul. Remain with me, O divine Lord, by the influence of thy all-powerful grace; take my whole being, and reign over me so absolutely, that I may never acknowledge any King or Master but thee. May I rather die than forget thy infinite goodness and unspeakable mercies: may these same *mercies give thee glory*, and may they *follow me all the days of my life*. (Ps. cvi. 8

xx. 6.) In the strength of the heavenly nourishment I have received, may I walk steadily in the paths of virtue, until I come to that happy region where I shall eternally sing, *Benediction, and glory and wisdom, and thanksgiving, honour, and power, and strength to our God, for ever and ever. Amen* (Apoc. v. 12.)

A Prayer to be said three Days after Communion

I HAVE not forgotten, O my good God! the great happiness which I have so lately enjoyed in receiving the adorable Sacrament of thy Body and Blood. Penetrated with the sincerest gratitude for all the graces bestowed on me in my late Communion, I once more most humbly and fervently thank thee for them. As I never could thank thee sufficiently for such a favour, I offer thee thy own adorable Heart as a supplement for the insufficiency of my gratitude and love. O divine Heart of Jesus! which was pierced for me on the cross, that I may at all times find a refuge in thee, receive me now, for I never more sincerely desired to consecrate myself to the service of my Creator, to love him fervently, and to live for him alone. I never dreaded my own inconstancy and weakness more than at present; for, alas! I know that I am still capable of offending thee, my divine Saviour, even after all thou hast done for me. It appears to me now that I am determined, firmly determined, to remember and to observe the sacred obligations of my baptism—to renounce the devil, the world, the flesh, and my own will —to prefer death itself to the misfortune of offending thee—and to prove by my conduct that the grace of my last communion has not been received in vain. But how long will these dispositions last? I have made thee many promises before, and have ungratefully broken them. Alas, my God! shall I be so unfortunate as to lose the fruit of my communion, and again relapse into sin? No, thou wilt not permit it;—if I distrust myself, it is to trust more firmly in thee. I have received the adorable sacrament which fortified the martyrs; why then should it not fortify me? Thou art as willing to be my sovereign strength as thou wert to be theirs. Into thy hands then I recommend my whole being—with all the confidence of a child I cast myself into the arms of my divine, indulgent Parent. In thy sacred heart, O Jesus! I place all my resolutions, particularly those of suffering all that can be endured, rather than offend thee mortally, and of making every necessary effort to correct my habitual faults. I most humbly implore, through thy divine Heart, and the intercession of thy blessed Mother, the grace to persevere in these my good purposes. *Amen.*

It will be an excellent means of advancing in virtue, to make choice, after your communion, of some one of your faults to correct, at least in part, before you are next to have the happiness of communicating, beginning by those that appear exteriorly, because they give disedification and bad example. Consider, also, what virtue you most stand in need of; whether it be attention and respect at prayer; more docility and obedience to superiors; more patience, forbearance, and condescension with your companions; more exactness to truth; more attention to your improvement, and the good employment of your time, &c.; and then determine, with God's assistance, to produce a great many acts of the virtue you select, that you may present them to Jesus Christ when he next visits you in the holy communion.

MEDITATIONS

FOR THE THREE DAYS AFTER COMMUNION

First Day.

On the Sentiments which the holy Communion should produce in our Souls.

I. *Point*.—Consider with astonishment the excessive liberality with which Jesus Christ has treated you, by this one Communion you are infinitely elevated above all that the world calls great—you are happier than if you enjoyed all the delights of the universe—

richer than if you possessed all its treasures—and more dignified than if you were its sole sovereign. Ah! if you understood the gift of God, if you had a just idea of your own dignity, how soon would you despise every thing in this world! Penetrated with gratitude for the greatness of the benefit you have received, you should exclaim with the Royal Prophet: What shall I render to the Lord for all he has done for me? how shall I testify my gratitude? Do not on this important matter deceive yourself as many do. Do not imagine that so great a benefit as a Communion is worthily acknowledged by the most fervent expressions of thanksgiving. It is not those who say, Lord, Lord, that shall enter into the kingdom of heaven; nor is it those that multiply acts of gratitude, who afterwards prove themselves truly grateful for the happiness of communicating. "Sincere gratitude for any benefit," says St. Thomas, "consists chiefly in esteeming the benefit as it deserves, and in endeavouring to make our benefactor an adequate return." This is seldom thought of by the generality of communicants; they would be ashamed of treating an earthly friend or benefactor with indifference; they would reproach themselves with insensibility, if they received favours from a fellow-creature without feeling them, and would be delighted at an opportunity of repaying them with gratitude. It is God alone, in this mystery of love, whose goodness is scarcely ever felt or acknowledged, and whose most precious favours do not often induce his servants to make him even a trifling return. Let not this be your case; be you at least that thankful Samaritan, whose first care was to cast himself at the feet of his Benefactor, penetrated with gratitude for the favour he had received, and disposed no doubt to acknowledge it to the best of his power. Return this day to give glory to Him, who has given you his precious body and blood, his soul and divinity, and thus rendered you in some respect an object of envy to the angels themselves, since they never received that mark of infinite love. Beg of God most earnestly to enlighten your mind, that you may understand the greatness of the favour conferred on you; and also to touch your heart, that you may feel your obligation of acknowledging it by every means in your power.

II. *Point.*—Cast yourself in spirit at the feet of your Creator, and present to him the sacrifice of thanksgiving which he deserves, *viz.* a voluntary, unreserved oblation of your whole being. Can that be too much for him who has created you to his image and likeness, and redeemed you with his precious blood? or rather, what can be enough for him who has loved you so far as to give you himself? If you would really and entirely belong to God, you should make a two-fold sacrifice—a sacrifice of your body with all its senses, and of your heart and soul with all their powers and affections. First, you should consecrate your body to God; that is, you should in future bear in mind the union you have contracted with God, and respect in yourself, the temple of the Divinity—a temple, of which he has so lately taken possession; consecrated by his presence, purified by his blood, and enriched with the most precious gifts of his holy spirit. This is the sacrifice to which St. Paul exhorts all Christians, but particularly communicants, when he says: *I beseech you, brethren, by the mercy of God, that you present your bodies a living sacrifice, holy, pleasing to God.* (Rom. xii. 1.) Reflect also, that as a material temple is not alone consecrated to God internally, but is known before it is entered to be a house of God, by its external solemnity; so should your modesty and christian deportment manifest to every one that you are really consecrated to God, and become the living temple of Jesus Christ. To animate you to this meritorious consecration of your senses to God, consider how strongly St. Chrysostom recommends it, when he says: It is not just that those eyes which have beheld the divine and sacred Host should afterwards delight in the vanity and idle follies of the world—that those lips, which received and touched the God of heaven, should ever be profaned by frivolous discourses—that your tongue, on which the body of Jesus Christ reposed, should ever become instrumental in lessening the reputation of others, or in wounding charity. Present your resolutions on this head to God through the glorious Queen of Virgins. Set before your eyes, and resolve in every action of your life, to imitate this incomparable model of your sex, whom St. Anselm describes as having "nothing disagreeable in her looks, nothing inconsistent in her words, nothing imprudent in her actions;—whose deportment was not assuming; whose voice was not loud or arrogant; and whose exterior modesty was a finished portrait of her interior purity." O most blessed Virgin! take me under thy protection, and preserve me from defiling by sin the temple of thy only beloved Son.

III. *Point.*—Consider that your immortal soul was created by God for himself; stamped with his own sacred image; redeemed with his blood, adorned with his graces, enriched with his merits, and often strengthened with that sacrament of life which you have so lately received. Its value must then be great, since God himself did not think it too dearly purchased by the blood of his only Son. Yes, you cannot be too deeply convinced that your immortal soul is your great and only treasure; to save *that*, no pains can be excessive, no security too great;—if *that* be lost, all is lost; and if you be so happy as to save *that*, though you lose all the rest, all is gained. *What* will *it profit a man if he gain the whole world, and lose his own soul?* (Matt. xvi. 26.) What does it now avail many of the damned, to have been on earth honoured, loved, respected, endowed with such beauty, talents, wit, or accomplishments as made them the idols or envy of all around them? Alas! what does all that avail them now, since they unfortunately lost their souls ?—Dwell on this irreparable misfortune, and you will soon feel the justice and necessity of curbing your passions, and leading a virtuous life. Your last words, perhaps, may be a recommendation of your soul into the hands of God; but remember that the best, the only means of securing for it an asylum in the bosom of its Creator, is by frequently consecrating all its powers to his honour and glory; by making use of your memory to recall the benefits and mercies of God; by employing your understanding in meditating on his holy law, that you may model your life on all it prescribes; and by renouncing your will so perfectly, as to have no other will than the will of God. But the victim of thanksgiving which God peculiarly requires from you, is your heart and all its affections. This is the sacrifice which will give value to every other, and without which all others would be vain;—it is that which above all others you should endeavour to make perfectly, because it is the offering which God himself condescends to ask; *Son, give me thy heart.* Consider how early you were taught to say: *My God, I give thee my heart.* These are the first words you daily utter, still perhaps you have not yet really offered your whole heart to God. Ah! delay no longer: to whom does it so justly belong? who ever loved you so much as God? who can make you happy, but God? O divine Lord! how true it is, that I have never been satisfied but when I endeavoured to serve thee, to act for thee, to give myself to thee. How sincerely I regret having ever cast away a single thought, a single affection, or a single moment of my existence, on any object less than thee, my Creator and my God! Penetrated with gratitude for that infinite mercy which induced thee to give thyself to me in the adorable Eucharist, I most fervently wish that I could make thee a sacrifice worthy of thyself; but as that is impossible—as thou knowest my poverty, and wilt be content with the little I can give permit me to offer thee my whole being, my body, my soul, my life, my actions, my will, and above all, my heart and affections. O my God! accept this oblation, in union with the sacrifice which Jesus offered thee on the cross, and in union with the early consecration which his blessed Mother made of herself to thee in the Temple.

Second Day.

On the Imitation of Jesus Christ.

I. *Point.*—Consider attentively, that as one of the chief ends for which Jesus gives himself to us in the holy Communion, is to unite us to himself, and to make us one with him, those who communicate are much more strictly bound than all others to endeavour to resemble their Redeemer. St. Thomas says, that in the holy Eucharist Jesus Christ applies his most sacred body like a seal on the heart of man, to revive that adorable image of the Divinity to which we were created; and to transform his creatures into himself, by imprinting on the soul the image of his adorable perfections, and infusing into the heart abundant graces to imitate his virtues. To become a perfect imitation of Jesus Christ, you should conform your judgment, your opinions, your ideas, your heart, feelings, and all your affections, to those of your divine Lord—thinking and reasoning like Jesus, and judging of all things here below as he judged of them. The thoughts of Jesus were always directed to God, or bent on something relative to the glory of God. How do you act in this respect? Have you ever reflected on the benefit and even necessity of banishing idle or useless thoughts? Are you convinced, that to repress those, and substitute a frequent and respectful recollection of God, would be the best guard you could have against those thoughts of vanity or pride which are so common and so sinful when indulged? Jesus Christ judged of all things as God judges of them.

he viewed the things of this world in the light of God, and pronounced on every thing passing in it accordingly. He valued what God values, and despised all that God despises. His adorable heart, inflamed with love for God, and desire for his glory, was incapable of a single sentiment of joy, of sorrow, of fear, of hope, of consolation, or sadness, but according as the interests, the glory, the worship of his heavenly Father were concerned. Examine your mind and heart on this most perfect and adorable model. Be ashamed of the trifles with which you have been hitherto delighted, or the insignificant incidents at which you have been grieved. Consider, what would Jesus have thought of them, how he would have regarded what you so much value or so greatly apprehend. O my divine and adorable Master! instead of looking on all things as thou seest them, and as I myself shall see them after death, I have consulted my interests, my passions, my imagination, and the corrupt maxims of the world, in forming my opinions and ideas. I have unfortunately sought after those very things which thou didst shun—I loved what thou didst hate—I have hated what thou didst love. Thou didst pronounce those blessed and happy who suffer, and I have always considered them as objects of compassion—thou didst despise and flee from the riches, honours, and pleasures of this world, and I have desired and esteemed them as great advantages. O my God! enlighten me to see and detest my folly.

II. *Point.*—Consider, that the first lesson which Jesus Christ gives you in his early years, is the necessity of becoming more virtuous, more rational, as you become older; for *Jesus*, as the Gospel says, *increased in grace and wisdom with God and man.* (Luke ii. 52.) Learn from this, that as every day, every hour the Almighty adds to your life, every grace, every instruction you receive, should advance you in the road of solid virtue. In particular, every time you have the happiness of communicating, you should grow, like Jesus in grace and wisdom before God and man; that is, God should discern in your heart, and those with whom you associate should witness in your conduct, an increase of the fear and love of God. Those faults and failings which were excusable some years ago, before you were admitted to the holy Communion, become serious at present. Examine whether you may not unfortunately have lost much of the fervour with which you first approached the adorable Eucharist, and never forget that not to go forward in virtue, is to go back.

Jesus Christ, while yet a child, is found among the Doctors in the Temple, asking them questions, and listening to the word of God with profound veneration. Did the eternal Son of God, the Fountain of all Knowledge, require instruction? Was there any thing for him to learn, or any person on earth who could teach him? Certainly not; but on this occasion he would teach you with what ardour you should seek after instruction—how thankfully and respectfully you should receive it—how highly you should value an opportunity of hearing the word of God. He would also impress on your mind an essential duty of youth, which is, to venerate age, and love the society of the virtuous. But the chief virtue which characterized the youth of Jesus Christ was obedience; so strongly would he recommend this to you, that he has scarce permitted any other account of his early years to reach us, than that he was subject to his blessed mother and his reputed father. He obeyed them in all things, at all times, with cheerfulness and exactness: consequently, to imitate your adorable model in this important point, you must resolve to respect and love your parents, or those who hold their place; to submit to their authority with docility, because they are deputed by God to command you; and with confidence, because they have also received light to direct your inexperience. Remember, that Jesus Christ was not less submissive to the orders of

Herod, one of the most wicked of men, than he was to those of his blessed mother, the most perfect of creatures, because it was God alone whom he obeyed in all superiors. Impress this lesson on your mind, and guard against a fault so common to youth, *viz.* that of obeying only those who may please you, and totally forgetting that duty with regard to others. If you do not respect the authority of God in all your superiors; if you do not love God in them all, and remember that it is he who inspires your parents themselves with their tenderness towards you, and their solicitude in providing for your welfare, you can never acquire that amiable docility, which is a virtue so necessary to youth, that without it you cannot become virtuous, learned, or happy. O Jesus! my God, impress on my heart the image of thy divine childhood; thy purity, simplicity, obedience, and docility! infuse into my soul the horror thou hadst of sin, that I may dread it as the only real evil, the only obstacle to my resembling thee.

III. *Point.*—Consider, that the hidden life of Jesus Christ is a model which you should continually study, because it was during those years that Jesus has given you *an example, that you should follow his footsteps.* (1 Pet. ii. 21.) During thirty years of subjection and labour, Jesus deigned in a peculiar manner to become the model of all Christians. Contemplate that model attentively, and consider with astonishment, that he who had descended from heaven to instruct, convert, and save the whole universe, employed the greater part of his life in seclusion, showing no otherwise the perfection of the Divinity which resided in him, than by obeying his parents, serving and assisting them, and fulfilling in all things the will of his heavenly Father. The accomplishment of that adorable will was the only object of his most vehement desires; it was so necessary to his happiness, that he himself declared it to be his food, the support of his existence, the end of his mission on earth. This pure, upright, and divine intention of accomplishing the will of God, so dignified and enhanced the merit of our Redeemer's actions, that one word, one sigh, one tear, one thought of Jesus Christ, was more meritorious in the sight of God, than the labours and austerities of all the saints. Learn then, from the hidden life of Jesus, that lesson of perfect conformity to the will of God, by which alone you can resemble him, and attain true sanctity. Resolve, in every stage of your life, to place all your perfection in being about the business of your heavenly Father; that is, in faithfully discharging the duties which Providence has allotted you, whatever they may be. If you be firmly convinced that this faithful, cheerful, persevering discharge of duty, is true sanctity, and a real imitation of Jesus Christ, you will carefully avoid that disedifying system of devotion pursued by many of your sex, who say long prayers; spend, or rather lose much time in chapels; who frequent the sacraments, yet whose hands are empty before God, because they do their own will, and not his; because their devotion is little better than sloth, which leads them, under cover of piety, to neglect those domestic duties which God had allotted them, and which should be their conscientious pursuit and their glory.—(*See the Holy Woman*, Prov. xxxi. 10.)

In the public life of Jesus Christ, which was a series of miracles and wonders, humility, patience, mortification, meekness, and unexampled charity, were lessons which he never ceased to preach to the world. The imitation of Jesus Christ in this respect is a point of the utmost importance, because charity was a favourite virtue of Jesus—the virtue to which he sacrificed his life—the virtue by which he would have his real followers distinguished—and the virtue also which St. Francis of Sales calls the peculiar fruit of a good communion. Resolve, then, that the fruits of your having been so lately united to the God of Charity should appear evident by your gentleness, patience, forbearance, silence on the defects of others, and endeavours to serve and oblige all, particularly those who may appear to you least amiable or deserving. Conclude this meditation, by fervently and humbly begging of God to impress the truths it contains so deeply on your heart, that your ideas and conduct may, in future, be happily regulated by them.

Third Day

On the Danger of not corresponding with the Graces received in the holy Communion.

I. *Point.*—Consider, that Christians in general frustrate more or less the designs of Christ, in instituting this mystery of love; some by constantly relapsing into mortal sin after their Communion; others by committing venial sins habitually, or by persevering in their ordinary failings, and taking no pains to amend their lives.

As to the first description of relapsing sinners, *viz.* those who banish Jesus from their hearts by grievous sin, their misfortune is so great, that it can never be excessively dreaded, or sufficiently deplored. They are compared by the holy fathers to the Jews, because, like them, they receive Jesus Christ with feelings of joy and gratitude, but shortly after crucify him by sin; they are even likened to Judas, the most unfortunate of all men, because, like him, they no sooner communicate, than they betray their Lord and divine Guest. Alas! would it not be better that such persons never communicated, never received those graces of which they never profit? Do you most earnestly beg of God to enlighten your mind, and give you a clear idea of the dreadful risk which relapsing sinners run, and also to penetrate your heart with a sincere horror of their ingratitude. To conceive their danger, you need only reflect on those awful words of St. Paul, who says, that *it is impossible for those who were once enlightened, have tasted also the heavenly gift, and were made partakers of the Holy Ghost, and are fallen away, to be renewed again to penance;* (Heb. vi. 4. and 6.) that is, sincere conversion becomes extremely difficult for those who, though fully enlightened by instruction, frequently nourished with the heavenly gift of Christ's sacred body, and also strengthened by the Sacrament of Confirmation, nevertheless persevere in a fatal habit of repenting, confessing, communicating, and then relapsing; salvation for them must indeed be most difficult, if not impossible. Why? because the ordinary means of salvation becomes useless to them: the bread of the strong does not fortify their souls, therefore the sacraments, which are a source of grace and salvation to other sinners, become the chief subject of their condemnation. As to their ingratitude, what can be more ungrateful, than to trample on the sacred blood which purified their souls! to insult a God again who so often received them with mercy! Ah! I will never be guilty of such ingratitude—I will never expose my soul to such danger; but I must not depend on my own strength; though I trust in the mercy of God, that the spirit of sin has gone forth from me, yet has he not perhaps already said that *he would return?* (Luke ix. 24.) Does he not perceive, with envy and rage, that my soul is, as the Gospel says, *swept and garnished?* (Ibid.) That it is purified by a good confession, and adorned with the robe of sanctifying grace; with the ornaments of virtuous desires and holy resolutions? Has not that wicked spirit determined to disturb the happiness I now enjoy, and to tempt me again with seven times more violence than before? O my God! my strength! my refuge! thou knowest that the least temptation would be too strong for me, if I be abandoned to myself. O stay with me, then, my God! protect me from mine enemies; and rather take me

23*

out of the world, than permit me to commit one mortal sin.

II. *Point.*—The second description of relapsing sinners, are those who communicate regularly, yet continue to commit venial sins deliberately, and persevere in a course of tepidity and negligence. Those are persons whose example you should most carefully guard against, because you would be more likely to imitate them than notorious sinners. The danger of persevering in ordinary faults and habitual negligence, requires even more serious reflection on your part, than the misfortune of falling into grievous sin; because, as yet the fear and love of God must have sufficient influence over your mind, to make you tremble at the idea of committing mortal sin after communion; but it is too common at your age, for relapses into venial sin to appear much less criminal and dangerous than they really are. That you may conceive how important it is to profit of each of your communions, reflect seriously on the parable of the slothful servant in the gospel, who buried the talent he received from his master. Take particular notice, that he is not accused of having made bad use of it: his only crime is, not having made any use of so favourable a means for promoting his own interests. On his master's return, he is not found richer than before, though he could have become so; he frustrates the benevolent designs of his Lord, and on that account alone he is treated with the utmost severity, and deprived of the talent bestowed on him, which is transferred to another. This is a clear and striking figure of those who receive the adorable Eucharist, yet bury that precious talent; that is make no use of it for advancing the business of their salvation; who, after years spent in regularly frequenting the sacraments, are not perceived to have corrected one single fault, or acquired one single virtue. This dangerous and disedifying system is chiefly attributed to your sex, and perhaps with too much justice; for how many women, to the disgrace of religion and scandal of their neighbour, continue from one communion to another as proud and vain, as negligent in their spiritual exercises, and thoughtless of their domestic duties; as attached to the vanities of the world and to their own will; as impatient and peevish, talkative and uncharitable, slothful and idle, as if they never communicated. O! how much have those to fear, who thus destroy with one hand what they build up with the other! Such persons injure the cause of religion much more than declared sinners. One young person, who frequents the sacraments without becoming more faithful to God, more useful and amiable in her family, more edifying to her neighbour, gives more scandal than twenty others, whose heads, it is true, appear turned with the vanities and pleasures of the world, but whose example has no weight, because they never received the benefit of instruction, the help of the sacraments, or perhaps even the light of faith. Consider these truths seriously: beg of God most earnestly to penetrate your heart with a holy fear of the account you will have to render for the very Communion you have just made. Resolve to make every effort necessary on your part for profiting of so great a grace; be on your guard against your accustomed faults; endeavour at least to lessen their number, that when you next communicate, your divine Lord may have no cause to reproach and punish you like the slothful servant of the gospel. O my God! by that infinite mercy which caused thee to die for my salvation, and that infinite love which induced thee to visit me in thy adorable Sacrament, deign to preserve me from exposing myself by negligence or sloth to the loss of the blessing I have received.

III. *Point.*—After having seriously considered the ingratitude and misfortune of relapsing sinners, you must already have firmly resolved never to become one of their unhappy number. This firm, determined resolution, should be the happy effect of the union you have so lately contracted with Jesus Christ, and of all the graces you have received this last week. But perhaps you have already often determined to serve God, and made the same resolution after each of your Communions, which is now recommended to you; whence came it then that you have been so negligent? Why have you fallen away from your first fervour? Why are you now the very same as you were when you first received your Saviour in this adorable mystery? It is because your resolutions hitherto have been only vague and verbal resolutions, such as relapsing sinners themselves seldom fail to make, such as many of the damned frequently have made. But if you sincerely intend to avoid being ranked among relapsing sinners, which you are as yet too young to merit altogether, you would do well to dwell on the following reasons or motives for perseverance.—First, Consider that your divine Redeemer, whom you have received in the Sacrament of his Love, will at all times be as great, as good, as amiable, as merciful, as worthy of your whole heart, as he now appears; consequently, though you may change, though your fervour and desire to advance in virtue may lessen in a month hence, perhaps in less, you should nevertheless persevere in your good resolutions, for the same reasons which caused you to make them. You should say to yourself; is not God the same now as when I felt that he deserved any exertion I could make for his sake? None of the truths of religion have changed—death is just as uncertain—judgment as terrifying—hell as formidable—eternity as long, as when they made such deep impression on my mind.—Secondly, Reflect on the difficulty you will certainly find in returning to God, if once you completely fall off from your present good purposes. How much did it perhaps cost you to enter into yourself—to examine your conscience—to prepare for your late Confession and Communion.

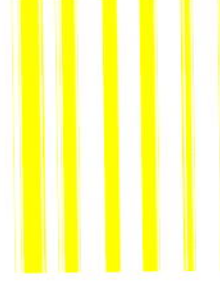

Would you then, by relapsing, furnish as much, or rather ten times more uneasiness, remorse, and difficulty for a future occasion, and at length for the bed of death?—Thirdly, Consider the uncertainty of your having a wish, or even an opportunity to approach the sacraments, if the grace you have just received be abused. A desire to be reconciled to God depends on a peculiar grace, of which those who relapse deserve to be deprived; and as to time, how do you know whether you may not die in a week or a month?—Whether your late Communion may not be your last? These, and many other good reasons for continuing to act as you are now determined to do. will strengthen your resolution, if you seriously reflect on them, whenever you feel tempted to relapse. Remember, however, that your best resolutions will be vain, if you were not also resolved to adopt the best means calculated to ensure perseverance. Those are many, but the chief are, first, such a horror of sin, as will dispose you to suffer all that could be endured in this world, rather than offend God mortally.—Secondly, great care in avoiding the commission of venial sins deliberately, and with a clear, distinct view that you are going to offend God. This point is of so much consequence, that you should take care not to pass it over lightly, because those multiplied venial faults, though slight in themselves, are most dangerous in their consequences. You would not consent to swallow a small quantity of poison frequently, though you were sure it would not kill you; why, then, should you, on any occasion, consent, by a deliberate venial fault, to swallow even a small portion of the deadly poison of sin? Alas! it is by doing so frequently, that many who began well, became so weak in virtue, that they were overcome by the first temptation, and miserably fell into mortal sin; because, as your catechism tells you, venial sin, (particularly of habit and deliberation) leaves the soul feeble and drowsy, and exposes her to fall into mortal sin. The other means of persevering are, attention to the presence of God, exactness in the discharge of your duties, but chiefly, and above all, fervent prayer. Perseverance is the most difficult, the most rare, and the most necessary of virtues; you should therefore earnestly and daily implore it of Him who is the giver of all good gifts.

Conclude your meditation, by begging that peculiar assistance from God, without which you can do nothing, and placing your resolutions in the adorable Heart of Jesus, and in the sacred hands of your blessed and glorious Patroness, the Mother of God.

Preparation *for* Confirmation.

It is not necessary to say much here in the way of Instruction for Confirmation. You already know from your Catechism, that the Sacrament you are about to receive was instituted to make you a "*strong and perfect Christian;*" that it derives its name from its chief effect, which is to confirm and fortify in the path of virtue—that its minister is a Bishop only—its matter chrism, solemnly blessed on Holy Thursday—its form, "*I sign thee with the sign of the Cross; I confirm thee with the chrism of salvation, in the name of the Father, and of the Son, and of the Holy Ghost, Amen.*" That it imprints an indelible character on the soul—that the heavenly Spirit it imparts is the Holy Ghost, the third Person of the adorable Trinity —and lastly, that its effects are to produce in the soul such strength, fortitude, and courage, as to enable Christians to persevere steadily in virtue, and to profess their faith in all circumstances, even before tyrants and persecutors, if called upon to do so. All those points, and every thing else necessary to be known concerning your holy religion, have been fully explained to you; so that, as far as regards instruction, you are already prepared for Confirmation; but that part of the preparation which is most essential, and which no one can make for you, is that of acquiring the proper dispositions for the Sacrament. On those the fruits of Confirmation depend: without them, as you well know, you would receive nothing from the sacrament but the character, and be denied all the gifts and graces bestowed on those who are duly disposed. Endeavour therefore to prepare with great fervour for the happiness you expect. The following details will assist you in disposing yourself for so solemn an action. They will also be useful to many who were confirmed before, as it often happens, that persons receive this sacrament when very young, ignorant, or otherwise badly disposed. If you be of this number, you should endeavour to repair your loss, and prepare to assist at the administration of the sacrament as fervently as if you had never received it. Sincerely desire on your part to receive the Holy Ghost; do all that depends on you to prepare your soul for the coming of that Divine Spirit, and then confidently hope that the gifts and graces of Confirmation, which were not granted you on receiving that sacrament, owing to the want of proper dispositions, will be now infused into your soul, and that the Almighty will forget and pardon in his mercy the sins and ignorance of your youth; more particularly as children are not always accountable for faults committed in approaching the sacraments, before they were sufficiently instructed.

On the other hand, if you be among those who were fully instructed before Confirmation, and who, through the mercy of God, have no grounds to fear any serious defect in your dispositions, when you were confirmed, you may, nevertheless, have much to reproach yourself with, as to your conduct afterwards, and very great need of renewing the promises and resolutions you then made. Consequently, there is no one who should look on the ceremony of her companions' Confirmation as a matter which does not concern her; on the contrary, the administration of this sacrament should make each of those who were confirmed, examine whether her conduct, since her Confirmation, has really been that of a strong and perfect Christian. You know that those who assist at the administration of this sacrament, participate in the gifts and graces of the Holy Ghost, in proportion to the sincerity of their desires for that happiness, and the efforts they shall have made to merit so great a blessing. You should therefore rejoice, when an opportunity occurs of renewing your sacred engagements with God, and endeavour to profit of it to the utmost of your ability. If you have been confirmed, accompany your companions, as far as depends on you, in the following preparation for and thanksgiving after Confirmation: these exercises will, of course, be particularly attended to by those who are expecting to receive the sacrament.

Preparation for Confirmation, as well as for the holy Communion, is divided into distant and immediate preparation. The distant preparation consists, first, in becoming fully instructed in the principles of the Christian Faith and Doctrine, and ardently desiring to receive the Holy Ghost. The instruction you have received, and the desire you also probably feel in a great measure; at least, it will not be difficult to excite it in your heart, when you consider attentively, that Confirmation imparts that same Divine Spirit who descended on the Apostles—that Spirit of Light, who in a moment taught them all truth—that Spirit of Charity, who inflamed them with such transports of love—that Spirit of Wisdom, who spoke by their tongues, and converted thousands—that Spirit of Strength and Fortitude, who banished every shadow of their natural timidity and fear—that sweet, consoling Spirit, who alone could comfort them for the absence of their Divine Master. How many spiritual advantages may you also expect from the visit of such a guest; advantages in some measure similar to those derived from it by the Apostles. They sincerely loved their Lord and Master, they wished to serve him, to preach his gospel, to promote his glory; yet until the descent of the Holy Ghost, they had not the courage or strength to oppose their enemies, or proclaim to the world those truths for which they afterwards laid down their lives. You also have formed many resolutions of leading a life worthy of a Christian; but how little ground have you for depending on yourself; how soon would you forget all your good purposes; how little courage and resolution would you have in overcoming yourself, if God did not mercifully impart to you peculiar graces of strength, light, fervour, and perseverance! Now, where could you hope more confidently for those graces than from the Sacrament you are going to receive? Confirmation is peculiarly instituted for the purpose of conferring them. O how ardently should you desire to receive such spiritual assistance! How grateful should you be to God, who, knowing your weakness and inconstancy, has mercifully provided it for you.

The immediate preparation necessary for Confirmation is pointed out by the conduct of the Apostles before the descent of the Holy Ghost. After having been purified from sin, and inflamed with the love of God by their long and intimate communication with Jesus Christ, they returned to Jerusalem immediately after the ascension of their Divine Master. There they spent ten days retired in the cenacle, persevering with *one accord in prayer*, (Acts i. 14.) and earnestly supplicating the descent of the promised Comforter. Whence you perceive that immediate preparation for Confirmation consists, first, in being in a state of grace; secondly, in spending some time in retirement; and thirdly, in earnestly begging of God, by fervent prayer, to give you his Holy Spirit, and to dispose your heart for his reception. You are fully aware of the absolute necessity of the first of those dispositions, since you know that Confirmation is a Sacrament of the living, which would not only be unprofitable, but injurious to a soul dead in mortal sin *The Holy Spirit of Wisdom*, says the Scripture, *will not enter a malicious soul, nor dwell in a body subject to sin*, (Wisd. i. 4.) Your first concern, then, should be, to make your confession with all the dispositions you know to be necessary for obtaining pardon from God, and all the graces annexed to the sacrament.

Situated as you are now, it is not necessary to remind you of the second immediate preparation for Confirmation, *viz.* a short retreat in imitation of the Apostles. You will conform to the general rule in that respect, and would do well to observe the few recommendations given for the time of retreat, to those preparing for their first communion.

The third immediate preparation is an increased desire to receive the Holy Ghost, and persevering supplications to obtain that great gift from God. To comply with this duty of prayer, you should, in the first place, discharge with great fervour your accustomed spiritual exercises, as well as the additional devotions of retreat; secondly, you should earnestly implore the Divine Spirit to descend on you with his seven-fold gifts. This will be best done by the following or any other short aspirations frequently repeated in the course of the day.

Come, O Holy Ghost! replenish my heart, and enkindle in it the fire of thy love.

O Divine Spirit! take full possession of my whole being.

O sacred Light! enlighten my understanding.

Divine fire of Love! inflame my heart.

O Spirit of heavenly Fortitude! strengthen me, and inspire me with Christian courage.

O Spirit of Truth! come, and teach me all truth; come and show me the vanity of the world; come, and make me a strong and perfect Christian.

Thirdly, beseech the Almighty with earnestness and humility to impart to you his heavenly Spirit. Call to mind the consolatory promise which Jesus Christ made, that his *heavenly Father will give his good Spirit to them that ask it.* (Luke xi. 13.) Lastly, address yourself to the Holy Ghost himself; implore with confidence his descent into your heart, and also those seven-fold gifts which are the peculiar graces conferred by Confirmation. Your Catechism, which explains their separate effects, tells you that they serve as a great help to virtue, and to make us perfect in the ways of God: therefore you should earnestly beg them of Him who is the giver of every perfect gift. For this intention you would do well to say daily the following short prayers, with the hymn *Veni Creator Spiritus*, eight or ten days before you receive the Sacrament of Confirmation.

A Prayer before Confirmation.

O God of infinite goodness! who wert graciously pleased at my baptism to make me thy child, and to imprint on my soul the character of a Christian, mercifully pardon my having hitherto so badly corresponded with thy unbounded mercies; receive my fervent thanksgiving for all the favours bestowed on me from my birth to this moment, particularly for my being now ranked among those who are to be peculiarly consecrated to thee by the Sacrament of Confirmation. Thou offerest me the greatest of thy gifts; thou art about to seal my soul with the sacred character of a soldier of Christ, in addition to that which already distinguishes me as a Christian. O my good and merciful Father! encouraged by such special marks of predilection, I venture to implore with confidence that thou wouldst thyself infuse into my heart all the dispositions necessary for becoming the residence of thy holy Spirit. Alas! my God, I am far from possessing those sentiments of faith, love, humility, and fervour, which should now animate my soul; but it will be easy for thee to grant them to me I most sincerely detest every sin of my life, and every fault, or even imperfect inclination which may be an obstacle to the graces thou desirest to bestow on thy unworthy child. Do thou deign to purify me from every stain, by applying to my soul the infinite merits of thy death and passion. I purpose most sincere to serve thee with fidelity from this day forward; bu I feel that I am too weak to execute my resolutio, if left to myself; therefore, I conjure thee to impart to me thy holy Spirit, that, like the Apostles, I may be endued with strength from on high, and inspired with courage and resolution to prove myself in reality thy follower. I desire to receive this most precious favour; but do thou render this desire still more ardent, and accept, on my behalf, the fervent desires which animated the heart of thy blessed Mother and the Apostles previous to the descent of the Holy Ghost, and let their perfect dispositions in every other respect atone and supply for my deficiencies.

Prayer to the Holy Ghost, to beg the Descent of that divine Spirit with his seven-fold Gifts.

O HEAVENLY SPIRIT! whom I earnestly desire to receive in the Sacrament of Confirmation, merci fully deign to descend on me with all thy gifts and graces. Grant me, I conjure thee, the gift of *Wisdom*, that I may despise in future the vain pleasures of the world, and take delight in the service of God. Grant me the gift of *Understanding*, that I may comprehend the truths which my holy religion teaches—the gift of *Counsel*, that I may discover and avoid the snares of the devil and the world—the gift of *Fortitude*, that I may steadily execute my good resolutions, and imitate the glorious example of many of my age and sex, who preferred torments and death, rather than to offend God. Bestow on me the gift of *Knowledge*, that I may discern and faithfully execute the will of God in all circumstances—the gift of *Piety*, that my heart may be penetrated with tender love for God and for all that regards his most holy service—the gift of *Fear*, that my soul may be filled with a salutary apprehension of the divine judgments, and dread nothing so much as to fall unprepared into the hands of the living God. O eternal Light! O infinite Charity! O increated Wisdom, who replenishest the hearts of the faithful, and kindlest in them the fire of thy love! O holy Spirit! who didst inspire the prophets, who presidest over the Church, who convertest sinners, and sanctifiest millions that listen to thy inspirations, despise not my youth, my ignorance, and weakness; in a moment thou couldst enlighten the darkest understanding, and soften the hardest heart. O! come then into my heart; come, heavenly Spirit; and do not delay.

O sacred Virgin! Spouse of the Holy Ghost, whose pure soul was the chosen tabernacle of that heavenly Spirit, and who above all creatures wert plentifully enriched with his choicest gifts and graces, intercede for me, and by thy powerful prayers prepare me for the happiness I so sincerely desire.

Glorious Apostles! who received the plentitude of the Divine Spirit, obtain for me by your prayers a share in the perfect dispositions which prepared you to receive that consolatory Spirit.

The CEREMONY *of* CONFIRMATION.

ON the morning of your Confirmation, renew with redoubled fervour your desire to be replenished with the Holy Ghost. Assist at the holy Sacrifice of the Mass with particular devotion, and offer up the adorable Victim of our Altars to atone for all the sins of your life, and to obtain any disposition which the all-seeing eye of God may discern to be still wanting in your heart.

After the holy Sacrifice is concluded, call to mind the explanation which has been given you of ea ceremony used in the administration of the Sacrament of Confirmation, that thereby you may receive it with more devotion and reverence; then devoutly join in the prayers offered for you by the Bishop in administering the Sacrament. The ceremony is as follows: First, the Bishop turning towards those to be confirmed, says:

May the Holy Ghost come down upon you, and the power of the Most High keep you from all sin.

R. Amen.

Signing himself with the sign of the ✠ Cross, he goes on:

Bish. Our help is in the name of the Lord.

R. Who made heaven and earth.

Bish. O Lord, hear my prayer.

R. And let my cry come unto thee.

Bish. The Lord be with you.

R. And with thy spirit.

Then he extends his hands over those to be confirmed, and addresses a solemn prayer to the Eternal Father, begging, through Jesus Christ his divine Son, that he would send down his holy Spirit, with all his gifts and graces, into their souls.

Bish. Let us pray. O almighty and everlasting God! who hast vouchsafed to regenerate these thy servants by water and the Holy Ghost, and who hast given them the remission of all their sins, send forth upon them thy seven-fold holy Spirit, the Paraclete from heaven.

R. Amen.

Bish. The spirit of wisdom and of understanding

R. Amen

Bish. The spirit of counsel and of fortitude.

R. Amen.

Bish. The spirit of knowledge and of piety.

R. Amen.

Bish. Replenish them with the spirit of thy fear, and sign them with the sign of the ✠ Cross of Christ, in thy mercy, unto life everlasting: through the same

Jesus Christ thy Son our Lord, who liveth and reigneth with thee in the unity of the same Holy Spirit one God, world without end. Amen.

Then the Bishop, making the sign of the Cross on the forehead of each of those who are to be confirmed with holy chrism, and calling her by the name she has chosen, says: *N.* I sign thee with the sign of the Cross, and confirm thee with the chrism of salvation, in the name of the Father✠, and of the Son✠, and of the Holy✠Ghost.

After which, he gives the person confirmed a slight stroke on the cheek, saying at the same time, *Peace be with thee.*

As soon as you return to your place, after having been confirmed, raise your heart to God in sentiments of the most lively gratitude. Imagine you are among the Apostles after the descent of the Holy Ghost, and join most devoutly in the transports with which they glorified God. You need not be recommended to observe the most edifying recollection and modesty while the Bishop continues to administer the Sacrament. The adorable guest you have received will excite you to sentiments of the most profound veneration and humility, particularly when you consider how unworthy you are of his presence; you may employ those few moments in reflecting on your happiness, and thank God for it in any terms your devotion may suggest. The sentiments of the heart are at all times preferable to any set form, but more particularly at a time when you may humbly hope that they are suggested by the divine Spirit of God himself.

After all have been confirmed, the Bishop washes his hands; in the mean time the following Anthem is said: Confirm, O Lord, that which thou hast wrought in us from thy holy temple which is in Jerusalem. Glory be to the Father, and to the Son, and to the Holy Ghost. As it was in the beginning, &c.

"Confirm, O Lord," &c. as above.

Then the Bishop standing, turned towards the altar

says the following prayers, in which you should devoutly join.

Bish. Show us, O Lord, thy mercy

R. And grant us thy salvation.

Bish. O Lord, hear my prayer.

R. And let my cry come unto thee.

Bish. The Lord be with you.

R. And with thy spirit.

Bish. *Let us pray.* O God, who gavest the Holy Ghost to thy Apostles, and hast been pleased to ordain that by them and their successors that same divine Spirit should be given to the rest of the faithful, mercifully look down upon what we thy servants have done, and grant that the hearts of these thy faithful, whose foreheads we have anointed with the sacred chrism, and signed with the sign of the Cross, may, by the same Holy Spirit coming down unto them, and by his vouchsafing to dwell in them, be made the temple of his glory, who with the Father and the Holy Ghost liveth and reigneth God, world without end. Amen.

Then the Bishop concludes the ceremony by giving a solemn Benediction to all present in these words:

Behold, thus shall every man be blessed who feareth the Lord. May the Lord bless ✠ you out of Sion, that you may see the good things of Jerusalem all the days of your life, and that you may live with him for all eternity. Amen.

When preparing for Confirmation, you were instructed in the obligations you were about to contract by that sacrament, you did not of course neglect reflecting on their importance, and resolving to comply with them to the utmost of your power. Now, however, that you have been confirmed, you would do well to renew those good resolutions, and again consider the motives which induced you to form them. Jesus Christ promised that the Holy Ghost should recall to the minds of the Apostles all whatsoever he had said to them:—the presence of the same Divine

Spirit will assist you also to recollect, to comprehend, and to improve, from the instructions you have received in his name.

The Apostles, whom you already chose for your models in preparing for confirmation, exemplify in their conduct after the descent of the Holy Ghost, the two principal fruits you should draw from the sacrament you have just received: First, they became courageous soldiers of Jesus Christ. Before the descent of the Divine Spirit, they were so timid, that the most courageous amongst them was by a few words intimidated into a denial of his Divine Master and all abandoned Jesus Christ in his dangers and humiliations: but no sooner had they received the promised strengthening Spirit, than they boldly professed themselves followers of Him whom so short a time before they had shamefully abandoned; they preached the sacred name of Jesus aloud to those who had but him to death. As St. Chrysostom says: "they were assailed by all descriptions of persons, and threatened with all sorts of torments, fire, sword, and wild beasts: yet, like generous champions of Christ, they treated them all with as much contempt as if they were painted enemies." Consider these glorious models, and remember, that you have now been signed with the sign of the Cross, and thereby peculiarly enlisted under its banner, to fight the battles of Christ; first, against the world, by opposing its false maxims and dangerous customs; secondly, against the flesh, by combating your passions, bad habits, and evil inclinations; thirdly, against the devil, by resisting his temptations and suggestions. This is the glorious warfare in which you are now engaged: it will require many sacrifices and much courage; but you have received graces in proportion, since you have been visited by the same strengthening Spirit who comforted, fortified, inspired, and sanctified the Apostles.

The second effect produced in the Apostles by the

descent of the Holy Ghost, was their wonderful change, from wavering and imperfect disciples of Christ, into strong and perfect Christians. They had always been followers of our Redeemer, and were sincerely attached to his divine person; but they were still subject to many failings; they were frequently influenced by the false maxims of the world; desirous of its honours, and so dull, as scarce ever to comprehend thoroughly the heavenly doctrine which Christ so often preached to them, concerning the contempt of the world, or the love of the cross. It was not so after they received the Holy Ghost; no sooner had that Spirit of Light descended on them, than they were literally changed into new men; their understandings were opened, so that they perfectly comprehended those divine lessons of virtue which the gospel teaches, but which before appeared to them so many mysteries. Their false notions were rectified, so that they valued and sought after the sufferings and humiliations from which they once fled, and considered it a folly to glory in any thing beside a close resemblance with their crucified Master. "O!" exclaims St. Leo, "how quickly is that learned which God deigns to teach!" As this same powerful Master has now blessed you with his presence, and speaks to your heart, his divine lessons should produce in you also this second effect of Confirmation, which is, to render you a strong and perfect Christian. What is it to be a strong and perfect Christian? Remember it well, and imprint it on your mind, that the sacred character you have just been sealed with may not tend to your eternal condemnation. It is to glory in your name of Christian; it is to follow Christ, from whom you derive that glorious name; to profess his doctrine, not only in words, but by the tenour of your life; to value nothing so much as virtue; to dread nothing so much as sin; to despise the world, to scorn being a slave to its opinions, its menaces, or its deceitful promises; and above all, to show forth in your conduct the twelve fruits of the Holy Ghost, which should be the lasting and solid effects of Confirmation in those who worthily receive that sacrament, and who correspond with the graces it confers: therefore, as you have reason to trust in the mercy of God, that you did not fail in any of the essential dispositions for Confirmation, you have now only to profit of the great gift you have received, and to let every one see that this sacrament has produced in you the fruits of the Holy Ghost, *viz.* Charity, Joy, Peace, Patience, Longanimity, or Perseverance, Goodness, Benignity, Mildness, Fidelity, or Sincerity, Modesty, Continency, and Chastity. You know the meaning of those virtues, and the method of exercising them; but you should particularly attend to those which peculiarly appertain to your sex and present age; such as *Charity*, which does not merely consist in loving God, but also in loving your neighbour for his sake;—*Patience*, which is exercised on a thousand little occasions that too often serve to irritate those who did not correct their tempers in their youth;—and *Mildness*, which is so peculiarly necessary and attractive in your sex;—*Modesty*, that amiable virtue, which renders those who are so happy as to possess it, silent and retiring, diffident of their abilities and opinions, reserved in their manners, and strictly careful in regulating their words, actions, and desires, according to the exact rules of Christian decorum, despising, with the wisdom and generosity of a Christian, all the follies, fashions, and customs of others. These virtues in particular, are the fruits you should draw from your Confirmation; they are the ornaments of your sex; without them, every gift from nature, every advantage from education, every accomplishment, would expose you rather to contempt, danger, and ridicule, than to esteem or admiration. Beg them most earnestly, from the heavenly Spirit you have received and also implore the other fruits of his holy presence, particularly *Charity*, which is the perfection of every virtue, and which in itself contains them all. For this intention, and in thanksgiving for the inestimable advantages you have received, say devoutly the following prayer every day for a week or fortnight after Confirmation.

A Prayer after Confirmation.

Is it possible, O my good and merciful Creator, that thou hast so far overlooked my misery and unworthiness, as to make my soul the tabernacle of thy Holy Spirit! Can I believe that I am now honoured with the presence and enriched with the gifts and graces of the Holy Ghost? Yes, I firmly hope that thou hast not been deaf to my petitions; I hope I am now in possession of that sacred gift I so ardently desired. O my God! accept the praises of thy angels and saints in thanksgiving for thy unbounded mercies in my regard. May the blessed Mother of thy Divine Son, and the glorious choir of Apostles, thank thee for me. May the Cross of Jesus Christ, with which my forehead has been signed, defend me from all my enemies, and save me at the last day. May the inward unction of sanctifying grace, figured by the chrism with which I have been anointed, penetrate my soul, soften my heart, strengthen my will, and consecrate my whole being to thy service.

O heavenly Spirit! third person of the adorable Trinity! whom I have received, and most fervently adore, deign to take eternal possession of my soul, create and maintain therein the purity and sanctity which becomes thy temple. O Spirit of *Wisdom!* preside over all my thoughts, words, and actions, from this hour to the moment of my death. Spirit of *Understanding!* enlighten and teach me. Spirit of *Counsel!* direct my youth and inexperience. Spirit of *Fortitude!* strengthen my weakness. Spirit of *Knowledge!* instruct my ignorance. Spirit of *Piety!* make me fervent in good works. Spirit of *Fear!* restrain me from all evil. Spirit of *Peace!* give me thy peace: I neither desire nor ask the peace which the world gives—the false peace found in pleasure and self-gratification—but the solid, lasting peace, which I know from my own experience is only found in the service of God. Teach me in future to place all my glory, all my happiness and peace in serving my good God, who has so tenderly loved me—in combating for Jesus my Saviour, who has chosen me for his soldier, and in listening to and obeying thy voice, O Divine Spirit! who hast deigned to make my soul thy habitation. Heavenly Spirit! dwelling within me, let thy sacred presence change my heart, and influence the whole tenour of my future life. Let all my works be fruits of *Charity;* infuse into my heart the *joy* of a good conscience, and teach me to delight in the service of God, and to despise the false joys of the world. Give me grace to preserve *peace* with God, my neighbour, and myself:—give me *patience* to bear with all the ills of this life;—make me *persevere* in the service of God, and enable me to act on all occasions with *Goodness*, *Benignity*, *Mildness*, and *Fidelity*. Let the heavenly virtues of *Modesty*, *Continency*, and *Chastity*, adorn the temple thou hast chosen for thy abode. O Spirit of Purity! by thy all-powerful grace preserve my soul from the misfortune of sin, which for all eternity will be distinguished by the double title and sacred character of a Christian by Baptism, and a soldier of Jesus Christ by the Sacrament of Confirmation. Amen.

On the Presence *of* God.

There is no practice of piety so universally neglected by young persons, as that of reflecting on the presence of God, or in other words, the recollection of the divine presence. To that question of the Catechism which asks, *Where is God?* they all readily answer, *that God is every where;* yet nothing is so rare with them as to think of God any where but in his temple, or even to reflect that it is a duty to do so at any time but at prayer. You perhaps, no less than others, are negligent in this respect: you receive the blessings of the Almighty without thinking of their source. From morning till night you are guarded from a thousand dangers by his watchful Providence, nourished and clothed by his infinite liberality; yet seldom, perhaps never, during the day, do you reflect on the presence and goodness of your Benefactor, or raise your heart in thanksgiving. This is worse than thoughtlessness—it is great ingratitude, which you would be sorry to be guilty of towards a fellow-creature. But the chief cause why young persons who are instructed, and otherwise well disposed, do not aim at this virtue, is, that they fancy it is some high point of perfection reserved to the saints, and beyond their age and abilities. This false notion which they generally entertain of its great difficulty, is an error, in which it is the interest of the devil to keep them; because it is certain, that the enemy of their salvation could not succeed in half his attempts against them, if they did not quite forget the presence of God. If this be your idea also, you will perceive how great your mistake is, when you learn that the real practice of this virtue merely consists in three things, which are possible to every one.

First, in never committing any deliberate fault, *because God is present;* calling to mind, when you are tempted to sin, that God is looking on, to see whether you love him sufficiently to overcome yourself, and the devil, for his sake.

Secondly, in offering each of your actions to God, with a pure intention of pleasing him.

Thirdly, in frequently raising your heart to God in the course of the day, by any of those short acts of love, thanksgiving, supplication, &c. which are called *ejaculations.*

This method of acquiring an habitual recollection

of God is not, you perceive, any thing beyond your comprehension or ability; on the contrary, circumstanced as you are at present, you should find it extremely easy. The regulations to which you are now obliged to conform, are precisely calculated to habituate you to the practice of those three points in which the virtue of the presence of God consists.

You are under the eye of some person whom you would not grieve or displease, by committing any fault in her presence; her company is no impediment to your recreation; on the contrary, it contributes to your pleasure, and it only proves a restraint when you are tempted to act wrong. In the very same manner should the presence of God influence your conduct during your life. It should prevent your committing deliberate faults, yet never appear a gloomy or troublesome restraint, as so many young persons falsely imagine it to be.

Beside the general oblation of the thoughts and actions of the day, included in your morning prayers, you have a public offering made of your studies and other such occupations, before their commencement. This is to habituate you to that purity of intention, and recollection of God, which is the second requisite for walking worthily in his divine presence.

The aspiration which is made aloud for all when the clock strikes, is intended to remind you of the divine presence, and to teach you the holy practice of frequently raising your heart to God in the midst of your studies and other occupations; therefore it will be entirely your own fault if you do not enter the world with a happy facility of remembering Him who never forgets you—a holy horror of committing any fault in the presence of Him who could that instant punish it—and a confirmed habit of offering all your actions to that divine Being, who will not let a cup of cold water given for his sake go unrewarded.

On the Sign *of the* Cross.

There is nothing which can more effectually assist you to recollect the presence of God, and remind you of the duty of consecrating all that you say or do to his honour and glory, than the frequent and devout use of the sign of the Cross. This sacred sign has always been used by the Church to signify, that all graces and spiritual assistance are derived from the cross and passion of Jesus Christ. When accompanied with corresponding sentiments, it is an excellent form of prayer, a fervent act of faith, of hope, and of charity, beside being a public and solemn profession of our belief in those mysteries of our religion, which we must all believe and profess in order to be saved; namely, the Unity and Trinity of God, the Incarnation, Death, and Resurrection of our Saviour.

The sign of the Cross should always be dear to you as the sign of a Christian, the badge of a Christian, and the glory of a Christian—as the distinctive mark of Christ's true followers,—as a memorial of the sufferings of Christ on the Cross, and of your own deliverance from eternal death by and through those sufferings. To merit, by an application of this saving sign, the fruits of that Cross and Passion which it represents, you should accustom yourself to make it devoutly, frequently, and openly. You should make it *devoutly*, that is, with gratitude for the blessings which you enjoy through that Passion, and with sincere sorrow for your sins. Remember that a precipitate, disrespectful, as it were half method of signing yourself with the Sign of the Cross, is in reality to dishonour it, and to liken yourself to those who professedly deride and contemn it. Next, you should make the Sign of the Cross *frequently*. This is inculcated by the example of the primitive Christians, who by this sacred sign consecrated themselves to God, and implored his blessing in every action. It is also strongly recommended by all the great saints and fathers of the Church; among the rest, by the devout St. Ephrem, who says, speaking on this subject: "Cover thyself with the sign of the Cross, as with a shield, signing with it thy limbs and thy heart. Arm thyself with this sign at thy studies, and at all times, for it is the conqueror of death—the opener of the gates of paradise—the great guard of the Church. Fail not to carry this armour about with thee in every place, every day and night, every hour and moment. Whether thou art at work, or eatest, or drinkest, or travellest, or whatsoever else thou dost, sign and arm thyself with the saving Sign of the Cross. Sign with it thy bed; and whatever thou usest, sign it at first with the Sign of the Cross, in the name of the Father, and of the Son, and of the Holy Ghost. This is an invincible armour, and no one can hurt thee, if thou art armed with it." Endeavour to reduce this strong admonition so fervently to practice, that your most devout and ordinary actions, the beginning and end of all your duties, may be the Sign of the Cross;—but be particularly exact in following the directions of your Catechism on this head, and never fail to make it with faith, devotion, and confidence, *in all temptations and dangers, and before and after prayer.*

Lastly, you should make the Sign of the Cross *openly*, because it is by this sign that you show yourself a Christian, and prove that you do not blush at the Cross and humiliations of your God and crucified Saviour. "While others," says a pious author, "boast of ribbons and stars, which are worn and gazed on because they are badges of worldly honour, conferred by the great ones of the earth; you should think it the greatest happiness, the greatest honour, to bear that holy ensign of the King of kings, which is expressive of his greatest mysteries." Therefore, far from refraining from this sacred sign, which would point you out as a Christian to utter strangers in the furthest quarter of the globe you should always make it openly and without hesitation. Remember, however, that you are to be guided in this most particularly by prudence, which should direct and accompany every action to make it virtuous. You cannot make the Sign of the Cross too frequently, or too openly at present, nor perhaps in future, if you be in the bosom of a Catholic and pious family; because you will be sure of that sacred sign being duly reverenced; but there are occasions in which it would be more prudent to refrain from making the sign of the Cross *outwardly*, as often as you are now accustomed to make it. For example, to make the Sign of the Cross when the clock strikes, as you are now in the habit of doing, may perhaps expose that sacred sign, as likewise the cause of piety in general, to laughter and derision. Therefore, on *that account*, through respect for the Sign of the Cross, and not from any apprehension of drawing ridicule on yourself, you would do better to confine yourself to that elevation of heart to God, and simple thought of the passion which should always accompany the outward Sign of the Cross, to make it meritorious and salutary. Be careful, however, not to confound those occasions with others in which your not making the Sign of the Cross may be taken, if not for a denial of your faith, at least for a wish to conceal it. Among those, you may, for example, consider the custom of blessing yourself before and after meals; because in all companies, though composed of different persuasions, Catholics are expected to make the Sign of the Cross. Then, and on all such occasions, you should call to mind, that those who deny Jesus Christ before men, shall be denied by him before his Father, (*St. Matt.* x. 33.) and do not hesitate to show yourself a Catholic by making the Sign of the Cross openly, devoutly, and with that generous, noble species of pride, which made St. Paul glory in this Cross of our Lord Jesus Christ, by which the world was crucified to him, and he to the world.

On Meditation.

It will be in vain for you to promise yourself any solid or permanent fruits from the best instructions and most Christian education, if you do not learn early to consider Meditation as one of your most important, indispensable duties, and as such persevere in it with the utmost exactness. A great deal depends on your conceiving such correct ideas of this holy exercise, as will prevent your being misled by the illusion of those who call Meditation an exercise of extreme difficulty, or else of too great sublimity for ordinary Christians. This opinion may easily be traced to the devil, the great enemy of all good; particularly as it is universally held by such as are most in the habit of listening to his suggestions. Those who pronounce most decidedly on the difficulty or impossibility of Meditation, are always the very persons who never even attempt it, and who certainly on that account alone, are of all others least qualified to give an opinion on an exercise of which they have no experimental knowledge. Still, notwithstanding the unfounded prejudices entertained against Meditation, nothing is more certain than that this exercise is absolutely necessary for those who would work out their salvation, and that it is so easy, and so adapted to the most limited understanding, that every person is capable of it.

Aware of this important truth, consider that Meditation is indispensably necessary, according to the unanimous opinion of the holy Fathers: St. Augustine and St. John Chrysostom assert, that reflection and consideration of the truths of salvation are the foundation of good works; and certainly it is clear to every one, that those who do not meditate or reflect on the maxims of the gospel, on their various duties, on the obstacles which impede their progress in virtue, and the means best calculated for removing them run a very great risk of forgetting those maxims, neglecting those duties, yielding to those obstacles, and slighting those means; consequently, of being lost eternally. On the contrary, those who meditate assiduously, morally insure their salvation; because Meditation naturally produces such good desires, holy affections, and efficacious resolutions, as at length excite to the execution of good designs, to the perfect amendment of life, and to the habitual practice of virtue. How consolatory is it to think that an exercise so necessary, is likewise so easy! In effect, nothing more is requisite for Meditation, than to be a reasonable creature, because Meditation is nothing more than an exercise of the three powers of the soul, memory, understanding, and will; that is, *an application of those three powers* to some particular subject, whether spiritual or temporal. There fore it is clear that Meditation, rightly understood, is not only easy, but universally practised, since all from the first to the last, have some object in view some scheme to accomplish, some business to pur sue; and there is no one, if he wishes to avoid being rash or foolish, who does not frequently reflect on and adopt the means most likely to insure success. The greatest saint is not distinguished from the greatest worldling precisely by meditating or reflecting more frequently and profoundly, but by the difference in the subject of his reflections. On the concerns of the soul alone Meditation is found troublesome and difficult. For example, what difficulty does a merchant find in meditating, that is, in reasoning and reflecting on commerce?—a farmer upon husbandry?—a tradesman upon his employment? Those persons frequently call to mind what they heard for or against the plans they pursue, and thus they exercise the *memory*;—they make serious reflections upon what they found profitable or the reverse; and consider frequently how far their plans are calculated to insure success, or expose them to failure: this is the exercise of the *understanding*.—

Lastly, however little capacity those persons may have, their reflections never fail to excite in their *will* hopes and desires of success, fears of danger, or sorrow for disappointment, which is the *exercise of the will;* and those same reflections afterwards urge them to take precautions against the accidents they foresee, and adopt such measures as may repair past losses, and insure ultimate advantage.

This is what is called *Meditation*, and is it not clear that it is practised by every description of persons? What, then, can hinder those who reflect, or meditate on temporal concerns, from doing the same in the momentous business of their eternal salvation? Why should not they, in the same manner, reflect on what may conduce to or hinder their attainment of eternal felicity? Why should not they examine well the state of their soul, its dispositions and inclinations, and consider what they ought to pursue or avoid? The whole secret is, to think of eternity as often, at least, as we do of time;—to feel as much interest for our soul as we do for our body;—and to be as willing to encounter difficulties and overcome obstacles for immortal treasures, as we are for perishable goods. But, alas! the want of these dispositions is precisely what constitutes the difficulty of Meditation on spiritual matters. *With desolation*, says the Holy Scripture, *is the land made desolate*, *because there is none that thinketh in his heart* on the danger he runs of eternal perdition, or on the means of saving him self from unspeakable misery. Still, as the dispositions for Meditation are acquired and perfected by the habit of this exercise, you cannot be too strenuously exhorted to adopt and persevere in the holy custom of devoting a short time daily to Meditation on some of those great truths of salvation, which at the hour of death, will most certainly appear to you as the only subjects worthy of your serious consideration.

The METHOD *of* MEDITATION.

1st. CALL to mind the presence of God, by a short act of faith, which teaches us that God is every where and profoundly adore and humble yoursel before that infinite Being, to whom no mortal is wor thy to speak.

2d. Make a short act of contrition, to cleanse your soul from sin, *that* being the great obstacle to com munication with God.

3d. Implore his divine assistance and the light of his Holy Spirit, to make the meditation you are going about in a manner pleasing to his divine Majesty, and profitable to your soul.

Then call to mind the Christian Truth, or mys tery, on which you desire to meditate. Thinking on that, to the best of your power, is the proper exercise of the *memory*. It is almost morally impossible but some reflection will arise, or present itself to your mind, concerning the truth you have present to your recollection. Any reflections, even one considera-tion, however simple, would suffice, if you dwell on it, and endeavour to penetrate it well. These re-flections will naturally lead you to consider the state of your soul, to draw from the truth on which you meditate, some conclusion for the reformation of your life. Thus you exercise your *understanding*.

From the understanding having been convinced and enlightened by reflection, the will must conse-quently be affected according to the nature of the objects reflected upon.—For example, such alarming truths as the rigorous justice of God,—Hell—or Eternity, will produce in our hearts, fear, horror, aversion, and sorrow. Those subjects that are amiable and attractive,—as the birth of the divine Infant Jesus,—the adorable Sacrament of our Altars, will, on the contrary, excite feelings of love, admi-ration, gratitude, desire, hope, and confidence; and in producing such acts consists the exercise of the *will*.

Preparatory Acts for Meditation.

O ETERNAL and omnipotent Being! before whom the Angels tremble, I firmly believe that I am in thy adorable presence, and I acknowledge, in the face of heaven and earth, that I am most unworthy of the honour and happiness of conversing with thy Divine Majesty. But, O dearest Lord, since I know it is thy will that I should pray, and that thou hast perhaps annexed my salvation to serious reflection on the truths of eternity, I approach to thee, notwithstanding my wretchedness, and beseech thee to accept on my behalf the divine dispositions of Jesus Christ my Saviour, when he entered the Garden of Olives to pray.—Eternal Father! I offer thee my memory, and entreat thee to banish from it every earthly idea. Adorable Jesus! I offer thee my understanding; deign to dissipate its darkness, and fill my soul with the light of thy grace. Divine Spirit! I offer thee my will, and beseech thee to render it conformable to thine, and to inflame it with the fire of perfect charity.

Act of Contrition.

I MOST sincerely regret, O merciful Father! every sin and fault of my whole life, particularly those which may at this moment prove an obstacle to the graces thou desirest to bestow on me in this meditation. O adorable Jesus! let thy infinite merits atone for my offences, and deign to efface them by thy precious blood, that my heart may be purified, and disposed to receive the impressions of thy grace. I renounce every thought or affection which may distract me in thy divine presence; and I conjure thee to grant, through the intercession of thy blessed Mother and my good Angel, that this meditation may conduce to thy honour and my salvation. *Amen.*

*** Meditations are generally divided into two or three parts; that is, the same subject is considered under different points of view, or else its principal circumstances are separately reflected on

The following Meditation on Death is divided into three points first, on the certainty of death; second, on the uncertainty of time, third, on the consequence of death. The method of exercising the three powers of the soul on this subject is pointed out clearly, that this one meditation may serve to instruct you in the plan to be pursued in reflecting on all other Christian Truths.

On Death.

I. Point.—*On the Certainty of Death.*

Exercise your *Memory*, by calling to mind that nothing is more certain, more inevitable than death. It is a solemn decree, pronounced without exception against all creatures, which condemns each and every one to die. It is an awful truth, which needs no elucidation, as the experience of every day and every hour proves that nothing is so certain, so unavoidable as death.

After your memory is fully possessed with the subject, exercise your *understanding* by the following or any other reflections which may present themselves on the foregoing truth. Consider, that death should make a deep impression on our hearts and minds, because it concerns every one without exception. There is no day nor hour in which many are not carried to the silent tomb—so that in eighty or ninety years hence, death will have swept away the millions who now cover the face of the earth; or if a few survive that period (which is but an instant compared to eternity) they will only linger for a moment on the verge of the grave, every instant expecting the stroke of death. This terrible truth, though universally believed, makes little impression on the generality of persons, because they forget their last end—they banish from their thoughts the idea of death, as if the forgetfulness of that most important of all events were a means of retarding its execution, and form schemes and projects without any reference to eternity: the greater number live as if they were never to die, and take as much pains for acquiring the riches, honours, and pleasures of this world, as if they were certain of remaining here always.

Apply these considerations to yourself. Death is to be my fate as well as that of others. I have already passed some years of my life; and where are those years? They are gone down as a shadow, and are already almost effaced from my memory: though I am now young, and perhaps have reason to hope for a long life; yet, were I to enjoy the longest that ever was spent on earth, it will certainly have an end; I shall die at last. It shall be said of me, as I have often heard it said of others; "*She is dead—she expired such a day—such an hour.*"

When you have seriously weighed this important truth, you will naturally feel astonished at the forgetfulness of death which prevails among Christians; you will contemn the pleasures of the world, which must shortly terminate, and compassionate the blindness of those who forget their last end, and thereby render their temporal death the commencement of eternal death. Above all, you will be penetrated with sentiments of regret, for having ever imitated their thoughtlessness; and thence will result a firm resolution of living henceforward in such a manner as may enable you to meet death with confidence and tranquillity.

Those sentiments, which are called the *affections of the will*, produced by meditation, you may simply indulge, expressing them to God mentally, or as follows.

O how great is the folly of those who never think of death until it has actually overtaken them! Why should the pleasures of this world be valued or sought after, since we are certain that death will put an end to them all? Why should its trials and pains be so much dreaded, since they also will end with death? Death is only terrible to the wicked—it is for the just the end of all their miseries, and the beginning of all their happiness. I can now render it one or the other for myself. O my God! imprint on my heart the thought of death, that I may learn to dread and also to desire its approach. Divine Jesus! teach me to tremble at the certainty of death, which has eternally separated so many from thee; teach me also to desire it, as the only means of being united to thee eternally. May I frequently remember my last end, that the salutary thought may prevent my offending thee, and thereby render the moment of my death far more desirable than terrific.

II. POINT —*The Uncertainty of the Hour of Death.*

Exercise of the *Memory.*—Call to mind those words of our divine Lord, which prove that death, though in itself the most certain of all events, is the most uncertain as to the time it may happen. You know not the day nor the hour—you know not when the Son of man will come—he will come like a thief in the night, when you least expect him.

Exercise of the *Understanding.*—Reflect, that as we are quite uncertain as to the moment of death, and cannot procure ourselves an additional day or hour of life, nothing can be more rash than to remain in a state in which we would not wish to be found at the hour of death. How many sinners are there living at present, who perhaps will experience the horrors of an unprovided death! Surely to depend on health, strength, or any thing else whatsoever, as a preservative from speedy death, is the most unaccountable of all follies. Jesus Christ himself has warned us that he would come when we do not expect him; thousands of persons who were in the enjoyment of health and spirits, yet were carried off without so much as an instant to call on God for mercy, or to prepare for appearing in his presence, should warn us of the danger we are in of being surprised by death, and convince us all that these great truths are not simple threats, as so many are inclined to consider them

Application of these Reflections to yourself.

It is then possible that I may not live another year, another week, or even another day. If death should come this moment, would it find me prepared to meet its summons? Am I in that state in which I should wish to be found at the moment of death? I need only consult my conscience. What does it reproach me with? what would I fear most, if I were to die in a day, or an hour? or if I were certain I had but another year to live, how would I spend it?

Exercise of the *Will.*—I have often deserved to be deprived by an untimely death of the graces and blessings which I abused; yet I have been spared through the infinite patience and goodness of God. O how sincerely I regret my folly, in exposing myself to the danger of being surprised by death in the state of sin! To be aware of the infinite importance of dying well, and also that every moment may be my last, should suffice to make me resolutely undertake all that I know is necessary for dying well. It is not when death actually seizes on me, that I should prepare for its approach; now is the time—I will carefully profit of it, since I know not how soon it may end. O divine Jesus! give me grace to be always ready for a summons, which I may every moment expect. I resolve most firmly to watch continually over myself, to perform my actions as a preparation for death; and, above all, to approach the sacraments each time as if it were to be the last. Alas! I do not know at this moment whether I may live to receive them again. O my God! penetrate my heart with a salutary contempt for this world, which may end to me this very day, and give me grace to value the opportunity I still enjoy of preparing for eternity

III. Point.—*On the consequence of Death.*

Exercise of the *Memory.*—Call to mind the principal consequence or effect of death with regard to this world and the next. First, death separates from all earthly objects, and reduces the body to a heap of dust and corruption; secondly, it presents the soul alone before God, to give an exact account of all her thoughts, words, actions, and omissions, from the first use of reason to the last moment of her existence.

Exercise of the *Understanding*.—Consider how very instructive the effects of death are with regard to this world, and how awful they are with respect to the next. No sooner has death put an end to the career of a soul on earth, than she is totally and eternally separated from the parents she so much loved; from the goods she possessed; from the friends with whom she was connected; from the pleasures and honours she enjoyed; from the very body she animated; in a word, from all that is temporal, from all things besides her sins and her good works, such as they may be at the moment of her separation from this world. She is no longer seen on earth, no longer heard; and in a short time no longer loved, or even thought of. Ah! how little do Christians reflect on these certain consequences of death! surely if they did, they would now treat the world as they will one day be treated by it;—they would sincerely despise it, and courageously forsake those pleasures and friends, amusements and vain honours, which will forsake them in the silent tomb. But after all, the privation of such advantages is not considered as a loss by Christians who are deeply impressed with the great truths of eternity. The consequences of death with regard to the next world, are to present the soul before God—to enlighten her with the pure light of truth—to show her clearly the nothingness of all that passes away with time; so that the loss or possession of God will then be the only object of her solicitude. She will be judged according to the Gospel—the Commandments—the duties of her situation in life—and a sentence of eternal happiness or eternal misery shall be pronounced on her accordingly.

Application of these Reflections to yourself.

I shall myself experience, sooner or later, these consequences of death. When I shall have expired, the first emotions of the few who may sincerely love me will be regret; but a very short time will suffice to console them, and wipe away their tears. I shall be forgotten, and in process of time not one on earth will know that I ever existed: even though I should be recollected, regretted, and loved after my death, of what use will that be to me in those terrible moments when I shall stand alone before God, obliged to render an exact account of all the thoughts, words, actions, and omissions of my life?

Exercise of the *Will.*—O how wise were those who, looking forward to the consequence of death, despised all earthly pleasures, and considered the opinion, praise, and honours of the world, as mere vanity! Where are all those who made so many sacrifices to the world? whose idol was their body, whose reputation among men was dearer to them than their innocence before God; who preferred the esteem of creatures to the friendship of their Creator? Alas! they are dead—their bodies are mouldered in the earth, and their souls burning in hell. While the names of the humble, mortified, retiring servants of God are handed down to posterity, the very names of those who served the world are forgotten. It is then the height of madness, to cleave to such vain and short-lived advantages as worldly pleasures or honours, and absurd in the extreme, to seek after the esteem of creatures! My God! give me grace to perceive daily more and more the nothingness of this world, that by a Christian life I may effectually dispose myself for appearing before thee, my God, my Sovereign Lord, to whom alone I will adhere during life, since thou alone wilt remain to me after death.

A Prayer after Meditation.

I THANK thee, O my God! with all the affection

of my heart, for having permitted me to converse with thee, and for all the graces thou hast bestowed on me during the holy time of meditation. Pardon me, I conjure thee, every distraction I have been guilty of, or any other fault I committed, and vouchsafe to enable me to accomplish the resolutions I have made in thy presence. Grant in particular, that the fruit of my meditation may be an increase of love for thee, and charity towards my neighbour; a lively sorrow for my past offences, and a heartfelt detestation of sin, and every occasion that may lead thereto. Accept, O Lord! a renewal of the consecration I have already made to thee of my whole being; of every day, hour, and moment of my remaining life; and vouchsafe to assist me so powerfully by thy grace, that I may endeavour in all things to copy thy sacred life, and thus fulfil the obligations I contracted at baptism.

On the predominant PASSIONS.

It is not usual, that in young persons, whose characters have not taken any settled form, any vice should have gained so decided an ascendency, as to enable themselves or others to discern clearly the nature of their predominant passion. Generally speaking, they should be more anxious to correct all their faults, than to find out the chief among them; as that is not discernible until they are placed amidst the busy scenes of the world. Still, as they cannot be made acquainted too early with the evil consequences of vice, it would be advisable for them to examine occasionally their dispositions, lest any evil propensity may take root in their hearts, thereby become the principle of their actions, and frustrate the ends proposed in the most Christian education.

The predominant passion of most persons is *Pride*, which never fails to produce not only thoughts of pride and vanity, but also such haughtiness of manner and self-sufficiency, as to render them absolutely disgusting and ridiculous. Incessantly endeavouring to attract admiration, and become the sole object of attention, they spare no pains to outdo others, to set themselves off, and by their conceited airs, their forwardness, their confidence in their own opinion, and neglect or contempt of that timid, gentle, retiring manner, so amiable and attractive, particularly in youth, they defeat their own purpose, and become as contemptible as they aim at being the contrary.

Many are so little sensible of the awful duties imposed by Christian *Charity*, as to be ever ready to blame, criticise, and condemn all who come under their observation. This is one of the most dangerous propensities, as the occasions for manifesting it occur incessantly, and frequently lead to mortal sin. The persons thus uncharitably disposed, talk continually of the faults of others, which they are always inclined to exaggerate, though often those defects exist only in the detractor's embittered imagination, which represents others in so unfavourable a point of view, as to subject their actions to the most unkind censure. To this may be added a satirical propensity, which criticises and turns every thing and every person into ridicule, sparing neither superiors, friends, enemies, nor even the most sacred characters, as Clergymen. This disposition never fails to make numerous enemies; and though occasionally encouraged by laughter and smiles of approbation, it nevertheless is generally as hated as it is hateful.

Those whose temper is violent and unrestrained, cannot be ignorant that *Anger* is their predominant passion—their frequent unreasonable and impetuous sallies of anger, on the slightest occasions, render intercourse with them as unsafe as it would be with a maniac.—Such dreadful and melancholy consequences have followed from even one fit of passion, as to render any family truly unhappy, who may possess a member with a violent temper. Those who feel inclined to this passion, should, while young, use all their efforts to overcome so dangerous a disposition. Reason, affection for their family, consideration for all those with whom they may be connected, and, above all, religion, furnish powerful motives and means for reducing any temper, however violent, to the standard of Christian meekness. The chief among those means is prayer, and the next, perhaps most efficacious, is absolute silence under all emotions of anger.

There are many other persons who, though they do not rank among the passionate, are nevertheless the pests, particularly of domestic society. Their predominant passion is a certain *ill-humour*, *fretfulness*, *peevishness*, *and irritability*, which pervades their words, manners, and even looks; and it is usually brought into action by such mere trifles, as leave no chance of peace to those who live in the house with them. Children and servants are the ordinary butts of their spleen; and even their best friends, their superiors themselves, are not always secure from their ill-tempered sallies, and their incessant complaints. In a word, their sourness, their dissatisfied, discontented manner, effectually embitters every society, and throws a gloom over the most innocent amusements. As this luckless disposition is peculiarly that of women, young persons cannot be too earnestly recommended to combat in youth any tendency thereto, lest they become, when older, the greatest torment of that society they are certainly intended to bless and ornament.

Sloth, which is the predominant passion of many persons, is alone one of those vices most difficult to correct. It shows itself by habitual indolence, and such negligence and apathy, that no duty, however serious, can rouse a person of this character to exertion. Days, weeks, and even years, pass over without any account of how they have passed; for though the indolent form many projects of amendment, yet those projects are never executed, because procrastination is the daughter of sloth. Any time but the present appears calculated for the discharge of duty, precisely because the most heroic efforts in prospect cost less than a single actual exertion. Thence it follows, that spiritual duties are so long neglected and deferred, that the torpor, which in youth could easily have been broken off, gains such an ascendency as to become almost unconquerable, and at length reduces the soul to that dreadful state generally called tepidity, which is only another word for sloth in spiritual matters. Then it is that every social and personal duty is abandoned; children, servants, affairs spiritual and temporal, order, cleanliness, every thing is neglected, and permitted to run into such disorder and confusion, as to render the persons degraded by this vice no less a disgrace to themselves, than to their friends and to society. In a word, there is no passion which leads more certainly to misery hereafter; for after all, the inanimate victim of sloth, who has lived without energy, without sentiment, almost without a soul, will at last be effectually roused by death, whose approach is terrible indeed to those who lead a useless inactive, idle, and consequently most sinful life.

Those whose predominant passion is *deceit*, are frequently not considered dangerous characters, until after they have given many persons cause to repent having had any intercourse with them. Their manners are generally as insinuating as their motives are base and interested. They are usually distinguished by a total disregard for truth; a base system of appearing to coincide with every one, the better to gain that confidence which they only intend to abuse; deceitful expressions—eternal manœuvring—equivocations—and so great an opposition to candour and plain dealing, as to adopt a thousand underhand means for carrying on their most simple and ordinary transactions, thereby engaging themselves and others in a labyrinth of difficulties, and spending their whole life in perplexities, entanglement, and hazard. Independently of religion, the natural desire we all have for happiness and security, should be motives enough for using efforts to counteract every tendency to this mean vice. It proves in general, sooner or later, its own punishment; for, notwithstanding the deep-laid schemes, the cunning and artifices of those who seem to live for the purpose of deceiving their fellow-creatures, yet the depravity and meanness of their motives in all their actions, are seen through much clearer and more frequently than they are aware. Beside, one lie or trick often requires many more to prop its crazy superstructure, and to invent those their mind must be incessantly on the rack; but as their craft is generally discovered, they are exposed to such contempt and distrust as deprive them of all credit. Even when by chance they intend to deal fairly and openly, they are carefully shunned, because a long habit of dissimulation has so indelibly stamped their character with the stigma of insincerity and knavery, as to render truth and falsehood equally disbelieved from their lips. In a word, they are invariably, in the close of life, so hated, despised, and distrusted, as to become outcasts in society, a burden to themselves, and almost as degraded and unhappy, even in this life, as they deserve to be.

The capital fault of some persons is inordinate, ungovernable *curiosity;* a vice which is a certain road to many sins, particularly in youth. It should, however, be observed, that there are two kinds of curiosity, one allowable, and even commendable, the other dangerous and sinful. They may be easily distinguished one from the other by their different effects. That species of curiosity which is innocent and desirable, especially in young persons, consists in a laudable desire of useful information; this thirst after knowledge, when well regulated, produces emulation, application to study, patience and perseverance in difficulties, good employment of time, and a love for the society and conversation of the learned. The vice of curiosity, on the contrary, is the bane of useful acquirement, because it consists chiefly in an eager desire to hear and see every insignificant trifle that passes, and gives persons so much to do with the concerns of others, as to leave them no leisure to attend to their own. Curious persons are always on the look-out for what is termed news; and as that levity and shallowness of mind which produces misguided curiosity, creates also a taste for unnecessary talk, they are never so well satisfied as when they have discovered a number of incidents to circulate among their friends and acquaintance. Their inquisitive air,—their prying and intrusive manners,—their incessant questions,—their eager impatience to be informed of every incident that takes place, and minute inquiries into the affairs of others, would lead to the idea that they were commissioned to investigate the origin, ancestors, names, tempers, fortunes, and faults of every individual who falls in their way. Even the secrets of families, which curiosity itself should respect, are not too impenetrable for the inquisitive, nor are the most insignificant domestic occurrences below their notice. On the contrary, to gain such information, they do not hesitate descending so low as to question children and servants; thereby giving occasion to innumerable crimes against charity, often against truth. Another propensity of curious persons is a desire to hear and see precisely those things which they have been told were dangerous, and to read every species of publication which they have been recommended to avoid, or know to be exceptionable. This contemptible disposition can only be rectified by many years' strict attention to the short rule of never interfering in what does not concern us, except when charity or duty dictates the contrary.

There are few persons, even amongst the best

Christians, who have not had occasionally to regret *offending with the tongue;* but the faults committed and mischiefs occasioned by those whose unbridled passion for *talk* is their predominant failing, can scarcely be estimated. This propensity generally characterizes persons of weak heads, vacant minds, and shallow understandings, who seem absolutely incapable of one instant's serious reflection, and know not what it is to think two minutes, even before they undertake to decide on the most important matters. Those who talk always, cannot hope always to talk sense, consequently their least material faults are absurd, random opinions, giddy, inconsistent expressions, and frequent faults against politeness and good-breeding; for the volubility of great talkers never allows others to deliver an opinion, or finish any sentence without helping them out. Their laughable and disgusting egotism, perpetual relations of their own unimportant adventures, ideas, or opinions, which they are too frivolous to perceive are interesting only in their own eyes; their system of laughing, whispering, and ridiculing, generally mark out great talkers as persons of little or no intellect, though they often do not want sense, if they could but prevail on themselves to be silent, and reflect ever so little on the necessity of making use of that gift. But those, however, are the least serious faults produced by excessive *love of talk.* Sins against charity, breaches of confidence, discovery of the secrets of others, indiscreet communication of their own affairs, and those of their families, to acquaintances, strangers, even to servants; remarks on the defects of others—breaches of truth—habitual exaggeration—loss of time—dissipation and levity, are all the infallible consequences of a passion for talking, beside the dreadful evils which unguarded repetition of stories has been known to produce in society, by disuniting the members of families—irritating and disgusting friends—breeding disturbances, &c.; evils which are much easier occa sioned than removed. Could those useless beings, whose occupation is talk, foresee the mischief which they occasion, even by one word, which often escapes their tongue and memory at the same time, how bitterly would they regret the dearly-bought pleasure of talking! how carefully would they study the virtue of silence and prudent restraint, and thus, spare themselves the regret of having unfeelingly published faults too true to be contradicted, and stories too mischievous in their effects to be easily remedied; thus inflicting wounds they cannot afterwards heal.

There are some persons who possess many amiable qualities, yet destroy the effect of them all by one predominant failing, a fund of *caprice* and *inconstancy*. Those persons rarely succeed in gaining one sincere friend; on the contrary, they seldom fail to disgust those whom they had at first attracted, because they frequently receive with marked reserve one day, those whom they treated with kindness the day before. On one occasion those changeable beings will scarce allow others to join in a conversation—the next, they will not by a single word manifest a desire to please. Their projects or undertakings are as variable as their ideas, and are never pursued with such steadiness as would encourage any rational person to join in them; nor can it ever be conjectured from the projects of one day or hour, what those of the next may be. They eagerly seek one moment after those objects which the next they despise; and are one day dissolved in vain joy, another oppressed with melancholy. But what is infinitely worse than all is, that this irrational capriciousness, beside rendering them the jest of others, and a burden to themselves, materially endangers their eternal salvation. Their ideas and feelings on spiritual matters are just as variable as on all other occasions; their plans of amendment and regularity, though frequently entered on with ardour, are as frequently abandoned; consequently there can be no persons so little likely to gain a crown, which is promised only to perseverance.

Selfishness is a common failing, and a peculiarly unamiable one, when it predominates in a character Those persons who make *self* their idol, are from morning till night occupied in providing for their own individual gratification and pleasure, and in taking measures for warding off from themselves every thing in the shape of trouble, inconvenience, provocation, &c.; thus they become almost the sole objects of their own thoughts, solicitudes, and exertions. They generally manifest their predominant failing to the least attentive observer, by an habitual inattention or indifference when the gratification of others is in question; —by an unfeeling insensibility for the misfortunes of their fellow-creatures, and by being the last to make an exertion for their relief. They seem almost incapable of taking part in the pains or pleasures of others; every species of misfortune or gratification pleases or grieves them, precisely only in as much as they perceive it is likely to affect them individually.

A turn for unrestrained *extravagance* is also a great fault when it predominates; it is directly opposite to generosity, with which it is confounded; for extravagant persons are generally deprived, by unnecessary expenses, of the means of obliging or relieving others; beside, they are much remarked for hard-heartedness, and insensibility to the wants of their neighbour; for a total neglect of the obligation of charity. and for being just as averse from supplying the real necessities of others, as they are prodigal in gratifying their own imaginary wants. Any tendency to this destructive passion should be guarded against, and if possible corrected even in early years, especially in female youth. It has been before observed, that on them, in a great measure, depends the happiness and peace of families, which should be a powerful motive for correcting every defect of temper and disposition; it may here be added, that on them depends materially the prosperity of their families, since economy and prudent management are necessary to the support, at least, of ordinary properties. But, unhappily, to them may be laid the ruin of many opulent fortunes; for females, generally speaking, are too much inclined to the passion in question—extravagance is too often their predominant failing. When this is the case, instead of considering the circumstances of their parents, they endeavour to keep pace with others of more opulent fortunes or exalted rank; disregarding, or perhaps not noticing the ridicule to which their foolish ideas and expenses expose them. They hurry, and even force their parents or husbands into the most extravagant and imprudent projects, and are never at rest until, at any expense, they have gratified their ambition, and attained the pinnacle of the mode with respect to houses, furniture, and dress; yet these are but a few of the mischiefs produced by ungoverned extravagance:—a little common sense would greatly assist religion in curing this mania.

Excessive *Parsimoniousness*, on the contrary, is the leading defect of others, and is infinitely a greater nuisance to domestic peace, than can be conceived by those who have not witnessed its effects. This fault of narrow-mindedness is frequently the characteristic of women, whose dispositions too often lead them to set such value on trifles, as to sacrifice for their preservation the greatest of all treasures, their own peace of mind, and that of their families. The duties of saving, economizing, and prudent management, devolve on them; but when a propensity to stinginess is indulged, and suffered to take root, their economy degenerates into downright avarice, and prudence into a sort of trifling, fidgeting vigilance, which is eternally on the watch to retrench, to save, to discover what may be done without, or to purchase for less than its value what is absolutely necessary. They regularly accost tradesmen, shop-keepers, &c. with a determination to bring down their prices, however just and moderate they may be; and carry on all their dealings at least with the appearance of a full and uncharitable conviction that every one intends to cheat them. All persons cannot labour too early in correcting every tendency to this degenerate propensity, which seldom produces more than trouble and anxiety —for certain it is, that the fretting and fuming of half-misers over mere trifles, is in the end very inadequately repaid by the miserable savings of the year.

A propensity to *extravagant Partialities* is a fault which frequently predominates in some warm, impetuous characters. Those persons are distinguished by a precipitate selection of favourites in every society; by an overflow of marked attentions to the objects of their predilection, whose interests they espouse, whose very faults they attempt to justify, whose opinions they support, whether right or wrong, and whose cause they defended often at the expense of good sense, charity, moderation, and even common justice. Wo to the person, whether superior or inferior, who ventures to dissent from them in opinion concerning the objects of their admiration; *that* alone exposes them to aversion and censure. The friendship or affection of such characters does not deserve to be valued, for it results not from discernment of merit, but blind prejudice; beside, they are remarkable for annoying those whom they think proper to rank among their favourites, both by expecting to engross their whole attention or confidence, and resenting every mark of kindness they may think proper to show to others. However, as their affections are in general as short-lived as they are ardent, no one person is likely to be tormented long with the title of their friend.

The foregoing are the chief among those passions to which the generality of mankind are subject. There are also a variety of other shapes, in which the capital sins separately predominate in different characters. It would not be easy to enumerate them, but you will not find it difficult, aided by the grace of God, to discover your capital enemy, provided you ardently beg that grace and light, and are sincerely desirous to overcome it to the utmost of your power. The following marks, by which you may discern your ruling passion, are pointed out by St. Chrysostom, and may assist your examination on this important point.—1st, Your predominant passion is that propensity, disposition, or failing, which is the ordinary cause of your faults and sins. 2dly, It is that which chiefly disturbs the peace of your soul, and occasions you most remorse and uneasy reflections. 3dly, That of which you are obliged to accuse yourself most frequently in confession. 4thly, That which gives occasion to the greatest conflicts in your soul, and which you feel most repugnance to overcome. 5thly, That which usually influences your deliberations, intentions, or projects, and which is the chief motive of all your actions: that, in a word, which is most untractable and deeply rooted in your heart· for if, when wounded on that point, you feel sensibly hurt, it is an evident mark that there is your predominant passion, your capital enemy, the greatest obstacle to God's grace, and to your eternal salvation.

DEVOTIONS

FOR EVERY DAY IN THE WEEK.

The practice of consecrating each day of the week to the honouring of some particular mystery, or saint, is conformable to a holy and ancient usage of the faithful. It is a devotion particularly calculated for assisting young persons to spend each day fervently, because their attention is better fixed, by being confined to one object at a time; and fervour is kept alive by the variety which occurs during the week.—You would do well to adopt this devotion.

The short Prayer affixed to each Practice you can say at your daily visit to the Blessed Sacrament, or at any convenient time in the morning; but recollect, that it is not by that Prayer the Mystery or Saint is to be principally honoured; it is much more by carefully avoiding sin, by purity of intention in your various duties, and by frequent use of the Aspiration annexed to each Practice, or any other your devotion may suggest.

Exercise for SUNDAY.—*Devotion to the adorable Trinity.*

THIS day is set apart by the Almighty himself to be kept holy; that is, to be sanctified by works of piety and particular devotion. You are instructed as to the method of sanctifying the Lord's Day. You know how much those deceive themselves, who fancy that they comply with this precept by hearing Mass; therefore you will be doubly culpable, if you ever yield so far to the bad example you may hereafter receive in this respect, as to make the Sunday a day of particular dissipation, rather than devotion You should remember, during your life, that the precept of sanctifying the Sunday, beside obliging to assist devoutly at the holy Sacrifice of the Mass, requires that the greater part of the day be devoted to works of piety; such as hearing a sermon, and the evening Office of the Church in your parish chapel, and spending some time in teaching the Catechism, or instructing the ignorant, either at home or abroad.

Beside those public duties of our holy religion, which should be common to all instructed Christians, your private practice for this day, particularly consecrated to the adorable Trinity, may be thanksgiving for the great blessings you have received from the three divine Persons at your baptism, when you were regenerated in the name of the Father, and of the Son, and of the Holy Ghost. Make a short reflection on the solemn engagements you then entered upon, and which you are now of an age to fulfil. Examine whether you really do what you then promised; whether you renounce the devil, by resisting his temptations; whether you renounce the world, by generously despising its follies; and whether you renounce the flesh, by conquering your sinful inclinations, your passions, or your bad habits; then implore pardon for your failings, resolve to amend them, and renew your baptismal vows in the following form.

Prayer.

O Blessed Trinity, Father, Son, and Holy Ghost. The source and fountain of all good! I most firmly believe in thee, I most humbly adore thee, and thank thee, with a grateful heart, for all the blessings and benefits I have received from thy infinite goodness! I most fervently consecrate and offer to thee an unreserved sacrifice of my whole being. O my God, who hast a right to every day, hour, and moment of my existence, accept as the first-fruits of this week the thoughts, words, and actions of this day, which I offer thee in testimony of my sincere desire to satisfy my obligation of keeping it holy; mercifully assist me to spend it in such a manner as may draw down thy blessing on the remainder of the week. Increase in my soul the heavenly virtues of Faith, Hope, and Charity, which I received at Baptism, and teach me to make Faith the rule of my conduct, that thereby it may avail me to life everlasting. Eternal Father! take possession of my memory; efface from it all images of vanity, and engrave therein the recollection of thy adorable presence. Eternal Son! enlighten my understanding, and conduct me in the path of salvation by the light of Faith. Holy Spirit! sanctify my will by the most ardent love; render it submissive under the contradictions of this life, and never permit that by attachment to my own ideas or judgment, I should forfeit the blessings of peace offered to men of good-will and obedient minds. Holy, adorable, undivided Trinity, by whose power, mercy, and providence I was created, redeemed, regenerated, and preserved to this moment, receive the oblation of my whole being, and take me out of the world rather than permit me to efface thy sacred image in my soul by mortal sin. I adore thee, O Holy Trinity, I worship thee, I most humbly give thee thanks for having revealed to man this glorious, this incomprehensible mystery, and for granting to those who persevere until death in the faithful profession of it, the reward of beholding and enjoying in heaven, what we now believe, and adore upon earth, one God in three persons, the Father, the Son, and the Holy Ghost. *Amen.*

Aspiration.—Glory be to the Father, and to the Son, and to the Holy Ghost; as it was in the beginning, is now, and ever shall be, world without end *Amen.*

Exercise for Monday—*Devotion for the Souls in Purgatory.*

It is a most pious and meritorious custom, to pray frequently for the souls in purgatory, and to offer up occasionally for those suffering friends of God the holy sacrifice of the Mass, the holy Communion, and other satisfactory works in our power. This devotion, though so well founded, is not as general and lively as it should be. There are many who would make any exertion or personal sacrifice to save a fellow-creature from much less pains than are endured in purgatory, yet who hear with unconcern of that prison of fire, where thousands are tormented; amongst whom are perhaps a parent, a brother, sister, or dear friend of theirs. This is generally owing to the weakness of our faith, and to our little notion of the intolerable pain reserved in the next world for a venial sin, for every slight fault or trivial imperfection which has not been atoned for in this life. You should endeavour from your youth to nourish the most tender compassion for those who are now absolutely incapable of assisting themselves, and who must remain separated from God until the last farthing is paid, either by their own sufferings, or by the interposition of the faithful Many powerful motives should induce you to be among the most fervent in assisting them: the chief are, that by this spiritual work of mercy you prove your love for God, you benefit your neighbour, and materially serve yourself. You prove your love for God, by interceding for those who are so dear to his Divine Majesty, and whom he so ardently longs to glorify for ever. You next perform an act of the greatest charity towards your suffering fellow-creatures, and by endeavouring to shorten their banishment, confer on them so great a benefit, that you cannot conceive its value, unless you could clearly see, as they do, what it is to be separated from God. Lastly, you essentially serve your own soul, by providing for yourself powerful advocates, who will not forget you when they stand before God.

These considerations should suffice to animate you to do all you can for the souls in purgatory. Devote then fervently the prayers, good works, and the various actions of the day, to their relief. Offer up, in particular, the holy Sacrifice of the Mass for this intention. You have a devout method of doing so in this book, and are already in the habit of saying the Beads of the Dead on Monday: but you should particularly impress on your mind, that sloth or negligence in the prayers or actions which you offer up for those suffering souls would frustrate your own intentions, and make you very unworthy of being heard on behalf of others. On the contrary, so far from benefiting those for whom you pray, you would only expose yourself to a severe purgatory in the same fire which torments them.

Prayer.

O God of all holiness! infinitely pure and adorable Being! how great must be thy horror of the least stain of sin, since thou punishest so rigorously in the flames of purgatory the venial faults of those whom thou so tenderly lovest Ah! mercifully enlighten my understanding, that the torments thou inflictest on the least offence in the other world, may teach me the enormity of sin, and penetrate my heart with compassion for those souls who are now enduring inexpressible pains, for such failings as perhaps I too often look on as trivial. My God, though thy justice banishes them from that kingdom where nothing defiled can enter, yet surely thy mercy has not forgotten them; no, thou art too good, too compassionate to abandon the work of thy own hands. Though the season for merit and repentance is now past for them, yet thou hast left them a resource in the prayers of thy servants on earth. Despise not then, O Lord, the supplication which I, thy unworthy child, now make for those who can no longer implore thy mercy for themselves. Remember, O infinite Goodness, that they are all the work of thy hands, redeemed by the precious blood of thy only Son; consider that they are the objects of thy infinite love, who burn with the most ardent desire to be united to thee. Have mercy on them then, O infinite mercy! and for thy own sake stretch forth to their relief those sacred hands by which they were formed; apply to them once more the merits of that adorable blood by which they were redeemed. I most humbly offer up, to implore this favour, the adorable Sacrifice of the Mass at which I shall assist this day, or to-morrow, all the Masses which will be celebrated throughout the world, together with the adorable actions, prayers, and infinite merits of Jesus Christ while on earth; to which I most humbly add all my thoughts, words, actions, prayers, and sufferings during this day. Mercifully accept this oblation, O Lord, on behalf of all who now suffer in purgatory; particularly those for whom thou desirest I should pray—those who are most dear to me—those to whose sufferings I may have been in any respect accessary—those who are most forgotten by others, and who have no one to pray for them. Give them all speedy repose and eternal rest, O merciful Father of all mankind! and give me the grace I stand in need of, for spending this day in such a manner as may, through thy infinite goodness, tend to the great object I dare to have in view, which is the repose of thy dear and suffering children.

Aspiration.—Give them, O Lord, eternal rest; and let perpetual light shine unto them.

Exercise for TUESDAY.—*On Devotion to your Angel Guardian*

ONE of the greatest proofs which the Almighty has given of his love for his creatures, is his having appointed angels to take charge of them through life—to watch over them—to protect them in danger—to admonish them—to pray for them, and never for an instant abandon them, until after death, when those blessed spirits resign their trust into the hands of Him from whom they received it. O how dear must one soul be to God! how precious must it be in his eyes, since he does not disdain to appoint an Angel for its guide and companion! Still, notwithstanding the greatness of the benefit, it is, like most other spiritual blessings, much less valued than it should be. There are many, who never think of the services they receive from the blessed Spirit who guards them, and who, on that account, are deprived of many spiritual advantages, which would be the fruit of more devotion to their Angel Guardians. This devotion is a debt of gratitude due from all Christians; but it is particularly to be recommended to young persons; because the inexperience, thoughtlessness, ignorance of duty, or strong passions, often attendant on youth, expose them to a thousand spiritual and corporal dangers, in which they would be much strengthened and often preserved by a solid devotion to their good Angel. Endeavour to excite this devotion in your heart, by reflecting on the many claims this heavenly Spirit has to your most tender gratitude and confidence. Call to mind the charity and zeal with which he took charge of your soul, when it was confided to him at your birth; the tender care with which he has since watched over you, bearing patiently with your ingratitude, grieving over your faults, reminding you of your duty, offering your prayers to God, and frequently imploring graces for you; beside other good offices, which surely merit on your part the most lively gratitude to God, and sincere devotion to your heavenly guide. This devotion, to be solid, should consist, first, in such profound respect for that pure spirit who constantly beholds you, as will restrain you from acting wrong, though you were quite concealed from human observation; since nothing should be done in the presence of an Angel, which you would not do before those whom you most respect. Secondly, it should consist in great confidence in your powerful advocate, recommending all your concerns to his intercession, beseeching him frequently to obtain for you the virtues you most want, the grace to conquer your faults, &c. And thirdly, it should consist in gratefully thanking him for the benefits daily received through his mediation. Endeavour to acquit yourself of those duties with fervour through life, but particularly on this day, which you specially dedicate to honour your Guardian Angel.

Prayer.

O Angel of God! my blessed Protector and most amiable Guardian! to whose care I have been committed by my Creator from the moment of my birth, unite with me in thanking the Almighty for having given me a friend, an instructor, an advocate, and a guardian in thee. Accept, O most charitable Guide! my fervent thanksgiving for all thou hast done for me; particularly for the charity with which thou didst undertake to accompany me through life; for the joy with which thou wert filled, when I was purified in the waters of baptism; and for thy anxious solicitude in watching over the treasure of my innocence. Thou knowest the numberless graces and favours which my Creator has bestowed on me through thee, and the many dangers, both spiritual and temporal, from which thou hast preserved me. Thou knowest how often thou didst deplore my sins, animate me to repentance, and intercede with God for my pardon. Ah why have I so little merited a continuance of thy zealous efforts for my salvation? Why have I so often stained my soul by sin, and thereby rendered myself unworthy of the presence and protection of an Angel, of so pure a spirit as thou art, who never sinned? Still, as my ingratitude and thoughtlessness have not lessened thy charitable interest for my salvation, they shall not diminish my confidence in thy goodness, nor prevent my abandoning myself to thy care, since God himself has intrusted thee with the charge of my soul. Penetrated with sorrow for the little progress I have made in virtue, though blessed with such a Master, and sincerely determined to correspond in future with thy exertions for my salvation, I most earnestly entreat thee, O protecting Spirit, to continue thy zealous efforts for my eternal interest; to watch over my youth, to direct my inexperience, to fortify my weakness, to shield me from the innumerable dangers of the world, and rather to obtain, by thy powerful prayers, that my life may be shortened, than that I should live to commit a mortal sin. Remember, O most happy Spirit! that it was one act of profound humility, and one transport of ardent love for thy Creator, that caused God to establish thee for ever in glory; obtain that those virtues may be early implanted in my soul, and that I may seriously endeavour to acquire the docility, obedience, gentleness, and purity of heart, which should be the favourite virtues of my present years. Conduct me safely through this world of sin and misery; watch over me at the awful hour of my death; perform for my soul the last charitable office of thy mission, by strengthening, encouraging, and supporting me in the agonies of dissolution, and then, as the Angel Raphael conducted Tobias safely to his father, do thou, my good Angel and blessed Guide, return with me to him who sent thee, that we may mutually bless him, and publish his wonderful works for a happy eternity. *Amen.*

Aspiration.—O my dear Angel Guardian, preserve me from the misfortune of offending God.

Exercise for WEDNESDAY.—*Devotion to St. Joseph.*

THIS glorious Patriarch has at all times been the peculiar object of the devotion, veneration, and confidence of the greatest saints. He has been looked on in every age as an example of real and exalted sanctity, as the model of humble souls, because he excelled in the heavenly virtue of humility; and as the patron and guide of contemplatives, because his life was one continual prayer. But though the great St. Joseph is the general advocate of all Christians, particularly of those who aspire to perfection, yet he appears much more peculiarly the patron and protector of youth. The Almighty, by selecting him for the various functions he exercised on earth, towards his divine Son, has pointed him out to all young persons as the deserving object of their respect and confidence; as their patron, their protector, and model. St. Joseph is the patron of youth, because he was chosen to watch over the childhood of Jesus Christ; to direct, provide for, and protect that Divine Child in his youth. He is the particular protector of young persons, because the Almighty intrusted to his care the helpless infancy of his Divine Son, and Jesus Christ himself so totally abandoned his sacred Person to his protection, that he was pleased to depend on him for the preservation of his life from the cruelty of Herod. Lastly, St. Joseph is the model of youth, for the virtues he particularly practised are precisely those which all young persons should imitate, *viz* great purity of heart; that is, such horror of sin as caused him to be called *a just man*;—great eneration and love for the Mother of God—an ardent attachment to the child Jesus—and a continual study and imitation of the obedience, humility, and other virtues which he witnessed in the conduct of his Divine Charge. Those are the reasons why this Saint has been chosen as your particular protector, and the festival of the Protection of St. Joseph selected for you as a day of extraordinary devotion. But you need not be told that it will avail you nothing to be among those who are particularly placed under the protection of St. Joseph, if you do not perform all that is necessary for meriting his patronage; therefore, to do your part, you should fervently devote yourself to that glorious Saint by the practice of solid devotion towards him; that is, by particularly honouring him during your life as your patron—by respecting him as your Father—by sincerely endeavouring to imitate his virtues, particularly his constant view of Jesus Christ—his love for the Blessed Virgin—his attachment to prayer—his respect for the presence of Jesus—his unbounded obedience. You should likewise firmly confide in his intercession (which St. Theresa says she never found to fail in any thing she recommended to his prayers)—and spend as fervently and piously as you possibly can this day, which you should every week consecrate to honour St. Joseph, with a view to obtain his powerful protection, not alone while you are young, but throughout your life, and also the grace of a happy death, for which he is specially invoked, on account of having himself expired in the most happy of all circumstances, in the arms of Christ, and under the immediate protection of the Blessed Virgin.

Prayer.

O GREAT St. Joseph! reputed Father of Jesus! and spouse of the Mother of God! thou art my special Patron, and the object of my sincere devotion, respect, and confidence. I rejoice, from the bottom of my heart, in the sublime favours bestowed on thee. I thank the Almighty for having honoured thee with the most glorious commission which was ever given to any creature, for having made thee the guardian of the life of Jesus—the protector of Him who watches over the world, the support and consoler of his most blessed Mother. O great Favourite of Heaven! if thou wert so exalted on earth, how great must thou be in heaven! If this wretched world was rendered a paradise for thee by the constant presence of Jesus, how happy must thou be, now that thou beholdest him in the splendour of his glory! I will, notwithstanding thy dignity and my unworthiness, approach thee with confidence, because I am convinced that the constant view of the eternal God become a child for our love, has filled thy heart with paternal tenderness for all those whom he honoured and instructed by the example of his early life. O glorious model and patron of God's greatest saints! thou dost not disdain to become the particular patron of youth, because the sacred infancy of Christ was the source of thy glory, and the object of thy tender devotion. Receive me then into thy venerable arms, for the love of the divine Infant who so often reposed on thy bosom. Take me as thy child, for the sake of him whose submission to thy will, and dependence on thy care, so exalted thee. I, on my part, most fervently offer thee my heart, and all my thoughts, words, and actions of this day, which I particularly consecrate to thee, as a small testimony of my respect and filial love. Present me, O blessed Saint! to Jesus, and obtain for me a share in the virtues and amiable dispositions of his divine childhood, that I may thereby become less unworthy to call thee my Father. Be thou, O glorious Guardian of the *Word made flesh!* my special protector; not alone amidst the many dangers of my youth, but throughout my life. Implore for me a particular devotion to thy Virgin Spouse, and the grace to imitate so faithfully her virtues and thine, that at the hour of my death, I may be entitled to look up to her and to thee with an humble confidence. When that awful hour of my departure from this world arrives, obtain for me, O glorious St. Joseph! a small share in the profound peace, holy confidence, and ardent love which the actual presence of Jesus and Mary infused into thy soul at thy consoling death, and do not cease to be my dear blessed protector, until I shall have happily joined thee in the kingdom of eternal rest. *Amen.*

Aspiration.—O glorious St. Joseph! obtain for me the grace of a holy life and a happy death.

Exercise for THURSDAY.—*Devotion to the Blessed Sacrament.*

THOUGH the adorable Sacrament of our Altar, which is the most precious of all our divine Redeemer's gifts to man—the most convincing proof of his love, and an abundant source of blessings, should be an object of universal devotion, yet very few among those who believe in the Real Presence of Jesus Christ in the Eucharist, correspond to the best of their power with the infinite love which he shows to all mankind in this adorable Sacrament. This, as well as most other spiritual evils, is caused by want of reflection; very few seriously reflect what it is to have a God so near them as our God is;—to have Jesus Christ himself reside among them—to be able at all times to visit, to converse with the King of Heaven, and to be certain of always finding, in the adorable Sacrament of the Eucharist, a good parent, ready to listen to and enter into all their concerns; a liberal Benefactor willing to enrich them, a Physician to heal them, a friend to advise them. Jesus Christ is all that, and infinitely more, to the happy few who know how to profit of his infinite mercy in remaining on earth. But how few are they! Do you at least reflect seriously, that if you be not among the small number of those who sincerely feel and endeavour to repay the love of Jesus in the Eucharist, you will be infinitely more culpable, more ungrateful than others, because Jesus Christ has granted you opportunities both for imbibing and practising devotion to the blessed Sacrament, of which the generality are deprived. While many others as deserving as you are, know little more concerning this ineffable Mystery than the Real Presence of Christ on the Altar, you are instructed in the end for which the Eucharist is instituted, and have been taught how to correspond with the merciful designs of Jesus Christ. The singular happiness and privilege of dwelling under the same roof with Jesus Christ, should be to you another strong motive for devotion to this adorable mystery. On this perhaps you seldom reflect; yet it is, notwithstanding, a great blessing, particularly when compared with the circumstances of the numbers who are situated many miles from a church, and who seldom, if ever, enjoy the advantages which you have constantly within your reach. Endeavour to prove your lively gratitude for these favours, and all the blessings you have ever received from the Holy Eucharist, by sincere and solid devotion to this adorable Sacrament. This devotion should consist in sentiments of respect, gratitude, and love towards Jesus present on our altars; in recurring with confidence and faith to this fountain of grace in all your necessities; in great recollection, modesty, and silence, whenever you are in the presence of this awful Sacrament; also in consecrating every Thursday to honour the blessed Sacrament; to thank God for so great a gift; to atone for all the irreverences which Jesus has ever suffered in this mystery of love; as likewise to implore graces, general and particular, for yourself and all mankind.

Prayer.

O MOST adorable Jesus whom thy own infinite

love induces to dwell among us, thy unworthy servants, in the adorable Sacrament of our Altars, receive, I beseech thee, my profound adoration. I firmly believe that thou art really present in the holy Eucharist, as powerful, as amiable, and as adorable as thou art in heaven; thou hast mercifully hidden the splendour of thy Majesty, lest it should deter us from approaching thy sanctuary. I believe thou dwellest on our altars, not alone to receive our adorations, but to listen to our petitions—to remedy our evils—to be the strength and nourishment of our souls, our powerful Helper, our Refuge, and our Sacrifice. I hope in that boundless mercy which detains thee among us poor weak sinners. I love that infinite goodness which induces thee to communicate thyself so liberally and so wonderfully to thy creatures. I thank thee for such a convincing proof of thy love, and ardently wish that I could worthily acknowledge all the blessings I have ever received from this fountain of grace and mercy. I sincerely regret that this precious pledge of thy love is received by the generality with such coldness and indifference. Alas! I myself have had too much share, by my ungrateful conduct, in wounding thy merciful heart on this altar, and am more guilty than others, since very few have been so much favoured; thou hast not only granted me abundantly the general blessings which this fountain of grace pours on the world, but thou hast provided me with the most favourable opportunities of loving and adoring thee in this august mystery. Thou hast placed me close to thy sanctuary, where I can recur to thee frequently, and daily behold the sacrifice on the altar. Ah! my good God! I am now convinced that thou deservest from me all the love that my heart is capable of feeling; therefore I humbly consecrate to thee all my affections, and firmly resolve from this moment to endeavour to imitate the respect, gratitude, and love, which always distinguished those among thy faithful servants, who were most peculiarly devoted to the august Sacrament of the Altar. Accept, O divine Jesus! the adorable Sacrifice of the Mass, and all the thoughts, words, and actions of this day, which I fervently offer in thanksgiving for the institution of this amiable Mystery; in atonement for all the insults, irreverences, and sacrileges which have ever been committed against it; and to implore for myself and all creatures a solid devotion to the holy Eucharist. Mercifully give efficacy to my ardent desire of worthily honouring thee in this adorable mystery, and grant me, through thy divine Heart, a share in the purity and fervour of the angels who day and night surround thy sanctuary, and of all those who ever loved thee most in this sacred mystery, that I may serve thee with sincerity and perseverance during my life, and be so happy at length, as to enjoy thee in the splendour of thy glory for a happy eternity. *Amen.*

Aspiration.—O living Bread! come down from heaven: be thou my support in this life, and my viaticum to a happy eternity.

Exercise for FRIDAY.—*Devotion to the Passion of our Lord.*

A GRATEFUL and feeling recollection of our divine Redeemer's Passion and Death should not be confined merely to one day in the week; every day, even every hour of our existence, should recall to our minds the torments which Jesus Christ voluntarily endured to save us from suffering eternally; or at least, every day should strengthen our gratitude for so great a benefit as that of our redemption, and our compassion for all that Jesus suffered on our account; but above all, it should increase our horror of sin, that great evil, which required such a remedy. The death of our merciful Mediator on Good Friday, has consecrated every Friday in a particular manner to the commemoration of his Sacred Passion; therefore you should on this day endeavour most fervently to animate and strengthen in your heart a grateful and solid devotion to the Passion of Jesus Christ, avoiding carefully that unfeeling insensibility, which makes so many look on a crucifix with as little sorrow and confusion as if they had no share in occasioning the excessive torments of the Divine Victim it represents You should early accustom yourself to think frequently of the sufferings of Christ, particularly when you make the sign of the cross, and look on a crucifix or any other representation of the passion. Secondly, you should be particularly exact in hearing Mass daily and devoutly, that being one of the best possible means of honouring the passion, since it is a commemoration and a renewal of the Sacrifice of the Cross. Thirdly, you should offer the holy Sacrifice of the Mass, and all the thoughts, words, and actions of every Friday, in union with the sufferings of Christ —to thank your Saviour for them—to obtain the conversion of sinners—and to beg of Jesus Christ, through the infinite efficacy of his sacred blood, that your heart may be early impressed with deep and lasting devotion to the passion. This devotion consists chiefly in sincere gratitude for that infinite love which induced Jesus Christ to endure such torments for your sake, as would separately have caused his death, if he had not preserved it by a miracle, to suffer more. Secondly, it consists in heartfelt contrition for the share your sins had in his sufferings, and a sincere, lively horror of sin in general; since those who deliberately offend their Redeemer, show that they are in the unhappy disposition of crucifying him again, if that were in their power :—lastly, in a fervent imitation of the virtues of Christ practised in the course of his Passion. As this last point is of most consequence, you should make it your particular practice, on every Friday, to consider the profound reverence with which Jesus prays in the Garden of Olives, that you may imitate it in all your spiritual duties. Reflect on the divine patience with which this meek Lamb endures the insults and cruelty of his enemies, and for his sake bear cheerfully with any little trial you may receive. Admire his profound silence, when accused of crimes it was impossible he could commit, and think yourself happy, if this day present you an opportunity of suffering a rebuke with gentleness and meekness, whether you have or have not merited it. Call to mind at your meals, the vinegar and gall presented to Jesus on the cross; compassionate the anguish of his afflicted Mother, who could not procure her divine Son a less bitter draught; and when you retire to rest think of the hard bed of the cross on which Jesus expired, and seek refuge in spirit in the adorable wounds of his sacred side.

Prayer.

O DIVINE and adorable Jesus! Saviour of mankind! I most humbly adore thee, and beseech thee to penetrate my soul with the most lively gratitude for that infinite love, which brought thee from heaven to suffer and die for me. O do not permit that I should ever be one of the ungrateful number who forget thy sufferings, or think of them with indifference. Ah! where should I be for all eternity, if thou hadst not loved me better than thy own life? Should not thy bitter sufferings fill my heart with compassion and sorrow, since they were occasioned by my sins? Yes, my adorable Saviour! divine Victim of my sins! I will at least think of thee, who hast never forgotten me. I will live for thee, who didst not refuse to die for me. I now most fervently offer to thee, in union with the oblation of thyself on the cross, the sacrifice of my whole being. I desire to accompany thee in spirit through all the stages of thy sufferings, and to commemorate them by the most sincere sentiments of gratitude for thy love, and sorrow for my sins and those of the world. Adorable Jesus! overwhelmed with sorrow for my sins in the Garden of Olives! give me the grace of sincere contrition and perfect conformity to thy holy will;—teach me, by thy wonderful patience in the midst of the most cruel insults, the virtue of meekness —let thy profound humiliations, when thou wert crowned with thorns, and clothed with a purple garment, animate me to conquer my pride, and despise sincerely the opinion of the world; associate me to the happy few who followed thee to Mount Cavalry, and beheld thee crucified. Thou didst end thy life, O merciful Jesus! in torments and humiliations, deprived of every thing this world calls pleasure or consolation; thou art my model. I know that thou art *the way, the truth, and the life;* that all who would be saved must walk after thee, and all who would reign with thee in heaven, must on earth take up their cross and follow thee. I believe these truths, and conjure thee, through thy sufferings from the moment of thy birth unto thy death, to strengthen me to bear whatever cross thou mayst send me. Thou hast not yet, it is true, honoured me with a great share in thy sufferings; thou hast spared the weakness of my age and virtue; but I know that if thou lovest me, I shall not pass through this life without sufferings. I am convinced that thou knowest what is best for me, therefore I now accept from thy hand, with resignation to thy holy will, all the trials and sufferings of my future life. I unite them beforehand to thy cross, and beg of thee to strengthen me now so powerfully by the graces thou hast purchased for me through thy death and passion, that I may never expose myself to eternal sufferings hereafter.

Aspiration.—I adore thee and bless thee, O Christ, because by thy cross thou hast redeemed the world.

Exercise for SATURDAY.—*Devotion to the Blessed Virgin.*

DEVOTION to the ever-glorious Virgin Mary is, in the opinion of some of the greatest Saints and Doctors, one of the most certain marks of a soul being likely to gain eternal happiness. The reason of this is, that a particular devotion to the mother of God, when rightly understood and reasonably practised, leads to the most perfect service of her divine Son, and at the same time renders the practice of virtue easy, by securing the peculiar protection and special intercession of the Blessed Virgin. She is the Mother, the Advocate, the Refuge, and the Hope of all Christians; but to those whom she discerns to be her sincerely devoted children, she is so peculiarly favourable, that her particular clients, such as St Bernard, St. Dominic, St. Aloysius, St. Stanislaus, have been distinguished even among the saints by the most sublime gifts of grace.

It should scarce be necessary to recommend to you a tender and ardent devotion to the Blessed Virgin. She who is the most perfect and most favoured of all creatures, the glory and model of your sex, the tender Mother of youth, and their powerful Advocate before God, should naturally attract your respect, love, confidence, and veneration. But as nothing is more common than a false idea of devotion to the Blessed Virgin, (particularly among young persons, who often think all consists in stated prayers in her honour, and a certain confidence in her intercession,) you should form a just and correct notion of this devotion, that you may not resemble those who honour the Blessed Virgin with their lips, but whose hearts and conduct are far from entitling them to call her their Mother.

To be truly devoted to the Blessed Virgin, you must first honour her with that respectful homage, which, though widely different from the honour paid to God, and infinitely inferior thereto, is nevertheless due to Mary, as the blessed Mother of your Redeemer, and the most perfect of God's creatures.

Secondly, you should confide in her, because she was given you by Jesus Christ for your Mother;—because she loves you with that pure and tender charity, which a thousand degrees surpasses all the tenderness of your own parents—and also because she is as able as she is willing to assist you in all circumstances, since no one could have so much interest in heaven, and influence over the heart of Jesus, as his dear and blessed Mother.

Thirdly, your devotion must consist in imitating her virtues. This is the real test of true devotion to Mary: it is so essential, that without it all the other means you may adopt for honouring the Mother of God will be vain. Dwell on this point, and consider how necessary it is for you in particular to imitate her, who is the model of your sex, and whose virtues you are obliged to practise, if you wish to save your soul. Consider also, how easy it is for you to imitate the Blessed Virgin, since her life was spent in the discharge of those very duties you have or will have to perform. She never worked a miracle; no extraordinary action is recorded of her—the Gospel mentions but one verbal lesson that she ever gave to man—all her sanctity consisted in discharging the duties of her state, and performing ordinary actions with more pure intention, more ardent love, more fervour, and altogether more eminent perfection than any creature who ever existed. Fix your eyes on her then, whom Jesus Christ himself gave you for your Mother and Model. For the present, you should dwell with particular attention on the lessons she teaches you in the early sacrifice she offered of her heart to God in her Presentation in the Temple. That festival was chosen as a day of special devotion for you, because it was then that the Blessed Virgin Mary became the Model of your present tender age; inviting you by her example, to make an early sacrifice of your heart to God, and to serve and love him from your earliest youth. It was during those years of seclusion from the world, that the glorious Virgin prepared herself, by the most fervent practice of all the virtues of her age and situation, for executing the great designs which the Almighty had formed in her regard. Follow her example, imitate the purity of life, innocence, humility, docility, and obedience, which sanctified the Blessed Virgin in the Temple. You are now separated from the world, as she was, and shielded from all its dangers;—you have time and opportunity for acquiring the habits of virtue, which your future circumstances may render necessary.

Hereafter the retired life of the Blessed Virgin in Nazareth, her silence, her love of labour, her charity, obedience, and cheerful submission to the hardships and inconveniences of her condition in life, will animate you to a faithful and cheerful discharge of the domestic duties you may have to fulfil; and in all the crosses and afflictions which must be expected in this life, the heroic constancy of your blessed Model at the foot of the cross will encourage and strengthen you How happy will you be, if you early adopt, and steadily persevere in this perfect method of honouring her, who, after God, deserves most the honour, veneration, respect, and gratitude of all creatures! How confidently may you then call her your Mother, and confide in her as such during your whole life! But more especially, what strong claims will this devotion to Mary give you to her powerful protection at the dreadful hour of death.

As real devotion to the Blessed Virgin is one of the most precious graces you could receive from God, and one that will require many sacrifices, and constant efforts to overcome your faults, you should frequently and earnestly beg of Jesus Christ to inflame your heart with an ardent love for her whom he so much loved, and to give you grace to imitate her heroic virtues. Offer for this intention, as well as in thanksgiving for all the favours bestowed upon Mary, the holy Sacrifice of the Mass, and all your thoughts, words, and actions on Saturdays. Let it be a day of particular fervour, and above all, be careful to avoid every deliberate fault on this day;

since you would grieve and offend the Blessed Virgin more by one wilful offence of her divine Son, than you could honour her by all your practices of devotion.

Prayer.

O ever-glorious Virgin Mary! most perfect and amiable of all creatures! I humbly cast myself at thy feet, and beseech thee to accept the sincere protestations of respect and veneration, which I now fervently present to thee. I reverence thee, O sacred Virgin! as the Mother of my Redeemer, and I fervently offer thee all the homage which is due to thee in that august quality. I confide in thee, I love thee, as the merciful advocate and tender Mother of all Christians; most earnestly desiring that I could collect in my heart alone, all the tender and respectful sentiments which ever animated thy most devoted servants. But to supply for my deficiencies I offer thee the filial tenderness with which Jesus Christ loved thee, and the respect and obedience with which, as thy dear Son, he deigned to honour thee. O Mother of Mercy! who wert never known to reject any one that had recourse to thee, receive me as thy child, for the sake of Him who confided me to thy care in his agony on the cross. Permit me to choose thee for my glorious Patroness, my dear Mother, and the object, next to God, of my respect, gratitude, and love. Ah! do not refuse to receive me under thy maternal care, and to grant me a place in thy amiable heart. Let me have the honour and happiness of being ranked from my youth among thy most devoted children; that by loving and serving thee, I may learn to serve and love God perfectly: and by endeavouring to imitate thee, I may imitate Jesus Christ, whose most perfect image thou art. Accept then the oblation I now make to thee of my heart, that thou mayest present it to Jesus Christ, in union with the early sacrifice thou didst make of thy pure heart in the Temple. O mercifully deign, most powerful Virgin, to obtain for me grace to make an early and perfect sacrifice of my heart and whole being to Him, for whose love and service alone I was created. Teach me, by thy early flight from the world, to dread and despise the world, and to profit of the advantage of my present situation, that thereby I may be prepared to meet the temptations and dangers to which I may be exposed. Obtain for me an abundant share in the heavenly dispositions of thy holy Heart, and beseech thy dear Son to impart to me in particular a lively horror of sin; purity of heart and mind; devotion towards thee, a love of retirement, fidelity in discharging the duties of my state, an ardent love for God, and that spirit of angelic modesty, which always distinguished thee, and marked thee out even exteriorly as the Temple of the Divinity. To obtain these great graces, and in thanksgiving for the favours bestowed on thee, my blessed model, I fervently offer the holy Sacrifice of the Mass, and the thoughts, words, actions, and various duties of this day. I conjure thee, by the maternal tenderness with which thou didst guard the sacred infancy of thy divine Son, to watch over me this day and every moment of my life; to be a mother, a refuge, and guide to me in all the difficulties, temptations, and dangers I may hereafter be exposed to; and when the dreadful hour of my death comes, O holy Mary, Mother of God, pray for me, support me, defend me, and plead for me so powerfully with God, that I may die in the friendship of my Creator, and reap for all eternity the happy fruits of having been sincerely devoted to thee. *Amen.*

Aspiration.—O clement, O pious, O sweet Virgin Mary! pray for me now, and at the hour of my death.

On NOVENAS.

By a Novena, is meant a devotion of nine days in honour of some mystery of our Redemption, to obtain a particular request or in honour of the Blessed Virgin, or any of the Saints; to beg their intercession in obtaining a favour from God. It may be made of any prayer according to each person's devotion, and is certainly a holy practice, which has often been found successful in obtaining favours from God. Those who perform it with the conditions necessary for prayer; in particular, with a lively hope of having their request granted, and perfect resignation, should it be refused, may be assured that Christ, who has said, *ask and you shall receive*, will grant them some grace or blessing as the fruit of their prayer, though in his infinite wisdom and mercy, he may refuse the particular favour which they implore. "If," says St. Augustine, "he seems deaf to their cries, it is only to grant their main desire, by doing what is more expedient for them." God alone knows what is good for us: how often is the refusal of our requests a far greater favour than would be the grant of them.

A NOVENA *in Honour of the Name of* JESUS.

OH! merciful Jesus, who didst in thy early infancy commence thy office of Saviour, by shedding thy precious blood, and assuming for us that name which is above all names; we thank thee for such early proofs of thy infinite love; we venerate thy sacred name, in union with the profound respect of the angel who first announced it to the earth, and unite our affections to the sentiments of tender devotion which the adorable name of Jesus has in all ages enkindled in the hearts of thy servants. Animated with a firm faith in thy unerring word, and penetrated with confidence in thy mercy, we now most humbly remind thee of the promise thou hast made, that when two or three should assemble in thy name, thou thyself wouldst be in the midst of them. Come, then, into the midst of us, most amiable Jesus! for it is in thy sacred name we are here assembled. Come into our hearts, that thy holy Spirit may pray in and by us; and mercifully grant us, through that adorable name, which is the joy of heaven, the terror of hell, the consolation of the afflicted, and the solid ground of our unlimited confidence, all the petitions we make in this Novena.

Oh! blessed Mother of our Redeemer! who didst participate so sensibly in the sufferings of thy dear

Son, when he shed his sacred blood, and assumed for us the name of Jesus; obtain for us, through that adorable name, the favours we petition in this Novena. Beg also, that the most ardent love may imprint on our hearts that sacred name, that it may be always in our minds, and frequently on our lips; that it may be our defence in temptations, and our refuge in danger, during our lives, and our consolation and support in the hour of death. *Amen.*

[*To this may be added the* Litany of Jesus, *p.* 66.]

A NOVENA *to the* SACRED HEART.

O SACRED and adorable Heart of Jesus! Furnace of Eternal charity. Ocean of infinite mercy! Consolation of the afflicted! Refuge of sinners! and Hope of the whole world! I most fervently adore thee, and unite my heart, my affections, and supplications, to the perpetual homage thou thyself renderest to the Divinity on our altars. Most amiable Heart! which hast loved us with an eternal love, supply thyself for my insensibility, and receive my desire at least of loving thee with all the ardour and sincerity thou so justly meritest. But remember, O adorable Heart! that thou hast not disclosed thyself to us only as an object of our adorations; thou desirest much more to engage our love, and to become the ground and motive of our tender confidence. For this end, thou wert pierced through with a lance on the cross; and for the same purpose thou remainest a daily victim of thy own love on our altars. O infinitely compassionate Heart of Jesus! which was overwhelmed with sorrow in the Garden of Olives, at the view of our spiritual and corporal miseries, I recur to thee now with all the confidence thou desirest I should repose in the extent of thy power and the riches of thy mercy. Convinced that those things which are impossible to human means are infinitely easy to thee, and relying with an humble, steadfast faith on the sacred words of Truth itself, that whatever we ask the Father in the name of Jesus should be granted, I now most humbly implore in that adorable name, in virtue of that promise, and through the abundant mercies of the sacred Heart of Jesus, the particular favour I petition for in this Novena (*Specify it.*)

O blessed St. Gertrude! and all ye glorious servants of Christ! who while on earth were particularly devoted to the sacred Heart of Jesus, join your prayers with mine, and implore from the divine Object of all your devotion the grant of the petition which I now make, and specially offer up through thy intercession. Beg likewise, from this adorable Heart, which has dominion over all hearts, and could in a moment change the most obdurate, to have compassion on those who are in the dreadful state of mortal sin, and to open to us all the treasures of its mercy at the hour of our death. *Amen.*

A Novena *to the* Blessed Virgin.

O most Holy Virgin! who wert chosen by the adorable Trinity from all eternity to be the most pure Mother of Jesus, permit me, thy humble and devoted client, to remind thee of the joy thou didst receive in the instant of thé most sacred incarnation of our divine Lord, and during the nine months thou didst carry him in thy chaste womb. I wish most sincerely that I could renew, or even increase that joy, by the fervour of my prayers. O tender Mother of the afflicted! grant me, under my present necessities, that peculiar protection thou hast promised to those who devoutly commemorate this ineffable joy. Relying on the infinite mercies of thy Divine Son; trusting in that promise which he has made, that those who ask should receive; and penetrated with confidence in thy powerful prayers; I most humbly entreat thee to intercede for me, and to obtain for me the favours which I petition for in this Novena, if it be the holy will of God to grant them; and if not, to ask for me whatever graces I most stand in need of. (*Here specify your requests.*)

I desire by this Novena, which I now offer in thy honour, to prove the lively confidence I have in thy intercession. Accept it, I beseech thee, in honour of that supernatural love and joy with which thy sacred heart was replenished during the abode of thy dear Son in thy womb; in veneration of which, I offer thee the sentiments of my heart, and these nine *Hail Maries.*

Repeat the *Hail Maries* nine times, and then say the following

Prayer.

O MOTHER of God! accept these salutations, in union with the respect and veneration with which the Angel Gabriel first hailed thee full of grace. I wish most sincerely, that they may become so many gems in the crown of thy accidental glory, which will increase in brightness to the end of the world. I beseech thee, O Comfortress of the afflicted! by the joy thou didst receive in the nine months of thy pregnancy, to obtain for me the grant of the favours which I have now implored through thy powerful intercession. For this end, I offer thee all the good works which have ever been performed in thy honour. I most humbly entreat thee, for the love of the amiable heart of Jesus, with which thine was ever so inflamed, to hear my humble prayers, and to obtain my requests.

A NOVENA *to* ST. JOSEPH.

O GLORIOUS descendant of the Kings of Juda! inheritor of the virtues of all the Patriarchs! just and happy St. Joseph! listen to my prayer. Thou art my glorious protector, and shalt ever be, after Jesus and Mary, the object of my most profound veneration and tender confidence. Thou art the most hidden, though the greatest saint, and art peculiarly the patron of those who serve God with the greatest purity and fervour. In union with all those who have ever been most devoted to thee, I now dedicate myself to thy service; beseeching thee, for the sake of Jesus Christ, who vouchsafed to love and obey thee as a son, to become a father to me; and to obtain for me the filial respect, confidence, and love of a child towards thee. O powerful advocate of all Christians! whose intercession, as St. Teresa assures us, has never been found to fail, deign to intercede for me now, and to implore for me the particular intention of this Novena. (*Specify it.*)

Present me, O great Saint, to the adorable Trinity, with whom thou hadst so glorious and so intimate a correspondence. Obtain that I may never efface by sin the sacred image according to the likeness of which I was created. Beg for me, that my divine Redeemer would enkindle in my heart, and in all hearts, the fire of his love, and infuse therein the virtue of his adorable infancy, his purity, simplicity, obedience, and humility. Obtain for me likewise a lively devotion to thy Virgin Spouse, and protect me so powerfully in life and death, that I may have the happiness of dying as thou didst, in the friendship of my Creator, and under the immediate protection of the Mother of God.

Lord, have mercy on us.
Christ, have mercy on us.
Lord, have mercy on us.
Holy Trinity, one God, have mercy on us.
Holy Mary, Spouse of St. Joseph, *Pray for us.*
St. Joseph, confirmed in grace, *Pray for us.*
St. Joseph, Guardian of the Word Incarnate,
St. Joseph, Favourite of the King of Heaven,
St. Joseph, ruler of the family of Jesus,
St. Joseph, Spouse of the ever-blessed Virgin,
St. Joseph, nursing father to the Son of God,
St. Joseph, example of humility and obedience,
St. Joseph, mirror of silence and resignation,
St. Joseph, patron of innocence and youth,

Pray for us.

St. Joseph, exiled with Christ into Egypt,
St. Joseph, intercessor for the afflicted,
St. Joseph, advocate of the humble,
St. Joseph, model of every virtue,
St. Joseph, honoured among men,
St. Joseph, union of all Christian perfections,

Pray for us

Lamb of God, &c.

V. Pray for us, O holy St. Joseph.

R. That we may be made worthy of the promises of Christ.

Let us pray.

ASSIST us, O Lord! we beseech thee. by the merits of the Spouse of thy most holy Mother, that what our unworthiness cannot obtain, may be given us by his intercession with thee: who livest and reignest with God the Father in the unity of the Holy Ghost, world without end. *Amen.*

A NOVENA *to* ST. PATRICK.

O BLESSED Apostle of Ireland! glorious St. Patrick! who didst become my father and benefactor long before my birth, receive my prayers, and accept the sentiments of gratitude and veneration with which my heart is filled towards thee. Thou wert the channel of the greatest graces to me; deign then to become also the channel of my grateful thanksgivings to God for having granted me, through thee, that precious gift of faith, which is dearer than life. O most blessed father, and patron of my country! do not, I beseech thee, despise my weakness. Remember, that the cries of little children were the mysterious invitation thou didst receive to come among us. Listen then to my most humble supplications; I unite them to the praises and blessings which will ever follow thy name and thy memory throughout the Irish Church; I unite them to the prayers of the multitude of my ancestors, who now enjoy eternal bliss, and owe their salvation, under God, to thy zeal and charity.

They will eternally share thy glory, because they listened to thy word, and followed thy example. Ah! since I am descended from saints, may I blush to differ from them; may I begin from this moment to love God with all my heart, and serve him with all my strength. For this end I most humbly beg thy blessing, O great St. Patrick! and thy particular intercession, for obtaining whatever grace thou seest to be most necessary for me, and also the particular intentions of this Novena. (*Name them.*)

O charitable Shepherd of the Irish Flock! who wouldst have laid down a thousand lives to save one soul, take my soul, and the souls of all Christians, under thy special care, and preserve us from the dreadful misfortune of sin. Thy zealous preaching provided us the blessings of religious instructions which we now enjoy; obtain that none of us may receive them in vain. Thou didst teach our ancestors how to connect the pursuit of virtue with that of science; deign also to take my studies under thy protection, and to obtain for me the grace to sanctify them by a pure motive of pleasing God and my superiors. I most humbly recommend to thee this country, which was so dear to thee while on earth. Protect it still; and above all, obtain for its pastors, particularly those who instruct us, the grace to walk in thy footsteps, that they may share in thy eternal bliss.

Lord, have mercy on us, &c. &c.
Holy Mary, Mother of God,
St. Patrick,
St. Patrick, Apostle of Ireland
St. Patrick, vessel of election,
St. Patrick, model of Bishops,
St. Patrick, enemy of infidelity,
St. Patrick, profoundly humble,
St. Patrick, consumed with zeal,
St. Patrick, example of charity,
St. Patrick, glory of Ireland,
St. Patrick, instructor of little ones,

Pray for us.

St. Patrick, our powerful protector,
St. Patrick, our compassionate advocate,
Lamb of God, &c. &c.

V. Pray for us, O glorious St. Patrick.

R. That we may be made worthy of the promises of Christ.

Let us pray.

O God, who didst send among us thy blessed servant St. Patrick, to instruct and save us, and didst infuse into his heart so great a share of thy own tenderness, charity, and zeal, listen, we beseech thee, to the prayers which we now offer up in union with the prayers of our glorious patron and father in heaven, and grant us, through his intercession, the intentions of this Novena, and the grace rather to die than offend thee.

A Novena *to* St. Charles Borromeo.

O glorious St. Charles! the father of the clergy, and the perfect model of holy prelates! thou art that good pastor, who, like thy divine Master, didst give up thy life for thy flock, if not by death, at least by the numerous sacrifices of thy painful mission. Thy sanctified life on earth was a spur to the most fervent, thy exemplary penance was a reproach to the slothful, and thy indefatigable zeal was the support of the Church. O great Prelate! since the glory of God and the salvation of souls are the only objects of solicitude to the blessed in heaven, vouchsafe to intercede for me now, and to offer up for the intention of this Novena, those fervent prayers which were so successful while thou wert on earth. (*Here specify your requests.*)

Thou art, O great St. Charles! among all the Saints of God, one in whose intercession I should most confide, because thou wert chosen by God to promote the interests of religion, by promoting the Christian education of youth. Thou wert, like Jesus Christ himself, always accessible to little ones; for whom thou didst thyself break the bread of the word of God, and procure for them also the blessings of a Christian Education. To thee, then, I have recourse with confidence, beseeching thee to obtain for me the grace to profit of the advantages I enjoy, and for which I am so considerably indebted to thy zeal Preserve me by thy prayers from the dangers of the world; obtain that my heart may be impressed with a lively horror of sin; a deep sense of my duty as a Christian; a sincere contempt for the opinion and false maxims of the world; an ardent love for God, and that holy fear which is the beginning of wisdom.

Lord, have mercy on us, &c. &c.
Holy Mary, Mother of God,
Queen of Apostles,
St. Charles,
St. Charles, imitator of Christ,
St. Charles, faithful follower of Christ crucified,
St. Charles, replenished with the spirit of the Apostles,
St. Charles, consumed with zeal for the glory of God,
St. Charles, Father and Guide of the Clergy,
St. Charles, the light and support of the Church,
St. Charles, a model of humility and penance,
St. Charles, most desirous of the salvation of souls,
St. Charles, most zealous for the instruction of youth,
St. Charles, Patron of the Ursuline Schools,
Pray for us.
Lamb of God, &c.

V. Pray for us, O glorious St. Charles.
R. That we may be made worthy of the promises of Christ.

Let us pray.

PRESERVE thy Church, O Lord, under the continual protection of thy glorious Confessor and Bishop, St.

Charles, that as he was eminent for the discharge of his pastoral duties, so his prayers may make us zealous in the love of thy holy name: through Jesus Christ our Lord. *Amen.*

A Novena *to* St. John the Baptist.

Precursor of our divine Lord, destined by the Eternal One to prepare his ways, thy seat must be high in Heaven, for on earth thou wert truly exalted.—Thou hast been pronounced the greatest of those born of woman, by the great Searcher of hearts. Thy miraculous birth and extraordinary life, thy austere penance and burning zeal, proclaim thee great; and were all these wanting, thy purity and profound humility would point thee out as one truly exalted. When thou camest into the world, thou didst come as the friend of thy Creator; and whilst on earth, thou didst never offend him. Though thou didst administer baptism to Jesus Christ, thou still didst own, with due humility, that you were not worthy to loose the latchet of his shoe. As the reward of thy humility, Christ himself hath praised thee, and the whole world to the end of time will glory in thy birth. In thee we behold a miracle of God's grace and power; and we conjure thee to raise in our behalf that glorious voice, which, from the wilderness, pierced the heavens, and was heard at the throne of the Most High. We beg of thee to implore for us the intentions of this Novena.—N. N.

O, Holy Anchoret, as thou wert by excellence the friend of the Saviour, thou canst obtain from him whatsoever thou wishest, for he ardently loved thee. Take me, then, under thy special protection; obtain for me the graces I stand in need of, and, more especially, perfect obedience to the voice of those who preach to us the necessity of true penance. O thou who wert a burning fire, obtain for us, through thy powerful intercession, a portion of that which is enkindled by the preaching of those whom God has commissioned to point out to us the way to eternal happiness. Teach us to know ourselves, teach us to know our God, and his son Jesus Christ our Lord. Obtain for us that we may be frequent and worthy partakers of the Holy Communion. Grant that we may approach with that angelic purity which enabled thee to discover the Lamb of God, though he was then unknown to the world. O Holy Martyr of Jesus, though I am not worthy to shed my blood for him as thou hast, I conjure thee to intercede for me, that I may live and die in the practice of Christian penance, and in the faithful observance of every duty which the law of God imposes on me.

A Prayer to St. Augustine.

O glorious St. Augustine! the light and oracle of the faithful! I most fervently join with the whole Church of Christ in thanking the Almighty for having chosen thee to become a peculiar object of his love, and an everlasting monument of his tender mercies. Illustrious penitent! thy admirable conversion proves to the whole world, that no crimes are too great for the God of all mercies to pardon—no heart too corrupt for his love to purify—and no obstacle too strong for his grace to overcome. Penetrated with veneration for thy virtues, I choose thee for my Father, my Protector, and my Advocate. I most humbly beseech thee to have compassion on my youth, and to protect me in those dangers which thou well knowest are attendant on my inexperienced age. O blessed victim of charity! obtain that I may seriously consecrate my heart to my Creator, and faithfully observe that great commandment of charity, so deeply engraven on thy heart. Thou wert the son of thy mother's precious tears, the conquest of her prayers, and afterwards the faithful imitator of her virtues; obtain for me the most profound respect and tender affection for my parents, gratitude for their care, and the grace to profit of the advantages which their solicitude for my eternal welfare has provided for me. I recommend to thee, in a particular manner, O great Saint! all those unhappy souls, who are in the dreadful state of mortal sin, and conjure thee, by the unceasing tears thou didst shed over thy own wanderings, to procure them the grace of conversion, and to obtain for me such horror of sin, that I may avoid it as the only real evil, and thereby merit to behold for all eternity that increated Beauty who was too long hidden from thy view, and eternally love that infinite Goodness, whom thou didst bitterly regret having loved too late. *Amen.*

A prayer to St. Angela, *Foundress of the Ursuline Order.*

Most blessed St. Angela! who art now in possession of that eternal crown which is promised to those who instruct others unto justice, permit me to have recourse to thee, as to my glorious Patroness, and to choose thee for my special Advocate before the throne of God. In union with all those happy souls, who, under God, are indebted to thee for the glory they now enjoy in heaven, I thank God for having raised thee up, to provide for millions the great blessings of religious instruction. How grateful should I be for the happiness of being ranked among the number who now enjoy the fruits of thy charity and zeal. O glorious Patroness and Mother of the weakest portion of Christ's flock! do not abandon thy charge, now that thou seest more clearly than ever the dangers to which youth are exposed. I entreat of thee, by that lively zeal for God's glory, which caused thee to devote thy life to the instruction of the ignorant, to take me as thy child, and to obtain for me the grace to profit of the blessings which the Almighty has bestowed on me through thee. Procure for me by thy prayers a docile heart—a lively horror of sin—sincere love of God and my neighbour—and so great a share in that tender compassion for the poor which distinguished thee, that I may never neglect an opportunity of affording them any spiritual or corporal assistance in my power. Teach me, by thy example, to practice works of mercy, that like thee I may find mercy, and join thee for all eternity in praising and blessing that good God, who has exempted me from the miseries suffered by many of my more deserving fellow-creatures. *Amen.*

A Prayer to St. Ursula.

O glorious St. Ursula! blessed Martyr of Jesus Christ! who didst despise the riches and dignities of this world for the love of God, and wert so happy as to lay down even thy life for his sake, take me under thy powerful protection—shield me by thy prayers from the dangers of the world, and teach me by thy example how to triumph over its temptations. I am not worthy to lay down my life for him who died for me; yet, as I know that I may have many temptations, to suffer from the world and my own corrupt inclinations, I have recourse to thee with confidence, to implore, through thy intercession, the strength to resist and overcome them all; and to remember, on all occasions, that the life of a Christian, if not laid down for Christ by martyrdom, should at least be sacrificed to his glory by penance and self-denial. Thou art, O great Saint! my special Patroness, therefore I humbly recommend to thee all my undertakings, and beg of thee, as thou wert so particularly gifted by God with the power of persuading others to the practice of virtue, to obtain for me the grace to love and fulfil the duties of a Christian, and to endeavour by good example to engage others in the service of God. O glorious Martyr! whose death was an act of the most perfect charity, be thou my protectress in my last moments, and intercede for me now, that I may prepare for them by the fervent practice of those solid virtues, which alone will furnish ground for confidence in the mercy of God on the bed of death.

A Prayer to St. Aloysius, *for young Students.*

Angelical youth Aloysius! who art, by the appointment of Christ's Vicar on earth, the Patron of those who apply to study, thou hast illustrated the Church by a holy contempt of worldly greatness, but still more by the innocence and sanctity of thy life allow me to choose thee as the particular patron of my studies, and to resolve most sincerely to follow the example thou hast left me of diligence and piety Receive me as thy client, and through the love which animated thy heart for Jesus and Mary, vouchsafe to assist me in the pursuit of virtue and learning. Obtain for me purity of body and mind, and a filial confidence in the ever-blessed Virgin. Defend me against the dangers of the world; direct me in the choice of a state of life; and obtain for me those powerful graces which will preserve me from the guilt of mortal sin; that assisted by thy patronage, and animated by thy example, I may lead so holy a life in this world, as to be associated with thee in the company of angels for all eternity. *Amen.*

On the Choice of a State of Life.

THE most exalted sanctity is attainable in every state and condition of life, provided that it is embraced in compliance with the will of God, and its particular obligations faithfully discharged, for his love. This is evident from the example of many who sanctified themselves in situations which appear least calculated for that end; such as on the throne or in the army. God, as a good Father of the great family of mankind, allots to each the station he would have him occupy. It is in corresponding with the designs of God in this important point, that most security and facility of salvation are commonly found, because there are graces annexed to each condition of life, which tend to lessen its difficulties, and to assist in the discharge for its obligations; and those graces, it may be supposed, are only bestowed on such as God calls to serve him in that particular condition. Whence you may perceive that it is, at least, a great imprudence to take so important a step rashly

Those who precipitately embrace any state of life without consulting their own inclinations and ability by reflection, without consulting the Almighty, and endeavouring to discover his will by prayer, and the advice of a director, run great risk of taking a false step, which may be followed by much temporal misery and great danger to their salvation. However, as in very early youth much reflection on this point would be little better than idle thoughts, your duty for the present is, to abandon yourself into the hands of God as to futurity, which you may not live to see; to avoid as a great sin, those promises of embracing any state of life which indiscreet fervour, or rather real presumption may dictate, and occasionally to beg of God to direct your choice whenever you may be called on to make it, and never permit you to act in so important a step contrary to his holy will. This may be done by the following prayer.

A Prayer to beg the Divine Direction in the Choice of a State of Life.

O Almighty God! whose wise and amiable Providence watches over every human event, deign tc be my light and my counsel in all my undertakings particularly in the choice of a state of life. I know that on this important step my sanctification and salvation may in a great measure depend. I know that I am incapable of discerning what may be best for me; therefore I cast myself into thy arms, beseeching thee, my God, who hast sent me into this world only to love and serve thee, to direct by thy grace every moment and action of my life to the glorious end of my creation. I renounce most sincerely every other wish, than to fulfil thy designs on my soul, whatever they may be; and I beseech thee to give me the grace, by imbibing the true spirit of a Christian, to qualify myself for any station thy adorable Providence may hereafter assign me. O my God! whenever it may become my duty to make a choice, do thou be my light and my counsel, and mercifully deign to *make the way known to me wherein I should walk, for I have lifted up my soul to thee.* (Ps. cxlii. 8.) Preserve me from listening to the suggestions of my own self-love, or worldly prudence, in prejudice to thy holy inspirations. Let *thy good Spirit lead me into the right way*, (Ibid. 9.) and thy adorable Providence place me, not where I may be happiest, according to the world, but in that state in which I shall love and serve thee most perfectly, and meet with most abundant means for working out my salvation. This is all that I ask, and all that I desire; for what would it avail me to gain the whole world, if, in the end, I were to lose my soul, and be so unfortunate as to prefer temporal advantages and worldly honours to the enjoyment of thy divine presence in a happy eternity?

A Prayer to implore the divine Light before any particular Undertaking.

O ADORABLE JESUS! I come to thee before I commence this undertaking, to implore thy assistance, and to consecrate it, through thee, to the glory of thy heavenly Father. Thou knowest that I can do nothing of myself; assist me, then, I beseech thee, to accomplish the will of God—that divine will, which was so dear to thee, as to be thy food while thou wert on earth. Direct me particularly in the affair I am going about, and teach me to act in a manner pleasing to thy divine Majesty—or rather do thou thyself deign to act in and by me: deign to govern me by thy wisdom—to support me by thy power—and by thy infinite goodness to direct all my exertions, on this occasion, to thy greater glory and my own eternal salvation.

A Renewal of the Baptismal Vows.

O MY God and my Lord, humbly prostrate in spirit before thy divine Majesty, I adore thy sovereign justice and thy infinite mercy. I am penetrated with fear at the consideration of thy awful judgments, and my own great ingratitude for all thy benefits, since I was ranked by baptism among thy children, raised to the glorious dignity of a Christian, and thus entitled to enjoy thee eternally in heaven. I was not then sensible of the precious grace bestowed on me, nor of the awful obligations I contracted when I promised to renounce the devil, the world, and the flesh. But I am now fully sensible of both; I most humbly thank thee for having brought me safely to the waters of baptism, and I detest from the bottom of my heart every thought, word, and action of my life which has been unworthy of a Christian. Thou knowest, O my God, how often I have stained the robe of innocence with which I was then clothed, and how frequently I have violated my sacred promises; but thou seest the contrition of my heart, and the sincerity with which I now renew, in the presence of heaven and earth, my profession of faith in the doctrines proposed to my belief by the holy Catholic Church, as well as the promises made for me when I was regenerated in the waters of baptism. I firmly believe in God the Father Almighty, Creator of heaven and earth—in Jesus Christ his only Son, our Lord, who was born, and suffered for us—in the Holy Ghost—the Holy Catholic Church--the Communion of Saints—the Forgiveness of Sins—the Resurrection of the Body, and Life Everlasting. I renounce the world, with its pomps, vanities, and false maxims, which I despise, because they are accursed by thee. I renounce the flesh, with all its temptations, and sincerely resolve to endeavour to amend my faults, to conquer my passions, and to sacrifice all that is most dear to me, rather than again deliberately sully that robe which I promised to carry unstained before the judgment-seat of Christ. O my good God, who didst love me before I could love thee, and didst apply to my soul the merits of Jesus Christ when I was unable to implore that favour; look on me with compassion, and grant me all those graces which will enable me to keep my baptismal engagements without reproof. Increase in my soul the heavenly virtues of faith, hope, and charity, which I received at my baptism, and teach me to make faith the rule of my conduct, that it may avail me to life everlasting, through the infinite mercies and merits of my Lord and Saviour Jesus Christ, who with thee and the Holy Ghost liveth and reigneth, one God world without end. *Amen.*

A Prayer for deceased Parents.

O ALMIGHTY GOD, my good Father! thou who gavest to us, in our parents, only a weak image of thy own tender solicitude and watchful providence over each of thy creatures, receive my fervent thanksgivings for all the blessings thou didst bestow on me in and through them, to whom, under thee, I am indebted for my being. It was thou, O Lord, who gavest, and thou hast taken away; nor shall that stroke which deprived me of parents (of a father, of a mother) prevent my blessing thy holy name. I am not an orphan while I can call thee my Father, and look up with confidence to that Blessed Virgin whom thy divine Son gave me for a Mother when expiring on the cross; on the contrary, the less resource I have on earth, the more claim I have on thy protection, my good Father, who art in heaven. To thee, then, I raise my heart into the arms of thy mercy I cast my whole being; with all the confidence of a child, I run to thee, and implore thy protection in my journey through this wretched life. To thee, I offer my most humble and fervent supplications for the repose of my dear deceased parents. I trust, O my God! that they have found favour in thy sight, and that they now repose in thy bosom, and rejoice in thy adorable presence. But, O God of all holiness! if they be not as yet in possession of that glory for which they were created —if any stain of sin exclude them still from the kingdom where nothing defiled can enter, O let the earnest prayer of their child prevail on their behalf; or rather, let the sacred blood which Jesus Christ shed for them, cancel all their debts, and purify them from every stain. Give them, O my God, eternal rest for the sake of him who died for them. Let perpetual light shine on them, and let the view of thy ancient beauty and adorable perfections fill them speedily with ineffable joys. Hear my voice for them, O Lord, for they cannot now plead for themselves; deign to give me in the dear parents I have had on earth, protectors and advocates in heaven, and mercifully grant me the grace to dispose myself by a holy life for being re-united to them in a happy eternity through the infinite merits of Jesus Christ our Lord. *Amen.*

An Universal Prayer for all things necessary to Salvation

O MY God, I *believe* in thee, do thou strengthen my faith. All my *hopes* are in thee, do thou secure them I *love* thee, with my whole heart, teach me to *love* thee daily more and more. I am *sorry* that I have offended thee; do thou increase my *sorrow*.

I *adore* thee as my first beginning. I *aspire* after thee as my last end. I give thee *thanks* as my constant Benefactor. I *call* upon thee as my sovereign Protector.

Vouchsafe, O my God, to conduct me by thy *wisdom*, to restrain me by thy *justice*, to comfort me by thy *mercy*, to defend me by thy *power*.

To thee I desire to consecrate all my thoughts, words, actions, and sufferings; that henceforward I may think of thee, speak of thee, willingly refer all my actions to thy greater glory; and suffer willingly whatever thou shalt appoint.

Lord, I desire that in all things thy *will* may be done, because it is thy *will*, and in the manner thou willest.

I beg of thee to enlighten my *understanding*, to

inflame my *will*, to purify my *body*, and to sanctify my *soul*.

Give me strength, O my God, to expiate my *offences* to overcome my *temptations*, to subdue my *passions*, and to acquire the *virtues* proper for my state.

Fill my heart with a tender *affection* for thy goodness, a *hatred* for my faults, a *love* for my neighbour and a *contempt* of the world.

Let me always remember to be submissive to my *superiors*, condescending to my *inferiors*, faithful to my *friends*, and charitable to my *enemies*.

Assist me to overcome sensuality by *mortification*, avarice by *alms-deeds*, anger by *meekness*, and tepidity by *devotion*.

O my God, make me *prudent* in my undertakings, *courageous* in danger, *patient* in afflictions, and *humble* in prosperity.

Grant that I may be ever *attentive* at my prayers, *temperate* at my meals, *diligent* in my employments and *constant* in my resolutions.

Let my conscience be ever *upright* and *pure*, my exterior *modest*, my conversation *edifying*, and my comportment *regular*.

Assist me, that I may continually labour to overcome *nature*, to correspond with thy *grace*, to keep thy *commandments*, and to work out my *salvation*.

Discover to me, O my God, the nothingness of *this world*, the greatness of *heaven*, the shortness of *time* and the length of *eternity*.

Grant that I may prepare for *death*, that I may fear thy *judgments*, that I may escape *hell* and in the end obtain heaven, through Jesus Christ. *Amen.*

The Rosary *of the* Blessed Name of Jesus.

In the name of the Father, and of the Son, and of the Holy Ghost. *Amen.*

Thou, O Lord, wilt open my lips.

And my tongue shall announce thy praise.

Incline unto my aid, O God.

Glory be to the Father, and to the Son, and to the Holy Ghost.

As it was in the beginning, is now, and will be for ever. *Amen.*

The five Mysteries of the first Part.

I. The Incarnation of our Lord Jesus Christ.

The Meditation.—The Son of God assumes human flesh out of the pure blood of the blessed Mary, ever Virgin, and is made man in her womb.

O Jesus, Son of David, have mercy on us. (*Ten Times.*)—Glory, &c.

II. The Birth of our Lord Jesus Christ.

The Meditation.—The Saviour of the world is born for our redemption; his Mother remaining a Virgin.

O Jesus, Son of David, have mercy on us. (*Ten Times.*)—Glory, &c.

III. The Circumcision of our Lord Jesus Christ.

The Meditation.—Our Saviour being eight days old, begins to suffer for our sins, and his blood already flows for us. He is circumcised according to the law, as if he had been himself a sinner.

O Jesus, Son of David, have mercy on us. (*Ten Times.*)—Glory, &c.

IV. Our Lord Jesus Christ is found in the Temple.

The Meditation.—Our Saviour being twelve years old, shows himself more than mortal by his knowledge and wisdom, teaching the teachers of the Jews

O Jesus, Son of David, have mercy on us. (*Ten Times.*)—Glory, &c.

V. The Baptism of our Lord Jesus Christ.

The Meditation—The Saviour of the world is baptized by St. John. The Eternal Father declares him to be his Son.

O Jesus, Son of David, have mercy on us. (*Ten Times.*)—Glory, &c.

The Prayer.

O Jesus, whose name is above all names, that in the name of Jesus every knee may bend, of those that are in heaven, on earth, and in hell. Who at the time appointed by the Eternal Wisdom, assumedst flesh in the womb of the blessed Mary, ever Virgin, and thus became the Son of David, whose birth gladdened men and angels. Who began so early to suffer for us, and to shed on our account that blood that washeth away the sins of the world. Whose immortal wisdom appeared at the age of twelve years. To whose baptism all heaven was attentive: grant to us to celebrate those mysteries to thy honour and our own salvation. Who with the Father and the Holy Ghost livest and reignest, one God, for all eternity. *Amen.*

The five Mysteries of the second Part.

I. Our Saviour washes his disciples' feet.

The Meditation.—Our Saviour, to show us an example of humility, and how much we ought to serve each other, descendeth so low, as to wash the feet of his disciples, though he is the God whom heaven and earth adore.

O Jesus of Nazareth, King of the Jews, have mercy on us. (*Ten Times.*)—Glory, &c.

II. The Prayer of our Lord Jesus Christ in the Garden.

The Meditation.—Our Saviour, knowing his Passion to be now at hand, is so affected with the thoughts of it, and so oppressed with the load of our sins, that he prays to his Almighty Father, that the bitter cup might pass away from him

O Jesus of Nazareth, King of the Jews, have mercy on us. (*Ten Times.*)—Glory, &c.

III. Our Saviour is apprehended.

The Meditation.—Our Saviour, as if he had been no more than mortal man, yields to the power of men, and permits himself, for our redemption, to be apprehended, as if he were a malefactor.

O Jesus of Nazareth, King of the Jews, have mercy on us. (*Ten Times.*)—Glory, &c.

IV. Our Saviour carries his Cross.

The Meditation.—Our Saviour, being torn with scourges, and pierced with thorns, to expiate our sins, is obliged to carry the cross on which he is to die, and moves on, labouring in sorrow, towards the place of his crucifixion.

O Jesus of Nazareth, King of the Jews, have mercy on us. (*Ten Times.*)—Glory, &c.

V. The Descent of our Saviour into Hell.

The Meditation.—The soul of our Saviour being separated by death from the body, descends to the place where the saints were expecting his redemption

The Prayer.

O Jesus, whose name is above all names, that in the name of Jesus every knee may bend, of those that are in heaven, on earth, and in hell. Whose mysterious humiliations and sorrows, appointed for thee, on account of our sins, appeared in thy washing of the feet of thy servants and creatures; in thy distress and prayer, and bloody sweat; in thy being secured and brought before courts as a criminal; in thy bearing the load of the cross; and in the separation of thy soul from the body, and its descent to the regions below; grant to us to celebrate those mysteries to thy honour and our own salvation. Who with the Father and the Holv Ghost livest and reignest, one God, for all eternity. *Amen.*

The five Mysteries of the third Part.

I. The Resurrection of our Lord Jesus Christ

The Meditation.—The soul of our Lord Jesus Christ which had been separated from the body, is re-united to it by a miracle of the Almighty power, and that body which had been dead, rises to die no more.

O Jesus, Son of the living God, have mercy on us (*Ten Times.*)—Glory be to the Father, &c.

II. The Ascension of our Lord Jesus Christ.

The Meditation.—Our Lord Jesus Christ ascends into the highest heaven, where the Saviour of mankind sits at the right hand of God the Father Almighty.

O Jesus, Son of the living God, have mercy on us. (*Ten Times.*)—Glory be to the Father, &c.

III. Our Lord Jesus Christ sends down the Holy Ghost.

The Meditation.—Our Saviour, now seated at the right hand of God, his Almighty Father, sends down the Holy Ghost to inspire and animate his disciples, that they may be qualified to publish to mankind his cross and his glory.

O Jesus, Son of the living God, have mercy on us. (*Ten Times.*)—Glory be to the Father, &c.

IV. Our Lord Jesus Christ crowning the blessed Saints.

The Meditation.—Our Saviour having, by his passion, resurrection, and ascension, opened a way for the sons of Adam to heaven, which they had lost by sin, bestows on his Mother and his Saints a crown of immortal glory.

O Jesus, Son of the living God, have mercy on us (*Ten Times.*)—Glory be to the Father, &c.

V. Our Lord Jesus Christ coming to judgment.

The Meditation.—Our Saviour will come in power and majesty, to judge the living and the dead, and to return to every one according to his works.

O Jesus, Son of the living God, have mercy on us (*Ten Times.*)—Glory be to the Father, &c.

The Prayer

O Jesus! whose name is above all names, that in the name of Jesus every knee may bend, of those that are in heaven, on earth, and in hell: whose body that was nailed to the cross for mankind, the Almighty raised from death glorious and immortal; who by thy ascension triumphed over death, and held captivity captive. Who according to thy promise, sent down the Spirit that proceedeth from the Father and the Son, the comforter and the enlivener: who stretching forth the bounty of thy almighty hand, shed upon the chosen children of Adam that glory that neither eye hath seen, nor ear hath heard, nor hath it entered into the heart of man; and who will come forth in power and majesty to judge the living and the dead, before whose throne all mortals will appear, grant us to celebrate those mysteries to thy honour and our own salvation: who with the Father and the Holy Ghost livest and reignest, one God, for all eternity. *Amen.*

N. B. The repeating the above prayers or meditations is not absolutely necessary. Those who cannot meditate on the mysteries, let them say the creed beforehand in this Rosary and in that of the blessed Virgin.

On the Rosary *of the* Blessed Virgin.

The devotion called the Rosary, is a pious orm of prayer, so much esteemed by the most learned and holy servants of God, as to be styled by one among the rest, "An abridgment of the Gospel, a history of the life, sufferings, and triumphant victory of Jesus Christ, and an exposition of all our Redeemer did in the flesh, which he assumed for our salvation." It consists of fifteen *Our Fathers* and a hundred and fifty *Hail Maries*, to commemorate the fifteen principal mysteries of our Redeemer's sacred life, and also to honour his blessed Mother, who had so great a share in all that concerned her dear Son. This pious practice is not as general as it should be; young persons, in particular, are more subject to distraction and indevotion in saying the Rosary, than in any other spiritual exercise; owing partly to the frequent repetition of the same prayer, but much more to the little attention they pay to the sense of the words they pronounce. Some children, perhaps, may not be sufficiently acquainted with the explanation of the few prayers contained in the Rosary, to give their minds occupation while they recite them; but that cannot be your case; therefore, as you are already in the habit of saying a part of the Rosary every day, you will be much less excusable than others, if you acquit yourself of that duty with the disedifying precipitation and indevotion unfortunately too common at your age. To avoid this, you should endeavour to conceive a due esteem for this holy exercise, and to impress upon your mind that the Rosary, though so easy, so simple, and thereby so adapted to your capacity, is the most perfect, the most sublime, and most profitable of all vocal forms of prayer. It is the most sublime, because it is composed of the most holy and excellent prayers which were ever conceived or pronounced; and it is also the most profitable, because those prayers, from their divine origin, are more pleasing and acceptable to God than all other prayers put together. The first is the *Our Father*, that heavenly form of prayer left us by our Redeemer, drawn up not by angels or saints, but by Jesus Christ himself, in which he deigned to teach us how we ought to pray. In that one prayer, which is so short and so easy that all persons may be capable of learning it, are contained not only, as your Catechism says, all those things you should ask or hope for of God, but also all the sublime acts of adoration, praise, thanksgiving, love, and confidence, comprised in all the other books of devotion which were ever written; all other prayers being only a paraphrase or explanation of *the Lord's Prayer.*

The second is the *Hail Mary*, composed in heaven, dictated by the Holy Ghost, delivered to the faithful by the Angel Gabriel, by St. Elizabeth, and the Church of God, containing in the first part an act of praise and thanksgiving for the great mystery of the Incarnation, and in the second an humble petition for the powerful prayers of the Mother of God, now and at the hour of death.

The third is the Doxology, or *Glory be to the Father*, a sacred verse, which contains an act of supreme adoration to the ever blessed Trinity, and presents to the Majesty of God, not the glory which proceeds from the weak praises of his creatures, nor even the glory that results to God from all the labours and great actions of the Saints, but that eternal glory which the Almighty, as God, possesses in and by himself; which he has enjoyed from the beginning and will enjoy for eternity, and which so little depends on his creatures, that it would not be diminished if all mankind were destroyed.

When you reflect on the sublime excellence of those three prayers which are the first that children learn but often the last they understand, you must perceive not only the sanctity of the Rosary which is composed of such prayers, but also the respect, humility, confidence, and devotion with which it should be said.

Endeavour then to excite those sentiments in your heart, by reflecting for a moment before you begin your Beads, on the justice and merit of giving that small testimony of your veneration for the mysteries of your redemption, and devotion to the Mother of God. Think also of the consolation it will be to you on your death-bed, to have said your Beads devoutly, and thereby implored, upwards of fifty times every day, the assistance of the B essed Virgin, for that dreadful hour when you will so much stand in need of her powerful intercession, yet perhaps not be able even to pronounce her name.

In saying the *Our Father*, think how unworthy any creature is to repeat those very words which the sacred lips of Jesus first pronounced, and endeavour to say it with the utmost humility, love, and confidence; convinced that, by saying that prayer in a proper disposition, you can please God more, and obtain more graces, than if you were to run through all the books of devotion which were ever written. The sentiments which should accompany the repetition of the *Hail Mary*, are pointed out by a holy and learned writer, who says, that "when an Angel anciently appeared to Patriarchs or Prophets, he was received with due honour, as being exalted above them both by nature and grace; but that when an Archangel visited Mary, he was struck with *her* superior dignity and pre-eminence, and approaching, saluted her with admiration and respect. Though accustomed to the lustre of the highest heavenly spirits, yet he was dazzled and amazed at the dignity and spiritual glory of her whom he came to salute Mother of God, while the attention of the whole heavenly court was with rapture fixed upon her. With what humility then should we, worms of the earth and base sinners, address her in the same salutation!" As to the Doxology, or *Glory be to the Father*, it should suffice to animate your devotion in saying it, to reflect that this verse is so much esteemed by the Church, as to be added to all the Hymns, Canticles, and Psalms of her Offices, and thereby daily repeated by her ministers upwards of a hundred times.

The Beads may be said with or without those short considerations and prayers, called the Mysteries of the Rosary; but when you are at liberty to choose a method, you would always do well to make use of them, repeating the Mystery before each *Our Father* to reflect on it as well as you can during the ten *Hail Maries*, and then conclude each decade with the *Glory be to the Father* and corresponding prayer. That is the very best means you could adopt for restraining your imagination, preventing the distractions which may involuntarily follow from the repetition of the same prayers, and exciting the sentiments of devotion which have been pointed out to you as necessary for saying the Beads devoutly. However, when for want of leisure, or for any other cause, you are obliged to omit the Mysteries of the Rosary, you may very profitably substitute a shorter method, which consists in naming each mystery, or simply calling it to mind at the beginning of the decade, and also the virtue it peculiarly inculcates; afterwards imploring that virtue through the intercession of the Blessed Virgin by the ten *Hail Maries*. Both methods are divided and arranged according to the days of the week on which they should be said, as follows:—

The Rosary *of the* Blessed Virgin.

In the Name of the Father, and of the Son, and of the Holy Ghost. *Amen.*

V. Hail Mary, full of grace, the Lord is with thee.

R. Blessed art thou amongst women, and blessed is the fruit of thy womb, Jesus.

V. Thou, O Lord, wilt open my lips.

R. And my tongue shall announce thy praise

V. Incline unto my aid, O God.

R. O Lord, make haste to help me.

V. Glory be to the Father, and to the Son, and to the Holy Ghost.

R. As it was in the beginning, is now, and ever shall be, world without end. *Amen. Alleluia.*

Except from Septuagesima *to* Easter; *then say*, Praise be to thee O Lord King of Eternal Glory.

THE JOYFUL MYSTERIES.*

The Annunciation.—Let us consider that an Angel was sent from Heaven to declare to the Blessed Virgin, the choice which God had made of her, to be the Mother of the Eternal Word: she receives this declaration with the most profound humility, and the Son of God becomes incarnate in her by the invisible operation of the Holy Ghost.

Hail Mary, ten times—Glory, &c.

The Prayer.—We acknowledge thee, O holy Virgin, to be the real Mother of God, and hail thee full of grace; we joyfully repeat the praises first given thee by the angel, and since continued by the entire Church. In becoming Mother to the Incarnate Word thou becomest a Mother to us also; may we ever feel the effects of thy kindness. *Amen.*

The Visit paid to St. Elizabeth.

Let us represent to ourselves the Blessed Virgin going with haste into the mountains of Judea, to visit her cousin St. Elizabeth, where, at her arrival, St. John the Baptist, yet unborn, exults in the presence of his Redeemer, and is sanctified in his Mother's womb.

The Prayer.—Most holy Virgin, who in this mystery didst eminently display the greatest humility and charity; obtain for us of God, that our souls may be frequently visited by thy dear Son, and in some degree experience those impressions which his presence once made on his blessed precursor.

The Nativity of our Lord.

Let us represent to ourselves the Redeemer of the world born in a stable, and laid in a manger, be-

* These are said on all Mondays and Thursdays; on the Sundays of Advent, and after Epiphany, until Lent.

cause there was no room for him in the inn at Bethlehem. Let us rejoice in the advantages of this humiliation, and endeavour to practise the lessons he here teaches.

The Prayer.—O most pure Mother of God, we sincerely rejoice in thy having given birth to the Desired of Nations, to the Saviour of the World. Beg of him, we beseech thee, that he would now graciously vouchsafe to be spiritually born in our hearts, enabling us by his grace, to imitate the virtues of his childhood; particularly his simplicity, innocence, docility, and contempt for the vanities of this world. *Amen.*

The Adoration of the Wise Men.

LET us prostrate ourselves with the wise men, to adore Jesus Christ in the arms of his blessed Mother: instead of gold, frankincense, and myrrh, let us offer him our minds, our hearts, and our whole being, without reserve.

The Prayer.—Most holy and immaculate Virgin! by the unspeakable comfort thou didst feel in the homage paid to our Redeemer, we entreat thee to present him in our name the offering we make of ourselves, that he may receive it more favourably through thee; that we may ever walk faithfully by the light of his grace, until we arrive at the possession of himself in heaven. *Amen.*

The finding of the Child Jesus in the Temple.

LET us participate in the joy which the Blessed Virgin must have felt, when, after having lost, without any fault of hers, the child Jesus in Jerusalem, and having sought him in much affliction during three days, she found him at length in the Temple amidst the Doctors, hearing them and questioning them.

The Prayer.—O most tender Mother of God! comfor of the afflicted! we earnestly conjure thee, by thy extreme delight on finding the child Jesus, for the anguish of having lost him, obtain for us the grace never to lose him by consenting to mortal sin nor to enjoy either pleasure or repose, while we thus oblige him to withdraw from us. *Amen.*

A short Method of reciting the ROSARY *of the* B. VIRGIN.

The JOYFUL MYSTERIES *for* Mondays *and* Thursdays.

The Annunciation—Virtue of humility.
The Visitation—Virtue of charity.
The Nativity—Virtue of detachment from the World.
The Purification—Virtue of purity.
The finding of our Lord in the Temple—Virtue of obedience.

THE SORROWFUL MYSTERIES.*

The Agony in the Garden.

BEHOLD our Saviour in the Garden of Olives, prostrate on the ground, bathed in a bloody sweat, accepting from his Father's hand the bitter chalice here offered to him. Let our prayers, our compunction and resignation, be animated by this Model.—*Hail Mary, &c.*

The Prayer.—O Mother of Him who was made man to save mankind! more sensibly affected by the suffering of thy Son than all his Martyrs were! obtain for us sincere contrition for our sins, persevering fervour in our prayers, and perfect resignation in all adversities.

The Scourging.

LET us contemplate how our Saviour Jesus Christ after being derided, calumniated, buffeted, and over

* These are said on Tuesdays and Fridays throughout the year and on Sundays in Lent.

Painted by Rubens.

The Redeemer of the World.

Published by Edward Dunigan, New-York.

whelmed with reproaches, was by Pilate's order most cruelly scourged, and in this mangled condition presented to the Jews.

The Prayer.—O MOTHER of Sorrows, whose heart was rent in the mangled flesh of thy Son! we beseech thee, by that love which induced him to shed his blood and give his life for us, to obtain, by thy intercession, that we may ever cautiously avoid those criminal pleasures and sensual gratifications, which our Redeemer would expiate by this bloody scourging. *Amen*

The Crowning with Thorns.

LET us figure to ourselves the indignities and insults offered to Jesus Christ: he is derided as a mock king, a reed is his sceptre, thorns are his crown, an old purple cloak is the robe of his royalty. Let his patience under these insults, instruct and console us under affronts and humiliations.

The Prayer.—O MOST meek and compassionate Virgin! whose anguish at these multiplied outrages could only be equalled by the feelings of Him who underwent them! obtain, we beseech thee, for us, that we may ever gratefully remember these tender proofs of his love; may his crown of thorns become our antidote against pride, and his patience under these insults our comfort and support in all our afflic tions. *Amen.*

The Carrying of the Cross.

BEHOLD our Saviour on his way to Mount Calvary, bending under the weight of his cross. Let us endeavour to console him under his sufferings, by carrying our cross courageously.

The Prayer.—MOST holy and generous Mother! who didst accompany thy dear Son even to Mount Calvary, feeling in thy love for him the anguish of his cross: may we, through thy prayers, follow him in the path which his blood has marked out; may we ever cheerfully carry all those crosses which his mercy, his providence, or his justice shall allot to us.

The Crucifixion.

Let us cast our eyes upon the Son of God, suspended by nails from the Cross, covered with wounds, bleeding at every pore, expiring in accumulated agony.

The Prayer.—O Virgin Mother! Victim of suffering and sorrow! who, motionless and silent at the foot of the Cross, wert doomed to sigh under the dying groans of thy Son, and mingle thy tears with his blood, transfixed with that sword of grief which holy Simeon had announced to thee: obtain for us, we most humbly beseech thee, that our hearts and affections be henceforth nailed to the Cross, that our lives be modelled by it, and our death sanctified by its influence. *Amen.*

A short Method of reciting the Rosary *of the* B. Virgin.

The Sorrowful Mysteries *for* Tuesdays *and* Fridays

The Agony in the Garden—Virtue of resignation
The Scourging of our Lord—Virtue of mortification.
The Crowning with Thorns—Virtue of humility.
The Carrying the Cross—Virtue of patience.
The Crucifixion—Virtue of the love of our enemies

THE FIVE GLORIOUS MYSTERIES.*

The Resurrection.

Let us consider the Son of God springing forth in a blaze of glory from the tomb; and implore the grace of a spiritual resurrection, as he has given us the model of one in his own person. *Hail Mary, &c*

* These are said on Wednesdays and Saturdays throughout the year, and on Sundays from Easter until Advent.

The Prayer.—Most holy Mother of God! by those transports of joy wherewith thou wert overwhelmed at the Resurrection of thy adorable Son, obtain for us, that we may participate in the glory of his immortal life; that we may so arise from the tomb of our sins and evil habits, as never more to return to them, but to walk hereafter in the newness of life. *Amen.*

The Ascension.

Let us call to mind how, on the fortieth day after his Resurrection, the Son of God ascended into heaven in the full display of his Majesty, in the presence of his disciples; and how he invites us to follow him thither by the fervour of our desires, if we wish hereafter to join him in the realms of glory.

The Prayer.—O holy Virgin! who didst more vehemently sigh after thy Son in heaven than all those who had attended him on earth, draw us to him by thy powerful intercession; that, disengaged more and more from the empty enjoyments of this world, we may every day advance in that path of virtue, which he and you have so edifyingly traced out for us. *Amen.*

The Descent of the Holy Ghost.

Let us commemorate how our Lord Jesus Christ, being seated at the right hand of his Eternal Father, sent, as he had promised, the Holy Ghost upon his Church, this divine Spirit coming down in the form of fiery tongues. Let us beseech him so to enlighten our minds, and inflame us with his love, that we may ever speak and act conformably to that law of grace, which he hath promulgated.

The Prayer.—Hail! O Virgin full of grace, and replenished on this day (of Pentecost) with a still greater abundance of heavenly gifts, behold in pity our manifold spiritual wants; obtain for us some sparks of that sacred fire which was shed upon thee, that, enlightened by the truths of the gospel. and animated by the ardour of divine love, we may ever sensibly feel the influence of this Holy Spirit. *Amen.*

The Assumption.

LET us consider, that the period appointed by the Eternal Wisdom being at length arrived, the Blessed Virgin quits the earth, to regain in heaven the company of her Son. Let us rejoice in her bliss and glory, begging that she may also conduct us thither by her prayers.

The Prayer.—O THOU, who by excellence art styled the Mother of holy love, it was in thy death and thy glorious Assumption that this love attained in thee the very summit of its perfection. Obtain for us, we beseech thee, the grace of a pure life, of a holy death. and a happy participation in supreme bliss. *Amen.*

The Crowning of the Blessed Virgin.

LET us reflect how the most perfect of Sons receives into heaven the most holy of Mothers; assigning to her the rank that was due to her merits and dignity, and crowning her with the brightest diadem of glory

The Prayer.—QUEEN of angels and men ! acknowledged as such in heaven and on earth, under the boundless authority of thy Son ; graciously accept the homage we have presented to thee in this Rosary. Look upon us as thy children ; lift up thy pure hands on our behalf, that we may ever feel the effects of thy patronage, and at length behold thee seated on thy throne of glory in the kingdom of heaven. *Amen.*

A short Method of reciting the ROSARY *of the* B. VIRGIN.

The GLORIOUS MYSTERIES *for* Sundays, Wednesdays *and* Saturdays.

The Resurrection—Virtue of faith.
The Ascension—Virtue of hope.

The Descent of the Holy Ghost—Virtue of charity.

The Assumption of the Blessed Virgin—Virtue of union with Christ.

The Crowning of the Blessed Virgin and Saints—Virtue of confidence in their prayers.

LITANY *of the* LIFE *and* PASSION *of* OUR LORD.

LORD, have mercy on us.—Christ, have mercy on us, &c.

Lord, have mercy on us.

Sacred Trinity of Persons in unity of Essence,

Have mercy on us.

Blessed Jesus, true God and true Man,

Through thy inflamed desire to redeem mankind,

Through thy unspeakable love, in making choice of the Blessed Virgin Mary for thy Mother,

Through thy blessed nativity and painful circumcision,

Through thy presentation in the temple, and flight into Egypt,

Through thy hidden life, thy fast in the desert, and thy labours for the conversion of sinners,

Through thy ineffable love, manifested in the institution of the sacrifice and sacrament of thy precious body and blood,

Through thy prayer in the garden, and thy bloody sweat,

Through thy being betrayed by Judas, insulted by the Jews, and scorned by Herod and his court,

Through thy cruel scourging, crowning with thorns, and exhibition to the people as a mock king,

Through thy carrying the cross, and thy agonizing crucifixion,

Through thy vehement thirst, and painful agony on the cross,

Have mercy on us

Through the compassion thou hadst for thy blessed Mother and beloved disciple, standing at the foot of the cross,
Through the separation of thy soul from thy body, and the wound in thy sacred side,
Through thy glorious resurrection and admirable ascension,
Through all thy sacred actions and sufferings during thy mortal life,

Have mercy on us.

V. Graciously hear our prayers, O Lord Jesus.
R. And let our cry come unto thee.

Let us pray.

O God, who, for the redemption of the world, didst vouchsafe to be born, to be circumcised, to be rejected by the Jews, and betrayed with a kiss; to be bound like a malefactor, and like an innocent lamb to be led to slaughter; to be ignominiously led before Annas, Caiphas, Pilate, and Herod; to be accused by false witnesses, scourged with whips, buffeted, defiled with spittle, crowned with thorns, stripped of thy garments, nailed to an ignominious cross, and placed between two thieves; to have vinegar and gall given thee to drink, and to have thy sacred side pierced with a spear, mercifully grant, O Lord, through these dreadful pains, and all the circumstances of thy passion and death, which I, though unworthy, commemorate, that I may be delivered from the pains of hell, and, with the good thief, be conducted by thee to the mansions of eternal light. *Amen.*

Soul of Jesus, sanctify me.
Blood of Jesus, wash me.
Passion of Jesus, strengthen me.
Wounds of Jesus, heal me.
Heart of Jesus, receive me
Spirit of Jesus, enliven me.
Love of Jesus, inflame me.
Mercy of Jesus, spare me
Cross of Jesus, support me.

Thorns of Jesus, crown me.
Sighs of Jesus, plead for me.
Agony of Jesus, atone for me.
Lips of Jesus, bless me in life and death, in time and eternity. *Amen.*

Litany *of the* Blessed Sacrament.

Lord, have mercy on us.
Christ, have mercy on us.
Lord, have mercy on us.
Living bread, that came down from heaven,
Hidden God and Saviour,
Wheat of the elect, and vine-bearing virgins,
Perpetual sacrifice, and clean oblation,
Lamb without spot, and immaculate feast,
Food of angels, and hidden manna,
Memorial of the wonders of God,
Word made flesh, dwelling in us,
Sacred Host, and Chalice of Benediction,
Mystery of faith, most excellent and venerable sacrament,
Atonement of the living and dead,
Heavenly antidote against the poison of sin,
Most wonderful of all miracles,
Most holy commemoration of the Passion of Christ,
Plenitude of all gifts,
Special memorial of divine love,
Overflowing fountain of divine goodness,
Most high and holy mystery,
Awful and life-giving sacrifice,
Bread made flesh by the omnipotence of the incarnate Word,
Sacrament of piety, sign of unity, and bond of charity,
Priest and Victim,
Viaticum of such as die in the Lord,
Pledge of future glory,

Have mercy on us

From an unworthy reception of thy body and blood,
From every occasion of sin,
Through the desire thou hadst to eat this Passover with thy Disciples,
Through thy precious blood, shed for us on the cross, and really present on our altars,
Through the five wounds thou didst receive in thy sacred body,

Deliver us, O Lord.

We sinners, *We beseech thee, hear us.*

That thou wouldst preserve and increase our faith, reverence, and devotion towards this admirable sacrament,
That by sincere confession we may be disposed for frequent and worthy communion,
That thou wouldst vouchsafe to deliver us from all tepidity, coldness, and obduracy,
That thou wouldst vouchsafe to impart to us the precious and heavenly fruit of this most holy sacrament,
That at the hour of death thou wouldst strengthen and defend us by this heavenly viaticum,

We beseech, &c.

Lamb of God, that takest away the sins of the world, *Spare us, O Lord.*
Lamb of God, that takest away the sins of the world, *Hear us, O Lord.*
Lamb of God, that takest away the sins of the world, *Have mercy on us, O Lord.*

Let us pray.

O God, who in this wonderful sacrament hast left us a memorial of thy death and passion, grant, we beseech thee, that we may so worthily reverence the sacred mysteries of thy body and blood, as continually to perceive in our souls the fruit of thy redemption. Who livest, &c. *Amen.*

Litany *for a* Happy Death

Lord, have mercy on us.
Christ, have mercy on us.
Lord, have mercy on us.

God the Father, who for our sake didst deliver up thy beloved Son to death, *Have mercy on us.*

God, the Son, who didst mercifully submit to the law of death, that we may thereby gain eternal life, *Have mercy on us.*

Holy Spirit, the great comforter of dying Christians, *Have mercy on us.*

O divine Jesus! when I shall be seized with my last illness, and warned to prepare for the approach of my Judge, *Then, merciful Jesus, have mercy on me.*

When my eyes, darkened with the mist of death, shall fix their last dying looks on thy crucified image,

When my pale and ghastly countenance shall fill others with compassion and terror,

When my ears, about to close for ever to all human discourse, shall await the dreadful sound of thy irrevocable sentence,

When my feet, unable to move, shall remind me that my earthly course is drawing to an end,

When my imagination, disturbed with gloomy and frightful phantoms, shall fill my heart with deadly horror,

When my soul, terrified at the view of my sins, and agonized with fear of thy rigorous justice, shall struggle with the angel of darkness,

When my heart, weakened and overwhelmed with the pains of sickness, shall be seized with the last agonies of death, and violently assailed with the last efforts of Satan,

When my friends, assembled round me, shall compassionate my sufferings, and weep for my approaching dissolution,

Then, merciful Jesus, have mercy on me.

When all my senses shall fail, and this world forever vanish from my view,
When the symptoms of death shall appear, and the last tears shall trickle down my cheeks,
When, tortured by the pangs of death, and oppressed with lengthened agony,
When the last heavy sighs of my heart shall press my soul to leave my body,
When my soul, fluttering at my lips, shall be on the point of beholding her Almighty Judge,
When my soul shall at length depart from this valley of tears, and leave my body pale, cold, and hideous,
When I shall stand all alone before my Judge, and behold at one glance all the sins of my life, and all thy claims, O my God, on my love,
When thou shalt pronounce that awful sentence, which no human power can revoke, and no human art elude,

Then, merciful Jesus, have mercy on me.

V. Through thy painful agony and precious death,
R. Deliver us, O Jesus!

Let us pray.

O God, who hast condemned our bodies to death, but hast given us immortal souls to enjoy thee eternally, and hast concealed from us the day and hour of our death, that we may always expect and prepare for our last hour; grant that a holy and penitential life may ensure for us the happiness of a tranquil death. O divine Jesus! whose precious death should lighten our sorrows, I fervently conjure thee, by the bitterness thou didst endure on the cross, when thy blessed soul was separated from thy adorable body, to be propitious to me and to all sinners in our last awful passage from time to eternity. *Amen.*

A short Prayer, which may be said daily for the Grace of a happy Death.

O most dear and adorable Jesus! who wast cruci

fied for the redemption of mankind, I beseech thee, by thy dolorous passion, by thy dreadful agony, by thy countless wounds, by the effusion of thy precious blood, by the recommendation of thy sacred soul into the hands of thy Eternal Father, and by thy ignominious death on the altar of the cross, that thou wilt graciously vouchsafe at my last hour to receive my spirit into the bosom of thy mercy. *Amen.*

THE THIRTY DAYS' PRAYER

To the B. V. Mary, in honour of the Sacred Passion of our Lord Jesus Christ, by the devout Recital of which, for the above Space of Time, we may hope to obtain any lawful Request.

It is particularly recommended as a suitable Devotion for Lent, and all Fridays throughout the Year.

Ever glorious and blessed Mary, Queen of Virgins Mother of Mercy, hope and comfort of dejected and desolate souls, through that sword of sorrow which pierced thy heart whilst thine only Son Jesus Christ our Lord suffered death and ignominy on the cross; through that filial tenderness and pure love he had for thee, grieving in thy grief, whilst from his cross he recommended thee to the care and protection of his beloved disciple St. John, take pity, I beseech thee, on my poverty and necessities; have compassion on my anxieties and cares, assist and comfort me in all my infirmities and miseries. Thou art the Mother of Mercy, the sweet consolatrix and refuge of the needy and the orphan, of the desolate and the afflicted. Look, therefore, with pity on a miserable forlorn child of Eve, and hear my prayer; for since, in just punishment of my sins, I am encompassed with evils, and oppressed with anguish of spirit, whither can I flee for more secure shelter, O amiable Mother of my

Lord and Saviour Jesus Christ, than to thy maternal protection. Attend, therefore, I beseech thee, with pity and compassion, to my humble and earnest request. I ask it, through the infinite mercy of thy dear Son; through that love and condescension wherewith he embraced our nature, when, in compliance with the divine will, thou gavest thy consent, and whom, after the expiration of nine months, thou didst bring forth from the chaste enclosure of thy womb, to visit this world, and bless it with his presence. I ask it, through that anguish of mind wherewith thy beloved Son, our dear Saviour, was overwhelmed on Mount Olivet, when he besought his Eternal Father *to remove from him*, if possible, *the bitter chalice* of his future passion. I ask it, through the three-fold repetition of his prayer in the Garden, from whence afterwards, with dolorous steps and mournful tears, thou didst accompany him to the doleful theatre of his sufferings and death. I ask it, through the welts and sores of his virginal flesh, occasioned by the cords and whips wherewith he was bound and scourged, when stripped of his seamless garment, for which his executioners afterwards cast lots. I ask it, through the scoffs and ignominies by which he was insulted, the false accusations and unjust sentence by which he was condemned to death, and which he bore with heavenly patience. I ask it, through his bitter tears and bloody sweat; his silence and resignation; his sadness and grief of heart. I ask it, through the blood which trickled from his royal and sacred head, when struck with his sceptre of a reed, and pierced with his crown of thorns. I ask it, through the excruciating torments he suffered, when his hands and feet were fastened with huge nails to the tree of the cross. I ask it, through his vehement thirst, and bitter potion of vinegar and gall. I ask it, through his dereliction on the cross, when he exclaimed, *My God! my God! why hast thou forsaken me?* I ask it, through his mercy extended to the good thief, and through his recommending his precious soul and spirit into the hands of his Eternal Father before he expired, saying, ALL IS CONSUMMATED. I ask it, through the blood mixed with water, which issued from his sacred side when pierced with a lance, and whence a flood of grace and mercy hath flowed to us. I ask it, through his immaculate life, bitter passion, and ignominious death on the cross, at which nature itself was thrown into convulsions, by the bursting of rocks, rending of the veil of the temple, the earthquake, and darkness of the sun and moon. I ask it, through his descent into hell, where he comforted the saints of the old law with his presence, and led captivity captive. I ask it, through his glorious victory over death, when he arose again to life on the third day, and through the joy which his appearance for forty days after gave thee, his blessed Mother, his apostles, and the rest of his disciples, when in thine and their presence he miraculously ascended into heaven. I ask it, through the grace of the Holy Ghost, infused into the hearts of the disciples, when he descended upon them in the form of fiery tongues, and by which they were inspired with zeal in the conversion of the world when they went to preach the gospel. I ask it, through the awful appearance of thy Son at the last dreadful day, when he shall come to judge the living and the dead, and the world by fire. I ask it, through the compassion he bore thee in this life, and the ineffable joy thou didst feel at thine assumption into heaven, where thou art eternally absorbed in the sweet contemplation of his adorable perfections. O glorious and ever blessed Virgin! comfort the heart of thy supplicant, by obtaining for me.* And as I am persuaded my divine Saviour honours thee as his beloved Mother, to whom he can refuse nothing, let me speedily experience the efficacy of thy powerful intercession, according to the ten-

* Here mention or reflect on your lawful request, under the reservation of its being agreeable to the will of God

derness of thy maternal affection, and his filial loving heart, who mercifully grantest the requests and compliest with the desires of those that love and fear him O most blessed Virgin! beside the object of my present petition, and whatever else I may stand in need of, obtain for me of thy dear Son, our Lord and our God, a lively faith, firm hope, perfect charity, true contrition, a horror of sin, love of God and my neighbour, contempt of the world, and patience and resignation under the trials and afflictions of this life. Obtain likewise for me, O sacred Mother of God! the great gift of final perseverance, and the grace to receive the last sacraments worthily at the hour of death. Lastly, obtain, I beseech thee, for the souls of my parents, brethren, relations, and benefactors, both living and dead, life everlasting. *Amen.*

A Method of honouring the Mysteries of the Life and Passion of our divine Lord, arranged for the different Hours of the Day, commencing at Five in the Morning, and ending at Ten at Night.

THE following devout practice is recommended to all persons, being very simple and easy, yet calculated to procure for us the greatest spiritual blessings, particularly to facilitate the union of our hearts with the sacred heart of Jesus, and our intentions and actions with those of our divine Redeemer On this union depends not only our advancement in virtue, but likewise our happiness here and hereafter. This is proved from the words of Jesus Christ himself, who tells us expressly that *without him we can do nothing*, and that *if any one goeth to the Father, it must be by him.* He is the *door* through which all must enter. He is *the way*—in any other path than that which his example has traced for us, we must necessarily go astray. He is *the truth*—no other maxims no other words than his, *are spirit and life.* He is *the vine*—to bear any fruit we must *abide in him.* The most heroic actions, divested of his spirit, are as a body without a soul, for *those who gather not with him, scatter;* on the contrary, the most trifling actions performed for his love, and united with his merits, are highly meritorious, and most acceptable in the sight of heaven.

This simple devotion will particularly assist all those who are desirous to walk in the divine presence, and to conform their lives more perfectly to Jesus Christ, whose wisdom will then instruct them—whose light will direct them—whose infinite merits will enrich them—whose consoling presence will support them—whose love will inflame them—and whose bitter sufferings will atone for their daily and multiplied transgressions.

The method of observing this little exercise is, first, when the clock strikes, to make a fervent offering of the ensuing hour to the commemoration of the mystery appointed for it by the following, or any other aspiration—"Divine Jesus, I offer thee my heart, and all my thoughts, words, and actions, during this hour, to honour thy N. N., and desire to spend it in union with the perfect dispositions of thy adorable heart during that stage of thy sacred life or passion." Secondly, to endeavour to practise some little act of virtue, during the hour, in honour of the mystery to which it is devoted, such as charity, patience, forbearance, &c.

It may be necessary to observe that this practice does not require any effort, or strained attention of the mind—the more simply it is performed the better, and it will be found by experience that it is perfectly compatible with exterior duties, and even the most distracting occupations.

The Mysteries of the Life and Passion of our Lord.

	o'clock
The eternal generation of the Word in the bosom of his Father, and his incarnation in time in the womb of the blessed Virgin.	5
His nativity and circumcision.	6
His manifestation to the Wise Men, and his presentation in the Temple.	7
His flight into, and return from Egypt.	8
His being found in the Temple, and his hidden life.	9
His baptism and retreat in the Desert.	10
His public life, preaching, miracles, and labours for the conversion of sinners.	11
His last supper, and the institution of the blessed sacrament.	12
His prayer and agony in the garden.	1
His seizure by his enemies, and his being abandoned by his disciples.	2
His appearance before Annas and Caiphas, and the blow he received from a servant of the High Priest.	3
His denial by St. Peter, and his sufferings during the night of his passion.	4
His being dragged through the streets of Jerusalem to the tribunals of Pilate, and his mockery before Herod.	5
His scourging and crowning with thorns.	6
His carrying the cross and crucifixion.	7
His agony and death.	8
His resurrection and ascension.	9
His rest in heaven from all his labours, and that which he enjoyed in the bosom of his Father from all eternity—his repose in time in the womb of his blessed mother, in the crib at Bethlehem, and during his mortal life—that which he still takes in the adorable sacrament, and in the hearts of all his faithful servants throughout the world.	10

DEVOTIONS FOR THE SICK.

A Prayer in the beginning of Sickness.

O MY God, I accept of the sickness with which thou art pleased to visit me, as a special favour from thy divine Majesty. I accept of all its circumstances and consequences, in satisfaction for my sins. Thou hast given me health and strength, O Lord, and thou hast taken them away; may thy holy name be for ever blessed. I most humbly adore all thy divine appointments, and resign myself entirely to the direction of thy wise providence, acknowledging that thou treatest me with too much indulgence. I deserve far greater sufferings than those I now endure, and merit pains infinitely greater than the pains of hell, where I would long since have been, had not thy pure mercy interposed between my soul and thy justice. Alas! how many are now suffering in those unquenchable flames, for crimes less than mine! My pains are nothing in comparison to theirs. I have no reason to complain.—O may thy holy will be done on earth, as it is in heaven. I offer myself with an entire submission, to suffer whatever thou pleasest, as long as thou pleasest, and in what manner thou pleasest Rebuke me not, O Lord, in thy fury, nor chastise me in thy wrath; but have regard to my weakness. Thou knowest how frail I am; that I am nothing but dust and ashes; deal not with me according to my sins, neither punish me according to my iniquities; but according to the multitude of thy most tender mercies have compassion on me. O! let thy justice be tempered with mercy; and let thy heavenly grace come to my assistance, to support me under this illness. Confirm my soul with strength from above, that I may bear, with fortitude and Christian patience, all the pains, disquiets, and difficulties of my sickness. Preserve me from temptation, and be thou my defence against the assaults of the enemy; grant also, that if this illness is to be my last, I may not be deprived of those helps, which thou hast in thy mercy prepared to strengthen my soul on its passage to eternity; that being perfectly cleansed from all my sins, I may believe in thee, trust in thee, love thee, and through the merits of thy passion and death, be admitted into the company of the blessed, where I may praise thee for ever. *Amen.*

Short acts for the Sick.

O LORD, I accept this sickness from thee; and entirely resign myself to thy blessed will, whether for life or death.

O Lord, I offer to thee all that I now suffer, or have yet to suffer, in union with the sufferings of my Redeemer.

I adore thee, my God, and my all, as my first beginning, and last end; I submit all the powers of my soul to thee; and I desire to pay thee the most perfect homage. I will praise thee always, in sickness as in health; I will join with thy whole church in blessing thee for ever.

I give thee thanks for all the blessings thou hast bestowed on me, through Jesus Christ thy Son; but above all, for having loved me from eternity, and for having redeemed me with his precious blood.

I believe, O Lord, all those truths which thou hast revealed, and which thy holy Catholic Church proposes to my belief. Thou art truth itself, who neither canst deceive, nor be deceived; in this faith I desire to live, and in the same, by thy grace, I am firmly resolved to die. I hope most firmly in thee, my God; expecting the pardon of all my sins, through the merits of Jesus Christ my Saviour. In thee, O Lord, have I put my trust; let me not be confounded for ever.

I love thee, my God, with my whole heart, and above all things; at least I desire so to love thee; I abandon myself entirely to the disposal of thy will.

I forgive from my heart, all those who have at any time offended or injured me; and I humbly ask pardon of those whom I have at any time offended.

Have mercy on me, O God! according to thy great mercy; and according to the multitude of thy tender mercies, blot out my iniquities.

Who will give water to my head, that night and day I may bewail my transgressions?

O Lord, be merciful to me a sinner; Jesus, Son of the living God, have mercy on me.

I commend my soul to God my Creator, who made me out of nothing; to Jesus Christ, my Saviour, who redeemed me with his precious Blood; to the Holy Ghost the Comforter, who sanctified me in Baptism Into thy hands, O Lord, I commend my spirit.

O holy Mary, Mother of God, pray for me a sinner, now and at the hour of my death. O all ye Saints and Angels of God, make intercession for me. *Amen.*

A Prayer before receiving the Viaticum.

O DEAR Jesus, I adore thee with all my heart! I give thee thanks for that infinite love which thou didst show to poor sinners, in dying for them on the cross, and for thy unspeakable goodness, displayed in the institution of thy adorable Sacrament. To this heavenly banquet thou art now pleased to invite me; but how can I approach! I who have so ungratefully offended thee, and who have lived so unworthy of the name of a Christian. I acknowledge, O God, that I am a sinner, a poor miserable sinner; thou alone art my hope, to thee I raise my eyes, who art rich in mercy; who art my advocate and most powerful mediator. I commit my cause into thy hands; help me now in my distress; let thy precious blood, the infinite treasure of thy merits, supply all my deficiencies, while I partake of this sacred food. Thou knowest my weakness, and the depth of my unworthiness; hou seest how unfit I am, through the multitude and enormity of my sins, to appear before thy judgment seat; I tremble at that dreadful hour, when I shall clearly see the extent of my ingratitude. What shall I do then, O divine Lord? what shall become of me, if my iniquities are to decide my eternal destiny? O good Jesus, let thy infinite merits accompany me to that place of terror; let all thy mercies plead on my behalf; I have nothing to trust to in myself, yet upon thy infinite goodness I have every reason to rely; my sins cry aloud for justice, but thy precious blood cries still louder for mercy. On this mercy I depend; and in this hope I desire to die; come, dear Jesus, now into my soul, and possess it for ever.

Short Acts of Thanksgiving, after having received the Viaticum.

Glory and thanksgiving be to thee, O Lord, who in thy sweetness hast been pleased to visit my poor soul. Now let thy servant depart in peace according to thy word.

Now thou art come to me, I will not let thee go; I willingly bid farewell to the world, and with joy I go to thee, my God.

Nothing more, O dear Jesus, nothing more shall separate me from thee; in thee I will live in thee I will die, and in thee I hope to abide for ever.

I desire to be dissolved, and to be with Christ, for Christ is my life, and to die will be my gain.

Now I will fear no evils, though I walk in the shadow of death, because thou art with me, O Lord: as the hart pants after the fountains of water, so does my soul after thee; my soul thirsts after the fountain of living water: O when shall I come, and appear before the face of my God!

Give me thy blessing, O divine Jesus, and establish my soul in everlasting peace; such peace, as only thou canst give; such peace, as it may not be in the power of my enemy to destroy.

O that my soul were at rest in thy happiness, and in the enjoyment of thee, my God, for ever.

What more have I to do with the world? And in Heaven, what have I to desire, but thee, my God?

Into thy hands I commend my spirit; receive me, sweet Jesus! In thee may I rest; and in thy happiness rejoice without end. *Amen*

A Prayer before Extreme-Unction.

O Lord Jesus Christ, who in thy great mercy hast instituted the Sacrament of Extreme-unction for the benefit of the sick, grant, I beseech thee, that it may heal my soul, fortify me against temptation, support me in the hour of anguish, and prepare me for a happy passage to eternity, or for whatever may be thy divine appointment. If thou foreseest that my health will be conducive to thy greater glory, and expedient for my eternal salvation, let this be the means to restore it. Dispose of me as thou knowest best; all I desire is the accomplishment of thy will; give me health or sickness, life or death; give me whatever thou pleasest; not my will, but thine be done; it is a greater happiness to fulfil thy adorable will, than to enjoy ten thousand lives. How happy should I be, if the destruction of my body could repair the injuries I have offered to thy divine Majesty! My eyes, alas! have seen vanities; my ears have been open to sinful and unprofitable discourse; my tongue has many ways offended in speaking and tasting; my hands have contributed to innumerable follies; my feet have gone astray in the paths of iniquity. By this holy unction, and by the prayers of thy Church, pardon me, O Jesus, all the sins I have committed by the gratification of my senses. Let those avenues through which sin has made its way into my soul, be now closed to the world; let my eyes be open to thee alone; my ears attentive to thy sacred word; my tongue solely employed in soliciting for mercy. Let my prayers ascend like incense in thy sight; let my hands be lifted up to Heaven for pardon; let my feet walk in thy ways, and let my heart be the living temple of the Holy Ghost

Into thy hand, O dear Jesus, I commend my spirit In thee I will live; in thee I will die; in thee I will abide; and in thee I hope to possess eternal rest for ever and ever. *Amen.*

A Prayer after Extreme-Unction.

O MY God, thou hast nourished me with the adorable Sacrament of thy body and blood, and hast now enabled me to receive the rites of thy Church, preferably to so many others, who were carried off by a sudden and unprovided death. For these, and all other blessings, I offer thee the pure and perfect thanksgiving thou receivest from thy blessed Mother and all the saints. I do not desire to be freed from my pains; thou knowest what is best for me; give me patience to suffer whatever thou pleasest, and as long as thou pleasest. If it be thy divine pleasure to inflict on my weak body still greater punishments than those I now suffer, my heart is ready, O Lord, my heart is ready to accept them, and to suffer in whatever manner and measure shall be conformable to thy holy will. This one grace I most ardently beg of thee, my God, that I may die the death of thy Elect, and be admitted, after the sufferings and tribulations of this transitory life, into the kingdom of thy glory, there to see and enjoy thee, in the company of the blessed, for all eternity. *Amen.*

Preparation for Death.

LORD, have mercy on her.
Christ, have mercy on her, &c. &c.
Holy Mother of God,
All ye holy Angels and Archangels,
All ye blessed company of the just,
All ye holy Patriarchs and Prophets,
All ye holy Apostles and Evangelists.
All ye holy Disciples of our Lord,
All ye holy Martyrs,
All ye holy Bishops and Confessors,

Pray for her

All ye holy Virgins and Widows, *Pray for her.*
All ye holy Saints of God, make intercession for her.
Have mercy, O Lord! and spare her.
Have mercy, O Lord! and hear her.
From all her offences, and the punishment due to them,
From all the snares and temptations of the devil,
From all impatience and repining at thy just chastisements,
From dejection of spirit, and diffidence in thy mercies,
From all undue fear of death, and immoderate desires of life,
From distraction of mind, and neglect of preparation for eternity,
By thy Cross and Passion,
By thy Death and Burial,
By thy glorious Resurrection and Ascension,
By the grace of the Holy Ghost, the Comforter,
In the hour of death, and in the day of judgment,

Deliver her, O Lord.

We sinners, beseech thee hear us.

That it would please thee to comfort her in her anguish, and enable her to look to a happy futurity We beseech thee, hear us.

That it would please thee to remind her of all thy mercies, and encourage her to confide in thy goodness. We beseech thee, &c.

That thou wouldst vouchsafe to grant her the grace to forgive those by whom she may have been offended, and to satisfy those whom she may have injured in word or deed. We beseech thee, &c.

That being thus reconciled to thee, and all creatures, she may with assured hope, and steadfast faith, receive the sacrament of thy blessed body, and by this heavenly food be strengthened against the pangs of death. We beseech thee, &c.

That patient submission under the pains of sickness, may expiate the punishment due to her sins, diminish her love of this world, and increase her desire of the happiness which awaits the just. We beseech thee, &c.

That she may readily acquiesce in the orders of thy providence, both in life and death. We beseech thee, &c.

Son of God, we beseech thee hear us.

Lamb of God, &c. &c.

Lord, have mercy on us, &c.

Our Father, &c.

O Lord, hear my prayer.

And let my cry come unto thee.

Let us pray.

ALMIGHTY and eternal God, in whose hands are life and death, whose infinite wisdom disposes all things advantageously for those who love thee, behold thy servant whom thou hast laid on the bed of sickness; comfort, we beseech thee, her afflicted spirit; increase her faith, strengthen her hope, and perfect her charity. Enable her to sanctify all her sufferings, by patient resignation, and if thy mercy shall restore her to health, may she carefully correct all that is displeasing in thy sight. If it please thee to call her out of this world, grant that she may pass safely through the shades of death transported by thy holy angels into the mansions of bliss, where no fear shall trouble her, no pain afflict her, no grief disquiet her mind; but pure delight, unspeakable joys, and perfect security shall be for ever confirmed to her, through Christ our Lord. *Amen.*

Prayers for the Agonizing.

DEPART, Christian soul, out of this world, in the name of God, the Father Almighty, who created thee; in the name of Jesus Christ, Son of the living

God, who suffered for thee; in the name of the Holy Ghost, who sanctified thee; in the name of the Angels, Archangels, Thrones, and Dominations, Cherubim and Seraphim; in the name of the Patriarchs and Prophets, of the holy Apostles and Evangelists, of the holy Martyrs and Confessors, of the holy Monks and Hermits, of the holy Virgins, and of all the Saints of God; let thy place be this day in peace, and thy abode in holy Sion, through Christ our Lord. *Amen.*

God of mercy, God of goodness! who, according to the multitude of thy mercies, forgivest the sins of such as repent, and graciously remittest the guilt of their past offences, mercifully regard this thy servant N. and grant her a full discharge from all her sins. Renew, O merciful Father, whatever is corrupt in her through human frailty, or by the snares of the enemy; make her a true member of the Church, and let her partake of the fruit of thy redemption. Have compassion, Lord, on her sighs, take pity on her tears, and admit her to the Sacrament of thy reconciliation, who has no hope but in thee. Through Christ our Lord. *Amen.*

I recommend thee, dear Sister, to Almighty God, and leave thee to his mercy, whose creature thou art, that having paid the common debt by surrendering thy soul, thou mayest return to thy Maker, who formed thee out of the earth. Let, therefore, the holy Angels meet thy soul at its departure; let the court of the Apostles receive thee; let the triumphant army of glorious Martyrs conduct thee; let the crowds of joyful confessors encompass thee; let the choir of blessed Virgins go before thee; and let a happy rest be thy portion in the company of the Patriarchs; let Jesus Christ appear to thee with a mild and cheerful countenance, and give thee a place among those who are to be in his presence for ever. Mayest thou be a stranger to all that is punished with darkness, chastised with flames, and condemned to torments. May all the ministers of Hell be filled with confusion and shame, and let no evil spirit dare to stop thee in thy way. Christ Jesus be thy deliverer, who was crucified for thee; Christ Jesus deliver thee from death, who vouchsafed to die for thee; Christ Jesus, Son of the living God, place thee in his garden of Paradise; and may he, the true Shepherd, own thee for one of his flock; may he absolve thee from all thy sins, and place thee on his right hand, in the inheritance of his elect. We pray it may be thy happy lot, to behold thy Redeemer face to face; to be for ever in his presence, and in the vision of that truth which is the joy of the blessed. *Amen.*

Let us pray.

WE recommend to thee, O Lord, the soul of this thy servant, and beseech thee, Jesus Christ, Redeemer of the world, that as in mercy to her thou becamest man, so now thou wouldst vouchsafe to admit her into the number of the blessed. Remember, Lord, she is thy creature, not made by strange gods, but by thee, the only true and living God; for there is no other God but thee, none that can work thy wonders. Let her soul find comfort in thy sight, and remember not her former sins, nor any of those excesses which she has fallen into, through the violence of passion and corruption. For although she has sinned, yet, she has still retained true faith in thee, Father, Son, and Holy Ghost; she has had zeal for thy honour, and faithfully adored thee, her God, and the Creator of all things.

Remember not, O Lord, we beseech thee, the sins and ignorance of her youth; but according to thy great mercy, be mindful of her in thy eternal glory Let the Heavens be opened to her, and the angels rejoice with her. Receive, O Lord, thy servant into thy kingdom. Let the Archangel St. Michael, the chief of the heavenly host, conduct her. Let the holy Angels of God meet her, and bring her into the city of the heavenly Jerusalem. May blessed Peter the Apostle, to whom were given the keys of the kingdom of Heaven, receive her. May holy Paul the Apostle, who was a vessel of election, help her. May St. John, the beloved Disciple, to whom God revealed the secrets of Heaven, intercede for her. May all the holy Apostles, to whom was given the power of binding and loosing, pray for her. May all the blessed and chosen servants of God, who, in this world, have suffered torments for the name of Christ, pray for her, that being delivered from this body of corruption, she may be admitted into the kingdom of Heaven; through the assistance and merits of our Lord Jesus Christ, who liveth and reigneth with the Father and the Holy Ghost, world without end. *Amen.*

If further prayers are required, any of the Penitential Psalms may be said.

Immediately after the sick person has expired, the following Responsory is said.

Come to her assistance, all ye Saints of God; meet her, all ye Angels of God; receive her soul, and present it now before its Lord. May Jesus Christ receive her, and the Angels conduct her to her place of rest; may they receive her soul, and present it now before its LORD.

Grant her, O Lord, eternal rest,
And let perpetual light shine on her.
Lord have mercy on us.
Christ have mercy on us.
Lord have mercy on us.
Our Father, &c.
And lead us not into temptation, &c.
Grant her, O Lord, eternal rest, &c.
From the gates of Hell,
Deliver her soul, O Lord.
May she rest in peace.
Amen.
O Lord, hear my prayer.
And let my cry come unto thee

Let us pray.

To thee, Lord, we recommend the soul of thy servant N., that being dead to this world, she may live to thee; and whatever sins she has committed through human frailty, we beseech thee, in thy goodness, mercifully to pardon, through Christ our Lord. *Amen.*

THE SEVEN PENITENTIAL PSALMS.

Proper to be recited on Fasting Days, and at other penitential Times.

Anth. Remember not, O Lord, our offences, nor those of our parents, and take not revenge on our sins.

Psalm vi. *Domine, ne in furore.*

1. David, in deep affliction, prays for a mitigation of the divine anger, 4. in consideration of God's mercy; 5. his glory; 6. his own repentance; 8. by faith triumphs over his enemies.

O Lord, rebuke me not in thy indignation, nor chastise me in thy wrath.

Have mercy on me, O Lord, for I am weak: heal me, O Lord, for my bones are troubled.

And my soul is troubled exceedingly: but thou, O Lord, how long?

Turn to me, O Lord, and deliver my soul; O save me for thy mercy's sake.

For there is no one in death that is mindful of thee, and who shall confess to thee in hell?

I have laboured in my groanings; every night I will wash my bed, I will water my couch with my tears.

My eye is troubled through indignation; I have grown old among all my enemies.

Depart from me, all ye workers of iniquity: for the Lord hath heard the voice of my weeping.

The Lord hath heard my supplication: the Lord hath received my prayer.

Let my enemies be ashamed, and be very much troubled: let them be turned back, and be ashamed very speedily. Glory be, &c.

Psalm xxxi. *Beati quorum.*

1 Blessings of remission of sins; 3. misery of impenitence; 6. confession of sins bringeth ease, 8. safety, 14. joy.

Blessed are they whose iniquities are forgiven, and whose sins are covered.

Blessed is the man to whom the Lord hath not imputed sin, and in whose spirit there is no guile.

Because I was silent, my bones grew old; whilst I cried out all the day long.

For day and night thy hand was heavy upon me: I am turned in my anguish, whilst the thorn is fastened.

I have acknowledged my sin to thee; and my injustice I have not concealed.

I said I will confess against myself my injustice to the Lord, and thou hast forgiven the wickedness of my sin.

For this shall every one that is holy pray to thee, in a seasonable time.

And yet in a flood of many waters, they shall not come nigh unto him.

Thou art my refuge from the trouble which hath encompassed me: my joy, deliver me from them that surround me.

I will give thee understanding, and I will instruct thee in this way in which thou shalt go; I will fix my eyes upon thee.

Do not become like the horse and the mule, who have no understanding.

With bit and bridle bind fast their jaws, who come not near unto thee.

Many are the scourges of the sinner, but mercy shall encompass him that hopeth in the Lord.

Be glad in the Lord, and rejoice ye just: and glory, all ye right of heart. Glory be, &c.

Psalm xxxviii. *Domine, ne in furore.*

1 **David's** extreme anguish; 15. he hopeth in God; 18. his resignation, grief; 22. fervent prayer.

Rebuke me not, O Lord, in thy indignation, nor chastise me in thy wrath.

For thy arrows are fastened in me; and thy hand hath been strong upon me.

There is no health in my flesh, because of thy wrath; there is no peace for my bones, because of my sins.

For my iniquities are gone over my head; and as a heavy burden are become heavy upon me.

My sores are putrefied and corrupted, because of my foolishness.

I am become miserable, and am bowed down even to the end; I walked sorrowful all the day long.

For my loins are filled with illusions; and there is no health in my flesh.

I am afflicted and humbled exceedingly; I roared with the groaning of my heart.

Lord, all my desire is before thee: and my groaning is not hid from thee.

My heart is troubled, my strength hath left me, and the light of my eyes itself is not with me.

My friends and my neighbours have drawn near, and stood against me.

And they that were near me stood afar off; and they that sought my soul used violence.

And they that sought evils to me spoke vain things, and studied deceits all the day long.

But I, as a deaf man, heard not; and was as a dumb man not opening his mouth.

And I became as a man that heareth not; and that hath no reproofs in his mouth.

For in thee, O Lord, have I hope; thou wilt hear me, O Lord my God.

For I said, Lest at any time my enemies rejoice over

me: and whilst my feet are moved, they speak great things against me.

For I am ready for scourges; and my sorrow is continually before me.

For I will declare my iniquity; and I will think for my sin.

But my enemies live, and are stronger than I; and they that hate me wrongfully are multiplied.

They that render evil for good, have detracted me, because I followed goodness.

Forsake me not, O Lord my God; do not thou depart from me.

Attend unto my help, O Lord the God of my salvation. Glory be, &c.

Psalm L. *Miserere.*

1. David prayeth for remission of his sins; 8. for perfect sanctity 17. God delighteth not in sacrifice, but a contrite heart; 19. he prayeth for the building of a temple in Jerusalem, figuratively the exaltation of the Church.

Have mercy on me, O God, according to thy great mercy.

And according to the multitude of thy tender mercies, blot out my iniquity.

Wash me yet more from my iniquity, and cleanse me from my sin.

For I know my iniquity, and my sin is always before me.

To thee only have I sinned, and have done evil before thee; that thou mayest be justified in thy words, and mayest overcome when thou art judged.

For behold I was conceived in iniquities; and in sins did my mother conceive me.

For behold thou hast loved truth; the uncertain and hidden things of thy wisdom thou hast made manifest to me.

Thou shalt sprinkle me with hyssop, and I shall be cleansed; thou shalt wash me, and I shall be made whiter than snow

To my hearing thou shalt give joy and gladness and the bones that have been humbled shall rejoice.

Turn away thy face from my sins, and blot out all my iniquities.

Create a clean heart in me, O God; and renew a right spirit within my bowels.

Cast me not away from thy face; and take not thy Holy Spirit from me.

Restore unto me the joy of thy salvation, and strengthen me with a perfect spirit.

I will teach the unjust thy ways; and the wicked shall be converted to thee.

Deliver me from blood, O God, thou God of my salvation; and my tongue shall extol thy justice.

O Lord, thou wilt open my lips; and my mouth shall declare thy praise.

For if thou hadst desired sacrifice, I would indeed have given it; with burnt-offerings thou wilt not be delighted.

A sacrifice to God is an afflicted spirit; a contrite and humbled heart, O God, thou wilt not despise.

Deal favourably, O Lord, in thy good-will with Sion; that the walls of Jerusalem may be built up.

Then shalt thou accept the sacrifice of justice, oblations, and whole burnt-offerings; then shall they lay calves upon thy altar. Glory be, &c.

PSALM CI. *Domine, exaudi.*

1 The extreme affliction of the Psalmist; 12. the eternity and mercy of God; 19. to be recorded, and praised by future generations; 26. the unchangeableness of God.

HEAR, O Lord, my prayer, and let my cry come to thee.

Turn not away thy face from me; in the day when I am in trouble, incline thine ear to me.

In what day soever I shall call upon thee, hear me speedily.

For my days are vanished like smoke; and my bones a grown dry like fuel for the fire.

I am smitten as grass, and my heart is withered; because I forgot to eat my bread.

Through the voice of my groaning my bone hath cleaved to my flesh.

I am become like to a pelican of the wilderness; I am like a night-raven in the house.

I have watched, and am become as a sparrow, all alone on the house-top.

All the day long my enemies reproach me; and they that praised me did swear against me.

For I did eat ashes like bread; and mingled my drink with weeping.

Because of thy anger and indignation; for having lifted me up thou hast thrown me down.

My days have declined like a shadow; and I am withered like grass.

But thou, O Lord, endurest for ever; and thy memorial to all generations.

Thou shalt arise and have mercy on Sion; for it is time to have mercy on it, for the time is come.

For the stones thereof have pleased thy servants, and they shall have pity on the earth thereof.

And the gentiles shall fear thy name, O Lord; and all the kings of the earth thy glory.

For the Lord hath built up Sion; and he shall be seen in his glory.

He hath had regard to the prayer of the humble; and he hath not despised their petition.

Let these things be written unto another generation; and the people that shall be created shall praise the Lord.

Because he hath looked forth from his high sanctuary; from heaven the Lord hath looked upon the earth.

That he might hear the groans of them that are in fetters; that he might release the children of the slain.

That they may declare the name of the Lord in Sion and his praise in Jerusalem.

When the people assembled together, and kings to serve the Lord.

He answered him in the way of his strength; declare unto me the fewness of my days.

Call me not away in the midst of my days: thy years are unto generation and generation.

In the beginning, O Lord, thou foundedst the earth; and the heavens are the works of thy hands.

They shall perish, but thou remainest: and all of them shall grow old like a garment.

And as a vesture thou shalt change them, and they shall be changed; but thou art always the self-same, and thy years shall not fail.

The children of thy servants shall continue; and their seed shall be directed for ever

Glory be to the Father, &c.

Psalm cxxix. *De profundis.*

An excellent model for sinners imploring the divine mercy.

Out of the depths I have cried to thee, O Lord; Lord, hear my voice.

Let thy ears be attentive to the voice of my supplication.

If thou, O Lord, wilt mark iniquities, Lord who shall stand it?

For with thee there is merciful forgiveness: and by reason of thy law I have waited for thee, O Lord.

My soul hath relied on his word; my soul hath hoped in the Lord.

From the morning watch even until night, let Israel hope in the Lord.

Because with the Lord there is mercy, and with him plentiful redemption.

And he shall redeem Israel from all his iniquities.

Glory be, &c

PSALM CXLII. *Domine, exaudi.*

1. David prayeth for favour in judgment; 3. represents his distress; 7. he prayeth for grace, 9. for deliverance, 10. for sanctification, 12. victory over his enemies.

HEAR, O Lord, my prayer; give ear to my supplication in thy truth; hear me in thy justice.

And enter not into judgment with thy servant: for in thy sight no man living shall be justified.

For the enemy hath persecuted my soul: he hath brought down my life to the earth.

He hath made me to dwell in darkness, as those that have been dead of old; and my spirit is in anguish within me: my heart within me is troubled.

I remembered the days of old, I meditated on all thy works: I mused upon the works of thy hands.

I stretched forth my hands to thee: my soul is as earth without water unto thee.

Hear me speedily, O Lord; my spirit hath fainted away.

Turn not away thy face from me, lest I be like unto them that go down into the pit.

Cause me to hear thy mercy in the morning; for in thee have I hoped.

Make the way known to me wherein I should walk; for I have lifted up my soul to thee.

Deliver me from my enemies, O Lord, to thee have I fled; teach me to do thy will, for thou art my God.

Thy good spirit shall lead me into the right land; for thy name's sake, O Lord, thou wilt quicken me in thy justice.

Thou wilt bring my soul out of troubles: and in thy mercy thou wilt destroy my enemies.

And thou wilt cut off all them that afflict my soul; for I am thy servant. Glory be to the Father, &c.

Anth. Remember not, O Lord, our offences, nor those of our parents; and take not revenge on our sins

Devotions *to the* S. Heart *of* Jesus.

The Devotion to the Sacred Heart of Jesus is now, through the mercy of God, so generally known, and so universally established, as to render any explanation of its nature quite superfluous. It is therefore only necessary to specify, that those who become members of the Association contract the following obligations; not, however, under pain of sin of any kind, but under the penalty of forfeiting the Indulgences and other graces annexed to this Devotion.

First, a *Pater*, *Ave*, and *Credo*, are to be said daily, with the following aspiration:—

O Heart of Jesus, I implore
That I may love thee more and more.

Secondly, an hour is to be spent before the Blessed Sacrament, on any day in the year, chosen by each member on her entrance into the Association; which hour, beside being registered in any community privileged to receive members, can be noted in the following billet of Association, to prevent forgetfulness.

"I have chosen from to spend before the Blessed Sacrament, to repair the outrages committed against the adorable Heart of Jesus in this Mystery of Love."

An Act of Consecration to the Sacred Heart of Jesus.

O sacred Heart of Jesus! to thee I devote and offer up my life, thoughts, words, actions, pains, and sufferings. My entire being shall henceforward only be employed in loving, serving, honouring, and glorifying thee. Be thou, O most sacred Heart! the sole object of my love, the protector of my life, the pledge of my salvation, and my secure refuge at the hour of death. Be thou also, O most bountiful Heart! my justification at the throne of God, and screen me from his anger, which I have so justly merited. In thee I place all my confidence, and, convinced as I am of my own weakness, I rely entirely on thy compassion.

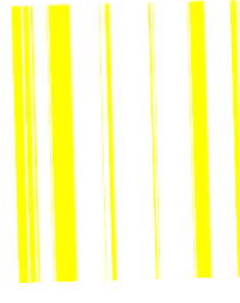

ate mercy. Annihilate in me all that is displeasing and offensive to thy pure eyes. Imprint thyself like a divine seal on my heart, that I may ever remember my obligations, and never be separated from thee. May my name also, I beseech thee, by thy tender goodness, ever be fixed and engraved in thee, O Book of Life!—and may I be a victim consecrated to thy glory, ever burning with the flames of thy pure love, both in time and in eternity. In this I place all my happiness, this is all my desire, to live and die in no other quality but that of thy devoted servant. *Amen.*

The Litany *of the* Sacred Heart.

Lord, have mercy on us.—Christ, have mercy on us, &c.
Lord, have mercy on us.
Christ, hear us.—Christ, graciously hear us, &c.
God the Father of heaven, *Have mercy on us.*
God the Son, Redeemer of the world, *Have mercy on us.*
God the Holy Ghost, *Have mercy on us.*
Holy Trinity, one God,
Heart of Jesus!
Heart of Jesus, formed in the womb of the most blessed Virgin,
Heart of Jesus, hypostatically united to the Eternal Word,
Heart of Jesus, Sanctuary of the Divinity, and Tabernacle of the most holy Trinity,
Heart of Jesus, Temple of Sanctity, and Fountain of all Graces,
Heart of Jesus, most meek and humble,
Heart of Jesus, most chaste and obedient,
Heart of Jesus, furnace of love, and source of contrition,
Heart of Jesus, treasure of wisdom and goodness,

Have mercy on us.

Heart of Jesus, throne of mercy, and abyss of all virtues,
Heart of Jesus, sorrowful in the garden, and spent with a bloody sweat,
Heart of Jesus, saturated with reproaches, and consumed for our sins,
Heart of Jesus, made obedient ever unto the death of the cross,
Heart of Jesus, pierced with a lance, and the refuge of sinners,
Heart of Jesus, fortitude of the just, and comfort of the afflicted,
Heart of Jesus, main strength of the tempted, and the terror of the devils, *Have mercy on us*
Heart of Jesus, sanctification of hearts, and perseverance of the good,
Heart of Jesus, hope of the dying, joy of the blessed, and delight of all the saints,
Lamb of God, who takest away the sins of the world, *Spare us, O Jesus! &c.*
Lamb of God, who takest away the sins of the world, *Hear us, O Jesus!*
Lamb of God, who takest away the sins of the world, *Have mercy on us, O Jesus!*

V. O most sacred heart of Jesus, have mercy on us.

R. That me may worthily love thee with our whole hearts.

Let us pray.

O God! who out of thy immense love hast given to the faithful the most Sacred Heart of thy Son our Lord as the object of thy tender affection; grant, we beseech thee, that we may so love and honour this pledge of thy love on earth, as by it to merit the love both of thee and thy gift, and be eternally loved by thee and this most blessed heart in heaven. Through the same Jesus Christ our Lord. *Amen.*

Through thy sacred Heart O Jesus! overflowing

with all sweetness, we recommend to thee ourselves and all our concerns, our friends, benefactors, parents, and relations, our superiors, and enemies: take under thy protection this house, city, and country: extend thy care to all such as lie under any affliction, and to those who labour in the agony and pangs of death; cast an eye of compassion on the obstinate sinner, and more particularly on the poor suffering souls in purgatory; as also on those who are engaged and united with us in the holy confederacy of honouring and worshipping thee. Bless these in particular, O divine Jesus! and bless them according to the extent of thy infinite goodness, mercy, and charity. *Amen.*

A Reparation of Honour to the Sacred Heart, to be made on the Feast itself, or at any other time, in presence of the Blessed Sacrament.

O MOST amiable and adorable Heart of Jesus! centre of all hearts, glowing with charity, and inflamed with zeal for the interest of thy Father and the salvation of mankind! O heart, ever sensible of our misery, and ever in motion to redress our evils; the real victim of love in the holy Eucharist, and a propitiatory sacrifice for sin on the altar of the cross! since the generality of Christians make no other return for these thy mercies, than contempt of thy favours, forgetfulness of their obligations, and ingratitude to the best of benefactors, is it not just, that we thy servants, penetrated with a deep sense of such indignities, should, as far as is in our power, enter on a due and satisfactory reparation of honour to thy most sacred Majesty? Humbled, therefore, in mind before heaven and earth, we solemnly declare our sincere detestation and abhorrence of such conduct. Inexpressible, we know, was the bitterness with which the multitude of our sins overwhelmed thy tender heart; insufferable the weight of our iniquities, which pressed thy face to the earth in the garden of Olives, and insurmountable thy anguish, when expiring with love, grief, and agony, on Mount Calvary, in thy last breath thou wouldst reclaim sinners to their duty and repentance. This we know, O dear Redeemer! and would most willingly redress these thy sufferings by our own, or share with thee in thine.

O merciful Jesus, ever present on our altars, and with a heart open to receive all who *labour and are burdened!* O adorable Heart of Jesus! source of true contrition! impart to our hearts the true spirit of penance, and to our eyes a fountain of tears, that we may bewail our sins, and those of the world. Pardon, divine Jesus! all the injuries, reproaches, and outrages offered to thee through the course of thy holy life and bitter passion. Pardon all the impieties, irreverences, and sacrileges which have been committed against thee in the sacrament of the Eucharist from its first institution. Graciously receive the small tribute of our sincere repentance as an agreeable offering in thy sight, in requital for the benefits we daily receive from the altar, where thou art a living and continual sacrifice, and in union with that bloody holocaust thou didst present to thy eternal Father on Mount Calvary.

Divine Jesus! give thy blessing to the ardent desire we now entertain, and the holy resolution we have taken of ever loving and adoring thee in thy sacrament of love the Eucharist, thus to repair, by a true conversion of heart, and zeal for thy glory, our past negligences and infidelity. Be thou, O adorable Heart! who knowest the clay of which we are formed, be thou our mediator with thy heavenly Father whom we have so grievously offended; strengthen our weakness, confirm our resolution, and with thy charity, humility, meekness, and patience, cover the multitude of our iniquities; be thou our support, our refuge, and our strength, that nothing henceforward in life or death may separate us from thee. *Amen.*

DEVOTIONS *to the* HEART *of* MARY.

O MOST amiable Heart of Mary! which of all hearts most perfectly resembles the Heart of Jesus, and is thereby worthy of the love and respect of all creatures, to thee I fervently consecrate my heart, and I choose thee, after the heart of Jesus, for the object of my imitation and confidence. I beseech thee, O sacred Virgin! by all the graces which were bestowed on thee by thy divine Son, to give me a passage through thy blessed heart to the Heart of Jesus. Lead me thyself into that adorable sanctuary, that I may learn to practise the virtues which rendered thee so faithful a copy of Him who was meek and humble of heart. Thou knowest that I wish most sincerely to venerate, to love, and to imitate that divine heart, which was the source of all thy merit and happiness, as well as the only object of thy love; but as I feel my own weakness, I have recourse to thee, beseeching thee to present my heart to Jesus in union with thine; that in consideration of thy perfections and merits, my miseries and sins may be overlooked, and my heart for ever consecrated, through thee, to the perfect love of my Creator. I choose thee now, O holy Heart of Mary, for my advocate and model, that thy prayers may assist me to imitate thee, and thereby conform my heart to that of my divine Saviour. Thou wert, O most pure Heart! happily inaccessible to the monster sin! yet thou art penetrated with humiliation and sorrow for the sins of the world: obtain that my heart may be truly contrite for my own sins, and may love God sufficiently to feel and deplore the sins of others. Thou wert replenished with the meekness and mercy of the Heart of Jesus, and consumed with his most ardent love; therefore through thee I most firmly hope to receive a share in those virtues; and above all, the grace to detest the vice of pride, which would render me so hateful to the adorable Heart of Jesus, and to practise that sincere humility which can best liken me to my Saviour and to thee. In thee, O blessed Heart of Mary! I will confide during my life, and in thee also I confidently hope to find a secure refuge and powerful advocate at the hour of my death

---

Litany of the Heart of Mary.

LORD have mercy on us, &c.
Heart of Mary,
Heart of Mary, according to the Heart of Jesus,
Heart of Mary, united to the Heart of Jesus,
Heart of Mary, sanctuary of the Holy Ghost,
Heart of Mary, temple of the Divinity,
Heart of Mary, tabernacle of the Word incarnate,
Heart of Mary, always exempt from sin,
Heart of Mary, always full of grace,
Heart of Mary, blessed among all hearts,
Heart of Mary, illustrious throne of glory,
Heart of Mary, abyss and prodigy of humility,
Heart of Mary, glorious holocaust of divine love,
Heart of Mary, nailed to the cross of Jesus,
Heart of Mary, comfort of the afflicted,
Heart of Mary, refuge of sinners,
Heart of Mary, hope of the agonizing,
Heart of Mary, seat of mercy,
Pray for us.

Lamb of God, &c.

V. Pray for us, O holy Mother of God.

R. That we may be made worthy of the promises of Christ.

Let us pray.

O DIVINE JESUS! who tenderly lovest the most holy of virgins, and art reciprocally loved by her, grant, we beseech thee, through the intercession of thy blessed

Mother, and by the resemblance her sacred Heart bore to thine, that we may ever return due love and affection for her care and tenderness in our regard, who, with the Father and the Holy Ghost, livest and reignest, world without end. *Amen.*

The Seven DOLOURS, *or chief Sufferings of the* BLESSED VIRGIN MARY.

I.

O MOST afflicted Virgin, permit me to commemorate the sorrow which filled thy heart, when on presenting thy divine Son in the temple, holy Simeon foretold that a sword should pierce thy soul, thereby announcing the share thou shouldst have in the sufferings of thy dear Son. I most devoutly compassionate thy grief on this occasion, and beseech thee, O glorious Queen of Martyrs! to obtain for me, through the sufferings of Jesus Christ, which were the great cause of thy dolours, a sincere and lively horror of sin, an ardent love of God, a tender practical devotion towards thee, and a happy death under thy special protection.

II.

O MOST holy and afflicted Virgin! permit me to commiserate the sorrow which filled thy maternal Heart, when thou didst see thy divine Infant persecuted by his own creatures, and wert obliged to flee into Egypt, to save him from the fury of Herod. I most devoutly compassionate thy grief on that occasion, and beseech thee, O glorious Queen of Martyrs! to obtain for me, through the sufferings of Jesus Christ, which were the great cause of thine, a sincere and lively horror of sin, an ardent love of God, a tender and practical devotion towards thee, and a happy death under thy special protection.

III.

O most afflicted Virgin! permit me to commemorate the sorrow which filled thy maternal heart, when thou wert separated from thy divine Son, who remained for three days absent from thee after thy journey to Jerusalem. I most devoutly compassionate thy grief on that occasion, and beseech thee, O glorious Queen of Martyrs! to obtain for me, through the sufferings of Jesus Christ, which were the great cause of thy dolours, a sincere and lively horror of sin, an ardent love of God, a tender and practical devotion towards thee, and a happy death under thy special protection.

IV.

O most holy and afflicted Virgin! permit me to commemorate the sorrow which filled thy maternal heart, when thou didst follow thy dear Son to Mount Calvary, and beheld him sinking under the weight of the cross and of our sins. I most devoutly compassionate thy grief on that occasion, and beseech thee, O glorious Queen of Martyrs! to obtain for me, through the sufferings of Jesus Christ, which were the great cause of all thy dolours, a sincere and lively horror of sin, an ardent love of God, a tender and practical devotion towards thee, and a happy death under thy special protection.

V.

O most holy and afflicted Virgin! permit me to commemorate the sorrow which filled thy maternal heart, when thou didst stand by the cross of Jesus witness all his torments, and see him at length expire for the sins of the world: I devoutly compassionate thy grief on that occasion, O glorious Queen of Martyrs! and beseech thee to obtain for me, through the sufferings of Jesus Christ, which were the great cause of thine, a sincere and lively horror of sin, an ardent ove of God, a tender and practical devotion towards thee, and a happy death under thy special protection.

VI.

O MOST holy and afflicted Virgin! permit me to commemorate the sorrow which filled thy maternal heart, when the adorable body of thy divine Son was taken down from the cross, and laid in thy arms. I most devoutly compassionate thy grief on that occasion, and beseech thee, O glorious Queen of Martyrs! to obtain for me, through the sufferings of Jesus Christ, which were the great cause of thy dolours, a sincere and lively horror of sin, an ardent love of God, a tender and practical devotion towards thee, and a happy death under thy special protection.

VII.

O MOST holy and afflicted Virgin! permit me to commemorate the sorrow which filled thy maternal heart, when the sacred body of Jesus was taken from thy arms, and laid in the sepulchre. I most devoutly compassionate thy grief on that occasion, and beseech thee, O glorious Queen of Martyrs! to obtain for me, through the sufferings of Jesus Christ, which were the great cause of thy dolours, a sincere and lively horror of sin, an ardent love of God, a tender and practical devotion towards thee, and a happy death under thy special protection.

The LITANY *of* LORETTO.

KYRIE eleison.
Christe eleison.
Kyrie eleison.
Christe audi nos.
Christe exaudi nos.

LORD, have mercy upon us. *Christ, have mercy upon us.* Lord, have mercy upon us. *Christ hear us.* Christ graciously hear us.

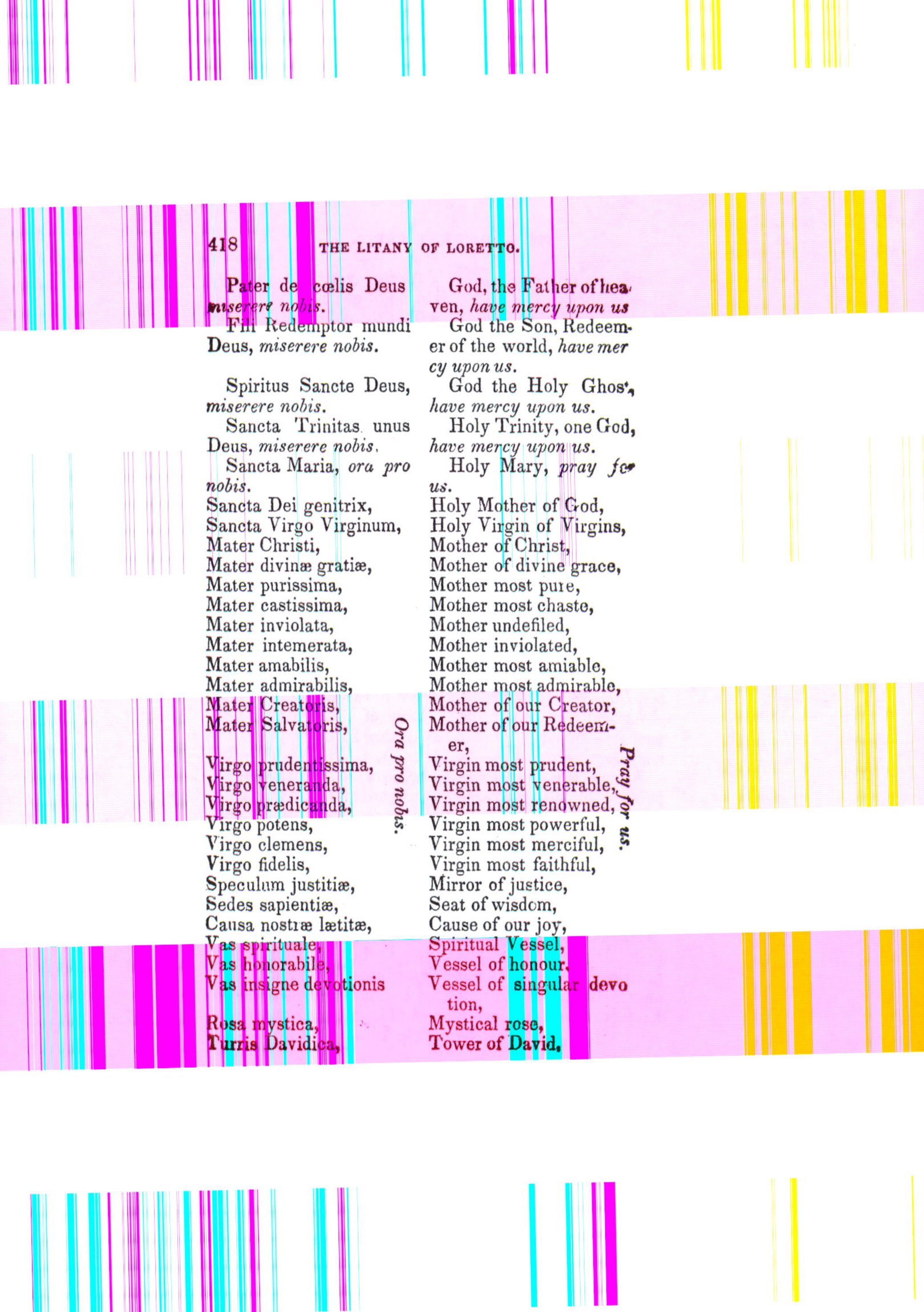

Pater de cœlis Deus *miserere nobis.*	God, the Father of heaven, *have mercy upon us*
Fili Redemptor mundi Deus, *miserere nobis.*	God the Son, Redeemer of the world, *have mercy upon us.*
Spiritus Sancte Deus, *miserere nobis.*	God the Holy Ghost, *have mercy upon us.*
Sancta Trinitas unus Deus, *miserere nobis.*	Holy Trinity, one God, *have mercy upon us.*
Sancta Maria, *ora pro nobis.*	Holy Mary, *pray for us.*
Sancta Dei genitrix,	Holy Mother of God,
Sancta Virgo Virginum,	Holy Virgin of Virgins,
Mater Christi,	Mother of Christ,
Mater divinæ gratiæ,	Mother of divine grace,
Mater purissima,	Mother most pure,
Mater castissima,	Mother most chaste,
Mater inviolata,	Mother undefiled,
Mater intemerata,	Mother inviolated,
Mater amabilis,	Mother most amiable,
Mater admirabilis,	Mother most admirable,
Mater Creatoris,	Mother of our Creator,
Mater Salvatoris,	Mother of our Redeemer,
Virgo prudentissima,	Virgin most prudent,
Virgo veneranda,	Virgin most venerable,
Virgo prædicanda,	Virgin most renowned,
Virgo potens,	Virgin most powerful,
Virgo clemens,	Virgin most merciful,
Virgo fidelis,	Virgin most faithful,
Speculum justitiæ,	Mirror of justice,
Sedes sapientiæ,	Seat of wisdom,
Causa nostræ lætitæ,	Cause of our joy,
Vas spirituale,	Spiritual Vessel,
Vas honorabile,	Vessel of honour,
Vas insigne devotionis	Vessel of singular devotion,
Rosa mystica,	Mystical rose,
Turris Davidica,	Tower of David,

Ora pro nobis. — *Pray for us.*

Turris eburnea,
Domus aurea,
Fœderis arca,
Janua cœli,
Stella matutina,
Salus infirmorum,
Refugium peccatorum,
Consolatrix afflictorum,
Auxilium Christianorum,
Regina angelorum,
Regina patriarcharum,
Regina prophetarum,
Regina apostolorum,
Regina martyrum,
Regina confessorum,
Regina virginum,
Regina sanctorum omnium,

Ora pro nobis.

Agnus Dei, qui tollis peccata mundi, *parce nobis, Domine.*

Agnus Dei, qui tollis peccata mundi, *exaudi nos, Domine.*

Agnus Dei, qui tollis peccata mundi, *miserere nobis.*

V. Ora pro nobis, sancta Dei genitrix.

R. Ut digni efficiamur promissionibus Christi.

Oremus.

Gratiam tuam, quæsumus, Domine, mentibus nostris infunde: ut qui angelo nuntiante, Christi Filii tui incarnationem cognovimus, per passion-

Tower of ivory,
House of gold,
Ark of the covenant,
Gate of heaven,
Morning star,
Health of the weak,
Refuge of sinners,
Comfortress of the afflicted,
Help of Christians,
Queen of angels,
Queen of patriarchs,
Queen of prophets,
Queen of apostles,
Queen of martyrs,
Queen of confessors,
Queen of virgins,
Queen of all saints,

Pray for us

Lamb of God, who takest away the sins of the world *spare us, O Lord.*

Lamb of God, who takest away the sins of the world, *hear us, O Lord.*

Lamb of God, who takest away the sins of the world, *have mercy upon us.*

V. Pray for us, O holy Mother of God. R. That we may be made worthy of the promises of Christ.

Let us pray.

Pour forth, we beseech thee, O Lord, thy divine grace into our hearts, that we to whom the incarnation of Christ thy Son was made known by the mesem ejus et crucem ad resurrectionis gloriam perducamur: per eundem Christum Dominum nostrum. Amen.

sage of an angel, may by his passion and cross be brought to the glory of his resurrection, through the same Christ our Lord. Amen.

The Litany *of the* Saints.

Anth. Remember not, O Lord, our offences, nor those of our parents, and take not revenge of our sins.

Kyrie eleison. Christe eleison. Kyrie eleison. Christe audi nos. Christe exaudi nos.	Lord, have mercy on us. Christ, have mercy on us. Lord, have mercy on us. Christ, hear us. Christ, graciously hear us.
Pater de cœlis Deus, *Miserere nobis.*	God, the Father of heaven, *Have mercy on us.*
Fili Redemptor mundi Deus, *Miserere nobis.*	God the Son, Redeemer of the world, *Have mercy on us.*
Spiritus Sancte Deus, *Miserere nobis.*	God the Holy Ghost, *Have mercy on us.*
Sancta Trinitas, unus Deus, *Miserere nobis.*	Holy Trinity, one God, *Have mercy on us.*
Sancta Maria, *Ora pro nobis.*	Holy Mary, *Pray for us.*
Sancta Dei genitrix, *Ora, &c.*	Holy Mother of God, *Pray for us.*
Sancta Virgo Virginum,	Holy Virgin of Virgins,
Sancte Michael,	St. Michael,
Sancte Gabriel,	St. Gabriel,
Sancte Raphael,	St. Raphael,
Omnes sancti Angeli et Archangeli, *Orate pro nobis.*	All ye holy Angels and Archangels,

Omnes sancti beatorum spirituum Ordines, *Orate, &c.*	All ye holy orders of blessed spirits,
Sancte J. Baptiste,	St. John Baptist,
Sancte Joseph,	St. Joseph,
Omnes sancti Patriarchæ et Prophetæ, *Orate, &c*	All ye holy Patriarchs and Prophets,
Sancte Petre,	St. Peter,
Sancte Paule,	St. Paul,
Sancte Andrea,	St. Andrew
Sancte Jacobe,	St. James,
Sancte Joannes,	St. John,
Sancte Thoma, *Ora pro nobis.*	St. Thomas,
Sancte Jacobe,	St. James,
Sancte Philippe,	St. Philip,
Sancte Bartholomæe,	St. Bartholomew
Sancte Matthæe,	St. Matthew,
Sancte Simon,	St. Simon, *Pray for us*
Sancte Thaddæe,	St. Thaddeus,
Sancte Mathia,	St. Matthias,
Sancte Barnaba,	St. Barnaby,
Sancte Luca,	St. Luke,
Sancte Marce,	St. Mark,
Omnes sancti Apostoli et Evangelistæ, *Orate, &c.*	All ye holy Apostles and Evangelists,
Omnes sancti Discipuli Domini, *Orate, &c.*	All ye holy Disciples of our Lord,
Omnes sancti Innocentes, *Orate, &c.*	All ye holy Innocents,
Sancte Stephane, *Ora, &c.*	St. Stephen,
Sancte Laurenti,	St. Laurence,
Sancte Vincenti,	St. Vincent,
Sancti Fabiane et Sebastiane, *Orate pro nobis.*	SS. Fabian and Sebastian,
Sancti Johannes et Paule, *Orate, &c.*	SS. John and Paul,
Sancti Cosma et Damiane, *Orate, &c.*	SS. Cosmas and Damian.

Sancti Gervasi et Protasi, *Orate, &c.*	SS. Gervase and Protase,
Omnes sancti Martyres, *Orate, &c.*	All ye holy Martyrs,
Sancte Sylvester, *Ora pro nobis.*	St. Sylvester,
Sancte Gregori,	St. Gregory,
Sancte Ambrosi,	St. Ambrose,
Sancte Augustine,	St. Augustine,
Sancte Hieronyme,	St. Jerom,
Sancte Martine,	St. Martin,
Sancte Nicolae,	St. Nicholas,
Omnes sancti Pontifices et Confessores, *Orate, &c.*	All ye holy Bishops and Confessors,
Omnes sancti Doctores, *Orate, &c.*	All ye holy Doctors,
Sancte Antoni, *Ora, &c.*	St. Anthony,
Sancte Benedicte,	St. Bennet, *Pray for us*
Sancte Bernarde,	St Bernard,
Sancte Dominice,	St. Dominic,
Sancte Francisce,	St. Francis,
Omnes sancti Sacerdotes et Levitæ, *Orate, &c.*	All ye holy Priests and Levites,
Omnes sancti Monachi et Eremitæ, *Orate, &c.*	All ye holy Monks and Hermits,
Sancta Maria Magdalena,	St. Mary Magdalen.
Sancta Lucia,	St. Lucy,
Sancta Agnes, *Ora, &c.*	St. Agnes,
Sancta Cæcilia,	St. Cecily,
Sancta Agatha,	St. Agatha,
Sancta Catharina,	St. Catharine,
Sancta Anastasia,	St. Anastasia,
Omnes sanctæ Virgines et Viduæ, *Orate, &c.*	All ye holy Virgins and Widows,
Omnes Sancti et Sanctæ Dei, *Intercedite pro nobis.*	All ye men and women, saints of God, *Make intercession for us.*
Propitius esto, *Parce nobis, Domine.*	Be merciful unto us, *Spare us, O Lord.*

Propitius esto, *Exaudi nos, Domine.*	Be merciful unto us, *Graciously hear us, O Lord.*
Ab omni malo, *Libera nos, Domine.*	From all evil, *O Lord deliver us.*
Ab omni peccato,	From all sin,
Ab ira tua,	From thy wrath,
A subitanea et improvisa morte,	From sudden and unprovided death,
Ab insidiis diaboli,	From the deceits of the devil,
Ab ira, odio, et omni mala voluntate,	From anger, hatred, and all ill-will,
A spiritu fornicationis,	From the spirit of fornication,
A fulgure et tempestate,	From lightning and tempest,
A morte perpetua,	From everlasting death,
Per mysterium sanctæ incarnationis tuæ,	Through the mystery of thy holy incarnation,
Per adventum tuum,	Through thy coming,
Per nativitatem tuam,	Through thy nativity,
Per baptismum et sanctum jejunium tuum,	Through thy baptism and holy fasting,
Per crucem et passionem tuam,	Through thy cross and passion,
Per mortem et sepulturam tuam,	Through thy death and burial,
Per sanctam resurrectionem tuam,	Through thy holy resurrection,
Per admirabilem ascensionem tuam,	Through thy admirable ascension,
Per adventum Spiritus Sancti Paracliti,	Through the coming of the Holy Ghost the Comforter,
In die judicii,	In the day of judgment,
Peccatores, *Te rogamus audi nos.*	We sinners, *Do beseech thee to hear us.*

Libera nos, Domine. — *O Lord, deliver us*

Ut nobis parcas,	That thou spare us,
Ut nobis indulgeas,	That thou pardon us,
Ut ad veram pœnitentiam nos perducere digneris,	That thou vouchsafe to bring us to true penance,
Ut Ecclesiam tuam sanctam regere et conservare digneris,	That thou vouchsafe to govern and preserve thy holy Church,
Ut dominum Apostolicum et omnes Ecclesiasticos Ordines in sancta religione conservare digneris,	That thou vouchsafe to preserve our apostolic prelate, and all ecclesiastical Orders in holy religion,
Ut inimicos sanctæ Ecclesiæ humiliare digneris,	That thou vouchsafe to humble the enemies of the holy Church,
Ut Regibus et Principibus Christianis pacem et veram concordiam donare digneris,	That thou vouchsafe to give peace and true concord to Christian Kings and Princes,
Ut cuncto populo Christiano pacem et unitatem largiri digneris,	That thou vouchsafe to grant peace and unity to all Christian people,
Ut nos metipsos in tuo sancto servitio confortare et conservare digneris,	That thou vouchsafe to confirm and preserve us in thy holy service,
Ut mentes nostras ad cœlestia desideria erigas,	That thou lift up our minds to heavenly desires,
Ut omnibus benefactoribus nostris sempiterna bona retribuas,	That thou render eternal good things to all our benefactors,
Ut animas nostras, fratrum, propinquorum, et benefactorum nos-	That thou deliver our souls, and those of our brethren, kins-

Te rogamus audi nos. — *We beseech thee to hear us.*

trorum, ab æterna damnatione eripias, *Te rogamus audi nos.*	folks, and benefactors, from eternal damnation, *We beseech thee to hear us.*
Ut fructus terræ dare et conservare digneris,	That thou vouchsafe to give and preserve the fruits of the earth,
Ut omnibus fidelibus defunctis requiem æternam donare digneris,	That thou vouchsafe to give eternal rest to all the faithful departed,
Ut nos exaudire digneris,	That thou vouchsafe graciously to hear us,
Fili Dei,	Son of God,
Agnus Dei, qui tollis peccata mundi, *Parce nobis, Domine.*	Lamb of God, who takest away the sins of the world, *Spare us, O Lord.*
Agnus Dei, qui tollis peccata mundi, *Exaudi nos, Domine.*	Lamb of God, who takest away the sins of the world, *Graciously hear us, O Lord,*
Agnus Dei, qui tollis peccata mundi, *Miserere nobis,*	Lamb of God, who takest away the sins of the world, *have mercy on us.*
Christe audi nos. Christe exaudi nos. *Kyrie eleison.* Christe eleison. *Kyrie eleison.* Pater noster, *in secreto.*	Christ, hear us. Christ, graciously hear us. Lord, have mercy on us. Christ, have mercy on us. Lord, have mercy on us. Our Father, *in secret.*
V. Et ne nos inducas in tentationem.	V. And lead us not into temptation.
R. Sed libera nos a malo *Amen.*	R. But deliver us from evil. *Amen.*

PSALM LXIX.

Deus in adjutorium meam intende; *Domine	Incline unto my aid, O God; *O Lord, make

ad adjuvandum me festina.

Confundantur et revereantur, *qui quærunt animam meam.

Avertantur retrorsum, et erubescant, *qui volunt mihi mala.

Avertantur statim erubescentes, *qui dicunt mihi, Euge, Euge.

Exultent et lætentur in te omnes qui quærunt te, *et dicant semper ; magnificetur Dominus, qui diligunt salutare tuum.

Ego vero egenus et pauper sum ; *Deus adjuva me.

Adjutor meus, et liberator meus es tu ; *Domine ne moreris.

Gloria Patri, &c.

V. Salvos fac servos tuos. R. Deus meus sperantes in te. V. Esto nobis Domine turris fortitudinis. R. A facie inimici. V. Nihil proficiat inimicus in nobis. R. Et filius iniquitatis non apponat nocere nobis. V. Domine non secundum peccata nostra facias nobis. R. Neque secundum iniquitates nostras retribuas nobis. V. Oremus pro Pontifice nostro *N*. R. Do-

haste to help me. Let them be confounded and ashamed *that seek my soul. Let them be turned backward, and blush for shame, *that desire evils to me. Let them be presently turned away blushing for shame, *that say to me, 'tis well, 'tis well. Let all that seek thee rejoice, and be glad in thee, *and let such as love thy salvation say always, the Lord be magnified. But I am needy and poor, *O God, help me. Thou art my helper and my deliverer : *O Lord, make no delay.

Glory be to the Father, &c.

V. Save thy servants. R. Trusting in thee, O my God. V. Be unto us, O Lord, a tower of strength. R. From the face of the enemy. V. Let not the enemy prevail against us at all. R. Nor the son of iniquity have any power to hurt us. V. O Lord, deal not with us according to our sins. R. Neither reward us according to our iniquities. V. Let us pray for our chief

minus conservet eum, et vivificet eum, et beatum faciat eum in terra, et non tradat eum in animam inimicorum ejus. V. Oremus pro benefactoribus nostris. R. Retribuere dignare Domine omnibus, nobis bona facientibus, propter nomen tuum, vitam æternam. V. Oremus pro fidelibus defunctis. R. Requiem æternam dona eis Domine, et lux perpetua luceat eis. V. Requiescant in pace. R. Amen. V. Pro fratribus nostris absentibus. R. Salvos fac servos tuos, Deus meus sperantes in te. V. Mitte eis Domine auxilium de sancto. R. Et de Sion tuere eos. V. Domine exaudi orationem meam. R. Et clamor meus ad te veniat.

Bishop *N.* R. Our Lord preserve him, and give him life, and make him blessed upon earth, and deliver him not to the will of his enemies. V. Let us pray for our benefactors. R. Vouchsafe, O Lord, for thy name's sake, to reward with eternal life all them who have done us good. V. Let us pray for the faithful departed. R. Eternal rest give to them, O Lord; and let perpetual light shine upon them. V. May they rest in peace. R. Amen. V. For our absent brethren. R. O my God, save thy servants trusting in thee. V. Send them help, O Lord, from thy holy place. R. And from Sion protect them. V. O Lord, hear my prayer. R. And let my cry come unto thee.

Let us pray.

O God, whose property is always to have mercy, and to spare, receive our petition: that we, and all thy servants who are bound by the chain of sins, may by the compassion of thy goodness mercifully be absolved.

Hear, we beseech thee, O Lord, the prayers of the suppliant, and pardon the sins of them that confess to thee; that in thy bounty thou mayest both give us pardon and peace.

Out of thy clemency, O Lord, show thy unspeakable mercy to us, that so thou mayest both acquit us of our sins, and deliver us from the punishments we deserve for them.

O God, who by sin art offended, and by penance pacified, mercifully regard the prayers of thy people making supplication to thee, and turn away the scourges of thy anger, which we deserve for our sins.

O Almighty and Eternal God, have mercy on thy servant *N.*, our chief Bishop, and direct him according to thy clemency, into the way of everlasting salvation; that by thy grace he may desire those things that are agreeable to thee, and perform them with all his strength.

O God, from whom are all holy desires, right counsels, and just works, give to thy servants that peace which the world cannot give; that both our hearts may be disposed to keep thy commandments, and the fear of enemies being removed, the times by thy protection may be peaceable.

Inflame, O Lord, our reins and hearts with the fire of thy holy Spirit, that we may serve thee with a chaste body, and please thee with a clean heart.

O God, the Creator and Redeemer of all the faithful, give to the souls of thy servants departed the remission of all their sins; that through pious supplications they may obtain the pardon which they have always desired

Prevent, we beseech thee, O Lord, our actions by thy holy inspirations, and carry them on by thy gracious assistance; that every prayer and work of ours may begin always from thee, and by thee be happily ended.

O Almighty and Eternal God, who hast dominion over the living and the dead, and art merciful to all whom thou foreknowest shall be thine by faith and good works; we humbly beseech thee that they, for whom we have determined to offer up our prayers, whether this world still detains them in the flesh, or the world to come has already received them out of their bodies, may by the clemency of thy goodness, all thy saints interceding for them, obtain pardon and full remission of all their sins, through our Lord Jesus Christ thy Son, who liveth and reigneth, &c. *Amen.*

V. O Lord, hear my prayer.

R. And let my cry come unto thee.

V. May the Almighty and most merciful Lord graciously hear us. R. *Amen.*

V. And may the souls of the faithful departed, through the mercy of God, rest in peace. R. *Amen*

THE COMMON

VESPERS ON SUNDAYS.

Our Father *and* Hail Mary *in silence.*

V. Deus in adjutorium meum intende.

R. Domine ad adjuvandum me festina.

V. Gloria Patri, et Filio et Spiritui Sancto. Sicut erat in principio, et nunce, et semper, et in sæcula sæculorum. *Amen. Alleluia.*

V. Incline unto my aid, O God.

R. O Lord, make haste to help me.

V. Glory be to the Father, and to the Son, and to the Holy Ghost. As it was in the beginning, is now, and ever shall be, world without end *Amen. Alleluia.*

From Saturday *before* Septuagesima Sunday, *till* Saturday *in* Holy Week, *instead of* Alleluia *is said:*

Laus tibi Domine, Rex æternæ gloriæ.

Ant. Dixit Dominus.

Praise be to thee, O Lord, King of eterna glory.

Anth. The Lord said

In Paschal Time the only Anthem to all the Psalms is Alleluia.

PSALM CIX.

1. DIXIT Dominus Domino meo : *Sede à dextris meis.

2. Donec ponam inimicos tuos : *scabellum pedum tuorum.

3. Virgam virtutis tuæ emittet Dominus ex Sion : *dominare in medio inimicorum tuorum.

4. Tecum principium in die virtutis tuæ, in splendoribus sanctorum : *ex utero ante luciferum genui te.

5. Juravit Dominus, et non pœnitebit eum : *tu es Sacerdos in æternum secundum ordinem Melchisedech.

6. Dominus à dextris tuis, *confregit in die iræ suæ reges.

7. Judicabit in nationibus, implebit ruinas ; *conquassabit capita in terra multorum.

8. De torrente in via bibet : *propterea exaltabit caput.

Gloria Patri, &c.

1. THE Lord said to my Lord ; *Sit thou at my right hand. 2. *Until I make thine enemies : *the footstool of thy feet. 3 The Lord shall send forth the sceptre of thy might from *Sion :* *rule thou in the midst of thine enemies. 4. Thine shall be the sovereignty, in the day of thy might, in the brightness of the saints : *from the womb, before the day-star, I begot thee. 5. The Lord hath sworn, and he will not repent : *thou art a priest for ever according to the order of *Melchisedech.* 6. The Lord on thy right hand, *hath crushed kings in the day of his wrath. 7. He shall judge the nations, he shall accomplish *their* ruin : *he shall crush heads in the land of many. 8. He shall drink of the brook in the way : *therefore shall he raise up his head.

Glory, &c.

Gloria Patri, &c. *is said at the end of every Psalm*

Ant. Dixit Dominus Domino meo, Sede à dextris meis.
Ant Fidelia

Anth. The Lord said to my Lord, Sit thou at my right hand
Anth True.

PSALM CX.

1. Confitebor tibi Domine in toto corde meo: *in consilio justorum, et congregatione.

2 Magna opera Domini: * exquisita in omnes voluntates ejus.

3. Confessio et magnificentia opus ejus; *et justitia ejus manet in sæculum sæculi.

4. Memoriam fecit mirabilium suorum, misericors et miserator Dominus: *escam dedit timentibus se.

5. Memor erit in sæculum testamenti sui: *virtutem operum suorum annuntiabit populo suo.

6. Ut det illis hæreditatem Gentium: *opera manuum ejus, veritas et judicium.

7. Fidelia omnia mandata ejus, confirmata in sæculum sæculi: *facta in veritate et æquitate.

8. Redemptionem misit populo suo: *mandavit in æternum testamentum suum.

9. Sanctum et terribile nomen ejus: *initium sapientiæ timor Domini.

10. Intellectus bonus omnibus facientibus eum:

1. I will praise thee, O Lord, with my whole heart: *in the assembly of the righteous, and in the congregation. 2. Great are the works of the Lord: *exquisite *and agreeable* to all his designs. 3. His work *is his* praise and glory; *and his justice remaineth for ever. 4. The merciful and gracious Lord hath appointed a memorial of his wonderful works: *he hath given food to them that fear him. 5. He will be for ever mindful of his covenant: *the greatness of his works will he publish to his people. 6. To give them the inheritance of the *Gentiles:* *the works of his hands are truth and justice. 7. True *and lasting* are all his ordinances, confirmed for ever and ever: *made in truth and justice. 8. He hath sent redemption to his people: *he hath appointed his covenant for ever. 9. Holy and awful is his name: *the fear of the Lord is the beginning of wisdom. 10. All understand it right, who prac-

*laudatio ejus manet in sæculum sæculi.

tise it: *his praise endureth for ever and ever.

Ant. Fidelia omnia mandata ejus; confirmata in sæculum sæculi.

Ant. In mandatis.

Anth. True are all his ordinances; confirmed for ever and ever.

Anth. In his commandments.

PSALM CXI.

1. Beatus vir qui timet Dominum: *in mandatis ejus volet nimis.

2. Potens in terra erit semen ejus: *generatio rectorum benedicetur.

3. Gloria et divitiæ in domo ejus: *et justitia ejus manet in sæculum sæculi.

4. Exortum est in tenebris, lumen rectis: *misericors, et miserator, et justus.

5. Jucundus homo qui miseretur et commodat, disponet sermones suos in judicio: *quia in æternum non commovebitur.

6. In memoria æterna erit justus: *ab auditione mala non timebit.

7. Paratum cor ejus sperare in Domino, confirmatum est cor ejus: *non commovebitur donec despiciat inimicos suos.

8. Dispersit, dedit pauperibus; justitia ejus manet in sæculum sæculi:

1. Blessed is the man that feareth the Lord: *in his commandments he shall take great delight.
2. Mighty on earth shall be his seed: *the generation of the righteous shall be blessed.
3. Glory and wealth shall be in his house: *and his righteousness endureth for ever and ever.
4. He is risen in darkness, a light to the upright: *he is merciful and just, compassionate.
5. Acceptable is the man that showeth mercy and lendeth, he shall order his words with judgment; *and he shall never give way.
6. The righteous man shall be in eternal remembrance: *he shall not fear an evil report.
7. His heart is ready to hope in the Lord: his heart is strengthened: *he shall not yield till he despise his enemies.
8. He hath

*cornu ejus exaltabitur in gloria.

9. Peccator videbit, et irascetur, dentibus suis fremet et tabescet: *desiderium peccatorum peribit.

distributed and given to the poor; his righteousness remaineth for ever: *his power shall be exalted in glory. 9. The sinner shall see it, and be enraged; he shall gnash his teeth and pine away: *the desire of sinners shall perish.

Ant. In mandatis ejus cupit nimis.

Anth. In his commandments he shall take great delight.

Ant. Sit nomen Domini.

Anth. Let the name of the Lord.

PSALM CXII.

1. LAUDATE pueri Dominum: *laudate nomen Domini.

2. Sit nomen Domini benedictum: *ex hoc nunc, et usque in sæculum.

3. A solis ortu usque ad occasum: *laudabile nomen Domini.

4. Excelsus super omnes gentes Dominus: *et super cœlos gloria ejus.

5. Quis sicut Dominus Deus noster, qui in altis habitat: *et humilia respicit in cœlo et in terra?

6. Suscitans a terra inopem; *et de stercore erigens pauperem?

7. Ut collocet eum cum principibus: *cum principibus populi sui.

1. PRAISE the Lord, ye servants *of the Lord:* *praise ye the name of the Lord. 2. Let the name of the Lord be blessed: *now and for evermore 3. From the rising of the sun to the setting thereof: *worthy of praise is the name of the Lord. 4. High is the Lord above all the nations: *and above the heavens is his glory. 5. Who is like unto the Lord our God, who dwelleth on high: *and beholdeth what is below in heaven, and on earth? 6. Who from the earth raiseth up the needy one: *and from the dunghill lifteth up the poor

8. Qui habitare facit sterilem in domo: *matrem filiorum lætantem.

one: 7. To place him with the princes: *with the princes of his people 8. Who maketh the barren woman to dwell in *her* house: *the joyful mother of *many* children.

Ant. Sit nomen Domini benedictum in sæcula.
Ant. Nos qui vivimus.

Anth. Let the name of the Lord be blessed for evermore
Anth. We who are alive.

PSALM CXIII.

1. In exitu Israel de Ægypto: *domus Jacob de populo barbaro:
2. Facta est Judæa sanctificatio ejus: *Israel potestas ejus.
3. Mare vidit et fugit: *Jordanis conversus est retrorsum.
4. Montes exultaverunt ut arietes: *et colles sicut agni ovium.
5. Quid est tibi mare, quod fugisti? *et ut Jordanis, quia conversus es retrorsum?
6. Montes exultastis sicut arietes? *et colles sicut agni ovium?
7. A facie Domini mota est terra: *a facie Dei Jacobi.
8. Qui convertit petram in stagna aquarum: *et rupem in fontes aquarum.
9. Non nobis Domine,

1. When *Israel* went out of *Egypt:* *the house of *Jacob* from a barbarous people: 2. *Judæa* became his sanctuary: **Israel* his empire. 3. The sea saw *them*, and fled · the *Jordan* ran back *to its fountain-head.* 4. The mountains skipped like rams, *and the hills like the lambs of ewes. 5. What ailed thee, O sea, that thou didst flee? *and thou, O *Jordan*, that thou didst run back *to thy fountain-head?* 6. Ye mountains, that ye skipped like rams? *and ye hills like the lambs of ewes? 7. At the presence of the Lord the earth trembled: *at the presence of the God of *Jacob.* 8. Who changed the rock into pools of water: *and the stony hill

non nobis: *sed nomini **tuo** da gloriam.

10. Super misericordia tua, et veritate tua: *nequando dicant Gentes, ubi est Deus eorum?

11. Deus autem noster in cœlo: *omnia quæcumque voluit, fecit.

12. Simulacra Gentium argentum et aurum: *opera manuum hominum.

13. Os habent, et non loquentur: *oculos habent, et non videbunt.

14. Aures habent, et non audient: *nares habent, et non odorabunt.

15. Manus habent, et non palpabunt: pedes habent, et non ambulabunt: *non clamabunt in gutture suo.

16. Similes illis fiant qui faciunt ea: *et omnes qui confidunt in eis.

17. Domus Israel speravit in Domino: *adjutor eorum, et protector eorum est.

18. Domus Aaron speravit in Domino: *adjutor eorum, et protector eorum est.

19. Qui timent Dominum speraverunt in Domino: *adjutor eorum, et protector eorum est.

20. Dominus memor

into fountains of water.
9. Not to us, O Lord, not
to us; *but unto thy own
name give *all* the glory.
10. For thy mercy's sake,
and for thy sure promise:
*never let the *Gentiles*
say, Where now is their
God? 11. For our God is
in heaven: *he hath done
all things whatsoever he
pleased. 12. The *idols*
of the *Gentiles* are *but*
silver and gold: *the
works of the hands of
men. 13. They have
mouths, but they shall not
speak: *they have eyes,
but they shall not see.
14. They have ears, but
they shall not hear: *they
have nostrils, but they
shall not smell. 15. They
have hands, but they shall
not feel; they have feet,
but they shall not walk:
*neither shall they cry
out with their throat. 16.
Let those that make them,
become like unto them,
*and all that put their
trust in them. 17. The
house of *Israel* hath hoped
in the Lord; *he is their
help, and their protector.
18. The house of *Aaron*
hath hoped in the Lord:
*he is their help and their
protector. 19. They who

fuit nostri: *et benedixit nobis.

21. Benedixit domui Israel: *benedixit domui Aaron.

22. Benedixit omnibus qui timent Dominum: *pusillis cum majoribus.

23. Adjiciat Dominus super vos: *super vos et super filios vestros.

24. Benedicti vos a Domino: *qui fecit cœlum et terram.

25. Cœlum cœli Domino: *terram autem dedit filiis hominum.

26. Non mortui laudabunt te Domine; *neque omnes qui descendunt in infernum.

27. Sed nos qui vivimus, benedicimus Domino: *ex hoc nunc et usque in sæculum.

fear the Lord, have hoped in the Lord: *he is their help, and their protector. 20. The Lord hath been mindful of us: *and hath blessed us. 21. He hath blessed the house of *Israel:* *he hath blessed the house of *Aaron.* 22. He hath blessed all who fear the Lord: *the little with the great. 23. May the Lord still heap *his blessings* on you: *on you and on your children. 24. Be ye blessed by the Lord: *who made both heaven and earth. 25. The heaven of heavens is the Lord's *abode:* *but the earth he has given to the sons of men. 26. The dead shall not praise thee, O Lord: *nor any of those who are gone down to hell. 27. But we, who are alive, bless the Lord: *now, and for evermore.

Ant Nos qui vivimus benedicimus Domino.

Ant. Tempore Paschali, *Alleluia, Alleluia, Alleluia.*

Anth. We who are alive, bless the Lord.

Anth. In *Paschal time,* Alleluia, Alleluia, Alleluia.

Instead of the foregoing, the following is occasionally sung.

PSALM CXVI.

1. LAUDATE Dominum omnes gentes: *laudate eum omnes populi.

2. Quoniam confirmata est super nos misericor-

1. PRAISE the Lord all ye nations: *praise him all people.

2. Because his mercy is confirmed upon us

dia ejus: *et veritas Domini manet in æternum.	*and the truth of the Lord remaineth for ever.

The little chapter. 2 Cor. 1.

BENEDICTUS Deus, et Pater Domini nostri Jesu Christi, Pater misericordiarum, et Deus totius consolationis, qui consolatur nos in omni tribulatione nostra.	BLESSED be the God and Father of our Lord Jesus Christ, the Father of mercies, and God of all consolation, who comforteth us in all our tribulations.
R. Deo gratias	R. Thanks be to God.

The HYMN, *Lucis Creator.*

LUCIS Creator optime,	CREATOR of the radiant light,
Lucem dierum proferens,	Dividing day from sable night:
Primordiis lucis novæ,	Who with the light's bright origin,
Mundi parens originem.	The world's creation didst begin.
Qui mane junctum vesperi,	Who of the morn and ev'ning ray
Diem vocari præcipis.	Mad'st measur'd light and call'd it day;
Illabitur etrum chaos;	Black night begins to cloud the spheres,
Audi preces cum fletibus.	Vouchsafe to hear our sighs and tears.
Ne mens gravata crimine,	Whilst with our crimes we burden'd are,
Vitæ sit exul munere;	And fall'n a prey to Satan's snare;
Dum nil perenne cogitat	Whilst fading pleasures us deceive,
Seseque culpis illigat.	Let not our souls our bodies leave.

Cœleste ulset ostium:	Let us at heaven foi mercy knock,
Vitale tollat præmium;	Let us the gates of life unlock:
Vitemus omne noxium;	Whatever's evil let us fly,
Purgemus omne pessimum.	And punish past iniquity.
Præsta, Pater piissime;	Most clement Father, lend thine ear,
Patrique compar Unice;	Co-equal Son, receive our prayer:
Cum Spiritu Paraclito,	O holy Spirit, hear our cry.
Regnans per omne sæculum. *Amen.*	Who reign all three eternally. *Amen.*
V. Diragatur Domine, oratio mea.	*V.* Let my prayer ascend, O Lord,
R. Sicut incensum in conspectu tuo.	*R.* Like incense in thy sight.

The HYMN, *Iste Confessor.*

ISTE confessor Domini, colentes	THIS Christ's Confessor, whose great fame
Quem pie laudant populi per orbem:*	The faithful through the world proclaim,*
Hac die lætus, meruit beatas	With glory did this day ascend
Scandere sedes.	To joys that never end.

*If it be not the Day of his Decease, say from**

Hac die lætus meruit supremos	Deserves that we should on this day
Laudis honores	The highest praises pay.
Qui pius, prudens, humilis, pudicus,	A pious prudence, actions mild,
Sobriam duxit sine labe vitam.	Chaste manners, not with crimes defil'd.

Donec humanos animavit auræ Spiritus artus.	Adorn'd his sober life, till death Deprived him of his breath.
Cujus ob præstans meritum frequenter, Ægra quæ passim jacuere membra, Viribus morbi domitis saluti Restituuntur.	His holy deeds did God so please, That ulcers, pains, and each disease, Obey'd him, and by pow'r divine Their place to health resign.
Noster hinc illi chorus obsequentem Concinit laudem celebresque palmas; Ut piis ejus precibus juvemur Omne per ævum.	For this we pious trophies raise, And sing this solemn hymn of praise; That by his prayers th' Amighty may His grace to us convey.
Sit salus illi, decus, atque virtus, Qui super cœli solio coruscans, Totius mundi seriem gubernat Trinus et unus. *Amen.*	To him be glory, power, and fame, Who rules the world's well-order'd frame: And fills the bright celestial throne, Mysterious three and one. *Amen.*
V. Justum deduxit Dominus per vias rectas.	*V.* The Lord hath led the just man through right ways.
R. Et ostendit illi regnum Dei.	*R.* And shown him the kingdom of God.
Ant. Amavit eum Dominus, et ornavit eum: stolam gloriæ induit eum et ad portas paradisi coronavit eum.	*Anth.* The Lord loved him, and adorned him; he clothed him with a robe of glory, and crowned him at the gates of paradise.

The Song of the B. V. Mary, *Luke* i. 46.

1. Magnificat *anima mea Dominum:

2. Et exultavit spiritus meus: *in Deo salutari meo.

3. Quia respexit humilitatem ancillæ suæ: *ecce enim ex hoc beatam me dicent omnes generationes.

4. Quia fecit mihi magna qui potens est: *et sanctum nomen ejus.

5. Et misericordia ejus a progenie in progenies, *timentibus eum.

6. Fecit potentiam in brachio suo: *dispersit superbos mente cordis sui.

7. Deposuit potentes de sede: *et exaltavit humiles.

8. Esurientes implevit bonis: *et divites dimisit inanes.

9. Suscepit Israel puerum suum: *recordatus misericordiæ suæ.

10. Sicut locutus est ad patres nostros: *Abraham, et semini ejus in sæcula.

Gloria Patri, &c.

1. My soul doth *magnify the Lord: 2. And my spirit hath rejoiced *in God my Saviour. 3. For he hath looked down on his lowly handmaid: *for behold from henceforth all generations shall call me blessed. 4. For he who is mighty hath done great things to me: *and holy is his name. 5. And his mercy from generation to generation, *is *shown* to those who fear him. 6. He hath exerted his strength by his *own* arm: *he hath disappointed the proud ones of the designs of their hearts. 7. He hath cast down the mighty ones from the throne: *and raised up the lowly ones. 8. He hath filled the hungry with good things: *but the rich he hath sent empty away. 9. He hath upholden his servant *Israel:* *being mindful of his mercy. 10. As he promised to our Fathers: *to *Abraham* and his seed for ever.

Glory, &c.

From Christmas-day to the Octave-day of the Epiphany.

Adeste Fideles.

THE NATIVITY OF OUR LORD.

Anthem.

Adeste, fideles!
Læti triumphantes,
Venite, venite in Bethlehem,
Natum videte
Regem angelorum.
Venite, adoremus;
Venite, adoremus Dominum.

Deum de Deo,
Lumen de lumine,
Gestant puellæ viscera,
Deum verum
Genitum non factum.
Venite, &c.

Cantet nunc Io!
Chorus angelorum,
Cantet nunc aula cœlestium,
Gloria
In excelsis Deo;
Venite, &c.

Ergo, qui natus
Die hodierna,
Jesu tibi sit gloria.
Patris æterni
Verbum caro factum,
Venite, &c.

With hearts truly grateful
Come, all ye faithful,
To Jesus, to Jesus in Bethlehem,
See Christ your Saviour,
Heaven's greatest favour.
Let's hasten to adore him,
Let's hasten to adore him,
Let's hasten to adore him,
our God and King.

God to God equal,
Light of light eternal;
Carried in virgin's ever spotless womb;
He all preceded,
Begotten, not created.
Let's hasten, &c.

Angels now praise him,
Loud their voices raising.
The heav'nly mansions with joy now ring,
To him who's most holy,
Be honour, praise, and glory.
Let's hasten, &c.

To Jesus, this day born,
Grateful homage return;
'Tis he, who all heav'nly gifts does bring
Word increated,
To our flesh united.
Let's hasten, &c.

We joyfully singing,
Grateful tributes bringing,
Praise him, and bless him in heav'nly hymns.
Angels implore him,
Seraphs fall before him.
Then e'er let us adore him—
our God and King.

Anthem from Trinity-Eve till Advent.

SALVE REGINA.

SALVE Regina, mater misericordiæ!—vita, dulcedo, et spes nostra salve!	HAIL, happy Queen, thou mercy's parent, hail! Life, hope, and comfort of this earthly vale.
Ad te clamamus, exules filii Hevæ.	To thee we *Eva's* wretched children cry,
Ad te suspiramus gementes et flentes in hac lacrymarum valle.	In sighs and tears to thee we suppliants fly.
Eja ergo advocata nostra illos tuos misericordes oculos ad nos converte.	Rise, glorious advocate, exert thy love, And let our vows those eyes of pity move.
Et Jesum benedictum fructum ventris tui, nobis post hoc exilium ostende,	O sweet! O pious maid! for us obtain, For us, who long have in our exile lain,
O clemens, O pia, O dulcis Virgo Maria.	To see thy infant Jesus and with him to reign.
V. Ora pro nobis sancta Dei genitrix.	*V.* Pray for us, O holy Mother of God.
R. Ut digni efficiamur promissionibus Christi.	*R.* That we may be made worthy of the promises of Christ.

From Advent to the Purification.

ALMA REDEMPTORIS.

ALMA Redemptoris Mater, quæ pervia cœli porta manes,	MOTHER of Jesus, heaven's open gate,
Et stella maris, succurre cadenti:	Star of the Sea, support the falling state
Surgere qui curat populo; tu quæ genuisti,	Of mortals: thou, whose womb thy Maker bore,
Natura mirante tuum sanctum genitorem:	And yet, strange thing! a Virgin, as before;

Virgo priùs ac posteriùs, Gabrielis ab ore.
Who didst from *Gabriel's* Hail! the news receive.

Sumens illud Ave, peccatorum miserere.
Repenting sinners by thy prayers relieve:

V. Angelus Domini nuntiavit Mariæ.
V. The angel of the Lord declared to *Mary.*

R. Et concepit de Spiritu Sancto.
R. And she conceived of the Holy Ghost.

After the Purification.

AVE REGINA.

AVE regina cœlorum,
HAIL *Mary!* Queen of heavenly spheres,

Ave domina angelorum,
Hail, whom the angelic host reveres!

Salve radix, salve porta,
Hail, fruitful root! Hail, sacred gate,

Ex qua mundo lux est orta;
Whence the world's light derives its date;

Gaude virgo gloriosa,
O glorious Maid! with beauty blest!

Super omnes speciosa:
May joys eternal fill thy breast!

Vale, O valde decora,
Thus crown'd with beauty and with joy,

Et pro nobis Christum exora.
Thy prayers for us, with Christ employ.

V. Dignare me, laudare te Virgo sacrata.
V. Vouchsafe, O sacred Virgin, to accept my praises.

R. Da mihi virtutem contra hostes tuos.
R. Give me strength against thy enemies.

From Holy Saturday till Trinity-Eve.

REGINA CŒLI.

REGINA cœli lætare, Alleluia.
TRIUMPH, O Queen of heav'n, to see, Allel.

Quia quem meruisti portare, Alleluia.	The sacred infant, born of thee, Alleluia.
Resurrexit sicut dixit, Alleluia.	Return in glory from the tomb, Alleluia.
Ora pro nobis Deum, Alleluia.	And with thy tears prevent our doom, Alleluia.
V Gaude et lætare Virgo Maria, Alleluia.	*V*. Rejoice and be glad, O Virgin *Mary*, Alleluia.
R. Quia surrexit Dominus vere, Alleluia.	*R*. For the Lord is truly risen. Alleluia.

Hymns for Benediction.

Pange lingua.

Pange lingua gloriosi.	Sing, O my tongue, adore and praise
Corporis mysterium,	The depth of God's mysterious ways:
Sanguinisque pretiosi	How Christ, the world's great King, bestow'd
Quem in mundi pretium,	His flesh conceal'd in human food,
Fructus ventris generosi,	And left mankind the blood that paid
Rex effudit gentium.	The ransom for the souls he made.
Nobis datus, nobis natus,	Given from above, and born for man,
Ex intacta virgine;	From virgin chaste his life began:
Et in mundo conversatus	He liv'd on earth, and preach'd to sow
Sparso verbi semine,	The seeds of heav'nly love below;
Sui moras incolatus	Then seal'd his mission from above
Miro clausit ordine!	With strange effects of power and love!
In supremæ nocte cœnæ,	'Twas on that ev'ning when the last

Recumbens cum fratribus,	And most mysterious supper past;
Observata lege plene	When Christ with his disciples sat,
Cibis in legalibus,	To close the law with legal meat;
Cibum turbæ duodenæ	Then to the twelve himself bestow'd
Se dat suis manibus.	With his own hands to be their food.
Verbum caro, panem verum,	The Word made flesh for love of man,
Verbo carnem efficit:	His word turns bread to flesh again,
Fitque sanguis Christi merum,	And wine to blood, unseen by sense,
Et si sensus deficit,	By virtue of omnipotence:
Ad firmandum cor sincerum	And here the faithful rest secure,
Sola fides sufficit.	Whilst God can vouch, and faith insure.
Tantum ergo sacramentum	To this mysterious table now,
Veneremur cernui:	Our knees, our hearts, and sense we bow:
Et antiquum documentum,	Let ancient rites resign their place
Novo cedat ritui:	To nobler elements of grace:
Præstet fides supplementum,	And faith for all defects supply,
Sensuum defectui.	Whilst sense is lost in mystery.
Genitori Genitoque	To God the Father born of none,
Laus et jubilatio:	To Christ his co-eternal Son,
Salus, honor, virtus quoque:	And Holy Ghost, whose equal rays

Sit et benedictio:	From both proceed, be equal praise:
Procedenti ab utroque,	One honour, jubilee, and fame,
Compar sit laudatio. *Amen.*	For ever bless his glorious name. *Amen.*
V. Panem de cœlo præstitisti eis. *Alleluia.*	*V.* Thou hast given them bread from heaven. *Allel.*
R. Omne delectamentum in se habentem. *Allel.*	*R.* Abounding with whatever is delicious. *Allel.*

The Prayer.

Deus, qui nobis sub sacramento mirabili passionis tuæ memoriam reliquisti; tribue, quæsumus, ita nos corporis et sanguinis tui sacra mysteria venerari, ut redemptionis tuæ fructum nobis jugiter sentiamus. Qui vivis.	O God, who in this wonderful sacrament hast left us a memorial of thy passion: grant us so to reverence the sacred mysteries of thy sacred body and blood, that our souls may be always sensible of the fruit of thy redemption. Who livest.

O Salutaris.

O Salutaris Hostia!	O Saving Host, that Heaven's gate
Quæ Cœli pandis ostium:	Laid'st open at so dear a rate:
Bella premunt hostilia:	Intestine wars invade our breast;
Da robur, fer auxilium.	Be thou our strength, support, and rest.
Uni trinoque Domino,	To God the Father and the Son,

Sit sempiterna gloria;	And Holy Spirit, Three in One,
Qui vitam sine termino,	Be endless praise: may HE above,
Nobis donet in patria.	With life eternal crown our love.

PANIS ANGELICUS.

PANIS angelicus fit panis hominum:	THE bread of angels, bread of man is made;
Dat panis cælicus figuris terminum:	The truth and substance now exclude the shade.
O res mirabilis! manducat Dominum	O strange effects of love! the sov'reign God
Pauper, servus et humilis.	Becomes the poor's, the slave's, the sinner's food.
Te, trina Deitas unaque, poscimus,	O Three in One, we humbly thee implore,
Sic nos tu visita, sicut te colimus:	To manifest thyself as we adore:
Per tuas semitas duc nos quo tendimus,	By thy own ways instruct us how to move,
Ad lucem quam inhabitas. Amen.	To find th' abyss of light, in which thou dwell'st above.
V. Posuit fines tuos pacem. Alleluia.	*V.* He hath placed peace in the borders. Alleluia.
R. Et adipe frumenti satiat te. Alleluia.	*R.* And filled thee with the fat of corn. Alleluia.

ECCE PANIS.

ECCE panis angelorum,	Lo! then, O man! involv'd in rapture see

Factus cibus viatorum :	The bread of angels thus made meat for thee :
Vere panis filiorum,	Meat to refresh the pilgrim in his way
Non mittendus canibus.	To the blest regions of eternal day :
	A sweet viatic and divine repast,
	True children's bread, to dogs not to be cast.
In figuris præsignatur,	Wrapt up in types the Lamb long figured lay,
Cum Isaac immolatur :	Till circling years the shadows drove away.
Agnus Paschæ deputatur,	In *Isaac* 'twas in lively figure slain,
Datur manna patribus.	And in the Paschal Lamb it bled again ;
	The ancient fathers too, in manna, eat
	In figure, this divine life-giving meat.
Bone Pastor, panis vere	Good Pastor ! thou true bread ! sweet Jesus, show
Jesu nostri miserere :	Thy tend'rest mercy on thy care below :
Tu nos pasce, nos tuere :	Feed and defend us here, that we may see
Tu nos bona fac videre	Good things with those who live and reign with thee
In terra viventium.	In heav'n's blest land, for ever there to spend,
	In pure celestial joys, joys ne'er to end.
Tu, qui cuncta scis et vales,	O thou, all-good all-pow'rful, and all-wise,

Qui nos pascis hic mortales;	Who feasts us here with thy own sacrifice,
Tuos ibi commensales,	Make us sit down with thee among the blest,
Cohæredes et sodales,	At thy own table in eternal rest;
Fac sanctorum civium. Amen.	Where we, with them, thy glory may adore, Companions and co-heirs for evermore. Amen.
V. Educas panem de terra. Alleluia.	*V.* May thou bring forth bread from earth. Allel.
R. Et vinum lætificat cor hominis. Alleluia.	*R.* And may wine give joy to the heart of man. Alleluia.

Ave verum.

Ave verum corpus, natum	Hail, Jesus! humbly we salute,
De Maria Virgine,	Of *Mary's* spotless womb the fruit;
Vere passum immolatum	Victim that on the cross was slain
In cruce pro homine.	For men, 'mid agony and pain.
Cujus latus perforatum	There where a lance hath pierc'd its side,
Unda fluxit cum sanguine:	Out flow'd of water, blood, a tide.
Esto nobis prægustatum	Give us, in death's last struggling pain,
In mortis examine.	The virtues of thy death to gain.
O dulcis, O pie,	O pious Jesus! Saviour meek!
O Jesu fili Mariæ	Have mercy on us mortals weak,
Miserere nostri. Amen.	O give us peace, eternal rest,

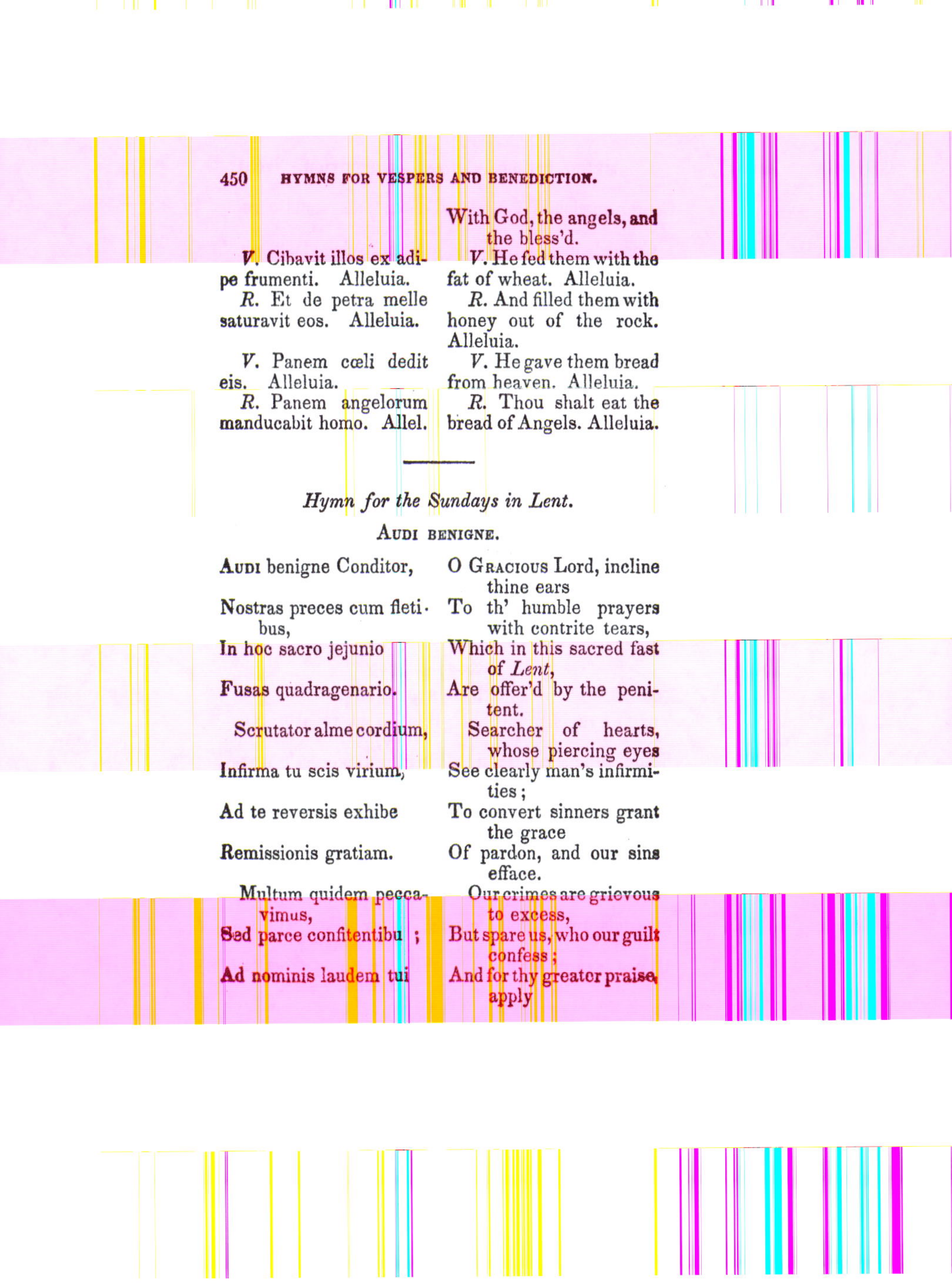

	With God, the angels, and the bless'd.
V. Cibavit illos ex adipe frumenti. Alleluia.	*V.* He fed them with the fat of wheat. Alleluia.
R. Et de petra melle saturavit eos. Alleluia.	*R.* And filled them with honey out of the rock. Alleluia.
V. Panem cœli dedit eis. Alleluia.	*V.* He gave them bread from heaven. Alleluia.
R. Panem angelorum manducabit homo. Allel.	*R.* Thou shalt eat the bread of Angels. Alleluia.

Hymn for the Sundays in Lent.

AUDI BENIGNE.

AUDI benigne Conditor,	O GRACIOUS Lord, incline thine ears
Nostras preces cum fletibus,	To th' humble prayers with contrite tears,
In hoc sacro jejunio	Which in this sacred fast of *Lent*,
Fusas quadragenario.	Are offer'd by the penitent.
Scrutator alme cordium,	Searcher of hearts, whose piercing eyes
Infirma tu scis virium,	See clearly man's infirmities;
Ad te reversis exhibe	To convert sinners grant the grace
Remissionis gratiam.	Of pardon, and our sins efface.
Multum quidem peccavimus,	Our crimes are grievous to excess,
Sed parce confitentibu ;	But spare us, who our guilt confess;
Ad nominis laudem tui	And for thy greater praise, apply

Confer medelam languidis.	To our sick souls a remedy.
Concede nostrum conteri	May saving fasts ob serv'd this Lent,
Corpus per abstinentiam;	Become the body's punishment;
Culpæ ut relinquant pabulum	That sin may thus unfed remain,
Jejuna corda criminum.	And th' heart from guilt thereof abstain.
Præsta beata Trinitas,	Grant, O most sacred Trinity,
Concede simplex Unitas;	Grant, O most perfect Unity,
Ut fructuosa sint tuis	That this our solemn abstinence
Jejuniorum munera. *Amen.*	May fruitful prove to mind and sense. *Amen.*
V. Angelis suis Deus mandavit de te.	V. God has given his angels a charge over thee.
R. Ut custodiant te in omnibus viis tuis.	R. To guard thee in all thy ways.

For Passion Sunday.

VEXILLA REGIS.

VEXILLA regis prodeunt!	BEHOLD the royal ensigns fly,
Fulget crucis mysterium,	Bearing the cross's mystery;
Qui vita mortem pertulit,	Where life itself did death endure,
Et morte vitam protulit.	And by that death did life procure.
Quæ vulnerata lanceæ	A cruel spear let out a flood
Mucrone diro, criminum,	Of water mixed with saving blood;
Ut nos lavaret sordibus,	Which gushing from our Saviour's side,

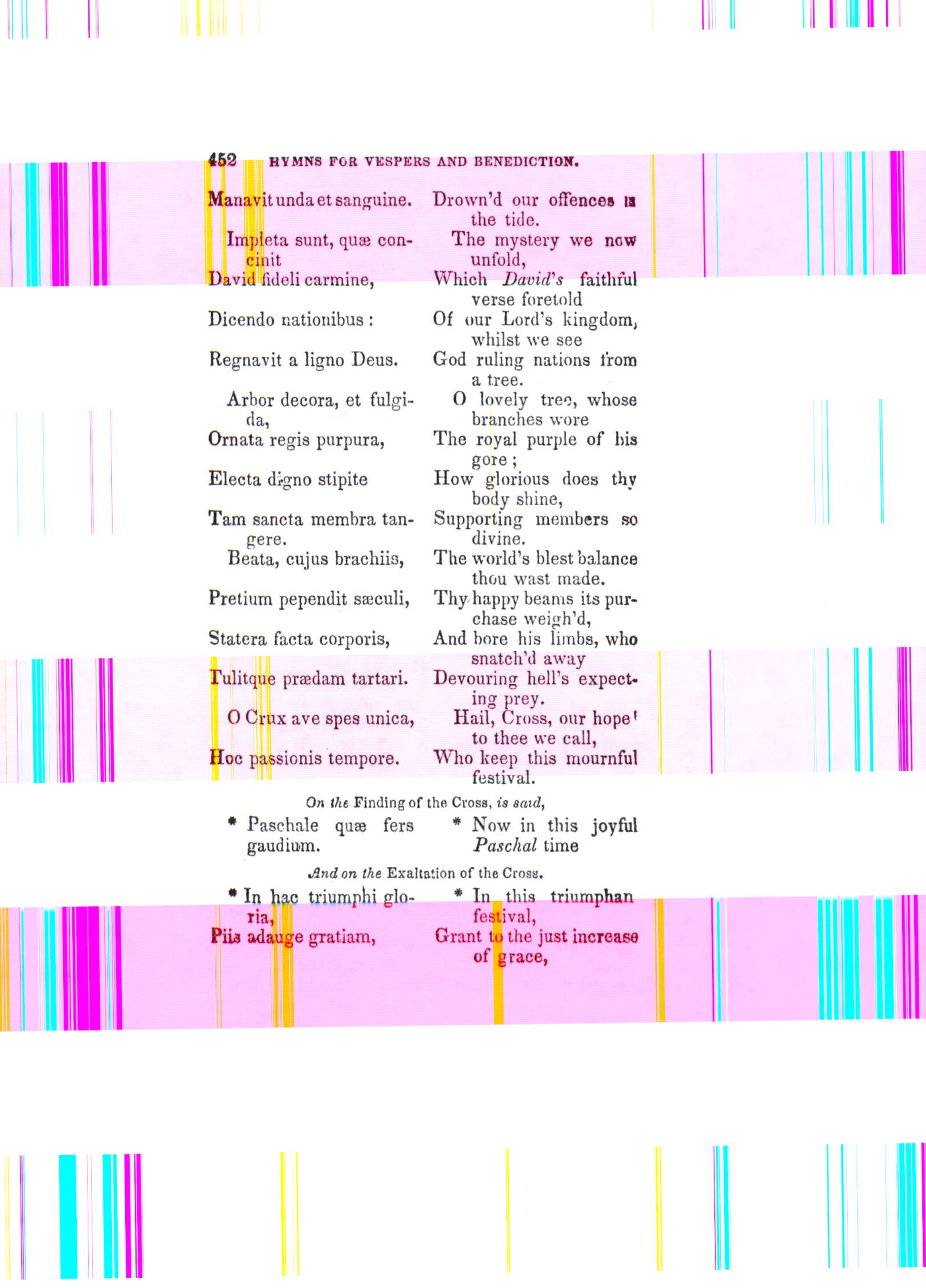

Manavit unda et sanguine.	Drown'd our offences in the tide.
Impleta sunt, quæ concinit	The mystery we now unfold,
David fideli carmine,	Which *David's* faithful verse foretold
Dicendo nationibus :	Of our Lord's kingdom, whilst we see
Regnavit a ligno Deus.	God ruling nations from a tree.
Arbor decora, et fulgida,	O lovely tree, whose branches wore
Ornata regis purpura,	The royal purple of his gore ;
Electa digno stipite	How glorious does thy body shine,
Tam sancta membra tangere.	Supporting members so divine.
Beata, cujus brachiis,	The world's blest balance thou wast made.
Pretium pependit sæculi,	Thy happy beams its purchase weigh'd,
Statera facta corporis,	And bore his limbs, who snatch'd away
Tulitque prædam tartari.	Devouring hell's expecting prey.
O Crux ave spes unica,	Hail, Cross, our hope! to thee we call,
Hoc passionis tempore.	Who keep this mournful festival.

On the Finding of the Cross, *is said,*

* Paschale quæ fers gaudium.	* Now in this joyful *Paschal* time

And on the Exaltation of the Cross.

* In hac triumphi gloria,	* In this triumphant festival,
Piis adauge gratiam,	Grant to the just increase of grace,

Reisque dele crimina.	And every sinner's crimes efface.
Te, fons salutis Trinitas,	Blest Trinity, we praises sing
Collaudet omnis spiritus:	To thee, from whom all graces spring:
Quibus crucis victoriam	Celestial crowns on those bestow,
Largiris adde præmium. *Amen.*	Who conquer'd by the cross below. *Amen.*
V. Eripe me, Domine, ab homine malo.	*V.* Deliver me, O Lord, from the wicked man.
R. A viro iniquo eripe me	*R.* From the unjust man deliver me.

The Plaint of the Blessed Virgin.

STABAT MATER.

STABAT mater dolorosa	BENEATH the world's redeeming wood
Juxta crucem lacrymosa	The most afflicted Mother stood,
Dum pendebat filius.	Mingling her tears with her Son's blood.
Cujus animam gementem	As that flow'd down from ev'ry part,
Contristatam et dolentem	Of all his wounds she felt the smart,
Pertransivit gladius.	What pierc'd his body pierc'd her heart.
O quam tristis et afflicta,	Who can with tearless eyes look on,
Fuit illa benedicta	When such a Mother, such a Son,
Mater unigeniti.	Wounded and gasping, does bemoan!
Quæ merebat, et dolebat,	O worse than *Jewish* heart, that could,
Et tremebat, cum videbat	Unmov'd, behold the double flood

Nati pœnas inclyti.

Quis est homo, qui non fleret,
Christi matrem si videret
In tanto supplicio?

Quis posset non contristari,
Piam matrem contemplari
Dolentem cum filio?

Pro peccatis suæ gentis
Vidit Jesum in tormentis,
Et flagellis subditum.

Vidit suum dulcem natum
Morientem, desolatum,
Dum emisit spiritum.

Eia mater fons amoris,
Me sentire vim doloris
Fac ut tecum lugeam.

Fac ut ardeat cor meum,
In amando Christum Deum,
Ut sibi complaceam.

Sancta mater istud agas,
Crucifixi fige plagas

Of *Mary's* tears, and *Jesu's* blood.

Alas! our sins, they were not his
In this atoning sacrifice,
For which he bleeds, for which he dies.

When graves were open'd, rocks were rent,
When nature and each element
His torments and her grief resent:

Shall man, the cause of all his pain
And all his grief, shall sinful man
Alone insensible remain?

Ah, pious mother, teach my heart,
Of sighs and tears the holy art,
And in thy grief to bear a part.

The sword of grief, which did pass through
Thy very soul, O may it now
Upon my heart a wound bestow.

Great Queen of Sorrows, in thy train
Let me a mourner's place obtain,
With tears to cleanse all sinful stain.

To heal the leprosy of sin,
We must the cure with tears begin,

Cordi meo valide.

Tui nati vulnerati,
Tam dignati pro me pati
Pœnas mecum divide.

Fac me vere tecum flere,
Crucifixo condolere,
Donec ego vixero.

Juxta crucem tecum stare,
Te libenter sociare,
In planctu desidero.

Virgo virginum præclara,
Mihi jam non sis amara,
Fac me tecum plangere.

Fac ut portem Christi mortem,
Passionis fac consortem,
Et plagas recolere.

Fac me plagis vulnerari,
Cruce hac inebriari,
Ob amorem filii

All flesh's corrupt without their brine.

Refuge of sinners, grant that we
May tread thy steps, and let it be
Our sorrow not to grieve like thee.

O may the wounds of thy dear Son
Our contrite hearts possess alone,
And all terrene affections drown.

Those wounds, which now the stars outshine,
Those furnaces of love divine,
May they our drossy souls refine;

And on us such impressions make,
That we of suff'ring for his sake
May joyfully our portion take.

Let us his proper badge put on,
Let's glory in the cross alone,
By which he marks us for his own.

That when the dreadful trial's come,
For every man to hear his doom,
On his right-hand we may find room.

Inflammatus et accensus,	O hear us, *Mary ! Jesus* hear !
Per te virgo sim defensus	Our humble pray'rs secure our fear,
In die judicii.	When thou in judgment shalt appear.
Fac me cruce custodiri,	Now give us sorrow give us love,
Morte Christi præmuniri	That so prepar'd, we may remove,
Confoveri gratia.	
Quando corpus morietur,	When call'd to seats of bliss above. *Amen.*
Fac ut animæ donetur	
Paradisi gloria.	
V. Tuam ipsius animam pertransivit gladius.	*V.* A sword has pierced thy own soul.
R. Ut revelentur ex multis cordibus cogitationes.	*R.* That the thoughts of many hearts may be revealed.

The Hymn *for* Easter

Alleluia, Alleluia, Alleluia.

O filii et filiæ

O filii et filiæ,	Praise by mortals now be given,
Rex cœlestis, Rex gloriæ,	On this day from death hath risen
Morte surrexit hodie, Alleluia.	The King of Glory, King of Heaven, Alleluia.
Et mane prima Sabbati.	The morn of Sabbath scarce did beam,
Ad ostium monumenti	When to his monument there came
Accesserunt discipuli, Alleluia.	Disciples who ador'd his name, Alleluia.
Et Maria Magdalene,	There *Mary Magdalen* anxious stood,

Et Jacobi, et Salome,	And *James*, and *Salome* the good;
Venerunt corpus ungere, Alleluia.	His body fain embalm they would, Alleluia.
In albis sedens angelus	The angel sat in white all rob'd,
Prædixit mulieribus,	And to the women he foretold:
In Galilea est Dominus, Alleluia.	In *Galilee* you'll see the Lord, Alleluia.
Et Joannes apostolus	The message scarce did greet his ear,
Cucurrit Petro citiùs,	Swifter than *Peter*, *John* drew near
Monumento venit priùs, Alleluia.	To the Lord's tomb, with hope, with fear, Alleluia.
Discipulis astantibus,	The disciples all assembled were;
In medio stetit Christus,	Among them Jesus did appear;
Dicens, pax vobis omnibus, Alleluia.	His peace he gave; remov'd their fear, Alleluia.
Ut intellexit Didymus	*Thomas* believed not, when 'twas said
Quia surrexerat Jesus,	That Christ had risen from the dead,
Remansit fere dubius, Alleluia.	Until he saw the wounds that bled, Alleluia.
Vide Thoma, vide latus,	My hands, my side, my feet, O see!
Vide pedes, vide manus:	*Thomas*, wounds that bled for thee:
Noli esse incredulus, Alleluia.	Renounce thine incredulity, Alleluia.
Quando Thomas vidit Christum	When *Thomas* Jesus had survey'd,

Pedes, manus, latus suum,	And on his wounds his fingers laid,
Dixt: Tu es Deus meus, Alleluia.	Thou art my Lord and God, he said, Al-el.
Beati qui non viderunt,	Blessed are they who have not seen,
Et firmiter crediderunt.	And yet, whose faith entire hath been,
Vitam æternam habebunt, Alleluia.	Them endless joy from pain shall screen, Alleluia.
In hoc festo sanctissimo	On this most solemn feast let's raise
Sit laus et jubilatio:	Our hearts to God in hymns of praise,
Benedicamus Domino, Alleluia.	And bless the Lord in all his ways, Alleluia.
Ex quibus nos humillimas	Our grateful thanks to God let's give,
Devotas atque debitas	In humblest manner, whilst we live,
Deo dicamus gratias, Alleluia.	For all the favours we receive, Alleluia.

Hymn for the Ascension.

SALUTIS HUMANÆ.

SALUTIS humanæ Sator,	O CHRIST, the Saviour of mankind,
Jesu voluptas cordium,	The light and comfort of the mind;
Orbis redempti conditor,	Creator of this earthly frame,
Et casta lux amantium.	Thy lover's chaste endearing flame.
Qua victus es clementia,	What strange excess of clemency
Ut nostra ferres crimina,	Prevail'd so far with guiltless thee,

Mortem subires innocens	That thou the sinner's load shouldst bear,
Ut morte nos ut tolleres?	And die to pay his forfeiture?
Jesu tibi sit gloria	To Jesus, who ascends the sky,
Qui victor in cœlum redis	Be glory for eternity:
Cum Patre et almo Spiritu,	To God the Father let's repeat
In sempiterna sæcula. Amen.	The same, and to the Paraclete. Amen.
V. Ascendit Deus in jubilatione. Alleluia.	*V.* God ascended in triumph. Alleluia.
R. Et Dominus in voce tubæ. Alleluia.	*R.* And the Lord at the sound of the trumpet. Alleluia.

Hymn for Pentecost.

VENI CREATOR.

VENI Creator Spiritus,	CREATING Spirit, come possess
Mentes tuorum visita,	Our souls, and with thy presence bless:
Imple superna gratia,	And in our hearts, fram'd by thy hand,
Quæ tu creasti, pectora.	Let thy celestial grace command.
Qui diceris Paraclitus.	Thou who art call'd the *Paraclete,*
Altissimi donum Dei;	The Almighty Father's gift complete;
Fons vivus, ignis, charitas,	The living fountain, fire and love,
Et spiritalis unctio.	And sacred unction from above.
Tu septiformis munere,	Thou finger of the Father's hand,

Digitus paternæ dexteræ,	Who dost a sev'nfold grace command :
Tu rite promissum Patris,	Thou promis'd, from the Highest sent,
Sermone ditans guttura.	In various language eloquent.
Accende lumen sensibus :	Purge with thy light our earthly parts,
Infunde amorem cordibus :	And with thy love inflame our hearts :
Infirma nostri corporis	Thus human weakness fortify
Virtute firmans perpeti.	With everlasting constancy.
Hostem repellas longiùs,	Far from us drive the infernal foe,
Pacemque dones protinùs,	And peace, the fruit of love, bestow :
Ductore sic te prævio	Thus having thee, our safest guide,
Vitemus omne noxium.	Let not our feet to evil slide.
Per te sciamus da Patrem	Let us by thee the Father own,
Noscamus atque Filium :	And to us let thy Son be known :
Te utriusque Spiritum	Let us believe in thee, who dost
Credamus omni tempore.	From both proceed the Holy Ghost.
Deo Patri, sit gloria,	To God the Father, and the Son,
Et Filio, qui a mortuis	Who rose from death, be glory done :
Surrexit ac Paraclito,	This praise for ever let's repeat,
In sæculorum sæcula. *Amen.*	To God the holy Paraclete. *Amen.*

V. Loquebantur variis linguis Apostoli, *Alleluia*.	*V*. The Apostles spoke in various tongues, *Alleluia*.
R. Magnalia Dei, *Alleluia*.	*R*. The wonders of God, *Alleluia*.

The Sequence for Pentecost.

VENI SANCTE SPIRITUS.

VENI Sancte Spiritus	COME Holy Ghost, send down those beams,
Et emitte cælitus	Which sweetly flow in silent streams,
Lucis tuæ radium.	From thy bright throne above.
Veni Pater pauperum:	O come, thou Father of the poor,
Veni dator munerum:	Thou bounteous source of all our store,
Veni lumen cordium.	Come fire our hearts with love.
Consolator optime,	Come thou of comforters the best,
Dulcis hospes animæ,	Come thou the soul's delicious guest,
Dulce refrigerium.	The pilgrim's sweet relief.
In labore requies,	Thou art our rest in toil and sweat,
In æstu temperies,	Refreshment in excessive heat,
In fletu solatium.	And solace in our grief.
O lux beatissima,	O sacred light, shoot home thy darts,
Reple cordis intima	O pierce the centre of those hearts,
Tuorum fidelium	Whose faith aspires to thee.

Sine tuo numine,	Without thy Godhead nothing can
Nihil est in homine,	Have any price or worth in man :
Nihil est innoxium.	Nothing can harmless be.
Lava quod est sordidum,	Lord, wash our sinful stains away,
Riga quod est aridum,	Water from heav'n our barren clay,
Sana quod est saucium.	Our wounds and bruises heal.
Flecte quod est rigidum,	To thy sweet yoke our stiff necks bow,
Fove quod est frigidum,	Warm with thy fire our hearts of snow,
Rege quod est devium.	Our wand'ring feet repeal.
Da tuis fidelibus,	O grant thy faithful, dearest Lord,
In te confitentibus,	Whose only hope is thy sure word,
Sacrum septenarium.	The seven gifts of thy spirit.
Da virtutis meritum,	Grant us in life t'obey thy grace,
Da salutis exitum,	Grant us in death to see thy face,
Da perenne gaudium. *Amen.*	And endless joys inherit. *Amen*

For the ASSUMPTION *of the* B. VIRGIN.

V. Exaltata est sancta Dei genitrix.	*V*. The holy Mother of Christ is exalted.
R. Super chorus angelorum ad cœlestia regna.	*R*. To the celestial kingdoms above the choirs of angels.

Hymn for the Feast of the Sacred Heart.

COR, ARCA.

COR, Arca legem continens	O SACRED Ark, bless'd heart of Jesus meek!
Non servitutis veteris,	In thee the law of grace, of peace, we seek.
Sed gratiæ, sed veniæ,	More holy far, than *Ark* that did contain
Sed et misericordiæ.	A law of rigour, slavery, and pain.
Te vulneratum caritas	For mortal's woes thy loving heart hath bled,
Ictu patenti voluit,	For sinner's wounds its healing influence shed.
Amoris invisibilis	Thy Father's glory hath thy heart all fir'd,
Ut veneremur vulnera.	To justice, love, a sacrifice expir'd.
Quis non amantem redamet?	Who shall refuse to thee the debt of love?
Quis non redemptus diligat,	Who that's redeem'd but shall look above,
Et Corde in isto feligat	To find in thy bless'd heart a place of rest
Æterna tabernacula?	From earthly cares, amid the just, the bless'd?
Decus Parenti et Filio,	Glory and praise to the Father, and the Son,
Sanctoque sit Spiritui,	To the Holy Ghost, to the Three in One.
Quibus potestas gloria,	To whom may power, honour, ever be,
Regnumque in omne est sæculum.	On earth, in heaven, thro' all eternity. Amen.
V. Haurietis aquas in gaudio. Alleluia.	*V.* You shall draw waters with joy. Alleluia.

R. De fontibus Salvatoris. Alleluia.	*R.* Out of the Saviour's fountains. Alleluia.

The Thanksgiving HYMN, TE DEUM.

TE Deum laudamus: Te Dominum confitemur.
Te æternum Patrem omnis terra veneratur.
Tibi omnes angeli, tibi cœli et universæ potestates,
Tibi cherubim et seraphim, incessabili voce proclamant
Sanctus, Sanctus, Sanctus, Dominus Deus Sabaoth,
Pleni sunt cœli et terra majestate gloriæ tuæ.
Te gloriosus Apostolorum chorus;
Te Prophetarum laudabilis numerus;
Te Martyrum candidatus laudat exercitus.
Te per orbem terrarum, sancta confitetur ecclesia,
Patrem immensæ majestatis:
Venerandum tuum verum, et unicum Filium;
Sanctum quoque Paraclitum Spiritum.
Tu Rex gloriæ Christe:
Tu Patris, Sempiternus es Filius.
Tu ad liberandum suscepturus hominem, non horruisti virginis uterum:
Tu devicto mortis aculeo, aperuisti credentibus regna cœlorum.
Tu ad dextram Dei sedes: in gloria Patris.
Judex crederis esse venturus:
Te ergo, quæsumus, tuis famulis subveni, quos pretioso sanguine redemisti.
Æterna fac cum sanctis tuis in gloria numerari.
Salvum fac populum tuum, Domine: et benedic hæreditati tuæ.
Et rege eos, et extolle illos usque in æternum.
Per singulos dies benedicimus te.
Et laudamus nomen tuum in sæculum: et in sæculum sæculi.
Dignare Domine, die isto: sine peccato nos custodire.
Miserere nostri, Domine: miserere nostri.
Fiat misericordia tua, Domine, super nos, quemadmodum speravimus in te.
In te Domine speravi: non confundar in æternum.

℣. Benedicamus Patrem et Filium, cum Sancto Spiritu.
℟. Laudemus et superexaltemus eum in sæcula.

Paraphrastical Translation of TE DEUM.

THEE, sovereign God, our grateful accents praise,
We own thee Lord, and bless thy wondrous ways.
To thee, Eternal Father, earth's whole frame,
With loudest trumpets sounds immortal fame.
Lord God of Hosts! to thee the heavenly powers,
With sounding anthems fill thy vaulted towers.
The cherubim thrice Holy, Holy, Holy, cry:
Thrice Holy all the seraphim reply,
And thrice returning echoes, endless songs supply.
Both heaven and earth thy Majesty display;
They owe their beauty to thy glorious ray.
Thy praises fill the loud Apostles' choir:
The train of prophets in the song conspire.
Legions of martyrs in the chorus shine
And vocal blood with vocal music join.
By these thy Church, inspir'd with heavenly art,
Around the world maintains a second part;
And tunes her sweetest notes, O God, to thee,
The Father of unbounded majesty;
The Son, ador'd copartner of thy seat,
And equal everlasting Paraclete.
Thou King of Glory, Christ of the Most High,
Thou co-eternal filial Deity:
Thou, who, to save the world's impending doom,
Vouchsaf'dst to dwell within a virgin's womb:
Old tyrant Death disarm'd; before thee flew
The bolts of heaven, and back the foldings drew.
To give access, and make the faithful way;
From God's right hand thy filial beams display.
Thou art to judge the living and the dead:
Then spare those souls, for whom thy veins have bled.
O take us up amongst the blest above,
To share with them thy everlasting love.
Preserve, O Lord, thy people, and enhance

Thy blessing on thine own inheritance.
For ever raise their hearts, and rule their ways:
Each day we bless thee, and proclaim thy praise
No age shall fail to celebrate thy name;
Nor hour neglect thy everlasting fame.
Preserve our souls, O Lord, this day from ill:
Have mercy on us, Lord! have mercy still.
As we have hop'd, do thou reward our pain:
We've hop'd in thee, let not our hope be vain.

V. Let us bless the Father, the Son, and the Holy Ghost.

R. Let us praise and extol him for ever.

Canticle *of* Zachary, *Luke* i. 68.

Benedictus Dominus Deus Israel: *quia visitavit, et fecit redemptionem plebis suæ.	Blessed be the Lord God of Israel, *because he hath visited and wrought the redemption of his people:
Et erexit cornu salutis nobis, *in domo David pueri sui.	And hath raised up a horn of salvation to us, *in the house of David his servant.
Sicut locutus est per os sanctorum, *qui a sæculo sunt prophetarum ejus:	As he spoke by the mouth of his holy prophets, *who are from the beginning:
Salutem ex inimicis nostris: *et de manu omnium qui oderunt nos.	Salvation from our enemies, *and from the hand of all that hate us.
Ad faciendam misericordiam cum patribus nostris: *et memorari testamenti sui sancti.	To perform mercy to our fathers; *and to remember his holy covenant.
Jusjurandum, quod juravit ad Abraham patrem nostrum, *daturum se nobis.	The oath which he swore to Abraham our father, *that he would grant to us.
Ut sine timore, de manu	That being delivered from the hand of our enemies, *we may

inimicorum nostrorum liberati *serviamus illi :

In sanctitate et justitia coram ipso, *omnibus diebus nostris.

Et tu puer, propheta Altissimi vocaberis : * præibis enim ante faciem Domini parare vias ejus.

Ad dandam scientiam salutis plebi ejus : *in remissionem peccatorem eorum.

Per viscera misericordiæ Dei nostri : *in quibus visitavit nos Oriens ex alto :

Illuminare his qui in tenebris et in umbra mortis sedent : *ad dirigendos pedes nostros in viam pacis.

serve him without fear : In holiness and justice before him, *all our days. And thou, child shalt be called the Prophet of the Highest : *for thou shalt go before the face of the Lord, to prepare his ways : To give knowledge of salvation to his people, *unto the remission of their sins : Through the bowels of the mercy of our God : *in which the Orient from on high hath visited us : To enlighten them that sit in darkness, and in the shadow of death : *to direct our feet in the way of peace.

Psalm L.

Miserere mei Deus, *secundum magnam misericordiam tuam.

Et secundum multitudinem miserationum tuarum, *dele iniquitatem meam.

Amplius lava me ab iniquitate mea ; *et a peccato meo munda me.

Quoniam iniquitatem meam ego cognosco : *et peccatum meum contra me est semper.

Tibi soli peccavi, et malum coram te feci : *ut justificeris in sermonibus tuis, et vincas cum judicaris.

Ecce enim in iniquitatibus conceptus sum : *et in peccatis concepit me mater mea.

Ecce enim veritatem dilexisti : *incerta et occulta sapientiæ tuæ manifestasti mihi.

Asperges me hyssopo

et mundabor: *lavabis me, et super nivem dealbabor.

Auditui meo dabis gaudium et lætitiam: *et exultabunt ossa humiliata.

Averte faciem tuam a peccatis meis: *et omnes iniquitates meas dele.

Cor mundum crea in me Deus: *et spiritum rectum innova in visceribus meis.

Ne projicias me a facie tua: *et spiritum sanctum tuum ne auferas a me.

Redde mihi lætitiam salutaris tuis: *et spiritu principali confirma me.

Docebo iniquos vias tuas: *et impii ad te convertentur.

Libera me de sanguinibus Deus, Deus salutis meæ: *et exultabit lingua mea justitiam tuam.

Domine labia mea aperies: *et os meum annunciabit laudem tuam.

Quoniam si voluisses sacrificium dedissem utique: *holocaustis non delectaberis.

Sacrificium Deo spiritus contribulatus: *cor contritum et humiliatum Deus non despicies.

Benigne fac Domine in bona voluntate tua Sion: *ut ædificentur muri Jerusalem.

Tunc acceptabis sacrificium justitiæ, oblationes et holocausta: *tunc imponent super altare tuum vitulos.

Gloria Patri, &c.

For the English Version of the Psalm Miserere, *see p.* 402.

Oratio.

Deus, qui culpa offenderis, pœnitentia placaris: preces populi tui supplicantis propitius respice: et flagella tuæ iracundiæ quæ pro peccatis nostris meremur averte. Per.

LITTLE OFFICE OF THE B. VIRGIN.

Hail Mary.

Incline unto my aid, O God.
R. Lord, make haste to help me.
Glory be to the Father, &c. Alleluia.
Anth. Whilst the king was

PSALM CIX.—*Dixit Dominus.* (See p. 429.)

Anth. While the king was on his couch, my spikenard yielded a sweet odour.

Anth. His left hand.

PSALM CXII.—*Laudate pueri Dominum.* (See p. 432.)

Anth. His left hand is under my head, and his right hand shall embrace me.

Anth. I am black.

PSALM CXXI.—*Lætatus sum.*

I REJOICED at those things which were said to me, we shall go into the house of the Lord.

Our feet were standing in thy courts, O Jerusalem

Jerusalem, which is built as a city, whose inhabitants are united together.

For thither did the tribes ascend, the tribes of our Lord, the testimony of Israel; to praise the name of our Lord.

Because seats sat there in judgment, seats upon the house of David.

Ask the things that are for the peace of Jerusalem, and abundance to them that love thee.

Let peace be made in thy strength, and abundance in thy towers.

For my brethren and my neighbours, I spoke peace of thee.

For the house of the Lord our God: I have sought good things for thee.

Glory be to the Father, &c.

Anth. I am black, but beautiful, O daughters of Jerusalem: therefore the king has loved me, and brought me into his chamber.

Anth. Winter is now past.

PSALM CXXIX.—*Nisi Dominus.*

IF our Lord builds not the house, they have laboured in vain that build it.

If our Lord keeps not the city, he watches in vain that keeps it.

It is in vain for you to rise before light: rise after ye have sat, you that eat the bread of sorrow.

When he shall give sleep to his beloved, behold children are an inheritance from our Lord; and the fruit of the womb is a reward.

As arrows in the hand of the mighty, so are the children of them that are rejected.

Blessed is the man that has filled his desire of them; he shall not be confounded, when he shall speak to his enemies in the gate.

Glory be to the Father, &c.

Anth. Winter is now past, the rain is gone and departed: Arise my love and come.

Anth. Thou art made fair.

PSALM CXLVII.—*Lauda Jerusalem.*

O JERUSALEM, praise our Lord: praise thy God, O Sion.

Because he has strengthened the locks of thy gates, he has blessed thy children in thee.

Who has set thy borders in peace: and fills thee with the fat of corn.

Who sends forth his speech to the earth; his word runs swiftly.

Who gives snow as wool; scatters mist as ashes.

He casts his crystal as morsels: before the face of his cold who shall abide?

He shall send forth his word, and shall melt them: his spirit shall breathe and the waters shall flow.

Who declares his word to Jacob, his justice and judgments to Israel.

He has not done so to any nation: and his judgments he has not made manifest to them.

Glory be to the Father, &c.

Anth. Thou art made fair and sweet in thy delicateness, O holy Mother of God

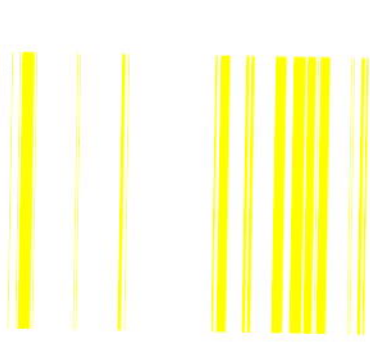

THE LITTLE CHAPTER. *Eccles.* 24

FROM the beginning, and before the world was I created, and unto the world to come, I shall not cease, and in thy holy habitation have I ministered before him

R. Thanks be to God.

THE HYMN. *Ave Maris Stella.*

BRIGHT Mother of our Maker, hail!
  Thou Virgin ever blest,
The ocean's star by which we sail
  And gain the port of rest.
While we this Ave thus to thee
  From Gabriel's mouth rehearse;
Prevail that peace our lot may be,
  And Eva's name reverse.
Release our long entangled mind,
  From all the snares of ill,
With heavenly light instruct the blind
  And all our vows fulfil.
Exert for us a mother's care,
  And us thy children own;
Prevail with him to hear our prayer
  Who chose to be thy Son.
O spotless maid! whose virtues shine
  With brightest purity;
Each action of our lives refine,
  And make us pure like thee.
Preserve our lives unstain'd from ill,
  In this infectious way;
That heaven alone our souls may fill
  With joys that ne'er decay.
To God the Father endless praise;
  To God the Son the same;
And Holy Ghost, whose equal rays
  One equal glory claim. *Amen.*

℣. Grace is poured forth on thy lips.
R. Therefore God has blessed thee for ever.

The *Anth.* O blessed Mother.
In the time of Easter—*Anth.* Triumph, O Queen

The Song of the Blessed Virgin Mary. Luke i. 46
(See p. 439.)

Anth. O blessed mother, and ever virgin, glorious queen of the world, make intercession for us to our Lord.

In the time of Easter.

Anth. Triumph, O Queen of heaven, to see, Alleluia
The sacred infant born of thee, Alleluia.
Return in glory from the tomb, Alleluia.
And with thy prayers prevent our doom, Alleluia.
Lord have mercy on us.
Christ have mercy on us.
Lord have mercy on us.
V. Lord hear my prayer.
R. And let my cry come to thee.

Let us pray.

Lord God, we beseech thee, grant that we thy servants may enjoy perpetual health of mind and body; and that by the glorious intercession of the ever-blessed Virgin Mary, we may pass from this present sorrow, to the enjoyment of everlasting gladness. Through our Lord, &c. *Amen.*

For the Saints.

Anth All ye saints of God, vouchsafe to make intercession for the salvation of us, and of us all.

V. Ye just, rejoice in our Lord, and be exceeding glad.

R. And glory, all ye right in heart.

Let us pray.

Protect, O Lord, thy people, and let the confidence we have in the intercession of thy blessed apostles Peter and Paul, and of thy other apostles, prevail with thee, to preserve and defend us for ever.

May all thy saints, O Lord, we beseech thee, every where assist us, that whilst we celebrate their merits, we may be sensible of their protection; grant us thy peace in our times, and repel all wickedness from thy Church: prosperously guide the steps, actions, and desires of us, and of all thy servants, in the way of salvation: give eternal blessings to those who have done good to us, and everlasting rest to the faithful departed. Through our Lord Jesus Christ thy Son, &c.

R. Amen.
V. Lord hear my prayer.
R. And let my cry come to thee.
V. Bless we our Lord.
R. Thanks be to God.
V. May the souls of the faithful, through the mercy of God, rest in peace.
R. Amen.

THE

OFFICE FOR THE DEAD

When the whole Office is said, it is recited in the manner of a Double, *viz.* the *Vespers* on the eve, and the *Invitatory*, *Matins*, and *Lauds*, on the following morning, concluding with one or more appropriate prayers: but at *Vespers* the Psalm *Lauda anima*, and at *Lauds* the *De Profundis* are omitted. On other occasions (when only one of the *Nocturns* and the *Lauds* are recited) there are but a word or two of the Anthems before each Psalm recited, and the whole Anthem at the end thereof.

VESPERS.

Anth. **I will please the Lord in the land of the living.**

Psalm cxiv Dilexi quoniam.

I have loved, because the Lord will hear the voice of my prayer.

Because he hath inclined his ear unto me: and in my days I will call upon him.

The sorrows of death have compassed me: and the perils of hell have found me.

I met with trouble and sorrow: and I called upon the name of the Lord.

O Lord, deliver my soul: the Lord is merciful and just, and our God showeth mercy.

The Lord is the keeper of little ones: I was humbled, and he delivered me.

Turn, O my soul, into thy rest: for the Lord hath been bountiful to thee.

For he hath delivered my soul from death; my eyes from tears, my feet from falling.

I will please the Lord in the land of the living.

Grant them eternal rest, O Lord:

And let perpetual light shine on them.

Anth. I will please the Lord in the land of the living.

Anth. Wo is me, O Lord, that my sojourning is prolonged.

Psalm cxix. Ad Dominum, cum tribularer.

In my trouble I cried to the Lord: and he heard me.

O Lord, deliver my soul from wicked lips, and a deceitful tongue.

What shall be given to thee, or what shall be added to thee, to a deceitful tongue?

The sharp arrows of the mighty, with coals that lay waste.

Wo is me that my sojourning is prolonged! I have dwelt with the inhabitants of Cedar; my soul hath been long a sojourner.

With them that hated peace I was peaceable: when I spoke to them they fought against me without cause.

Grant them eternal rest, &c.

Anth. Wo is me, O Lord, that my sojourning is prolonged.

Anth. The Lord keepeth thee from all evil; may the Lord keep thy soul.

PSALM CXX. *Levavi oculos.*

I HAVE lifted up my eyes to the mountains: from whence help shall come to me.

My help is from the Lord, who made heaven and earth.

May he not suffer thy foot to be moved; neither let him slumber that keepeth thee.

Behold he shall neither slumber nor sleep, that keepeth Israel.

The Lord is thy keeper, the Lord is thy protection upon thy right hand.

The sun shall not burn thee by day; nor the moon by night.

The Lord keepeth thee from all evil: may the Lord keep thy soul.

May the Lord keep thy coming in and thy going out, from henceforth, now, and for ever.

Grant them eternal rest, &c.

Anth. The Lord keepeth thee from all evil: may the Lord keep thy soul.

Anth. If thou, O Lord, wilt mark iniquities: Lord who shall stand it?

PSALM CXXIX. *De Profundis.* (See p. 405.)

Grant him eternal rest, &c.

Anth. If thou, O Lord, wilt mark iniquities: Lord who shall stand it?

Anth. Despise not, O Lord, the works of thy hands.

PSALM CXXXVII. *Confitebor tibi.*

I WILL praise thee, O Lord, with my whole heart for thou hast heard the words of my mouth.

I will sing praise to thee in the sight of the Angels. I will worship towards thy holy temple, and I will give glory to thy name.

For thy mercy, and for thy truth: for thou hast magnified thy holy name above all.

In what day soever I shall call upon thee, hear me: thou shalt multiply strength in my soul.

May all the kings of the earth give glory to thee: for they have heard all the words of thy mouth.

And let them sing in the ways of the Lord: for great is the glory of the Lord.

For the Lord is high, and looketh on the low; and the high he knoweth afar off.

If I shall walk in the midst of tribulation, thou wilt quicken me; and thou hast stretched forth thy hand against the wrath of my enemies; and thy right hand hath saved me.

The Lord will repay for me: thy mercy, O Lord, endureth for ever: O despise not the works of thy hands

Grant them eternal rest, &c.

Anth. Despise not, O Lord, the works of thy hands.

V. I heard a voice from heaven saying to me,

R. Blessed are the dead that die in the Lord.

Anth. All that my Father gives me shall come to me, and him that comes to me I will not cast out.

Canticle of the Blessed Virgin Mary. (See p. 439.)

Grant them eternal rest, &c.

Anth. All that my Father gives me, shall come to me; and him that comes to me, I will not cast out.

Our Father, &c. *in secret.*

V. And lead us not into temptation.

R. But deliver us from evil.

When the Office is not a Double, the following ***Prayers*** *are said, kneeling.*

Our Father, &c. *in secret.*

V. And lead us not into temptation.

R. But deliver us from evil.

When the Office is a Double, the following Psalm is omitted.

PSALM CXLV. *Lauda anima.*

PRAISE the Lord, O my soul, in my life I will praise the Lord : I will sing to my God as long as I shall be.

Put not your trust in princes : in the children of men, in whom there is no salvation.

His spirit shall go forth, and he shall return into his earth : in that day all their thoughts shall perish.

Blessed is he who hath the God of Jacob for his helper, whose hope is in the Lord his God : who made heaven and earth, the sea, and all things that are in them.

Who keepeth truth for ever ; who executeth judgment for them that suffer wrong ; who giveth food to the hungry.

The Lord looseth them that are fettered : the Lord enlighteneth the blind.

The Lord lifteth up them that are cast down . the Lord loveth the just.

The Lord keepeth the strangers : he will support the fatherless and the widow ; and the ways of sinners he will destroy.

The Lord shall reign for ever thy God, O Sion, unto generation and generation.

Grant them eternal rest, &c.

V. From the gates of hell.

R. Deliver their souls, O Lord.

V. May they rest in peace.

R. Amen.

V. O Lord, hear my prayer.

R And let my cry come to thee.

V The Lord be with you.

R. And with thy spirit.

Let us pray.

O GOD, by whose favour thy servants were raised o the dignity of bishops, (*or* priests,) and so honour ed with the apostolical functions, grant, we beseech thee, they may be admitted to the eternal fellowship of thy apostles in heaven. Through.

O GOD, the giver of pardon, and lover of human salvation, we beseech thy clemency, that the brethren, relations, and benefactors of our congregation, who are departed this life, may, through the intercession of the blessed Mary, ever a virgin, and of all thy saints, attain to the fellowship of eternal bliss.

O GOD, the Creator and Redeemer of all the faithful, give to the souls of thy servants, men and women, the remission of all their sins; that by pious supplications they may obtain the pardon they have always desired. Who livest and reignest, world without end.

R. Amen.
V. Eternal rest give to them, O Lord.
R. And let perpetual light shine on them.
V. May they rest in peace.
R. Amen.

On the Commemoration of All Souls, the last of the foregoing Prayers is said exclusively.

A Prayer on the Day of the decease of a Man or Woman.

ABSOLVE, we beseech thee, O Lord, the soul of thy servant N., that being dead to the world, he (*or* she) may live to thee: and whatever he (*or* she) has committed through human frailty, do thou wipe away by the pardon of thy most merciful goodness: through our Lord Jesus Christ thy Son, who livest and reignest with thee in the unity of the Holy Ghost, God, world without end.

R. Amen.
V. Grant them eternal rest, O Lord.
R. And let perpetual light shine on them.
V. May they rest in peace.
R. Amen.

A Prayer for a Bishop or Priest deceased. When it is for a Priest, the word Pontifical *is omitted, and* Priestly *introduced.*

O God, who among thy apostolic priests hast bestowed on thy servant N. the pontifical (*or* priestly) dignity; grant, we beseech thee, that he may also be joined with them in perpetual society. Through, &c.

For a Father and Mother deceased.

O God, who hast commanded us to honour our father and mother, have compassion, in thy mercy, on the souls of my father and mother, and forgive them their sins, and grant that we may meet in the joy of eternal bliss. Through, &c.

For a Father or a Mother.

O God, who hast commanded us to honour our father and mother, have mercy, through thy goodness, on the soul of my father, (*or* my mother,) and forgive him (*her*) his (*her*) sins, and grant I may see him (*her*) in the joy of eternal bliss. Through &c.

For a Mother deceased.

O God, who hast commanded us to honour our father and mother, have mercy, through thy goodness, on the soul of my mother, and forgive her her sins, and grant I may see her in the joy of eternal bliss. Through, &c.

For a Man deceased.

Incline, O Lord, thy ear to our prayers, in which we humbly beseech thy mercy, that thou wouldst place the soul of thy servant, which thou hast caused to depart from this world, into the region of peace and light; and unite in the fellowship of thy saints. Through, &c.

For a Woman deceased.

We beseech thee, O Lord, for thy goodness, have mercy on the soul of thy servant; and being freed from the corruption of mortality, restore her the portion of eternal salvation. Through, &c.

On an Anniversary Day. If it be for one Person only, it is to be said in the singular number.

O Lord, the God of pardon, give to the souls of thy servants, men and women departed, whose anniversary day of departure we commemorate, the seat of refreshment, the happiness of rest, and the brightness of eternal light. Through, &c.

For Brethren, Relations, and Benefactors.

O God, the giver of pardon, and lover of human salvation, we beseech thy clemency to grant that the brethren, relations, and benefactors of our congregation, who are departed this world, may, by the intercession of the blessed Mary, ever virgin, and of all thy saints, attain to the fellowship of eternal beatitude. Through, &c.

For the Dead in general.

O God, the Creator and Redeemer of all the faithful, give to the souls of thy servants, men and women, the remission of all their sins: that by pious supplications they may obtain the pardon which they have always desired. Who livest and reignest with God the Father, in the unity of the Holy Ghost, one God, world without end. R. Amen.

At Matins.

The following *Invitatory* is recited on *All-Souls Day*, and as often as the three *Nocturns* are said, as before directed in the rubric, page 471. At other times it is omitted, and the Office begins with the Anthem of the *Psalms* of the *Nocturn*, when only one *Nocturn* is said with the *Lauds* in the following order, *viz.* on *Monday* and *Thursday*, the first *Nocturn*; on *Tuesday* and *Friday*, the second *Nocturn*; on *Wednesday* and *Saturday*, the third *Nocturn*.

The Invitatory.

Come, let us adore the King, to whom all things ive.

Come, let us adore the King, to whom all things live

PSALM XCIV. *Venite exultemus.*

COME, let us praise the Lord with joy: let us joyfully sing to God our Saviour. Let us come before his presence with thanksgiving, and make a joyful noise to him with psalms.

Come, let us adore the King, to whom all things live.

For the Lord is a great God, and a great King above all gods: because the Lord repels not his people, for in his hand are all the ends of the earth: and the heights of the mountains are his.

Come, let us adore.

For the sea is his, and he made it: and his hands formed the dry land. Come let us adore and fall down: and weep before the Lord that made us. For he is the Lord our God: and we are the people of his pasture, and the sheep of his hand.

Come, let us adore the King, to whom all things live.

To-day, if ye shall hear his voice, harden not your hearts: as in the provocation, according to the day of temptation in the wilderness: where your fathers tempted me, they proved me, and saw my works.

Come, let us adore.

Forty years long was I offended with that generation, and I said: These always err in their hearts. And these men have not known my ways: so I swore in my wrath that they shall not enter into my rest.

Come, let us adore the King, to whom all things live.

Grant them eternal rest, O Lord, and let perpetual light shine on them.

Come, let us adore.

Come, let us adore the King to whom all things live

In the First Nocturn.

On Monday and Thursday.

Anth. Direct, O Lord my God, my way in thy sight.

Psalm v. *Verba mea.*

Give ear, O Lord, to my words, understand my cry.

Hearken to the voice of my prayer, O my King and my God.

For to thee will I pray: O Lord, in the morning thou shalt hear my voice.

In the morning I will stand before thee, and will see: that thou art not a God that willest iniquity.

Neither shall the wicked dwell near thee: nor shall the unjust abide before thy eyes.

Thou hatest all the workers of iniquity: thou wilt destroy all that speak a lie.

The bloody and the deceitful man the Lord will abhor: but as for me, in the multitude of thy mercy,

I will come into thy house: I will worship towards thy holy temple, in thy fear.

Conduct me, O Lord, in thy justice: because of my enemies, direct my way in thy sight.

For there is no truth in their mouth: their heart is vain.

Their throat is an open sepulchre: they dealt deceitfully with their tongues: judge them, O God.

Let them fall from their devices: according to the multitude of their wickednesses cast them out: for they have provoked thee, O Lord.

But let all them be glad that hope in thee: they shall rejoice for ever, and thou shalt dwell in them.

And all they that love thy name shall glory in thee: for thou wilt bless the just.

O Lord, thou hast crowned us, as with a shield of thy good-will.

Grant them eternal rest, &c.

Anth. Direct, O Lord my God, my steps in thy sight.

Anth. Turn to me, O Lord.

PSALM VI. *Domine, ne in furore.* (See p. 399.)

Grant them eternal rest, &c.

Anth. Turn to me, O Lord, and deliver my soul: for there is none in death who will be mindful of thee.

Anth. Lest at any time.

PSALM VII. *Domine, Deus meus.*

O LORD, my God, in thee have I put my trust: save me from all them that persecute me, and deliver me

Lest at any time he seize upon my soul, like a lion while there is no one to redeem me, nor to save.

O Lord, my God, if I have done this thing, if there be iniquity in my hands:

If I have rendered to them that repaid me evils, let me deservedly fall empty before my enemies.

Let the enemy pursue my soul, and seize it; and tread down my life on the earth; and bring down my glory to the dust.

Rise up, O Lord, in thy anger: and be thou exalted in the borders of my enemies.

And arise, O Lord my God, in the precept which thou hast commanded. And a congregation of people shall surround thee.

And for their sakes return thou on high. The Lord judgeth the people.

Judge me, O Lord, according to my justice, and according to my innocence in me.

The wickedness of sinners shall be brought to nought, and thou shalt direct the just: the searcher of hearts and reins is God.

Just is my help from the Lord: who saveth the upright of heart.

God is a just judge, strong and patient: is he angry every day?

Except you will be converted, he will brandish his sword: he hath bent his bow, and made it ready.

And in it he hath prepared the instruments of death: he hath made ready his arrows for them that burn.

Behold he hath been in labour with injustice; he hath conceived sorrow, and brought forth iniquity.

He hath opened a pit and dug it: and he is fallen into the hole he made.

His sorrow shall be turned on his own head: and his iniquity shall come down upon his crown.

And I will give glory to the Lord according to his justice: and will sing praise to the name of the Lord the most high.

Grant them eternal rest, &c.

Anth. Lest at any time the enemy seize upon my soul, like a lion, while there is none to redeem me, nor to save.

V. From the gates of hell,

R. Deliver their soul, O Lord.

Our Father, &c. *in secret.*

The First Lesson. Job vii.

Spare me, O Lord, for my days are nothing. What is a man that thou shouldst magnify him? or why dost thou set thy heart upon him? Thou visitest him early in the morning, and thou provest him suddenly. How long wilt thou not spare me, nor let me alone to swallow down my spittle? I have sinned, what shall I do to thee, O keeper of men? why hast thou set me opposite to thee, and I am become burdensome to myself? Why dost thou not remove my sin, and why dost thou not take away my iniquity? Behold now I shall sleep in the dust: and if thou seek me in the morning I shall not be.

R. I believe my Redeemer liveth, and that in the last day I shall rise from the earth, and in my flesh I shall see God my Saviour.

V. Whom I myself shall see, and not another, and my eyes shall behold. And in my flesh.

The Second Lesson. JOB X.

MY soul is weary of my life; I will let go my speech against myself, I will speak in the bitterness of my soul. I will say to God: Do not condemn me: tell me why thou judgest me so. Doth it seem good to thee that thou shouldst calumniate me, and oppress me, the work of thy own hands, and help the counsel of the wicked? Hast thou eyes of flesh: or shalt thou see as man seeth? Are thy days as the days of man, and are thy years as the times of men, that thou shouldst inquire after my iniquity, and search after my sin? And shouldst know that I have done no wicked thing, whereas there is no man that can deliver out of thy hands.

R. Thou who didst raise Lazarus stinking from the grave. Thou, O Lord, give them rest and a place of pardon.

V. Who art to come to judge the living and the dead, and the world by fire. Thou, O Lord.

The Third Lesson. JOB X.

THY hands have made me, and fashioned me wholly round about, and dost thou cast me down headlong on a sudden? Remember, I beseech thee, that thou hast made me as the clay, and thou wilt bring me into dust again. Hast thou not milked me and curdled me like cheese? Thou hast clothed me with skin and flesh: thou hast put me together with bones and sinews. Thou hast granted me life and mercy, and thy visitation hath preserved my spirit.

R. O Lord, when thou shalt come to judge the earth, where shall I hide myself from the face of thy wrath? For I have sinned exceedingly in my life.

V. I dread my misdeeds, and blush before thee: do not condemn me, when thou shalt come to judge. For I have sinned exceedingly in my life.

V. Grant them eternal rest, O Lord, and let perpetual light shine on them. For I have.

Here the Lauds are recited, when the first Nocturn only is said.

AT THE SECOND NOCTURN.

On Tuesday and Friday.

Anth. In a place of pasture he hath set me.

PSALM XXII. *Dominus regit me.*

THE Lord ruleth me; and I shall want nothing. He hath set me in a place of pasture.

He hath brought me up on the water of refreshment; he hath converted my soul.

He hath led me on the paths of justice, for his own name's sake.

For though I should walk in the midst of the shadow of death, I will fear no evils, for thou art with me

Thy rod and thy staff, they have comforted me.

Thou hast prepared a table before me, against them that afflict me.

Thou hast anointed my head with oil; and my chalice which inebriateth me, how goodly is it.

And thy mercy will follow me all the days of my life.

And that I may dwell in the house of the Lord, unto length of days.

Grant them eternal rest, &c.

Anth. In a place of pasture he hath set me.

Anth. The offences.

PSALM XXIV. *Ad te Domine levavi.*

To thee, O Lord, have I lifted up my soul. In thee O my God, I put my trust! let me not be ashamed.

Neither let my enemies laugh at me: for none of them that wait on thee shall be confounded.

Let all them be confounded that act unjust things without cause.

Show, O Lord, thy ways to me, and teach me thy paths.

Direct me in thy truth, and teach me: for thou art God my Saviour; and on thee have I waited all the day long.

Remember, O Lord, thy bowels of compassion; and thy mercies that are from the beginning of the world

The sins of my youth, and my ignorances, do not remember.

According to thy mercy remember thou me: for thy goodness sake, O Lord.

The Lord is sweet and righteous: therefore he will give a law to sinners in the way.

He will guide the mild in judgment: he will teach the meek his ways.

All the ways of the Lord are mercy and truth, to them that seek after his covenant and his testimonies.

For thy name's sake, O Lord, thou wilt pardon my sin; for it is great.

Who is the man that feareth the Lord? he hath appointed him a law in the way he hath chosen.

His soul shall dwell in good things: and his seed shall inherit the land.

The Lord is a firmament to them that fear him and his covenant shall be made manifest to them.

My eyes are ever towards the Lord; for he shall pluck my feet out of the snare.

Look thou upon me, and have mercy on me; for I am alone and poor.

The troubles of my heart are multiplied; deliver me from my necessities.

See my abjection and my labour; and forgive me all my sins.

Consider my enemies, for they are multiplied, and have hated me with an unjust hatred.

Keep thou my soul, and deliver me: I shall not be ashamed, for I have hoped in thee.

The innocent and the upright have adhered to me; because I have waited on thee.

Deliver Israel, O God, from all his tribulations.

Grant them eternal rest, &c.

Anth. The sins of my youth, and my ignorances do not remember, O Lord.

Anth. I believe to see.

PSALM XXVI. *Dominus illuminatio mea.*

THE Lord is my light and my salvation, whom shall I fear?

The Lord is the protector of my life; of whom shall I be afraid?

Whilst the wicked draw near against me to eat my flesh.

My enemies that trouble me have themselves been weakened, and have fallen.

If armies in camp should stand together against me, my heart shall not fear.

If a battle should rise up against me, in this will I be confident.

One thing have I asked of the Lord, this will I seek after; that I may dwell in the house of the Lord all the days of my life.

That I may see the delight of the Lord, and may visit his temple.

For he hath hid me in his tabernacle: in the day of evils, he hath protected me in the secret place of his tabernacle.

He hath exalted me upon a rock: and now he hath lifted up my head above my enemies.

I have gone round, and have offered up in his tabernacle a sacrifice of jubilation: I will sing, and recite a psalm to the Lord.

Hear, O Lord, my voice, with which I have cried to thee: have mercy on me, and hear me.

My heart hath said to thee: my face hath sought thee: thy face, O Lord, will I still seek.

Turn not away thy face from me: decline not in thy wrath from thy servant.

Be thou my helper, forsake me not; do not thou despise me, O God my Saviour.

For my father and my mother have left me: but the Lord hath taken me up.

Set me, O Lord, a law in the way, and guide me in the right path, because of my enemies

Deliver me not over to the will of them that trouble me: for unjust witnesses have risen up against me: and iniquity hath lied to itself.

I believe to see the good things of the Lord in the land of the living.

Expect the Lord, do manfully and let thy heart take courage, and wait thou for the Lord.

Grant them eternal rest, &c.

Anth. I believe to see the good things of the Lord in the land of the living.

V. May the Lord place them with the princes.

R. With the princes of his people.

Our Father, &c. *in secret.*

The Fourth Lesson. Job xiii.

Answer me: how many are my iniquities and sins? make me know my crimes and offences. Why hidest thou thy face, and thinkest me thy enemy? Against a leaf that is carried away with the wind, thou showest thy power, and thou pursuest a dry straw. For thou writest bitter things against me, and wilt consume me for the sins of my youth. Thou hast put my feet in the stocks, and hast observed all my paths, and hast considered the steps of my feet. Who am to be consumed, as rottenness, and as a garment that is moth-eaten.

R. Remember me, O God, because my life is but wind: nor may the sight of man behold me.

V. From the depths I have cried to thee, O Lord: Lord, hear my voice. Nor may.

The Fifth Lesson. Job xiv.

Man born of a woman, living for a short time, is filled with many miseries. Who cometh forth like a flower, and is destroyed, and fleeth as a shadow, and never continueth in the same state. And dost thou think it meet to open thy eyes upon such an one, and to bring him into judgment with thee? Who can make him clean that is conceived of unclean seed? Is it not thou who only art? The days of man are short, and the number of his months is with thee: thou hast appointed his bounds which cannot be passed. Depart a little from him, that he may rest, until his wished-for day come, as that of the hireling.

R. Wo is me, O Lord, because I have sinned exceedingly in my life: O wretch, what shall I do, whither shall I fly but to thee, my God: Have mercy on me when thou comest at the latter day.

V. My soul is greatly troubled; but thou, O Lord, succour it. Have mercy on me.

The Sixth Lesson. JOB XIV.

WHO will grant me this, that thou mayest protect me, in hell, and hide me till thy wrath pass, and appoint me a time, when thou wilt remember me? Shall man that is dead, thinkest thou, live again? All the days, in which I am now in warfare, I expect until my change come. Thou shalt call me, and I will answer thee: to the work of thy hands thou shalt reach out thy right hand. Thou indeed hast numbered my steps, but spare my sins.

R. Remember not my sins, O Lord, when thou shalt come to judge the world by fire.

V. Direct, O Lord my God, my way in thy sight: When thou shalt come to judge the world by fire.

V. Grant them eternal rest, O Lord, and let perpetual light shine on them: When.

Here the Lauds *are recited when the second Nocturn only is said.*

AT THE THIRD NOCTURN.

On Wednesdays and Saturdays.

Anth. May it please thee.

PSALM XXXIX. *Expectans expectavi.*

WITH expectation I have waited for the Lord, and he was attentive to me.

And he heard my prayers, and he brough me out of the pit of misery and the mire of dregs.

And he set my feet upon a rock, and directed my steps.

And he put a new canticle into my mouth, a song to our God.

Many shall see this, and shall fear: and they shall hope in the Lord.

Blessed is the man whose trust is in the name of the Lord: and who hath not had regard to vanities and lying follies.

Thou hast multiplied thy wonderful works, O Lord my God: and in thy thoughts there is no one like to thee.

I have declared and I have spoken: they are multiplied above number.

Sacrifice and oblation thou didst not desire; but thou hast pierced ears for me.

Burnt-offering and sin-offering thou didst not require: then said I, behold I come.

In the head of the book it is written of me, that I should do thy will: O my God, I have desired *it*, and thy law in the midst of my heart.

I have declared thy justice in the great church: lo, I will not restrain my lips, O Lord, thou knowest it.

I have not hid thy justice within my heart: I have declared thy truth and thy salvation.

I have not concealed thy mercy and thy truth from the great council.

Withhold not thou, O Lord, thy tender mercies from me: thy mercy and thy truth have always upheld me.

For evils without number have surrounded me; my iniquities have overtaken me, and I was not able to see.

They are multiplied above the hairs of my head: and my heart hath forsaken me.

Be pleased, O Lord, to deliver me; look down, O Lord, to help me.

Let them be confounded and ashamed together that seek after my soul to take it away.

Let them be turned backward and be ashamed, that desire evils to me.

Let them immediately bear their confusion, that say to me, 'Tis well, 'tis well.

Let all that seek thee rejoice and be glad in thee: and let such as love thy salvation, say always, the Lord be magnified.

But I am a beggar and poor: the Lord is careful for me.

Thou art my helper and my protector: O my God, be not slack.

Grant them eternal rest, &c.

Anth. Be pleased, O Lord, to deliver me: look down, O Lord, to help me.

Anth. Heal my soul, O Lord.

Psalm xl. *Beatus qui intelligit.*

Blessed is he that understandeth concerning the needy and the poor: the Lord will deliver him in the evil day.

The Lord preserve him and give him life, and make him blessed upon the earth; and deliver him not up to the will of his enemies.

The Lord help him on his bed of sorrow: thou hast turned all his couch in his sickness.

I said: O Lord, be thou merciful to me: heal my soul, for I have sinned against thee.

My enemies have spoken evils against me: when shall he die, and his name perish?

And if he came to see *me*, he spoke vain things, his heart gathered together iniquity to itself.

He went out, and spoke to the same purpose.

All my enemies whispered together against me: they devised evils to me.

They determined against me an unjust word: shall he that sleepeth rise again no more?

For even the man of my peace, in whom I trusted, who ate my bread, hath greatly supplanted me.

But thou, O Lord, have mercy on me, and raise me up again : and I will requite them.

By this I know that thou hast had a good-will for me : because my enemy shall not rejoice over me.

But thou hast upheld me by reason of my innocence : and hast established me in thy sight for ever.

Blessed be the Lord the God of Israel from eternity to eternity. So be it. So be it.

Anth. Grant them eternal rest, &c.

Anth. Heal my soul, O Lord, because I have sinned against thee.

Anth. My soul

PSALM XLI. *Quemadmodum desiderat.*

As the hart panteth after the fountains of waters. so my soul panteth after thee, O God.

My soul hath thirsted after the strong living God; when shall I come and appear before the face of God?

My tears have been my bread day and night, whilst it is said to me daily, where is thy God?

These things I remembered, and poured out my soul in me : for I shall go over into the place of the wonderful tabernacle, even to the house of God :

With the voice of joy and praise ; the noise of one feasting.

Why art thou sad, O my soul? and why dost thou trouble me?

Hope in God; for I will still give praise to him, the salvation of my countenance, and my God.

My soul is troubled within myself: therefore will I remember thee from the land of Jordan and Hermoniim, from the little hill.

Deep calleth on deep at the noise of thy flood-gates.

All thy heights and thy billows have passed over me.

In the daytime the Lord hath commanded his mercy ; and a canticle to him in the night.

With me is prayer to the God of my life. I will say to God, thou art my support.

Why hast thou forgotten me? and why go I mourning, whilst my enemy afflicteth me?

Whilst my bones are broken, my enemies who trouble me have reproached me.

Whilst they say to me, day by day, where is thy God?

Why art thou cast down, O my soul? and why dost thou disquiet me?

Hope thou in God, for I will still give praise to him: the salvation of my countenance and my God.

Grant them eternal rest, &c.

Anth. My soul has thirsted after the living God, when shall I come and appear before the face of the Lord?

V. Deliver not to beasts the souls that confess thee.

R. And the souls of thy poor forget not to the end

Our Father, &c. *All in secret.*

The Seventh Lesson. Job xvii.

My spirit shall be wasted, my days shall be shortened, and only the grave remaineth for me. I have not sinned, and my eye abideth in bitterness. Deliver me, O Lord, and set me beside thee, and let not any man's hand fight against me. My days have passed away, my thoughts are dissipated, tormenting my heart: they have turned night into day, and after darkness, I hope for light again. If I wait, hell is my house, and I have made my bed in darkness. I have said to rottenness; thou art my father: to worms; *you are* my mother and my sister. Where is now then my expectation, and who considereth my patience?

R. The fear of death troubles me: sinning daily and not repenting: because in hell there is no redemption, have mercy on me, O God, and save me.

V. O God, in thy name save me, and in thy strength deliver me; because in hell.

The Eighth Lesson. Job x x.

The flesh being consumed, my bone hath cleaved to my skin, and nothing but lips are left about my teeth. Have pity on me, have pity on me, at least you my friends, because the hand of the Lord hath touched me. Why do you persecute me as God, and glut yourselves with my flesh? Who will grant me that my words may be written? Who will grant me that they may be marked down in a book? With an iron pen, and in a plate of lead, or else be graven with an instrument in flint-stone? For I know that my Redeemer liveth, and in the last day I shall rise out of the earth. And I shall be clothed again with my skin, and in my flesh I shall see my God. Whom I myself shall see, and my eyes shall behold, and not another: this my hope is laid up in my bosom.

R. Judge me not, O Lord, according to my deeds, for I have done nothing worthy in thy sight: therefore I beseech thy majesty, that thou, O God, mayest blot out my iniquity.

V. Wash me, O Lord, yet more from my injustice, and cleanse me from my sin. That.

The Ninth Lesson. Job x.

Why didst thou bring me forth out of the womb? O that I had been consumed, that eye might not see me! I should have been as if I had not been, carried from the womb to the grave. Shall not the fewness of my days be ended shortly? Suffer me, therefore, that I may lament my sorrow a little: before I go and return no more, to a land that is dark and covered with the mist of death: a land of misery and darkness, where the shadow of death, and no order, but everlasting horror, dwelleth.

R. Deliver me, O Lord, from the ways of hell, who hast broken the brazen gates, and hast visited hell, and hast given light to them, that they might behold thee who were in the pains of darkness.

℣. Crying, and saying: thou art come, O our Redeemer. Who were.

℣. Grant them eternal rest, O Lord, and let perpetual light shine on them. Who were.

This is always said in the Week-day office. But the following Responsory *is said only on* All Souls' Day, *and when the three* Nocturns *are said together, as before, p.* 471.

R. Deliver me, O Lord, from eternal death, in that dreadful day, when the heavens and earth are to be moved: when thou shalt come to judge the world by fire.

℣. I tremble and do fear, when the examination is to be, and thy wrath to come, when the heavens and earth are to be moved; when thou.

℣. That day is the day of anger, of calamity, and of misery, a great day and very bitter. When thou.

℣. Grant them eternal rest, O Lord, and let perpetual light shine on them.

R. Deliver me, O Lord, from eternal death, in that dreadful day, when the heavens and earth are to be moved, when thou.

At Lauds.

Anth. The bones that have been humbled shall rejoice in our Lord.

Psalm L. *Miserere.* (See page 402.)

Grant them eternal rest, &c.

Anth. The bones that have been humbled shall rejoice in the Lord.

Anth. Hear.

Psalm LXIV. *Te decet hymnus.*

A hymn, O God, becometh thee in Sion: and a vow shall be paid to thee in Jerusalem.

O hear my prayer: all flesh shall come to thee

The words of the wicked have prevailed over us: and thou wilt pardon our transgressions.

Blessed is he whom thou hast chosen and taken to thee: he shall dwell in thy courts.

We shall be filled with the good things of thy house: holy is thy temple, wonderful in justice

Hear us, O God our Saviour, *who art* the hope of all the ends of the earth, and in the sea afar off.

Thou who preparest the mountains by thy strength, being girded with power: who troublest the depth of the sea, the noise of its waves.

The gentiles shall be troubled, and they that dwell in the uttermost borders shall be afraid at thy signs: thou shalt make the outgoings of the morning and of the evening to be joyful.

Thou hast visited the earth, and hast plentifully watered it; thou hast many ways enriched it.

The river of God is filled with water: thou hast prepared their food, for so is its preparation.

Fill up plentifully the streams thereof; multiply its fruits; it shall spring up and rejoice in its showers.

Thou shalt bless the crown of the year of thy goodness: and thy fields shall be filled with plenty.

The beautiful places of the wilderness shall grow fat: and the hills shall be girded about with joy.

The rams of the flock are clothed, and the vales shall abound with corn: they shall shout, yea, they shall sing a hymn.

Grant them eternal rest, O Lord.

Anth. Hear my prayer, O Lord; all flesh shall come to thee.

Anth. Thy right hand.

PSALM LXII. *Deus, Deus meus.*

O GOD, my God, to thee do I watch at break of day.

For thee my soul hath thirsted; for thee my flesh, O how many ways!

In a desert land, and where there is no way, and no water; so in the sanctuary have I come before thee, to see thy power and thy glory.

For thy mercy is better than lives: thee my lips shall praise.

Thus will I bless thee *all* my life long : and in thy name I will lift up my hands.

Let my soul be filled as with marrow and fatness : and my mouth shall praise thee with joyful lips.

If I have remembered thee upon my bed, I will meditate on thee in the morning : because thou hast been my helper.

And I will rejoice under the covert of thy wings ; my soul hath stuck close to thee : thy right hand hath received me.

But they have sought my soul in vain, they shall go into the lower parts of the earth : they shall be delivered into the hands of the sword, they shall be the portions of foxes.

But the king shall rejoice in God ; all they shall be praised that swear by him : because the mouth is stopped of them that speak wicked things.

PSALM LXVI. *Deus misereatur nostri.*

MAY God have mercy on us, and bless us : may he cause the light of his countenance to shine upon us, and may he have mercy on us.

That we may know thy way upon earth, thy salvation in all nations.

Let people confess to thee, O God : let all people give praise to thee.

Let the nations be glad and rejoice : for thou judgest the people with justice, and directest the nations upon earth.

Let the people, O God, confess to thee ; let all the people give praise to thee. The earth hath yielded her fruit.

May God, our own God bless us, may God bless us : and all the ends of the earth fear him.

Grant them eternal rest, &c.

Anth. Thy right hand, O Lord, has received me.

Anth. From the gate.

The Song of Ezechias. ISAIAS XXXVIII

I SAID: in the midst of my days I shall go to the gates of hell:

I sought for the residue of my years. I said: I shall not see the Lord God in the land of the living.

I shall behold man no more, nor the inhabitant of rest.

My generation is at an end, and it is rolled away from me, as a shepherd's tent.

My life is cut off as by a weaver: whilst I was yet but beginning he cut me off: from morning even to night thou wilt make an end of me.

I hoped till morning; as a lion so hath he broken all my bones.

From morning even to night thou wilt make an end of me. I will cry like a young swallow, I will meditate like a dove.

My eyes are weakened with looking upward:

Lord, I suffer violence, answer thou for me. What shall I say, or what shall he answer for me, whereas he himself hath done it?

I will recount to thee all my years in the bitterness of my soul.

O Lord, if man's life be such, and the life of my spirit be in such things as these, thou shalt correct me, and make me to live. Behold in peace is my bitterness most bitter.

But thou hast delivered my soul, that it should not perish; thou hast cast all my sins behind thy back.

For hell shall not confess to thee, neither shall death praise thee; nor shall they that go down into the pit, look for thy truth.

The living, the living, he shall give praise to thee, as I do this day: the father shall make thy truth known to the children.

O Lord, save me, and we will sing our psalms all the days of our life in the house of the Lord.

Grant them eternal rest, &c.

Anth. From the gate of hell, deliver my soul. O Lord.

Anth. Let every spirit praise the Lord.

PSALM CXLVIII. *Laudate Dominum.*

PRAISE ye the Lord from the heavens; praise ye him in the high places.

Praise ye him all his angels: praise ye him all his hosts.

Praise ye him O sun and moon: praise him all ye stars and light.

Praise him ye heavens of heavens: and let all the waters that are above the heavens, praise the name of the Lord.

For he spoke, and they were made; he commanded and they were created.

He hath established them for ever, and for ages of ages: he hath made a decree, and it shall not pass away.

Praise the Lord from the earth, ye dragons, and all ye deeps.

Fire, hail, snow, ice, stormy winds, which fulfil his word.

Mountains and all hills, fruitful trees and all cedars.

Beasts and all cattle: serpents and feathered fowls.

Kings of the earth, and all people; princes, and all judges of the earth.

Young men and maidens: let the old with the younger praise the name of the Lord: for his name alone is exalted.

The praise of him is above heaven and earth: and he hath exalted the horn of his people.

A hymn to all his saints: to the children of Israel, a people approaching to him.

PSALM CXLIX. *Cantate Domino.*

SING ye to the Lord a new canticle: let his praise be in the church of the saints.

Let Israel rejoice in him that made him: and let the children of Sion be joyful in their king.

Let them praise his name in choir: let them sing to him with the timbrel and the psaltery.

For the Lord is well pleased with his people: and he will exalt the meek unto salvation.

The saints shall rejoice in glory: they shall be joyful in their beds.

The high praises of God shall be in their mouth: and two-edged swords in their hands.

To execute vengeance upon the nations, chastisements among the people:

To bind their kings with fetters, and their nobles with manacles of iron.

To execute upon them the judgment that is written: this glory is to all his saints.

PSALM CL. *Laudate Dominum in sanctis.*

PRAISE ye the Lord in his holy places: praise ye him in the firmament of his power.

Praise ye him for his mighty acts: praise ye him according to the multitude of his greatness.

Praise him with sound of trumpet: praise him with psaltery and harp.

Praise him with timbrel and choir: praise him with strings and organs.

Praise him on high-sounding cymbals: praise him on cymbals of joy: Let every spirit praise the Lord.

Grant them eternal rest, &c.

Anth. Let every spirit praise the Lord.

V. I heard a voice from heaven saying to me

R. Blessed are the dead that die in the Lord.

Anth. I am the resurrection, and the life: he that believes in me, though he be dead, shall live; and every one that lives, and believes in me, shall never die.

The Song of Zachary. LUKE I. (See page 464.)

Grant them eternal rest, &c.

Anth I am the resurrection, and the life : he that believes in me, though he be dead, shall live ; and every one that lives, and believes in me, shall never die.

The following Prayers are said kneeling, when the Office is not a Double.

Our Father, &c. *in secret.*
V. And lead us not into temptation.
R. But deliver us from evil.

When the Office is a Double, the PSALM *De Profundis* (for which see p. 405) *is omitted.*

Grant them eternal rest, &c.
V. From the gates of hell.
R. Deliver their souls, O Lord.
V. May they rest in peace
R. Amen.
V. O Lord, hear my prayer.
R. And let my cry come to thee.
V. The Lord be with you.
R. And with thy spirit.

The Prayer *is recited as at the End of the* Vespers, (*page 475,*) *according to the Rank, Degree, or Sex of the Person for the Repose of whose Soul the Office has been said or sung.*

Some few of the many Reasons which must for ever attach a Roman Catholic to his Religion.

Why are you a Roman Catholic?

Because as I am convinced there can be but one true religion, so I am equally convinced that no other than the Roman Catholic Religion can be this true one.

Why do you think there can be but one true religion?

1st, Because reason itself shows it. 2dly, Because it is clearly declared in the Scripture.

How does reason show that there can be but one true religion?

It must appear evident, when we consider in what true

religion consists. The true religion is that pure and holy worship of God, which he himself approves and commands; which is really worthy of his infinite majesty; which is grounded on his unerring truth and his adorable sanctity. It is that religion whose doctrines are true, and whose precepts are holy. That such are the characters of the true religion cannot be contested. But it is plain that these characters cannot belong to more than one religion; for God cannot approve as pure, and holy, and worthy of him, any one religion, without disapproving every other that is contrary thereto. If the doctrine taught in one religion be true, the contrary doctrines taught in other religions must be false. If the precepts or rules of conduct inculcated by one religion lead to virtue and holiness, whatever is opposite to these must lead to vice and ungodliness. We cannot therefore admit different true religions, without attributing contradictions and inconsistencies to God himself. Whence it appears, that it is equally impossible there should be more than one true religion, as it is that there should be more than one true God.

How does it appear from Scripture, that there can be but one true religion?

Innumerable passages of the Scripture show it. But we shall content ourselves with a few that are plain to the weakest capacity.

1st, Jesus Christ came, as he says himself,* to gather all nations together, to bring back all who had been dispersed, that there might be but one sheepfold and one shepherd. It was therefore contrary to his intention, that people should be separated and divided into different sheepfolds, that is to say, into different communions.

2dly, He also came† to establish his spiritual kingdom throughout the whole earth. But how could the Eternal Wisdom, who had expressed in the most forcible terms,‡ the desolation threatening a kingdom divided in itself, expose

* "And other sheep I have that are not of this fold; them also I must bring, and they shall hear my voice; and there shall be one fold and one shepherd." *John* x. 16.

"And not only for the nation, but to gather together the children of God that were dispersed." *Ibid.* xi. 52.

"That they all may be one, as thou, Father, in me, and I in thee: that they all may be one in us: that the world may believe that thou hast sent me." *Ibid.* xvii. 21.

† All the Gospels.

‡ "And Jesus knowing their thoughts, said to them: Every kingdom divided against itself shall be made desolate; and every city or house divided against itself shall not stand." **Matt xii 25.**

his own kingdom to such a danger? Yet this he certainly would have done, had he authorized different religions, whose opposition to each other in belief, and in rule of conduct, must be an endless source of dissensions and divisions.

3dly. It was the constant prayer of our divine Saviour whilst on earth, that all his disciples should be *one*, as he and his heavenly Father were one. He must therefore have established that plan of worship which, uniting all in the same faith, same hope, and same love, could alone promote what he so earnestly had at heart.

4thly The Apostles were sent* by Jesus Christ to teach all nations the same heavenly doctrines he had taught them, to administer to them all the same baptism; and to preach to them all the same Christ or Redeemer. By which it is plain no room is left for variety or difference. Hence St. Paul declares, That there is but *one Lord, one Faith, and one Baptism*, Eph. iv. 5.

5thly. Jesus Christ established but one Church for all nations, as is evident from his own words to St. Peter:† You are *Peter, (or the Rock,)* and on this Rock I build my Church; (*not Churches;*) and also from these words: He *that will not hear the Church,* (not churches,) *let him be to thee as the heathen and the publican.* Now all must allow, if there be but one Church, there is but one religion.

As it seems evident, from the reasons alleged, that there can be, and that there is but one true religion, the great point to be discussed is, why you look upon the Roman Catholic Religion to be that only true one.

1st, Because it is the only religion that can unite all nations and all ages in the same religious sentiments.

2dly, Because it is the only religion that can afford people reasonable grounds of certainty with regard to their faith.

3dly, Because it is the only religion whose method of instructing is adapted to the nature of man.

* "All power is given to me in heaven and on earth.
"Go ye therefore, and teach all nations; baptizing them in the name of the Father, and of the Son, and of the Holy Ghost.
"Teaching them to observe all things whatsoever I have commanded you: and behold I am with you all days, even to the consummation of the world." *Matt.* xxviii. 18, 19, 20.

† "And I say to thee, that thou art Peter, and upon this rock I will build my church, and the gates of hell shall not prevail against it.
"And I will give to thee the keys of the kingdom of heaven; and whatsoever thou shalt bind on earth, shall be bound also in heaven; and whatsoever thou shalt loose on earth, shall also be loosed in heaven" *Matt.* xvi. 18, 19

4thly Because it is the religion which, of all others, shows best our Saviour's love for mankind, and holds him forth to us in the most amiable light.

5thly, Because it is the only Christian Society that can, in a manner plain to the weakest capacity, trace up its origin to Christ and his apostles.

6thly, Because it is the only Christian Society that has not violated the ninth article of the Creed.

How do you show that the Roman Catholic Religion is the only one that can unite all nations and all ages in the same religious sentiments?

The Roman Catholic Religion holds, that Jesus Christ has established a Church which is to extend to all nations, and last throughout all ages; in which he and his holy Spirit will always reside, and teach all truths to the end of time. That the Pastors of this Church, as being the successors of the Apostles, have from Christ's own mouth their divine commission to instruct and guide the faithful, together with his promise of being with them himself constantly till the end of the world. Whether these tenets be true, is not now the question—that shall be discussed in the sequel. But on these grounds it is that the Roman Catholic Church has always claimed as its prerogative, an authority derived from Christ, to which every individual must yield strict obedience and firm assent in religious matters.

This authority, constantly subsisting, is what prevents all difference or disunion in religion amongst Roman Catholics, and secures them from the danger of being, as St. Paul says,* *carried about by every wind of doctrine.* Because, as it lays down one and the same rule for all to follow, it must tend to unite all in the same religious sentiments.

But no such bond of union subsists in any other religion. For it is by rejecting and disclaiming any such authority, that those of other religions have from the beginning endeavoured, and still endeavour to justify their separation from the Roman Catholic Church. Their great principle is, that they are to judge and decide for themselves; the consequence whereof must be, and in fact is, a strange variety in religious belief, and a daily splitting and dividing into new sects.

Wherefore it appears evident, that the Roman Catholic Religion is not only calculated, but it is also the only religion calculated to unite all nations and ages in the same religious sentiments.

How do you show that the Roman Catholic Religion is the

* Ephes. iv. 14.

only one that can afford people reasonable grounds of certainty with regard to their faith?

Every one knows that the grounds of certainty a Roman Catholic has for his faith, is that authority of the Church which we have just been speaking of; whereas the grounds of certainty any other person has, is only his own judgment, or what is the same thing, that interpretation of Scripture, which in his opinion is the true one. Now the Roman Catholic is certain that the Church will not mislead him; but a person of any other religion has no reason to be certain but he may be misled by his own opinion or judgment; wherefore the former has reasonable grounds of certainty with regard to his faith; the latter has not.

But how do you show that the Roman Catholic has every reason to be assured the Church will not mislead him?

From the very nature of religion, the Roman Catholic sees the necessity of an authority, in order to decide all controversies that may arise, and to preserve union:—he knows, that without subordination there can be nothing but confusion in either church or state, and that, without an authority, which all are bound to acknowledge, there can be no subordination;—he sees, that shaking off the yoke of authority to become one's own guide in the affair of religion, must directly tend to pride, to obstinacy, and to every species of religious phrenzy;—he sees that those famous heresies which heretofore distracted the Christian world, have all arisen from this want of submission; that it is the essential character of every heresy, to be maintained in opposition to the Church's authority; which gave St. Augustin occasion to say, that *he might err, but would not be a heretic*;* meaning, that he was secured from heresy by his disposition of ready obedience to the Church. The Roman Catholic further sees, that the bulk of mankind through their ignorance, their weakness of understanding and their several avocations, being incapable of examining their Scriptures, or of judging for themselves, must unavoidably rely upon authority.

From these motives of plain reason and common sense, the Roman Catholic is sufficiently convinced, that to be guided by authority is his indispensable duty; if it be his duty, it is therefore what God requires of him; and surely by doing

* A heretic is one who has an opinion, for such is the etymology of the word. What is understood by having an opinion, is following one's own fancy and particular sentiment. A Catholic without maintaining any particular sentiment, follows unhesitatingly the doctrine of the Church, which Christ has promised to be with *all days, even to the end of the world.*

what God requires of him, he cannot go astray Thus, even without any help from Scripture, the Roman Catholic is assured he cannot be misled by following the authority of the Church.

This conviction of his mind, already so well grounded in reason, is fully strengthened and confirmed when he comes to read those clear and positive texts of Scripture,* which show—That Jesus Christ himself gave his authority to the Pastors of the Church†—that he commanded all to hear and obey them as himself—that he would take as offered to himself any contempt or disobedience shown to them—that in their functions of teaching and instructing, he himself would remain with them for all days until the end of the world. That he would send them the Spirit of Truth, who should abide with them and teach them all truth‡—that whoever would not hear the Church should be considered as a heathen and a publican—that the gates of hell should not prevail against the Church§—that the Church is the Pillar and Ground of Truth.

By these passages of Scripture, and many others that might be alleged, the Roman Catholic has, from the word of God himself, an entire and evident confirmation of what his own reason had already told him of his Church's Authority: whence with the fullest confidence he may rest assured that he cannot go astray under her guidance. Such are the grounds of certainty a Roman Catholic has with regard to his faith; and every person of candour must acknowledge they are just and reasonable.

* "Peace be to you: as the Father hath sent me, I also send you.

"When he had said this, he breathed on them, and he said to them: Receive ye the Holy Ghost.

"Whose sins you shall forgive, they are forgiven them: and whose sins you shall retain, they are retained." St. *John* xx. 21, 22, 23.

† "He that heareth you, heareth me; and he that despiseth you, despiseth me; and he that despiseth me, despised him that sent me." *Luke* x. 16.

‡ "And I will ask the Father, and he shall give you another Paraclete, that he may abide with you for ever.

"The Spirit of Truth, whom the world cannot receive, because it seeth him not, nor knoweth him: but you shall know him, because he shall abide with you, and shall be in you.

"I will not leave you orphans." *John* xiv. 16, 17, 18.

"The Holy Ghost, whom the Father will send in my name, he will teach you all things, and bring all things to your mind, whatsoever I shall have said to you." *Ibid.* 26.

§ "The House of God, which is the Church of the living God, the pillar and ground of the truth.' 1 *Tim.* iii. 15

Well, and how do you show that a person who differs from the Roman Catholic Church has reason to fear being led astray, by interpreting the Scripture according to his own opinion and judgment?

He surely has every reason to fear it, when he considers, that to mistake an opinion is what daily happens to thousands and thousands, in other less difficult matters as well as in religion. Is not this even what he himself must say of all those who, following their own opinion as he does, yet differ from him? Is it not even the nature of man, to be liable to error of judgment? And what privilege can he plead, to be exempt from the common lot of mankind? Is it that he seeks the truth with more candour and sincerity than others do? Such a notion, however he may flatter himself with it, must appear presumption and folly in the eyes of others. Moreover, by persuading himself he cannot go astray in his own interpretation of Scripture, he assumes to himself that infallibility he denies the Roman Catholic Church. Besides all this, he has to encounter against the certainty of his opinion, an argument which cannot possibly fail to make the deepest impression on an unbiased person. I mean, that the sense he gives the Scripture is contrary to the sense in which it is understood by all the wise and learned men the Roman Catholic Church comprises within its pale, and contrary to what is acknowledged to have been believed by all Christendom at least for several ages. If, after all this, he persists in saying that he is sure he is right in following his own opinion and judgment, we can only beseech God to give him what Solomon begged of the Almighty for himself, that is, *a docile heart.* But it is sufficiently plain to whoever is open to conviction, that he has no just cause to be assured he does not mistake in his opinion, and of course that he has no reasonable grounds of certainty with regard to his faith.

To sum up all in a word: Faith is of its own nature certain and infallible—opinion is not: whatever persuasion therefore is built on opinion, cannot be faith; hence there can be no true or real faith, but what is grounded on authority; that is, not only the authority of God revealing, (which all sects pretend to,) but also the authority of the Church, as the only sure channel through which the sense of revelation is conveyed to *us.*

How do you show, that the Roman Catholic Religion is the only one whose method of instructing is adapted to the nature of man?

The Roman Catholic Religion instructs by the method of authority and it is sufficiently clear, from what has been said in the answers to the foregoing questions, that this is the only method whereby,

First, The ignorant, the dull of apprehension, and those who have not leisure to examine the Scriptures, that is to say, the greater part of mankind, can be *at all* instructed; whereby,

Secondly, The learned themselves can be *so* instructed as to remove all fluctuation and doubt from their minds; whereby,

Thirdly, Both learned and ignorant are furnished with the same motives of belief, and the same foundation for their faith; whereby,

Fourthly, All heresies, schisms, and dissensions about religion are prevented; whereby,

Fifthly, The spirit of peace, of meekness, of humility, of diffidence in ourselves, of submission and obedience, that is to say, the characteristic virtues of a disciple of Christ, are inculcated, and are formed in us; whereby that pride and presumption of the human heart, which, as St. Paul says,* *exalted itself against the knowledge of God*, is beat down and subdued, *and bringeth into captivity every understanding to the obedience of Christ*. Whereby we are guarded against the wildness of imagination, the illusions of self-love, the spirit of party, the bias of education, the influence of prejudice, and so many sources of error and vice; whereby, in short, that holy, that rational, that amiable religion, which Jesus Christ brought down from heaven as a blessing to mankind, can be taught, can be enforced, and can be constantly maintained. Now as the method of instructing by authority, is that which answers all these heavenly purposes, and leads man to virtue and happiness in a manner conformable to his nature; and as the contrary method, whereby people are desired to shake off authority and judge for themselves, naturally leads to so great evils, and is so ill suited to the state and condition of mankind: it follows that the Roman Catholic Religion, which is the only one that instructs by authority, is also the only Religion whose method of instructing is adapted to the nature of man.

But does not this doctrine, which enforces the necessity and the obligation of being guided by Church authority, tend to make people the vassals and slaves of churchmen? Are we to hoodwink our reason, and blindly to follow whatever the clergy say? Are they not men as well as others, and as such, are they not liable to error? Might they not pervert their authority to bad purposes, and make us their dupes?

Objections of this sort, which indeed we but too often hear

* 2 Cor. x 5

proceed only from ignorance, pride, or passion;—they must immediately vanish, if we but calmly listen to the voice of reason. The authority we are obliged to submit to, is not that of any clergyman speaking or acting from himself; but it is the authority of the entire body of the Pastors of the Church. Each clergyman, in the discharge of his functions, acts as the Church's deputy. It is in her name, and by her authority, he instructs and guides the faithful committed to his care. The submission and obedience paid him in this capacity, is paid to the Church itself; and in obeying the Church, we obey Jesus Christ. Can this reasonable obedience (which regards only the concern of our souls) be called vassalage or slavery to churchmen? Or is it hoodwinking our reason, to submit to what is in fact the authority of God himself? That clergymen are only men, like others; that as such, they are liable to error; that they might possibly pervert their authority to bad purposes; all this is certainly true. But though they be of themselves liable to error, and capable of abusing their authority, we have nothing to fear by giving ourselves up to their guidance, as long as they preach only the doctrine of the Church, and confine their authority to spiritual matters, for which alone it was given. If, indeed, any clergyman should happen to prove such a traitor to his trust, as to give out a doctrine different from that of the Church, (a matter which would immediately spread an alarm,) or if he should be imprudent enough to enforce his authority, which is spiritual, in matters that are merely temporal, every one knows, that in the former case he must, and in the latter he may be disobeyed; because he then ceases to be invested with the authority of the Church and of Jesus Christ; and thus we are secured from the danger of being (what the enemies of our religion are so apt to call us) *dupes of the clergy.*

However, from all that has been said on this subject, no one can doubt but that, whilst a clergyman goes on in the ordinary course of those functions the Church has cut out for him, he is entitled to the respect and obedience due to the minister of the Church of Jesus Christ; this quality is never to be overlooked, on account of any frailties of the person; and obedience cannot be refused without overturning the very foundations of faith: hence a disposition of revolt against the clergy, of disobedience to their authority, of aversion and contempt of them, carries with it all the malice and guilt of heresy; for by such a disposition every heresy is already formed in its cause; and from thence each particular heresy flows as a stream from its source.

How do you show that the Roman Catholic Religion is the

religion which, of all others, shows best our Saviour's love for mankind, and holds him forth to us in the most amiable light?

From what has been already said, it plainly appears, that the Roman Catholic Religion is the only one that represents our Divine Redeemer as fulfilling the duties of the best of parents; in procuring us instructions the most proper and most suitable to our nature; in becoming even himself our instructor, and thus performing his loving promise, *that he would not leave us orphans;* in giving us (beside himself, the invisible guide) a visible one, we cannot mistake, that will guard us against going astray, and will direct us in that belief which, under pain of being eternally lost, is required of us. Our Divine Redeemer, however, is held forth to us by the Roman Catholic Religion, as providing us with the most precious food for the preservation of our spiritual life; no other, indeed, than his own ever adorable flesh and blood, which he gives for nourishment of our souls in the sacrament of the altar. Whoever considers this, and has a heart susceptible of the love of his God, though he were not convinced of the truth of the Roman Catholic Religion, yet he should naturally wish it was true; as it must be our greatest happiness in this life to have such visible tokens of our Saviour's love, in the secure means of salvation he has left us; and to be so firmly assured of the ardent desire he has of being for ever united with us in heaven, by the ways his love found out to be united with us in the closest manner on earth. Such is the amiable light in which our Saviour is held forth to us by the Catholic Religion; a light in which it is plain the tenets of any other religion will not allow us to view him.

How do you show that the Roman Catholic Church is the only Christian Society that can, in a manner plain to the weakest capacity, trace up its origin to Christ and his Apostles?

As the Roman Catholic Church is a body of Christians united in faith and communion with the Pope or Bishop of Rome; their visible head: a Roman Catholic therefore, in order to trace up his Church to Christ and his Apostles, has nothing more to do, than count back from the present Pope through the catalogue of his predecessors, till he comes to St. Peter, the first Pope and Bishop of Rome, to whom Christ* committed the care of feeding his lambs and his sheep; that is, his entire flock. In this catalogue of Popes, not one has broke off from the line of succession, but all continuing on in the same communion, governed each in his turn the Church he found established before him. Thus the Roman Catholic has a regular chain of head Pastors of

* John xxi. 15, 16, 17.

his Church—a chain, whose links are closely joined and hang one to the other, from the first to the last: and every one must perceive with what ease a Roman Catholic may, by only following this chain, trace his Church to Christ and his apostles.

But if we attempt to trace the origin of any other sect or society of Christians, we find ourselves stopped as soon as we come to the author of that sect, and the time of its forming a separate congregation:—here the chain is broken, the line of succession is cut short: from that time only, and not higher, can the origin of that sect or society of Christians be dated; just in the same manner (to use an example) as the Republic of Holland cannot be traced higher than about two hundred years ago, when the seven United Provinces shook off the yoke of Spain, and formed themselves into a separate state; and as also the American Republic began only the other day, by separating from the empire of Great Britain, and cannot therefore attempt to date its origin at any earlier period. Such exactly is the case of every Christian Society, except the Roman Catholic Church, whose origin reaches up to the apostles, whilst each of the others can go no higher than the time of its separation. And hence it appears plain to the weakest capacity, that it is only the Roman Catholic Church which can trace up its origin to Christ and his Apostles.

How do you show that the Roman Catholic Church is the only Christian Society that has not violated the ninth Article of the Creed?

The ninth article of the Creed is, *I believe the Holy Catholic Church, the Communion of Saints;* by which words we declare, that we hold as an article of our belief, a true Church of Christ constantly subsisting on earth, which is holy, which is Catholic, (that is, universal,) and which is that communion wherein the saints are found. Now it is plain, that breaking off from this Church, which we thus in the creed profess to believe, is certainly violating or going against the ninth article of the Creed. But the Roman Catholic Church stands totally free from this charge, having, as all the world knows, never broken off from that standing body of Christians, which in all ages has been called the Catholic Church; being in fact itself, that very Church that has all along subsisted and borne the name of Catholic:—every other society of Christians, on the contrary, has broken off from this standing body, has quitted its communion, and formed as its origin a new church and congregation separate from all that was before it. By which it is evident that every one of these sects, however they may attempt to assign reasons for their separation, have by this very separation violated the ninth article of the Creed.

To render this argument quite short and decisive, we may thus reason with each and every one of these sects:—At the time your church formed a separate communion, either there was a true Church of Christ subsisting on earth, or there was not:—If there was, your Church, by forming a separate communion, quitted and renounced this true church of Christ:—If you say there was not, then you give the lie to the Creed, in as much as you make it propose as the object of our belief, a thing that did not exist.

Thus, without further inquiry, we see at once, that all the different sects of Christians who are separated from the Roman Catholic Church, carry on the very face of them their own condemnation.

But is it not very uncharitable to believe, that the Roman Catholic Church, besides being the only true Church, is the only one in which salvation can be obtained?

It is by no means uncharitable to believe this; no more than it is uncharitable to believe any awful truth which God has revealed. No Christian can be justly charged with a want of charity, for believing that *many are called, but that few are chosen;* that *it is easier for a camel to pass through the eye of a needle, than for a rich man to enter into the kingdom of heaven;* that *he who will not believe, is already judged;* that *without faith it is impossible to please God;* that *there is but one Faith, one Lord, and one Baptism;* that *he who will not hear the Church, must be considered as the heathen and the publican;* or, in short, that Christ at the last day, shall thus sentence the reprobate: *Go, ye cursed, into eternal fire.* As the firm belief of all these, and the other terrifying truths which frequently occur in holy writ, and which are manifestly damnatory of the great majority of mankind, as well at this day as in all former ages, do not clash with charity; so neither does the doctrine of exclusive salvation. Our Saviour, who was charity itself; his Prophets and Apostles, who were animated with the same divine spirit, did all respectively deliver these formidable oracles, while their hearts glowed with the tenderest love of the unhappy objects who had fallen under God's displeasure Turks, Jews, Atheists, and the numberless infidel tribes may as justly upbraid with a want of charity every denomination of Christians who assent to the Athanasian Creed, or who admit the necessity of baptism and divine faith, as our separated brethren upbraid us Roman Catholics, for believing that there is only one true religion revealed by the God of Truth, and that the Roman Catholic Religion is that true one. If separated Christian communities have, in their own opinion, an indisputable claim to charity, while they unhesitatingly pronounce the Roman Catholic Religion *damnable* and *idolatrous*, though professed by the greater part of Christendom, it is doubtless because they conceive that such sentiments and language are dictated by truth, and because their conscience bears them testimony that they are sincerely well affected to Roman Catholics and infidels, while they thus, however reluctantly, condemn them. Now Roman Catholics feel warranted to assert their claim to the tenderest charity upon the very same grounds. To them it appears as undeniable as the very existence of the Godhead, that the Religion revealed by him, must be essentially One, consistent throughout, and perfectly accordant in all it prescribes and professes. To assert that God can declare to one body of Christians that certain points are to be believed, and to another that they are not to be believed, is to attribute to him what is incompatible with his very nature: it would authorize the infidelity of the Atheist, who may then triumphantly boast, that he can never be justly condemned for refusing to believe in a God who contradicts himself. It is not less incredible, that among the multitude of religions, more than one can be right. But while Roman Catholics, weighing maturely the distinctive qualities of the Church established by Jesus Christ, perceive that these qualities exclusively belong to that ancient and widely extended body of Christians in communion with the See of Rome; they at the same time declare, in the face of heaven and earth, that they are strictly bound to love their neighbour, and that every human being, let his religion, his practice, or his prejudice be what they may, is that very neighbour whom they are bound to love. They further with equal solemnity declare, that as to live in hatred of any denomination whatsoever of their fellow creatures, is to live in enmity with God, so to die in such hatred is to forfeit heaven, to die reprobated. Roman Catholics also, while they believe their own religion to be the only true one, are convinced that great numbers are comprised within its pale, who do not adhere to it by any visible bond of communion. All baptized infants; all innocent children of every religious persuasion; and all grown-up Christians who have preserved their baptismal innocence, though they make no outward profession of the Catholic faith, are yet claimed as her children by the Roman Catholic Church. Neither have we any difficulty in believing, with many individuals of our communion, that there are several in the British empire as well as in other countries, professing the religion by law established there, whose uniform integrity of life, whose ardent love of God, and sincere disposition to embrace the truth, if they but knew it, not only open for them the road to salvation, but afford them more solid grounds to expect that blessing, than those Roman Catholics have, who live in constant disobedience to the dictates of their religion, and who deny, by their practice, the faith which they profess.

Are Roman Catholics taught to believe or to assert, that all those of other religions will be damned?

No, most assuredly they are not. If ignorance, embittered by resentment, has ever given utterance to similar expressions, these are not the language of Roman Catholics as such; which fully appears by the foregoing answer, and is further manifest, from their being taught to believe, that God alone knows who shall be his by faith and good works: that many are not now the people of God, who shall one day be numbered in his inheritance; that many shall come from the East and from the West, and shall sit down with Abraham, and Isaac, and Jacob, in the kingdom of heaven, while the children of that kingdom shall be excluded. Moreover, final perseverance is a most profound secret, absolutely impervious to mortals; it is pent up in the bosom of the Deity. No man, without a special revelation, can ascertain what passes, at the moment of death, between the dying Christian and his God. It is ours earnestly to desire eternal happiness for every fellow-creature; to work out our salvation with fear and trembling; not to be high-minded, nor to judge others, that we ourselves be not judged; but to hope humbly for all, in the infinite mercies of God, through Jesus Christ.

But, at least, is it not very uncharitable in Roman Catholics, to abjure all manner of communication in religious exercises, with those of every other religion?

This abjuration, or refusal, so far from being uncharitable, is in their mind enforced by the truest charity. Convinced as Roman Catholics are, and firmly persuaded that there is, and that there can be, no other true religion than their own, they cannot consistently, nor candidly, nor lawfully approve, or even appear to approve, any other religion, which they certainly should appear to do, were they thus to join in these religious exercises, or frequent places of worship belonging to separated communions. Such temporizing conduct has the aspect of prevarication: it is, in short, betraying the truth of God. In their principles they must abhor it, as calculated to delude their separated brethren into an unfounded, and therefore into a most dangerous security. Charity here compels them to stand off. Besides, esteeming the gift of divine faith to be invaluable, in as much as, without faith, it is impossible to please God, they cannot innocently expose themselves to the danger of losing it.

But still, when those of other religions scruple not occasionally to attend at Roman Catholic Sermons, and at religious exercises in Roman Catholic places of worship, would there not be something more brotherly in returning this compliment, than in standing off with such rigour?

The preceding answer has anticipated a negative to this question; it is now in addition to be observed, that the principles of other religions allow of such communication; the principles of the Roman Catholic Religion peremptorily forbid it. Were a set of men, however individually respectable, to assemble as a deliberative body, with a view of reforming what they deem abuses in the constitution of Great Britain were these men to propose to the imperial parliament a coalition with the legislative body, whereby they should be entitled to assist at the deliberations of parliament, and the members of the legislature be admissible to sit with them in turn, every one is aware of the fate of such a proposal; and every one who is convinced of the essential unity of the Church, as well as of its necessary and indefectible identity, in every age, from its first establishment by Christ to the end of the world, must consistently reject, with at least equal aversion, every similar proposal of religious reciprocity.

Can it then be sinful, to listen to the word of God? Is not his word good in all places, and wherever it is preached?

The pure, unadulterated word of God, is certainly good in itself every where; but all is not the word of God which passes under that name; the original Hebrew, Chaldaic, and Greek manuscripts, are no longer in existence: there are a great number of copies indeed, and very many translations but copies can so far only be the word of God, as they are faithful transcripts of the originals; and translations are that word, no farther than they truly express the sense of it. Now it is undeniable, that numberless spurious copies are in circulation, corrupted by Jews, and ancient Eastern Heretics; so that, abstracting from the testimony of the Church, this authorized guardian of the Scriptures, and voucher of their authenticity, there can be no certain assurance that any individual copy or translation is indeed the word of God; a circumstance of such weight in the judgment of the great St. Augustin, as made him declare, that he would not receive the four Gospels, if not induced thereto by the authority of the Catholic Church. And if the Scriptures so far back as the time of St. Peter, when the living voice of the Apostles discriminated for the faithful the pure from the corrupt, could still be wrested by the unlearned and unstable to their own perdition, how much more liable are these Scriptures now to misconceptions and misrepresentations among the sects, where the authority of that Church is rejected, and where the Scriptures are presumptuously expounded according to the dictates of private judgment!

When it is also notorious, that various translations have, in many places, forced the word of God into such meanings, and into such language, as might best accord with the peculiar tenets of the translators,* or might best seem to warrant their defection from the Catholic Church, it becomes equally notorious, that arbitrary translations of that sort cannot be safely relied on, as the pure word of God.

Even among the English *reformed* translations, some of a later date have altered and superseded others, which in their day were publicly read as the pure word of God; these latter translations having been superseded in turn themselves by others still later. A petition was presented to King James the First by a number of zealous Protestants, wherein they represent, that in the translation of the Psalms, as found in the Book of Common Prayer, there were two hundred deviations from the truth; and the Petitioners grounded their objections against this book almost entirely upon the corruptions or mistranslations which they discovered in it, as set forth in a particular treatise, entitled *A Defence of the Minister's Reasons for refusal of subscribing.*

Mr. Carlisle, a Protestant writer of that period, abused the English translations, as having *depraved* the sense; *obscured* the truth; *deceived* the ignorant; *distorted* the Scriptures; and *preferred* darkness to light; *falsehood* to truth, &c. &c. &c.

The ministers of the Diocese of Lincoln, in their address to the King, charge the English translation with taking from and adding to the text, so as to change or obscure the meaning of the Holy Ghost. They further pronounce this same translation *absurd* and *senseless*, on which account they scruple to subscribe to it.

Mr. Broughton, a most decided Protestant, wrote about this time to the Lords of the Council, in order to procure, through their interference, a new translation, because the one then in use was, according to him, *full of errors*. In his *Advertisement of Corruptions*, he tells the Bishops, that their public translation of the Scriptures into English *perverts* the text of the Old Testament in eight hundred and forty-eight places. Very many faults of copies are to be found even in the Vatican and Alexandrian manuscripts of the Bible. In

* It is a fact, that Luther, Calvin, Zuinglius, Beza, Bucer, etc. etc. etc. assailed and censured, with the utmost asperity, each other's translation of the Bible. See their respective works.

the Greek New Testament alone, Mr. Mills has discovered thirty thousand various readings. But if instead of translations absolutely rejected by the Catholic Church, her Vulgate* alone were in use among the separated communions, that Vulgate, which she presents us from the faithful pen of the learned and laborious St. Jerom, and which the most distinguished opposers† of Catholicity have mentioned with respect, it would not yet be lawful for us Roman Catholics to commune in religious matters with separated sects, or to listen to their teachers as our spiritual guides.

And why?

Besides the reason heretofore assigned, Roman Catholics cannot discover in these teachers that transmissive spiritual authority, emanating through an unbroken chain of succession, from Christ himself and his Apostles; which authority they consider as essentially necessary in every preacher, to constitute him an orthodox minister of the word of God. For as a Roman Catholic cannot allow any other society of Christians to be the true Church, except that which acknowledges the spiritual pre-eminence of one chief Bishop, and holds communion with his See as of indispensable necessity; so, neither can a Roman Catholic conscientiously become a hearer of those, whose commission to preach or expound the gospel is not manifestly and actually derived from that authority. How shall they preach unless they be sent? Among all the illustrious personages under the old law, none took upon themselves the province of public instruction, but such as were called by God, as Aaron was. The prophet Jeremiah rests his own claim to credit, and the claim of the other prophets, upon this particular circumstance, that God had sent them. He repeats it with reiterated energy in many parts of his prophecy; insisting in other places, as often and with equal force, that the false prophets were not to be credited; because, though they spoke in the name of God, yet that God had not sent them. Our Redeemer, the great teacher of mankind, would be particularly characterized by this quality, as well in the noted oracle of the dying Patriarch, who announced the continuance of the sceptre in Juda, until he should come who was to be sent; as in the prophetic prayer of Moses: Send, O Lord, whom thou wilt send. Also

* St. Jerom undertook and executed this translation at the instance of Pope Damasus. He translated the Old Testament from the Hebrew, and revised the New Testament from the Greek. His labours on this occasion are highly extolled by St. Augustin

† Mr. Whitacre, Doctor Dove, Doctor Humphry, Doctor Covel, Molinæus, Pelican, and Beza, respectively allow that the Vulgate is pious and profitable to the Church, faithful to the original, preferable to all other Latin Translations, etc. etc. etc

in the words of his precursor: He whom God hath sent shall speak the words of God: wherefore Jesus Christ studiously exhibits this distinctive quality, as prominent in his own person: But I, says he, have a greater testimony than that of John; for the works themselves which I do, give testimony of me, that the Father hath sent me. When about to raise Lazarus from the dead, he clearly insinuates his motive in performing this miracle to be, that the surrounding multitude might believe that the Father had sent him. On another occasion he proves to the Jews, how justly he ought to be called the Son of God, because the Father had sanctified and sent him into the world. He declared, that eternal life consists in knowing the Father, the only true God, and Jesus Christ, whom he had sent. After all which, commissioning his Apostles to preach the gospel to the world, he says: As the Father hath sent me, I also send you. And in his last discourse on the eve of his death: Amen, Amen, I say to you, he that receiveth whomsoever I send, receiveth me; and he that receiveth me, receiveth him that sent me. The word apostle signifies a man sent. But when the chain of transmissive spiritual jurisdiction is broken by a separation from the visible body of Pastors united under one visible head, Roman Catholics cannot perceive that teachers, so separated, are really sent to instruct them: nor can they of course become their hearers.

Are heavy temporal inconveniences a sufficient excuse for Roman Catholics, when, through fear of incurring them, they yield compliance in this point?

Such compliance being repugnant to their religious principles, it cannot be fairly required of them, nor lawfully conceded, whatever temporal inconveniences may result from their refusal. Let all those who chance to be involved in such trying circumstances, whether placemen, servants, or dependents, be careful to prove, by their edifying conduct, by their honesty, their fidelity, and their uniform attention to their employer's interest and welfare, that the religion of their preference effectually inculcates every Christian Virtue in an eminent degree. No violence will then be offered to their consciences: they will be left at full liberty to adore their God in their own way: they must become respectable and respected in this very act of recusancy.

"*This shall be unto you a straight way, so that fools shall not err therein.*"—Isa. xxxv. 8

Prayer.

Most gracious and merciful God, who, of thy pure bounty, hast bestowed on me, in preference to so many

others, the precious gift of faith, which is the beginning of salvation; who hast made me, before reason could direct my choice, a member of the one only and true Catholic Church, wherein I am secured from error, and guided in the road that leads to eternal bliss. Grant, O my God, that I may never prove so ungrateful as to waver in this faith, or to contradict it by my conduct; but that, till the end of my life, firmly believing what it teaches, and earnestly endeavouring to comply with the duties it lays down, I may merit the eternal reward thou hast promised to those who persevere to the end in the profession of thy faith and the observance of thy commandments. This grace, O my God, I ardently implore, through the death and passion of my Saviour Jesus Christ, who, with thee and the Holy Ghost, liveth and reigneth, one God, world without end. *Amen.*

THE END.

www.ingramcontent.com/pod-product-compliance
Lightning Source LLC
LaVergne TN
LVHW021308110826
845150LV00003B/519

* 9 7 8 1 4 2 5 5 5 9 4 0 3 *